Faith Misplaced

FAITH MISPLACED

THE BROKEN PROMISE OF U.S.-ARAB RELATIONS: 1820–2001

USSAMA MAKDISI

PUBLICAFFAIRS
New York

Published in the United States by PublicAffairs™,
a member of the Perseus Books Group.

PublicAffairs books are available at special discounts for bulk purchases in the U.S. by corporations, institutions, and other organizations. For more information, please contact the Special Markets Department at the Perseus Books Group, 2300 Chestnut Street, Suite 200, Philadelphia, PA 19103, call (800) 810-4145, ext. 5000, or e-mail special.markets@perseusbooks.com.

Book Design by Trish Wilkinson

Library of Congress Cataloging-in-Publication Data

Makdisi, Ussama Samir, 1968–
Faith misplaced : the broken promise of U.S.-Arab relations: 1820–2001 / Ussama Makdisi. — 1st ed.
p. cm.
Includes bibliographical references and index.
ISBN 978-1-58648-680-8 (alk. paper)
1. Arab countries—Foreign relations—United States. 2. United States—Foreign relations—Arab countries. 3. Arab countries—Politics and government—1945– 4. United States—Foreign relations—1989– I. Title.
DS63.2.U5M3 2010
327.73017'4927—dc22 2010011357

First Edition

10 9 8 7 6 5 4 3 2 1

For Sinan and Nur

CONTENTS

INTRODUCTION

The American University of Beirut's most famous building, College Hall, was destroyed by a bomb in the early morning of November 8, 1991. The sound of the explosion jolted awake the quiet, religiously mixed neighborhood of Ras Beirut, which had long been identified with the American institution. The perpetrators of the College Hall attack are still at large. We will, in all likelihood, never know who planted the bomb, or why. Its single victim, a forty-nine-year-old university employee and father of four who happened to be sleeping in the building, became one more casualty—mourned and quickly forgotten—in what now appears to be the ever-widening conflict that ensnares America and the Arab world.

This conflict needs historical explanation. There is no American institution in the Middle East that has attained greater prestige than the American University of Beirut (AUB). For over a century, College Hall's clock tower had stood as a visible reminder of a peaceful American presence in the Arab world. Yet this same clock tower had also been witness to a tumultuous history that gradually yet relentlessly drove Americans and Arabs apart. During the Lebanese civil war, which began in 1975 and which had formally ended the year before the College Hall bombing, several American civilians had endured long spells in captivity; one

AUB president had been murdered and another abducted and held hostage; a U.S. ambassador to Lebanon had been kidnapped and killed; and the U.S. embassy as well as a U.S. Marine barracks near Beirut Airport had been blown up. Four decades, moreover, had elapsed since the first Arab-Israeli War, but only months since the United States had driven Iraq out of Kuwait, unveiling its military might in the post–Cold War era. Today a significantly larger College Hall stands in the original building's place. The rebuilt structure was expressly designed to evoke the memory of its predecessor. Its reconstruction was financed by hundreds of alumni, by various Lebanese, Arab, and American corporations, and by the tax dollars of the American people. The new College Hall is a monument built in hopeful defiance of our present difficult age.

This book recounts the story of the birth and transformation of the Arab idea of America, for which the fate of College Hall represents an apt metaphor. It does so as part of a wider chronicle of the encounters between Americans and Arabs that began in a sustained manner in the early nineteenth century, some fifty years before the original College Hall was built. It was then that American Protestant missionaries first set out to convert the peoples of the Orient and prepared the ground for a fascinating, evolving mutual discovery between Americans and Arabs. This history matters. Knowledge of it will alter substantially, if not drastically, the one-dimensional picture most of us have of the nature of U.S. engagement in the Middle East.

Rather than search for antecedents to the present conflict between Americans and Arabs, *Faith Misplaced* brings to the fore what has sadly been lost in the relationship between the two peoples and why. The book therefore opens with an account of the first American missionaries who traveled in 1819 to the Ottoman Empire, which encompassed most of what we today call the Arab world. It reveals the largely unknown story of a zealous group of young evangelical Protestants who sought out Arabs in order to convert them as part of their belief in an impending millennial age. Readers will follow these Americans, noting their assumptions, hopes, and frustrations as they struggled to adjust to what was a radically unfamiliar world. This first round of encounters between Americans and Arabs remains a study in cultural misunderstanding, but it laid the basis for a more enduring relationship between them. As Americans adjusted, indeed abandoned, their evangelical expectations, so too did Arab perceptions of the missionaries change dramatically for the better. Trial and error on both sides continually narrowed the cultural divide across a half-century. This led finally to a modus vivendi, best exemplified by the flourishing of the increasingly secular American schools and colleges that dominated the educational landscape of the late Ottoman Empire. As we shall see, these American institutions did not demand religious conversion, but inculcated an idealization of modern America.

Through their interactions with missionaries, their experience of American education, their writings in the new Arabic press, and their experience of emigration to the United States itself, Christian and Muslim Arabs came to discover America. I trace how and why a century ago Arabs were able to draw a picture of the United States as a benevolent great power that was neither imperialist nor covetous of the resources or lands of the Ottoman Empire.

The very fact that such a positive picture was initially drawn at all, and that American missionaries, not soldiers, constituted the first face of America to Arabs was immensely important in laying the foundations for what one American with long experience in the region once described as a "reservoir of goodwill." But this goodwill was neither universal nor arrived at naturally or inevitably. *Faith Misplaced* is not a romantic recounting of U.S.-Arab relations; it does not obscure the racial and religious tensions that marked different groups of Americans and Arabs as they adapted to a modernizing world. Yet it does highlight how Christian and Muslim Arabs, though they viewed European imperialism with trepidation and feared their own sectarianism, increasingly found themselves drawn to the allure of powerful Western nations. Above all, they were inspired by what they regarded as President Woodrow Wilson's promise of self-determination. Never has the star of America shone so brightly in the Arab world as it did during the era of the First World War. But as we shall see, this incipient Arab faith in America ultimately proved to be as misplaced as was the initial American missionary belief in the efficacy and universalism of rigid American evangelicalism.

The immediate aftermath of the First World War created the modern Middle East as we know it. Instead of granting independence to Arabs, as Egyptian and Syrian nationalists had hoped, Britain and France divided up the eastern Arab world in the form of so-called mandates and protectorates, that is, states that were subordinated, often violently, to either British or French tutelage. Many, if not most, of the conflicts that today rage in the Middle East can be traced back to key British and French decisions taken between 1916 and 1920. The American missionary presence in the area notwithstanding, the U.S. government did not yet consider the Middle East a strategically crucial part of the world. It acquiesced to the new colonial arrangement that laid the seeds for Arab disillusionment with America and the West. Without resorting to grand narratives that speak of undifferentiated religions, groups, and cultures, *Faith Misplaced* emphasizes a series of historical turning points that, in retrospect, clearly led us to our current unhappy circumstances. Choices, not fate, drive this tale.

Readers will note that this book tells two stories: the story of a growing Arab faith in America, and then the story of a sudden, ever more bitter disenchantment with it. The pivot is 1948 and the crucial U.S. role in helping to create and then defend the exclusively Jewish state of Israel in what had been historically a multi-religious land. This new state was built directly at the expense of Palestinian Muslims and Christians who had been the overwhelming majority of the population of the land until they were forced out of their homes. At a moment when the rest of the world was entering the age of decolonization, the Palestinians were made stateless. More than any other single factor, the presence of Israel has altered the course of U.S.-Arab relations and explains the narrative of this book. Israel's creation, in fact, coincided with the manifestation of a new, more overtly political and economic, oil-driven American involvement in the post–World War II Middle East that largely overshadowed America's previous, long-standing cultural presence and the largely voluntary and private relationships between Americans and Arabs rather than between states. Culture and religion remained salient after 1948 to be sure, but they could no longer be the driving force that they had been in the nineteenth century.

This book describes how the relationship moved from a fairly fluid and open set of cultural interactions in what is today Lebanon and Egypt to a more political and confrontational era defined most clearly by the question of Palestine. While, of course, U.S.-Arab relations involve far more than the Arab-Israeli conflict, it is impossible to address the problem of America's standing in the Arab world without squarely facing the political question that has haunted America's relationship with the Arabs most conspicuously and consistently for over sixty years. No matter how one turns the kaleidoscope of U.S.-Arab relations, one always returns, or is returned to, the picture of Palestine.

Rather than avoid this controversial issue, *Faith Misplaced* makes it the interpretive key with which to understand the relentless dynamic of post-1948 U.S.-Arab relations. The same language of human and national rights that legitimated the creation of Israel in the West also catapulted the question of Palestine to center stage in modern Arab politics, where it has largely remained ever since. We will discover why the loss of Arab Palestine, a historical episode largely ignored in the United States, captured the imagination of diverse Arab populations from North Africa to Yemen more strongly than any other Arab cause in the decolonizing age of the twentieth century.

My hope is to recognize, in other words, the nature of a tragedy that is still being played out in our own time. A resurgent postwar Western, and American, liberalism chose to put its faith in the redemptive meaning of a pioneering and militarily victorious new state of Israel. Yet it deemed insignificant the predicament of Palestinian Arabs, perceived as distant and abstract, in its eagerness to resolve Europe's Jewish "problem" and to make amends for the long history of Western anti-Semitism. This is surely one, though not the only, reason why the United States ultimately decided to break with the Arabs over Palestine despite strenuous and collective Arab pleas to Western nations, and particularly the United States, to understand Zionism from an Arab standpoint. These Arab protestations were echoed by prominent American educators, officials, and missionaries who resided in the Arab world.

There may indeed be cultural foundations for U.S. support for Israel, but part of what this book specifically illustrates is that cultures, whether American, Arab, or both in relation to each other, do not operate in a vacuum, nor are they unchanging. Indeed, it is at this point in the story that the two halves of *Faith Misplaced* come together. Although we today often automatically link Christian evangelicals to Israel and to chilling fantasies about Armageddon, most nineteenth-century American missionaries who worked in the Middle East, and who constituted several of the dramatic actors of the first chapters of this book, were not motivated by Christian Zionism. Many of their successors in the twentieth century became prominent educators or humanitarian workers and came to empathize with the Palestinian Arabs. They were able to puncture through the web of abstractions that pervaded how many Westerners viewed the Orient, the Holy Land, and the Middle East. As this book shows, while they struggled to make sense of their place in a nationalist and anticolonial Middle East, they could not shut their eyes to an unfolding calamity in which their government was playing a critical part.

There was indeed considerable debate within official U.S. circles about the role the United States ought to play in legitimating Israel and about the costs of such a decision to not only the missionary legacy built up over a century of trial and error but to America's strategic position in the Middle East. President Harry Truman and his successors, however, decided that they could both secure Middle Eastern oil and support Israel. They *chose* to defy the Arabs, not because they were anti-Arab or imperialist by nature, but because they made a basic calculation that the balance of domestic and foreign interests suggested one course of action. They hoped that Arab disillusionment would be short-lived, or at any rate, contained or mollified. Considered in the context of the Second World War, the fate of Arabs in Palestine appeared to them to be but a single problem among far greater ones that afflicted many parts of the world, and the ensuing Arab-Israeli conflict became for the United

States a sideshow of the Cold War. Truman's fateful decision in 1948, nevertheless, set the course and tone for U.S-Arab relations to the present day.

The last section of *Faith Misplaced* takes up a story that will be more familiar to readers well versed in current affairs, but it places recent events within a historical perspective. Arab intellectuals and politicians—including many individuals who had a deep and abiding faith in Western liberalism and who were confident of their ability to act as a bridge between cultures—were the first to put the case of Palestine before Western governments and, to a lesser extent, before Western publics. We follow how they failed in their attempts to make any headway and how they were stymied by deep divisions within the Arab world that rendered their own position as interlocutors between America and the Arab world, between East and West, steadily more untenable. As these most Westernized and liberal of Arabs looked on, conservative monarchies dependent on Western support were challenged by secular nationalist regimes that emerged in the wake of the Arab defeat of 1948 as part of a revolution against traditional elites and as a reaction to Western domination of Arab affairs.

The Suez crisis of 1956, when Egypt's charismatic new leader Gamal Abdel Nasser defied Britain and France and nationalized the Suez Canal, was a critical moment. More so than any other U.S. president before or after him, Dwight Eisenhower understood the problem of America's standing in the region. He sought to take a strong stand against European imperialism to underscore to the Arabs what he insisted was America's anticolonial nature. Yet Eisenhower found himself contending with two irreconcilable pressures: a nationalist reaction that swept across the Middle East and was personified in the secular Nasser on the one hand, and on the other hand, Israeli expansionism, broad pro-Israel sympathy within the United States as well as Cold War imperatives that further undermined America's historic engagement with the Arab world.

Eisenhower's dilemma was that he wanted to improve America's image among the Arabs, but he could not resolve the Palestinian question. He could restrain Israel, but he found himself unable and unwilling to restore the rights of the Palestinians. More clearly than any other U.S. leader, he understood how profoundly U.S.-Israeli relations impinged upon U.S.-Arab relations, but he was unable to alter the dynamic at work. By the same token, the most important Arab leaders of the day also desperately wanted a more fruitful relationship with the United States. They were undercut, however, by America's domestically driven embrace of Israel, as well as by the bitter internal rivalries of the Arab world. Ultimately, we see how Eisenhower committed the United States to weakening and overthrowing secular nationalist regimes in the area as America gradually took over from the British as the dominant outside power in the Middle East.

Faith Misplaced concludes with a reading of the implications of Nasser's crushing defeat at the hands of a U.S.-backed Israel in 1967. We thus follow how a general Arab faith in secular nationalism—or at the very least in the nation-states that claimed to be the standard-bearers of this nationalism, such as Egypt—began to wane at the same time as fundamentalist Saudi influence began to grow, aided by spectacular increases in oil revenue following the 1973 Arab-Israeli War. The comprehensive defeat of Egypt did not end Palestine's status as the paradigmatic Arab anti-imperialist cause. Instead, as our own era illustrates only too clearly, a number of Islamist movements came to the fore as Nasser's successor, Anwar Sadat, bowed Egypt out of the Arab-Israeli conflict in a separate peace. Buoyed by the Iranian Revolution of 1979, these Islamist movements have consistently used the unresolved plight of the Palestinians to represent themselves credibly as the authentic voice and conscience of the contemporary Arab world and to depict the United States as an enemy of this world.

Rather then easing with the passage of time, the basic difference over Palestine has hardened throughout the last decades as Arab disillusionment with American policy has given way to outright hostility and as American policymakers since 1967 have progressively abandoned even the pretense of neutrality or evenhandedness in their approach to the conflict. My book stops just short of the attacks of September 11, 2001, and the subsequent, ongoing U.S. military occupations of Afghanistan and Iraq. Although these topics are vitally important, the purpose of this book is to illustrate the historical foundation on which these more recent and more familiar events have been layered.

I have deliberately foregrounded Arab perspectives in the telling of this story because they have rarely, if ever, been highlighted in standard Western accounts of U.S.-Arab relations. Knowing how political leaders in Washington, Moscow, London, and Paris acted and how they viewed the Arab world is vital, and there is now a substantial corpus of works that delve into the Middle Eastern foreign policies of successive U.S. administrations. In a bibliographical essay at the end of this book, I enumerate these and other works that have analyzed various aspects of the Arab-Israeli conflict, American oil politics, Zionism and Israel, and the questions of Islamic fundamentalism and the problem of terrorism, especially after September 11, 2001. In more academic works, a series of impressive studies have explored facets of American cultural encounters with the Orient. The reader familiar with these works will easily detect their influence on my own book. Yet in most, if not all, standard English-language accounts of America and the Middle East, readers will be hard-pressed to find Arab voices taken seriously, and none do so across a span of two centuries.

Far too often, Western readers have been treated to any number of notions of what or who Arabs and Muslims are and what their cultures are supposedly all about; far less often have Arabs been presented fairly with their own understanding of their history, their lives, their aspirations, their politics, and their disappointments. Although a huge contemporary outpouring of Arabic thought and writing exists, glib generalizations still abound in the American mainstream about what "the Muslim" thinks, does, or says, as if such a Muslim type exists. Consider how often newspaper commentary moves effortlessly from the contemporary to the medieval when analyzing Islamist politics in a manner we almost never do when discussing, say, American evangelical politics. Arab government archives, it is true, are not nearly as accessible as those of Western governments, or Israel's for that matter, but there is nevertheless an abundance of Arab documentation, newspaper accounts, novels, and memoirs that are easily accessible. Many of these were either written in English or have been translated.

My goal, however, is not simply to provide an Arab side of the story, nor even to provide a comprehensive account of modern Arab history. There have been a number of important studies of Arab politics and contemporary history. However much *Faith Misplaced* highlights a range of Arab perspectives that has moved from the secular to the religious over a century, I have always believed that these perspectives cannot be analyzed as though they are sealed off from the Western ideas, assumptions, and actions that have so clearly shaped the modern context in which these Arab beliefs have been articulated. The Arab world does not operate in a vacuum. Let me be more specific. In the age of Western hegemony within which the actions depicted in the following pages largely unfold, there is no such thing as an entirely independent Arab or Muslim side that can be studied and judged without taking into account Western power.

This is not to deny that there is such a thing as Islamic fundamentalism or acts of terrorism committed by Arab groups. Nor does it mean that we can ignore the fair degree of Arab autonomy and agency that make *Faith Misplaced* a complex story. My goal is neither simply to condemn a Western colonial conspiracy nor to describe an alleged endemic Arab or Muslim problem with modernity. I am not interested in "blaming the West," but by the same token I am not invested in exculpating, obscuring, or justifying the enormous influence that Western states have had in shaping the possibilities and problems of the modern Middle East. Not for a moment can I pretend that there has been in this century or in the last any symmetry of power between Arabs and Americans—or for that matter, between Israelis and Palestinians.

I am even less interested in defending the dogmas of Arab nationalism or more broadly the religion of Islam. Rather, I explore what has been, in the twentieth century at least, a deeply unequal relationship—but a relationship nevertheless—that has bound Arabs, Israelis, Europeans, and Americans together. I do not doubt that many Arabs and Muslims have believed that they possessed, and still possess, purity of thought and deed, just as some also believe (and an even smaller group apparently act on the belief) that they are involved in an existential war against Western "crusaders" and that Muslims remain the collective target of a brutal, generalized Western assault.

Many Americans and Westerners have also put their faith in the late Harvard political scientist Samuel Huntington's crude description of a "clash of civilizations," or in a mythical object they name the "Arab mind," or in so-called Judeo-Christian values that by definition are separated from Muslim values (however much Muslims see themselves as part of the same Abrahamic tradition), or in the cultural and religious inferiority of Arabs and Muslims as a whole. Prejudice, alas, has always been part of history, whether Arab or American. But as a scholar who believes firmly in cause and effect, I can no more pretend that what is often today called Arab or Muslim "hatred" of the West, or an "Arab predicament," can be discussed independently of Western—and specifically British, American, and Israeli—actions.

In saying this, I am guided by the prescient words spoken in 1946 in Jerusalem by the eminent Arab historian Albert Hourani, whom we shall encounter again later in this book. In testifying before the Anglo-American Committee of Enquiry, which was charged with recommending a way out of the impasse over Palestine, Hourani reminded the assembled American and English commissioners of the nature of the ties that inexorably bind Arabs to the West.

> Arabs are faced today with a choice between paths: either they can go out towards the West and towards the world in openness and receptiveness, trying to take from the West what is of most value and greatest depth in its tradition, and blend it with what they have of their own, trying to establish a relationship of tolerance and trust between them and the Western nations with whom they are brought into contact, and trying to enter into the new world community on a level of equality and in spirit of cooperation. Or else they can turn away from the West

> and from the world, in spiritual isolation and in hatred, taking nothing from the outside world except the material means with which to combat it.

But Hourani, crucially, did not stop here. He continued,

> I believe the first path is the path that Arabs must follow, and that the responsible leaders among them want to follow. Nevertheless the attitude which the Arabs will take up towards the West is not entirely a matter for the Arabs themselves; it depends very largely upon the attitude which the West takes up towards them.[1]

At midcentury, then, Hourani captured perfectly the dilemma faced by modern Arabs in their encounter with more powerful Western nations. He was himself an exemplary product of the intersection of the two worlds. He was born in Manchester, England, in 1915 to Lebanese Presbyterian parents, who had themselves been converted by American missionaries. He graduated from Oxford's Magdalen College and taught at the American University of Beirut for two years before the Second World War. After the war, he returned to teach at St. Anthony's College in Oxford. He died in 1993, having established himself as one of the most influential professors of modern Middle Eastern history.

Readers may be surprised to learn of just how great a role Christian Arabs played in establishing themselves as bridges between cultures. They took the lead in discovering America, and later, as the bond between Arabs and Americans hung in the balance, they put forward the most articulate presentations of a secular and liberal Arab position on the key question of Palestine to their American and Western interlocutors. Far more than the rulers in the West whose decisions shaped their collective future, individuals such as Hourani understood that at the time the Arabs generally still maintained a hopeful attitude toward what they saw as American values of democracy and self-determination. Yet, as *Faith Misplaced* shows, these most liberal and Westernized Arabs were systematically ignored and overlooked. Sadly, the door was shut in their faces, and also in the faces of their secular Muslim Arab contemporaries and compatriots. We are still living with the consequences of this rebuff.

I was born in the United States but raised in the Arab world. Steeped in two cultures, I have been able to see America through Arab eyes and the Arabs through American ones. In some basic respects, I have followed the trajectory similar to that of several individuals who appear in this book. I lived in Lebanon during that country's civil war, acquired my higher education in the United States, achieved a doctorate at Princeton in history, and now teach at Rice University in Houston. Like Hourani and several of his contemporaries, such as Philip Hitti and George Antonius (whom we shall also presently encounter), I have been able to appreciate firsthand just how large is the gap between abstract representations of the Arab world and America and their more human reality, and how crucial it is to narrow it.

The bridge to cultural understanding cannot be built from one side alone; it needs individuals who can appreciate two perspectives with equal sensitivity. Hourani was one such figure, but he embodied an earlier and more innocent age when one could believe in the idealism of America and Britain and in their potential to shape positively and benevolently a newly independent Arab world. I, in contrast, have lived in an era when the intensity and virulence of the conflict between the United States and the Arab world have greatly elevated the stakes of knowledge about the historical development and transformation of the relationship between Americans and Arabs.

I am also deeply and personally entangled in the history that follows. My maternal great-great-grandfather was the first Arab pastor of the Protestant church in Beirut. My maternal great-grandfather traveled from Palestine to the United States and returned in 1910 an ordained Baptist minister. My mother's father emigrated to the United States from Jerusalem, was drafted and fought with the U.S. army in France during the First World War, became a U.S. citizen, and then returned to the

Arab world. He expanded his Jerusalem business to Egypt before moving finally to Lebanon. My paternal grandfather was a professor of Arabic at the American University of Beirut and was himself the son of a Protestant convert from the Orthodox Christian faith. My grandmothers on both sides took pride in their modern Protestant upbringing and yet instilled a sense of ecumenism in their children, my parents, who pursued their higher education at universities in the United States and who have also both taught at what were formerly American missionary institutions, AUB and Beirut University College (previously the Beirut College for Women and today the Lebanese American University). My uncle was a professor of English and comparative literature at Columbia University until his untimely death in 2003. Today my two brothers and I teach at American universities in Los Angeles, Houston, and Beirut, respectively.

Perhaps because I have lived in an openly multi-religious part of the Arab world during wartime, I have also inherited an acute sense of the innate similarity of people regardless of their religious affiliations and retain a faith (there, I have used the word again!) in the necessity and healing quality of constant secular criticism. The point of education is not to become satisfied with one's knowledge, but to test this knowledge at every opportunity, to sharpen it, to broaden it. The same goes for political conviction. The test of any position is not how sincerely it is held or how passionately it is argued, but how well it can deal with the introduction of new information—whether the argument becomes more nuanced and refined, collapses under the weight of its internal contradiction, or resorts to prevarication and denial. Having lived through a terrible and ultimately unresolved civil war in Lebanon, I have not only witnessed extreme polarization and violence but also recognized the shared fate and ultimately the remarkably similar though belated sense of disillusion and real regret over unnecessary conflict that have overtaken what were once bitterly opposed (but never monolithic) communities. And what goes for Christian and Muslim Lebanese applies equally well to Americans and Arabs.

By training, I am a historian. My most recent book, *Artillery of Heaven*, attempted to untangle the complex early missionary encounter that first bound Americans and Arabs together. In many ways, it constitutes a prelude to this book and represents my first sustained, scholarly attempt to traverse what has become—indeed, what has been made into—a chasm of misunderstanding that separates Americans from Arabs. This current endeavor very much follows in its path, although I have tried to gear this book to a general audience rather than to specialists in the field.

Some caveats are therefore in order. I have tried to keep footnotes to a minimum, restricting my citations to quotations and figures. I include at the end a brief bibliographical essay to indicate some of the more important sources and accounts that I have relied on in each chapter and to make suggestions for further reading. I use the word "Arab" with full understanding that Arab nationalism, like all nationalisms, is of recent vintage. In this book, I have tried to demarcate this nationalism as one of the many products of the transition from a nineteenth-century Ottoman world and its myriad forms of identification to the world of the smaller successor nation-states of Lebanon, Syria, Palestine, and Iraq that were established after the empire's collapse. Thus, the term "Syrian" in an Ottoman context refers to those Arabic-speaking men and women who regarded themselves as belonging to an area that we would today refer to as the separate, independent republics of Syria and Lebanon. These people were citizens of the Ottoman Empire. After 1920, however, and with the demise of the Ottoman Empire and the creation of the separate nation-states of Syria, Lebanon, and Palestine, the term "Syrian" refers exclusively to nationals of the state of Syria. "Syrian" was also a term that the mostly Christian immigrants to the United States used to distinguish themselves from Muslim "Turks." Today the descendants of these immigrants and newer immigrants to the United States are referred to as Arab Americans.

I use the terms "the Arab world" and "the Middle East" advisedly. These descriptions tend to create a sense of uniformity that is not always warranted and that often masks enormous variations of tradition, dialect, and historical experience. And yet I use the terms not simply for want of a better alternative but to indicate an Arab commonality that at certain moments and with specific key issues (Algeria in the 1950s until independence in 1962 and Palestine from at least the 1940s until today) or specific leaders (Gamal Abdel Nasser) becomes manifest and resonates powerfully across the region—though again, with a complexity and with contradictions that I have tried to note in the book.

I am also acutely aware that there are many sources I have not been able to track down, and many angles and topics that I could have fruitfully pursued or explored more comprehensively. Because my goal is to trace a trajectory over two centuries, I have chosen to focus on what I see as the most important encounters and locales that have defined an evolving Arab image of America. The first half of *Faith Misplaced* therefore privileges the original American mission to the Arab world and the emblematic product of this mission, the American University of Beirut, which overshadowed in scale and importance all other American cultural institutions in the Middle East. There were, of course, other missions that were also very important, and over the course of this book I mention them. Following a similar path, their experiences also generally struggled with the secularization of the meaning of America in the Middle East with which the first American mission and missionaries contended so obviously. The second half of the book, as I have explained, focuses on the dynamic of the Arab-Israeli conflict.

I do not pretend, in any case, to have exhausted the possibilities of research, but given the constraints of time, I am fairly confident that there is enough in the following pages to start a discussion on solid historical grounds. For I conceive this book, most basically, as an invitation to dialogue without, I hope, falling back into romantic clichés about either Americans or Arabs. If there is one major theme and point to this book, it is change. Faith in the possibility of future change is what sustains me in the desperate times in which we live.

The value of history stems from the lessons we draw from it. It stems as well from history's ability to inspire imaginations overwhelmed by the immediacy of the present. History writing does not change power politics, but it is a terrain of contestation like any other. Abolitionists were once called wishful thinkers, as were advocates of women's equality with men. And so too are those who today struggle for peace and justice in Palestine and the Middle East as a whole. The lesson I draw from the history of American and Arab encounters is, at one level, deceptively simple: Cultures change, as do the historical conditions that shape them. Nothing, in short, is inevitable, and thus we are not doomed as Arabs or as Americans to pursue a path of mutual incomprehension, let alone of mutual demonization. It is for precisely this reason that I have written *Faith Misplaced.* Not because I know things *will* change for the better, but because I know that they *can.*

1

RECLAIMING BIBLE LANDS

On an early November morning in 1819, two young missionaries, Pliny Fisk and Levi Parsons, boarded the schooner *Sally Ann* in Boston bound for the Mediterranean island of Malta. From there they were to proceed to Smyrna, but their final destination was Palestine. There they were to examine whether a mission station could be opened, and if Palestine proved unfeasible, then they were to settle anywhere in the region, "as Providence shall indicate."[1] The two men were, understandably, filled with anticipation. They were also burdened by expectations. They were the first American missionaries to attempt to evangelize the lands of the Bible, and the first charged with reclaiming them from what Fisk and Parsons saw as a withering infidel grasp. In both these endeavors, they ultimately largely failed. But they succeeded in something different, something they had not set out to do in any deliberate manner. They set in motion a long process of interaction between Americans and Arabs that gave birth to the first, great idea of America in the Arab world.

Fisk and Parsons worked for the American Board of Commissioners for Foreign Missions (ABCFM), whose ponderous name obscured a simple, yet extraordinary, ambition: to deliver the Gospel of Truth to *all* the world's "heathen." The ABCFM had been founded in 1810 as a result of the zeal of a few New England seminary students who, like young men in many parts of the world, were dissatisfied with mere academic pursuit. They wanted to change the world, not simply study it. From such visionary origins, the American Board rapidly established itself as the largest and most influential American foreign missionary organization, one that would send out more Americans to more foreign territories than any other missionary society in the nineteenth century.

As they contemplated evangelizing the region they called the Holy Land, Fisk and Parsons believed that they were fulfilling scriptural prophecy. Like almost every evangelical Protestant of the period, they were guided by an unshakeable belief that Islam was, along with Catholicism, destined to collapse as a prelude to the thousand-year, or millennial, reign of Jesus Christ.

Millennialism resonated with the American missionaries. It regarded disparate world events as preordained signs of an unfolding heavenly plan, and it outlined the missionary relationship to these events. Men such as Fisk and Parsons believed that they had an urgent duty to evangelize as many nations as possible. The more converts they won, the more manifest became God's plan for the salvation of Christians. His providence made the world accessible; the missionary task was to press home the advantage. The British conquest of India, the French Revolution, Napoleon's conquest of Egypt and occupation of Rome, the American Revolution, the expansion of the continental United States, the military decline of the Ottoman Empire—these were all indications to American missionaries that they could plausibly evangelize the world.

For the exuberant Parsons, as for many other evangelicals, the "restoration" of the Jews to Palestine was another important indication of Jesus Christ's imminent earthly reign. "Destroy, then, the Ottoman Empire," he exhorted his evangelical audience at Boston's Park Street Church in 1819 on the eve of his departure to the Holy Land, "and nothing but a *miracle* would prevent their [the Jews'] immediate return from the four winds of heaven."[2] But this solicitude for the Jews was profoundly ambivalent. Scriptural prophecy for Parsons pointed in one direction, scriptural history in another. Far from simply loving the Jews, Parsons described them as "degenerate children"; their hands, he insisted, were "imbued in the blood of the Son of God."[3] They had forsaken God and thus had been justly punished by him. Now, however, was a season for change. And so, like the Muslims and Christians of the East—indeed, like the Indians of North America and the islanders of Hawaii—the Jews could be redeemed, but only if they abandoned their religion, their faith, their way of being, and accepted salvation at a missionary's hand. The missionaries may have loved the Jews as they did all of God's creation, but it was a kind of love not easily appreciated by the people of the world whom they intended to convert.

On that same Sunday afternoon in 1819, Fisk also spoke from a pulpit. An eager audience had crowded into the pews of the Old South Church and spilled over into its aisles, its stairs, and both its galleries, so that many aged persons and ladies were forced to stand. The missionaries' intimate readings of the Bible had inevitably built up in their minds the expectation and burning desire to see, smell, and experience the real thing, to wander the streets of Jerusalem and to gaze upon the Cedars of Lebanon. Their audience shared their anticipation. Like many Americans, the missionaries came from fairly humble, rural backgrounds; the Bible unquestionably formed their moral and educational foundation and also shaped their literary and imaginative outlook. And like many Americans, they were swept up by a religious revival in the early part of the nineteenth century. Fisk and Parsons had each experienced a profound personal conversion that had transformed their lives. They had become born again in faith, and the basis for their desire and determination to see "living" faith flourish in Palestine—which the American Board described as the land of "ancient Promise and present Hope"[4]—lay in these singular acts of personal conversion, more so than in family, race, or nation.

Fisk made it clear to his listeners that there would be obstacles in the way of this new American mission to the Holy Land and that trials and tribulations awaited its pioneers. Islam, after all, was a formidable opponent, and its adherents were reputed to be fanatical. None of the assembled American evangelicals had actually been to Palestine, and their view of Islam, "natives," and the Holy Land was all the more ideological given this lack of contact. Palestine's importance to them was derived therefore almost solely from its location at the heart of a two-thousand-year-old biblical story, not from any knowledge or appreciation of Palestine's subsequent history. That Muslims—or "Mohammedans" or "Turks," as they were called—had conquered the area in the seventh century was known, but only as part of a general notion that with this conquest history there had effectively stopped.

Violent, oppressive, cruel, but above all lifeless and mechanical, Islam to the likes of Fisk and Parsons, and to the evangelical community that sustained them, could not possibly have been seen as a *faith* shared by millions, and Muhammad was in their eyes an imposter, not a prophet. They viewed Islam as a religion of the sword, not of the spirit, as an artifice rather than a natural part of Palestine's history. In the minds of many Americans, moreover, the repeated capture of U.S. sailors by Moroccan and Algerian corsairs and the demand for their ransom in the late eighteenth and early nineteenth centuries had helped consolidate a picture of a despotic region dominated by rapacious, often cruel, always turbaned bashaws. Numerous stories, plays, and poems were published about the so-called Barbary Wars and about the ordeals of "slavery" endured by American men and women in the East. But with the rise of a missionary spirit within America, there appeared, along with the inherited and distorted vision of Islam, a determination to redeem its followers and the other inhabitants of the Ottoman Empire as well.

Far more than their Puritan predecessors, Fisk and Parsons emphasized an active solicitude for the salvation of others. Parsons's infatuation with Jewish restoration notwithstanding, the Bible, crucially, had impressed upon the American missionaries the Christian message of universal, rather than tribal, salvation and redemption. They did not want to exclude Arabs or Turks or Persians or Jews and were certainly not oblivious to their presence; rather, they sought to win them back into God's favor, which they assumed these non-Christians to have lost. The missionaries called this "disinterested benevolence" because they were willing, they said, to sacrifice themselves in fulfilling God's command to go out and convert the world.[5]

Fisk therefore was not daunted by the immensity of his self-imposed task. His ambition reflected an age when nationalism as we know it was absent and when the hostility that today so deeply scars the relationship between American and Arab was unimaginable. The missionaries, at first flush, preached few of the values that liberal Americans today cherish in their great majority. They spoke not of secularism or tolerance, but rather of heathens, infidels, and nominal Christians. They sought not to spread democracy but to inculcate belief in the imminent second coming of Jesus Christ; they believed not in equality but in righteousness.

The United States was then but a fraction of its present size, with the Mississippi River effectively demarcating the western border, though not the territorial ambitions, of an expanding young republic. It had long been the contention of several influential colonial-era New England theologians, including Cotton Mather and Jonathan Edwards, that America had been favored by God. Mather, one of the most prolific writers in colonial America and son of an influential Puritan minister, had famously boasted in his epic of Puritan Christian conquest and settlement of the New World, *Magnalia Christi Americana*, that he wrote about the "*Wonders* of the CHRISTIAN RELIGION, flying from the depravations of *Europe*, to the *American Strand*."[6] Edwards believed that the renewal of mankind would begin in America, for God had led pious Christians to first discover and then prosper in it. America, for both the American Board and its zealous missionaries, contained the most Christian of churches. It was, in effect, the New Israel, and hence its citizens had a particular duty to enlighten not only America's Indian heathen but the world at large.

Fellow missionaries had already departed for Hawaii. Others worked to convert Indians in the face of white American racism and covetousness for Indian tribal lands in Georgia. Both Fisk and Parsons were inspired by the story of David Brainerd, an introspective young eighteenth-century missionary who had devoted himself to proselytizing Indians. Despite his harsh condemnations of Indian habits and his failure to master any Indian language or convert any significant number of Indians, Brainerd exemplified for American missionaries such as Fisk the very essence of Christian compassion and self-sacrifice.

In any event, Fisk and his audience expected that the men and women of the East would ultimately convert. The thought that they might not never seemed to occur to the evangelical throng that pressed into the church to hear what he had to say and willingly contributed to the missionary enterprise there and then $2,932.31—the equivalent of approximately $51,000 today. At the close of the ceremony, a gentleman even presented a bill of exchange for thirty pounds sterling to form either a Bible society or a school in Palestine. All was untried and untested, and yet there was no stopping the commencement of this American attempt to win the minds, and more particularly the hearts and souls, of the people of the region we today call the Middle East.[7]

Though the ABCFM was willing to throw caution to the wind for the sake of this new mission, many others derided the missionaries and what appeared to them to be a fool's errand. The missionary enterprise was explicitly premised on reclaiming the inhabitants of the Holy Land for Christ, but it was led by a few individual men, not by a great army. At the outset, neither Fisk nor Parsons knew any Arabic or Turkish or Persian or Armenian, and both young men had only the vaguest idea of the lands and cultures they had set out to transform. Their cause was religiously belligerent, yet the missionaries carried with them no weapons. Both Fisk and Parsons instead counted on their absolute faith that their God could erect an empire in the hearts of humans and compel a surrender to his will. They were careful to distinguish between the historical crusades—whose physical violence they condemned and which, in any case, they associated with a venal and bigoted Catholicism—and what they considered to be their own more noble form of spiritual warfare. Fisk told his listeners that Sabbath evening at the Old South Church that he yearned for "spiritual conquests" of Muslims.[8] Parsons described himself as embarking on a "spiritual crusade to the land of promise."[9] The two men departed from Boston Harbor on November 3, 1819.

Following an uncomfortable Atlantic crossing, Fisk and Parsons entered the harbor of Malta just before Christmas Eve. From there, as planned, they made their way to Smyrna, then a vibrant port city in the venerable Ottoman Empire, which stretched from North Africa through the Middle East and into the Balkans, binding together various provinces and peoples, among whom were Arabs, Armenians, Greeks, and Turks, under the dynastic rule of the Muslim Ottomans. The missionaries were relieved that they were free to travel around the Ottoman domains. Islam, as a religion, reigned supreme, but Christians, including the missionaries, and Jews were granted full religious autonomy to make sense of their own place in this diverse though unequal world.

In their letters home, however, the two men expressed anxiety about the daunting scope and scale of their self-appointed task. They had already started studying Italian; they wanted next to grapple with modern Greek, then probably Arabic, or possibly Turkish. "It is one thing to learn a language so as to sit down, and with the help of dictionaries read a well written book," they wrote. "It is quite another thing to learn a language so as to read it, speak it, write it, and understand it when spoken rapidly, and perhaps very indistinctly and very imperfectly."[10] And what they said about language, they may as well have said about culture. It is one thing to have studied it from afar, to have believed certain things about it, to have parsed it out, to have divided it up into simplistic rules of behavior and action. It is another thing altogether to come into contact with the real, living, complicated, unpredictable thing.

A year after the arrival of the two Americans, Parsons's health began to decline noticeably. Two years later, in February 1822, Pliny Fisk, "with a heart overflowing with grief," wrote home from Alexandria to announce the sad news that his bosom-friend and fellow missionary pioneer Levi Parsons had succumbed to disease.[11] Still, all had not been in vain. The missionaries had distributed many Bibles and other religious tracts. They had traveled extensively throughout the eastern Mediterranean and had had many hopeful conversations with priests, rabbis, and *shaykhs*. Parsons had visited Jerusalem in the company of Orthodox pilgrims, although he was unable to establish a missionary station there. Fisk, for his part, had learned modern Greek, although he was not exactly sure what to do with it, given the outbreak of a Greek rebellion against the Turks, which would eventually lead, but only after a bloody nine-year campaign, to Greek independence. The vast majority of the inhabitants of Palestine and Syria, in any case, spoke Arabic, and so Fisk commenced lessons in Arabic. In general, both Americans had been treated with a mixture of respect and curiosity in most parts of the empire in which they had traveled. Fisk therefore asked for reinforcements. From Paris, where he was studying Arabic with the Orientalist Sylvestre de Sacy, the Reverend Jonas King agreed to join the mission in 1822. And in December of that same year, two more missionaries, Isaac Bird and William Goodell, embarked from New York with their wives and headed east.

Although the missionaries led by Fisk were American and represented a proudly American organization, they were known to the Arabic-speaking population of Egypt and Syria as *al-Inkiliz*, or "the English ones."[12] They traveled under English protection, they spoke English, and they were Protestant, which at the time was associated firmly with England. In those first decades of the nineteenth century, the history and people of the United States, including their democracy and their slavery, their wars with Indians and their revolution against a British king, were, at best, only vaguely known across the Ottoman Empire. That there might be savages in its wilds who went without clothes, that it had been settled by English colonists, that it was very, very distant, that it seemed, in a word, exotic, was the most that some people—the better-educated sort—knew about America. The Ottoman governor of Tripoli in North Africa, for example, who granted safe passage in 1796 to the captain and crew of an American merchant vessel, described them as *müsteminler*, or aliens (as opposed to Eastern Christians and Jews, who were protected subjects of the empire) of a foreign nation "called America."[13] The Barbary conflicts were so remote and of such insignificance to most Arabs of the Ottoman Empire that they had not even bothered to coin a term for them.

The missionaries to Palestine themselves scarcely referred to the Barbary Wars. They were far more preoccupied with how to interact with, and convert, the native populations, over whom they had no real power. Although Morocco had been the first state in the world to recognize U.S. independence in 1778, the Ottoman Empire itself did not establish formal diplomatic relations with the United States until 1830. American merchants, nevertheless, carried out a steady trade with the Ottomans. They took with them processed materials such as cottons and rum and returned with figs, raisins, and Turkish opium—almost the entire Ottoman crop was being taken by 1828—that was then used in the New England–controlled China trade. The missionaries, for their part, needed to justify their presence in a land that had raised enormous expectations among evangelicals in America. Five years into the mission to reclaim the lands of the Bible, with nearly twenty thousand tracts and four thousand Bibles or parts thereof distributed, the Americans had yet to make a single Arab Christian convert.[14] A few Armenians had broken with their apostolic church, but by and large the mission had precious little to show for itself. The evangelical public at home in New England was eager for good news, anticipating the kind of reports they were receiving from Hawaii, which spoke wondrously of the smashing of idols and of great progress in the Christianization on the islands. Instead, the *Missionary Herald*, which covered news from American Board mission stations across the world, offered details about the tragic illness and death of Parsons. Readers also discovered other significant developments. Syria, not Palestine, became the main center of American missionary activity, and the slow and steady search for converts proved to be an ungratifying process.

As early as 1823, Pliny Fisk had sought to dampen hopes by declaring that the "man who goes into the wilderness to cultivate it does not expect to see flourishing cities rise at once."[15] But although mission supporters in America—who ultimately paid for missionary outfits and houses—were told that they had to expect a long battle with so entrenched a foe as Islam and, indeed, with the Oriental churches mired in age-old "superstition," their patience was being taxed.[16] The American Board secretary Jeremiah Evarts, who was desperately fending off domestic criticism of what appeared to be a hopeless mission to North American Indians, publicly defended his missionaries. Privately, however, he reproached them. No matter how great the difficulties in the Ottoman Empire, he reminded the missionary Jonas King, men "are apt to grow cold in the best of causes, and great and constant exertion is necessary to keep them from fainting."[17]

Fisk, the leader of the mission, tried to put a brave face on things. In addition to pleading for more patience, he proclaimed that Beirut, which was located "at the foot of mount Lebanon," was an ideal spot for the mission.[18] Instead of news about converts, he and his fellow missionaries sent hundreds of pages of vivid description of the Mediterranean city, the surrounding countryside, and the mountains of Lebanon, including its biblical cedars. Beirut, ancient *Colonia Julia Augusta Felix Berytus* and home to the eastern Roman Empire's most famous law school, boasted easy access to a largely Christian hinterland that was populated by both Greek Orthodox and Maronites. The former owed their ecclesiastical allegiance to the patriarch in Constantinople, the latter to the pope in Rome.

In the early nineteenth century, the city, which would grow first to become a provincial capital and then much later the capital city of the independent state of Lebanon, was a walled town with five gates. Its streets struck the missionaries as "narrow and dirty," and its houses, made of "mud, and of a soft, sandy, crumbling stone," appeared to them "dark, damp, and inconvenient."[19] The town possessed three large mosques and several smaller ones as well as Maronite, Roman Catholic, Greek, and Greek Catholic churches. Its population was estimated by Goodell in January 1824 to be not less than five thousand strong. Ships were forced to anchor about two miles from the city, but the cargoes they loaded there included silks, wines, tobacco, olives, figs, raisins, and other fruits. The cargoes they unloaded contained a variety of colonial commodities, such as sugar from the Antilles and Brazilian coffee as well as European manufactured goods, especially English textiles, much to the satisfaction of the English consul, Peter Abbott, with whom the missionaries established immediate contact and under whose protection they journeyed up into Mount Lebanon.

The foreignness of Beirut to the Americans was mirrored by the spectacle of unmistakably foreign men in clerical garb accompanied by their unveiled wives and children, with boxes and baggage in tow, arriving in town. There was no question of the missionaries fitting in: That was neither their objective nor their outlook. Their wives sewed their clothing from cloth sent to them by American missionaries in Malta, who also sent shoes and stockings. In a house they rented just beyond the walls of the city, they ate pork and sat on chairs and around tables rather than cross-legged on carpets. Then they set about trying to find Arabic tutors.

At first, the missionaries reported back that the local inhabitants were friendly. "The Arabs appeared very civil and friendly," wrote Bird and Goodell in their journal from Beirut. "Some of them gave us fruits as we passed the doors of their cottages, and invited us to stop and take coffee with them. The children generally appeared cleanly; and some of them, who have picked up a few Italian phrases said to us, 'Buon giorno,' (good morning) although it was near sun-set."[20] Fisk and King, the latter of whom traveled to more remote villages in order to learn Syriac, the liturgical language of the Maronites, reported similar receptions. The ruler of Mount Lebanon in this period was a wily emir by the name of Bashir Shihab. Fisk and King said about Bashir that "he knew something of America, and when we told him we were Americans, he gave us a salutation, and an expressive look, which flattered our national pride."[21]

The emir was himself a Maronite Christian, but he kept up both a mosque and a church in his mountain palace. He also welcomed the missionaries to his land; so too did various Maronite priests. Fisk and King even paid a visit to the newly elected Maronite patriarch, Yusuf Hubaysh, at his remote mountain monastery of Qannubin and offered him a Bible. He received them politely, although in all likelihood he mistook them for pilgrims. In these early days, there was virtually no hostility to the missionaries as individuals. But it is also clear that most of those who welcomed Fisk and his brethren had very little idea how serious was their determination to proselytize and how adept they would prove themselves to be in violating what was an unwritten, but cardinal, rule of coexistence in a multi-religious land: Do not openly blaspheme or insult other people's religions. In the small libraries of the monasteries scattered across Mount Lebanon that the American missionaries explored, the local chronicles recorded by Maronite priests and monks were laced with references to infidels and schismatics. But in their public dealings and everyday intercourse with those of other faiths, priests avoided giving offense and, in turn, expected no less of others; the saying in Mount Lebanon at the time was "Within each faith, God's help is needed."[22]

The American missionaries believed, however, that one did not need to learn a culture before trying to convert it. Certainly, Fisk and Bird diligently applied themselves to the study of Arabic. Yet, for the American missionaries, the mastery of Arabic was simply the means to a predetermined end. There was nothing, they maintained, that ought to prevent them in the meantime from trying to communicate what they believed were the inherent truths of the Gospels to the people of Syria, Palestine, and Mount Lebanon.

The Americans pursued two paths of mission almost immediately; the first was education. The homes of married missionaries became the setting for informal schooling. Bird and Goodell believed that their wives reflected "the intelligence and influence of the female part of the community in America."[23] They took in a few, apparently indigent, boys and girls and attempted to instill in them what the missionaries referred to as a proper Christian and civilized manner. This meant learning to read the Bible and other evangelical tracts and learning how to keep house or carry out various domestic chores. In July 1824, the missionaries established a more formal school for boys, and they hired a native Arabic speaker to teach the Bible in Arabic.[24]

The second path was direct proselytization, through both preaching to anyone who would listen and distribution of Bibles to any who would accept them. It was this path that the irrepressible Jonas King favored. Far more than home education, direct evangelization was in line with the missionary spirit that had carried the Americans several thousand miles to foreign shores. It had a more heroic, more masculine, and more dramatic aspect to it, and it was far more in line with the evangelical legacy of David Brainerd that they cherished.

King would often leave the missionary station at Beirut and head into mountain villages and there seek out the local priests. He would quiz them about the Bible, tease them for what he believed was their superstition, and expose how little they actually read, or encouraged others to read, the Bible. There was little doubt that King enjoyed these intellectual duels. Though he irritated their priests, the villagers of Mount Lebanon listened to King politely; some were intrigued by his message of salvation. Others pitied him because, as their Catholic priests informed them, he was "English" and thus had no religion. But they were also taken aback by the stridency of his evangelism and by his direct attacks on their traditional clergy.

It was precisely such an approach by the American missionaries—culturally deaf and arrogant, yet sincere and passionately embraced—that brought trouble to them. The most hostile reaction to their preaching came not from the Muslims, whom the missionaries were not allowed to convert directly, but from the Eastern Christian churches. In Mount Lebanon it was the Maronite patriarch who began the counterattack on the mission. He had been greatly embarrassed when the very men he had hosted at his monastery subsequently, and consistently, attacked his authority and faith.

The patriarch issued, in response, several proclamations banning any of his flock from accepting or reading the missionaries' Bibles. He also forbade any manner of religious discussion with those "from the sect of the English" whom he described as the "heretical followers" of Satan, the "enemies of the Roman Church, mother and teacher of all churches."[25] He accused the missionaries of deceit, of altering the Word of God, and of seducing the ignorant commoners of his faith. He said that they had enormous funds at their disposal to bribe and otherwise lure unsuspecting, simple-minded men and women into following their evil way. Their books, he commanded, were to be burned, and they were to be shunned. In the city of Aleppo, meanwhile, the Ottoman authorities, at the apparent urging of Eastern church leaders, demanded that the missionaries stop spreading "false" books (presumably their Bibles, which were based on a Roman version with the Apocrypha deleted) and warned them against either trying to convert Muslims or disturbing the tranquillity of any of their imperial subjects.[26]

The missionaries had struck a raw nerve. The religious pluralism of the Ottoman domains had never sanctioned freedom of speech, let alone presupposed equality between members of different religious communities.

But it did assume a subordination to Ottoman authority and an acceptance of the fait accompli of religious diversity. Because Protestant missionaries sought to attract adherents to their new, and as yet unrecognized, faith, they and their books were not considered a part of the religious order of the empire; rather, they were seen as a threat to its diversity. That there were only a few individual missionaries who prowled the patriarch's domains was not the point. They were "English" and thus embodied for him the much larger and more pernicious force of what he regarded as an ungodly Protestantism. They defied the Holy Roman Church to which he as a patriarch had pledged utter and total ecclesiastical submission. The Ottoman imperial system unquestionably privileged Islam over all other religions, but despite their subordinate status, Maronites and other communities, including the Armenians and Jews, were granted ecclesiastical autonomy and full control over marriage and inheritance in their communities. There was no native Protestant community, and therefore Protestantism had no legal standing—any man bold enough to embrace openly the views of the Protestant missionaries would have found himself legally as well as socially ostracized.

The Americans were trying to overturn a multi-religious society that was more than simply the sum of its parts. The Americans could only see separate "Maronites," "Mohammedans," "Druzes," "Jews," and "Armenians." Fisk, Goodell, Bird, and King could describe their manners and customs in great detail, but without appreciating the fact that ultimately these different communities also shared a common way of life. Christians and Muslims had long since reconciled themselves to living in proximity to others of different faiths. In Mount Lebanon, more immediately, men of ecclesiastical and secular rank of all religious faiths upheld a strict division between themselves and those whom they regarded as "ignorant" commoners. Hospitality, wrote the Scottish traveler David Urquhart in the midnineteenth century, "covers a multitude of sins."[27] To simply allow anyone to read and interpret the Bible was to open the door to utter confusion and chaos. It was to undermine the stability of the Maronite Church and therefore the Maronite nation, which had long survived in a hostile, Muslim-dominated world. In the face of such an existential threat, the patriarch was not interested in dialogue. He wanted to destroy the missionary threat.

The first great struggle between American missionaries and their Eastern Christian opponents unfolded with each side committed to vanquishing the other. There was no middle ground. The cultural clash was not so much between still inchoate American and Arab (or Muslim) identities, and certainly not between democracy and despotism, but far more obviously between opposing Christian readings of the world. Both were illiberal. The missionaries represented an evangelicalism that promoted freedom of conscience but also a deep hostility to—and a desire to overcome—other forms of faith that they disparaged, from liberal Protestantism in New England to Maronite Christianity in Mount Lebanon. As religiously intolerant as the American Board undoubtedly was, its leadership also vigorously promoted the possibility and necessity of assimilating Indians into white American society. It bitterly, though unsuccessfully, opposed the despoliation of Cherokee and other Indian tribes in Georgia. As the domestic missions to the Indians faltered and were eventually abandoned after 1830, when the U.S. government formally announced the deportation or "removal" of the Indians across the Mississippi, foreign missions became even more important as a proving ground for American benevolence and Christianity.

The Maronite patriarch personified a very different tradition. Far from trying to change others, he was interested exclusively in his own community. He may well have had a great fear of other religions, but he and his church had long accepted the impure world in which they lived. Two forms of explicit religious *intolerance* were set against one another—the American form was global in ambition, and the Maronite one was extraordinarily parochial in scope.

The missionaries refused to relent. King wrote a polemic in Arabic shortly before he left Beirut for good in September 1825. He called his testament a "Farewell Letter." In it, King explained to his Eastern Christian "friends" in Jerusalem, Ramle, Jaffa, Tyre, Sidon, Beirut, Dayr al-Qamar, Damascus, Aleppo, Tripoli, and Antioch why he could not become a Catholic. The Roman Church had not only corrupted the Word of God, he said, but during the Counter-Reformation it had sanctioned terrible oppression and cruelty. It had interrogated and tortured thousands of its Protestant opponents and was thus unworthy of the name Christian. King also laid out in very simple terms what Protestants believed. His "Farewell Letter" constituted the first public call for an Arab puritanism without any regard for local history, decorum, or sensibility: To be saved, his Eastern Christian "friends" had to become "true Christians" as individuals. Each had to read the Word of God and demonstrate faith in Jesus Christ. Each had to be born again spiritually after being graced by the Holy Spirit, which initial baptism pointed to but did not accomplish. Those who did not repent would face eternal punishment. If their families spurned the converts, so be it; if they were disinherited, persecuted, or even killed, so be it. The blood of martyrs, King intimated, would fertilize the soil of the Holy Land once more.[28]

Fate would have it that a young Maronite by the name of As'ad Shidyaq would become the center of this cultural clash. Highly educated and extremely bright, As'ad was introduced to Jonas King, who took an immediate liking to him. As'ad came from a prominent family, and many of his ancestors had worked for the Maronite Church. He himself had been groomed for the priesthood and had also taken a vow of submission to the authority of the patriarch. But as he taught the missionary Syriac and helped him translate his polemical "Farewell Letter," he soon found himself having a crisis of faith. As'ad was no longer convinced by Catholic dogma. He asked his patriarch for guidance and for some scriptural evidence that could refute various "English" objections to the Roman Church.[29]

The patriarch was stunned. He summoned As'ad to his monastery near Beirut in January 1826 and sought to convince him of the folly of embracing the missionaries' message. He declared that they had no church and no local standing, and he was perplexed to see an undeniably bright young man flirting with heresy and asking dangerous, even seditious questions about the pope's authority, the practice of confession, and the veneration of saints and icons—questions that went to the heart of the Maronite faith. But As'ad persisted in his protestations. The patriarch's advisers whispered in his ear that As'ad was insane, for who would defy the Word of God for the heretical "English"? Some among them advised the patriarch to bleed him; others urged him to punish the young man. Fearing for his life, As'ad escaped from the patriarch's monastery and made his way to Isaac Bird's house.

The respite was temporary. As'ad's own family was scandalized. Under intense pressure from family and community, As'ad agreed to leave the "English" and return to his own home. Very quickly, however, he was forcibly returned to the patriarch. This time Yusuf Hubaysh had his erstwhile charge taken to a remote monastery. As'ad attempted to escape several times, but each time he was caught. Then he was beaten and finally tortured. He was cast into a cell, denied his Bible, and weighed down by a heavy chain around his neck, as if he were a madman who had to be restrained for his own good. But the punishment illustrated something more visceral: Confronted with a failure to convince As'ad, the patriarch sought to compel his submission. The temptation to use brute force where persuasion had failed was simply too great for the Maronite leader. In his wretched prison cell, As'ad was tormented by his own wavering of faith. He felt betrayed by his community and was abandoned by the missionaries.

The illness and death of Pliny Fisk in October 1825 exacerbated the feelings of despondency within the small American missionary community. The mission had lost its anchor at the very hour of its severest test. Bird and Goodell in Beirut and the American Board in Boston tried, in whatever way they could, to rescue As'ad, but failed to do so. The ruling emir sided with the patriarch and scolded the missionaries for interfering in affairs of religion. By 1828 an upsurge in the Greek war of independence from the Ottomans forced Bird and Goodell and their families to quit Beirut. Fearing for their safety, the missionaries withdrew to the safety of Malta. They left behind a tiny group of native helpers and teachers and, of course, As'ad Shidyaq, who died alone in captivity.

American evangelical readers of the *Missionary Herald* had followed in detail the dramatic story of As'ad's captivity. For the very first time, an

Arab became an object of widespread American compassion. Even before As'ad died, the American Board publicized the story of the "martyr" As'ad Shidyaq to confound skeptics. It printed a small pamphlet—entitled simply *A Brief Memoir of Asaad Shidiak: an Arab young man, of the Maronite Catholic Church in Syria*—that went into several editions. Here at last was an Arab who had willingly embraced evangelical "truth." As'ad's own ambivalence about his conversion was ignored. The patriarch, predictably, was rendered as a stock figure, a cruel and bigoted tyrant, an evil man, a counterpoise to the Americans' sense of their own innate goodness.

The heroic American portrait of the life and death of As'ad Shidyaq covered up, but could not erase, a resounding missionary defeat. Maronite Christians—like all other communities of the region—refused to convert; Eastern Christian clerics were fully prepared to fight bitterly to preserve their inherited privileges, their customs, and their communities. The millennial phase of the American mission had sunk rapidly under the weight of its own expectations.

The missionaries lost their first battle to win the Arab converts principally because the Arabic-speaking Eastern Christian communities, especially the Maronites, had put up unexpectedly heavy resistance. But eventually they lost because they failed to recognize that the world was far more complex than their evangelical enthusiasm allowed. Reality would not bend to missionary zeal. "Look at the trees," an old Maronite priest tellingly rebuked Isaac Bird. "Each one bears its own fruit: the vine, the mulberry, the oak, each has its fruits peculiar to itself, and you cannot alter this course of nature. It would be foolish to attempt to make the vine bear mulberries, or the mulberry acorns, or the oak figs."[30]

The bitter struggle over As'ad Shidyaq broke the back of the first mission, but it also cleared the way for a new mission that was less overtly belligerent and thus ultimately more successful. In the aftermath of As'ad's death, the work of gathering together the nascent Protestant community began anew—and was given new impetus by the commercial treaty of 1830, which established the first formal diplomatic relations between the Ottoman Empire and the United States. The treaty led to the appointment of an American minister in Constantinople, and eventually American consuls were posted to Beirut, where over the course of the next two decades several additional men and women joined the growing mission. Most prominent among the American missionaries was Eli Smith, a graduate of Yale University who quickly established himself as the leader of the mission. If Jonas King's combative spirit had defined the first missionary decade, it was Smith's intensity of purpose that defined those that followed.

Understanding that the way forward through direct proselytization lay blocked, Smith turned to different tactics. He and his colleagues resigned themselves to a more constructive attitude, for they recognized that the foreseeable future allowed them to build only a small Protestant community alongside other faiths, not in place of them. The missionaries provided mountain villagers with rudimentary medical services and built up in Beirut the mission press that Smith had put in place by the mid-1830s; he ordered special Arabic fonts from the leading European foundry in Leipzig to inaugurate what would soon become a leading Arabic printing press in the eastern Mediterranean. The shift away from overt belligerence coincided with work on a new modern translation of the Bible into Arabic, which Smith initiated; the missionaries also instructed students in the English language and, in some places like Constantinople, where another mission of the American Board had been established in 1830, furnished young men with a practical education and secular skills. In addition, they lay the foundations for the first school for girls in the empire, opened by Smith's first wife, Sarah, in Beirut in 1834. The missionaries were by no means the only educators in the empire, but they would soon become legendary in this regard.

By the midnineteenth century, American missionaries had fanned out across major cities in the empire and in many of its villages. So ubiquitous were they that they began to be recognized and described for the first time as "American," as opposed to "English," by local priests and by the Ottoman government. American warships also became an increasingly frequent fixture in Ottoman ports. In 1848 naval captain William Lynch led an American expedition—with what he described as a crew of "young, muscular, native-born Americans"—to discover the source of the Jordan River.[31] The ship that bore him to the East had formerly been called the *Crusader* but was rechristened the *Supply*. Just as the stars and stripes fluttered over several missionary homes high in Mount Lebanon, so too did Lynch proudly hoist the American flag over the steel boats he had specifically designed and built for exploring the Dead Sea.

Following the establishment of a U.S. consulate in Egypt, a separate American mission under the control of the United Presbyterian Church of North America was inaugurated in Egypt in 1854. It concentrated on proselytizing the Coptic Christian minority, just as the Americans in Syria and Anatolia worked mainly among Christians who were subjects of the empire. The Presbyterian mission's contemptuous attitude toward "nominal" Christians and Muslims was essentially the same as the American Board's, as was its commitment to Bible-based literacy and education. Simultaneously, then, these different missionary movements helped identify the idea of America with missions. As important as Egypt was for the Presbyterian mission, it operated in the shadow of the more prestigious, more established, and more powerful American Board missions in Syria and Turkey. Without doubt, the Beirut station constituted the undisputed Arab jewel in the American missionary crown.

Far away from their homeland, the missionaries felt more American than ever in their Arab surroundings. They idealized America while setting down roots in foreign soil. They felt, as Sarah Smith confided to her parents, that the lands of the East demanded a suavity that did not sit well with the "sincerity of plain American manners."[32] Like the other Americans, she found the customs, manners, landscape, architecture, people, religions, and dress of the Orient bewildering, even repellent, in their diversity and difference. But she also expressed an anxious disquiet about the state of America and reminded evangelicals there of their obligations to help better and save what she and the American missionaries insisted were the less fortunate in the world. "I cannot tell you how much like a paradise America appears, as I view it from this land of darkness," wrote Smith. "And yet it seems to me as if its blessed inhabitants were dreaming, as it were, over a lost and guilty world. I know there are many who pray, and labor, and give, for its renovation; but are there many whose sole object it is to live especially and steadily for this end?"[33]

The missionaries continued to deplore both Islam and Oriental Christianity and still wanted to convert the multitude of Muslims and the "nominal" Christians. They still also looked to the Jews, although with markedly less intensity than they had at the outset of the mission because the Ottoman Jews constituted so small a population of the empire and, like other communities, they had generally resisted conversion. The naive spirit of Parsons and King began to dissipate—at least in public pronouncements and in dealings with the Arabs of Beirut, Mount Lebanon, and Syria.

The period of adjustment was not without its share of disappointments, hardships, and false starts. For many years the missionaries held out hope that the heterodox Druze community of Mount Lebanon might convert en masse. But like so many earlier fantasies of native conversion, this expectation proved illusory. Eli Smith and another missionary, Harrison Gary Dwight, conducted a survey of Anatolia and Persia. Their tour, together with the labors of William Goodell, who moved to Constantinople in 1830, would lay the basis for sustained and eventually tremendously significant American missionary work among the Armenians, a major Christian community of the empire whose church was founded at the beginning of the fourth century AD. But for now the Armenian ecclesiastics reacted with the same fury that had marked the Maronite response to the missionaries. The Americans also discovered the Nestorian (Assyrian) Christians and approved a mission to them centered in Urmia, in what is today northwestern Iran.

Above all, the pressure from the home front to make converts proved dispiriting. Rufus Anderson, the leader of the American Board who succeeded Jeremiah Evarts, fretted about the English-language instruction offered by the mission school in Beirut. Syrians, he opined, had become "so anglified in their ideas and tastes that they became disgusted with their countrymen, and even with their noble Arabian tongue, and were unfitted in great measure for doing good to their people."[34] It was an odd judgment from one who knew no Arabic, as well as a powerful reminder that the initial purpose of the American mission was evangelism, not education. Anderson decided to curtail English-language education in mission schools, bolstered in his belief by the fact that mission students in Beirut invariably used their newly acquired language skills to seek lucrative employment as interpreters rather than to evangelize among their own communities.

The missionaries on the ground were pulled in different directions. Some sympathized with Anderson. They were still filled with an unalloyed evangelical enthusiasm for mission that refused to make any significant concession to the foreign world in which they worked. Others were not so sanguine. Far more so than Anderson could appreciate sitting in America, they recognized that they could either pursue the slow and difficult work of evangelical conversion, in order to gradually build up native Protestant communities in the Ottoman Empire, or they could devote themselves to providing a more secular education, which was what the great majority of the local inhabitants greatly desired. The first path marginalized them in a society where all the major religious communities, and even its minor ones, were united in opposition to having their own converted; the second made them obviously relevant in a society that lacked any kind of educational system that could bring students of different religious denominations together and provide them with an education and language for the world.

The choice between relevance and irrelevance was not easily made by the missionaries, and indeed it was not, properly speaking, a choice that presented itself in this period in such clear terms. Most missionaries believed they could pursue both evangelical and secular goals without compromising either. The newly arrived midcentury Amherst graduate Daniel Bliss admitted that "sympathy and calves' foot jelly are no part in the 'Plan of Salvation,' but a great help in illustrating it."[35] A missionary seminary in the Lebanese mountain village of Abeih continued to teach mathematics, geography, astronomy, history, and natural philosophy, although, in line with Anderson's insistent belief, the overall emphasis was squarely on making science "subservient" to Christianity.[36]

In a suburb of Constantinople, another American Board missionary, Cyrus Hamlin, gambled on a thoroughly Westernized education for his pupils, which he strongly believed was the more effective way of spreading Christianity. He opened a school in 1840 that soon included a steam-powered flour mill and a bakery. He also had a vision that would lay the basis for one of the great new universities of the East. Anderson balked at so radical and secular a path, and the two men grew estranged from one another. Hamlin recognized that the local prestige of the mission was at stake—the name of America would rise or fall in relation to how much its missionaries could provide a real future for its converts and students and how far they could go in meeting local expectations for material improvement in their lives. For Anderson, who staked his reputation on a narrow evangelism and who had already seen the collapse of schemes to bring civilization to the Indians in North America, such considerations were irrelevant. They were also very expensive. Converts, he feared, might well be "mercenary" in their motivations.[37] The missionaries, he also feared, might be tempted to play God over the converts. Anderson had witnessed firsthand how the expanding American frontier, its temptations, riches, and lands, and its beguiling mantra of manifest destiny had already trampled underfoot many professed American ideals. The missionaries were men, and men were sinful. They might well become too possessive of secular institutions, too settled, too comfortable in their foreign worlds, and thus lose sight of their own original evangelical calling.

Portentous upheavals within the Ottoman Empire, however, augured a more successful missionary age. The Greek revolt, which had begun the year Fisk and Parsons arrived in the Levant and continued to unfold during the As'ad Shidyaq affair, led to the independence of Greece in 1830. Indeed, the Greek revolt had just ended when the ambitious Ottoman

Albanian–born governor of Egypt, Muhammad Ali, openly rebelled against imperial authority and sent his son Ibrahim Pasha to invade Syria in 1831. The Egyptians occupied Syria, including Mount Lebanon and Beirut, and in 1832 they attempted to march to Constantinople. The Ottoman Empire would have surely collapsed had it not been for British intervention. In 1840 the British navy thwarted Muhammad Ali's ambitions and restored an enfeebled but "legitimate" Ottoman authority to its Syrian provinces.

The Ottoman answer to its own evident military decline was the same one provided by other Eastern powers struggling to adapt to an age of Western hegemony. Just as Meiji Japan would do, the Ottomans embarked upon a wholesale reformation of their empire. Their initial concern, naturally, was to staunch the bleeding of territory by focusing on the military. But very quickly reform spread to clothing, education, land tenure, architecture, urban planning, and communications. Change inevitably encroached upon the foundational ideology of Muslim primacy that had defined the empire's character for several centuries. Beginning in 1839, the imperial rulers went out of their way to emphasize that they would treat all their subjects equally regardless of their religious affiliation. For an Islamic empire, this was a momentous and revolutionary ideological transformation. For the very first time, a Muslim empire implicitly acknowledged the political equality of Muslim, Christian, and Jewish subjects. Rather than emphasizing discrimination, the Ottomans tried to create a unifying, secular national ethos of Ottoman patriotism.

At the conclusion of the Crimean War of 1856, the sultan declared that he wanted to establish "a state of things conformable with the dignity of my empire and the position which it occupies among civilized nations." He issued an imperial decree that heralded a "new era." In this Ottoman version of the Emancipation Proclamation, the sultan declared his desire to promote the welfare of all his subjects, "who in my sight are all equal, and equally dear to me, and who are united to each other by the cordial ties of patriotism."[38] As in almost all such moments, reform contended with reaction. There was indeed a backlash in various parts of the empire to the unprecedented notion of equality, and Christians were massacred by Muslim mobs in cities such as Aleppo and Damascus in 1850 and 1860. Protestants too were often harassed and persecuted, but almost always by Eastern Christian prelates from whose communities they had seceded.

For the American missionaries, this revolutionary age of equality had two important outcomes. It confirmed their status as protected Americans whose safety was guaranteed not simply by diplomatic treaties but by the presence of European and American gunboats in various Ottoman harbors and the prestige of Western modernity in evidence all around them. And the new age witnessed the belated, official recognition in 1850 of Protestants as an autonomous and protected religious community in the empire. As foreigners, the missionaries relied on so-called Capitulations. Originally treaties granted by the Ottoman sultans in the sixteenth and seventeenth centuries, they offered Western mercantile communities resident in the empire exemptions from taxation and a guarantee of consular representation in case of disputes with Ottoman subjects. But in the present age of Western military supremacy, they were interpreted by missionaries, and by virtually all other Westerners, in a manner that placed them virtually beyond the reach of Ottoman law. American missionaries were immunized from the harshest moments of upheaval around them, just as they had been during the Greek revolt. They frequently reported that the local populace sought out their homes and schools as sanctuaries whenever tumult erupted. Smith, Hamlin, and others became stewards over native Protestants whose churches began to be organized across the empire.

The existential cultural clash that had marked the initial, heady American spiritual assault on the lands of the Bible had metamorphosed into a stable modus vivendi. The mutual ignorance and recrimination in which both Americans and their Maronite opponents had so enthusiastically engaged no longer seemed to unfold with the same immediacy. As'ad Shidyaq's tribulations now seemed to belong to a past age. When another highly educated Maronite Christian by the name of Butrus al-Bustani embraced Protestantism in the early 1840s, the missionaries initially feared a reprise of the As'ad Shidyaq affair. But the political climate had changed substantially. Toleration, not discrimination, was now the imperial mantra, and although the Maronite Church was bitterly disappointed in Bustani's conversion, it realized that a new age had dawned.

Bustani freely and openly collaborated with his American missionary patrons in Beirut. His wife Raheel, who had been raised in the house of Sarah Smith, was devoted to the Protestant mission and served as an exemplar of female piety in a world that the missionaries viewed as particularly antagonistic toward women. Bustani participated enthusiastically in a new organization independent of the American mission called the Syrian Society of Arts and Sciences; founded in Beirut in 1847, it met regularly until 1852. This society comprised mostly Arabs, but its presidents were American missionaries. It ran regular monthly meetings on questions of the arts and sciences, but it refused to delve into questions of religion. Its constitution reflected the signs of the times. American and Arab men of different backgrounds could at last find common ground; they could work together rather than against one another. They shared what appeared to be a common language of modernization.

Just as the local priests had adapted to the presence of an American mission in their midst, so too did the Americans belatedly recognize the complexity of their surroundings. From being radically out of place when Parsons and Fisk had first set out on their evangelical quest, the missionaries were now seen as legitimate representatives of America in the empire. The more established the missionaries became, the more they thrived in their unique position as interlocutors and translators of culture. They were America to the Arabs, and they presented the Arab world to Americans. Unlike the American Board's unsuccessful attempt to promote Indian-white coexistence in the United States, which was contested at every turn and proved to be a haunting failure, there was at this point very little to challenge the missionaries' view of the Arabs, or indeed their representation of America in the Arab world.

By the end of 1855, the American community in Beirut looked quite settled. The leader of the American Board, Rufus Anderson, was astonished at the expansion of the city and of the mission when he visited the city that same year. Missionary homes commanded superb vistas. The small, cramped walled city the first missionaries encountered in 1823 had spilled into the surrounding countryside; new suburbs had grown up, and the city had become the residence of several foreign consuls, including in 1850 an American consul. Palm and olive trees had given way to the lucrative mulberry crucial to an expanding silk market. A quarantine zone had also been constructed, and warehouses built to store cargoes of petroleum from America. Three schools—one of which was for girls—with over one hundred students in all constituted the heart of the mission. The Arabic press was in full production, turning out close to 1,700,000 pages of Scriptures and other evangelical tracts.[39] Smith had already translated up to the forty-fourth chapter of Isaiah, despite his faltering health. The seminary in Abeih housed twenty-five boys. Progress was measured, but Anderson at least was pleased. He could take solace that the birth pains of the American mission appeared to be over.

In their private correspondence and in writings meant for home evangelical audiences, the missionaries continued to be judgmental of the Ottoman Empire and its inhabitants. Like other Westerners in an era of manifest Western supremacy, the missionaries were enveloped by a web of language of their own making that characterized the Arabs—and other non-Western people—as dark, depraved, lost, primitive, backward, or savage. Those who refused to convert to their way of life and religion bore the brunt of missionary disdain.

Even the few hard-won converts were regarded as mere "babes in Christ." Though a native church had been founded in 1848 in Beirut, it was not until 1890 that the missionaries could bring themselves to appoint an Arab pastor over it, one Youssef Badr, who came from the Lebanese village of Shwayr and was a Greek Catholic Christian who gave up his job as a stonemason and converted to Protestantism when he decided to pursue an education at the missionary seminary in Abeih. There was a hard inequality in pay and in responsibilities between the so-called native teachers and the missionaries. The conventional wisdom among the missionaries was simple: Mount Lebanon, Palestine, and Syria—or "the Bible lands," as they referred to them—would continue to stagnate until they were revivified by Christian evangelism.

One such effort was the missionary William Thomson's spectacular transposition of biblical stories into the contemporary context of Palestine and Syria. In this work, appropriately entitled *The Land and the Book*, he proposed to guide his American readers through the "identical land" and the "same scenes" that they had read about for so long.[40] This biblical romance was predicated, however, on firsthand knowledge of the lands of the Bible and experience with its actual inhabitants. Despite his condemnation of the falsity and fanaticism of Islam and of what he saw as the vulgar and primitive "domestic economy" of the East, Thomson's discussion of the "Arabs" pushed his readers in a new direction. His intricate description of Muslims at prayer was biased, but it was also moving. It gave tentative form and humanity to what had been for most Americans simply a metaphor for despotism. Muslims, he added, "are rather afraid of any one who is especially sanctimonious and given to prayer—their prayers, I mean."[41] *The Land and the Book* became one of the most commercially successful nineteenth-century missionary accounts of the Holy Land.

Even more than Thomson, the missionary Cornelius Van Dyck sought to embrace and thrive in a new and unfamiliar environment. Van Dyck, born to Dutch parents but raised in Kinderhook, New York, joined the Syria mission as a medical missionary in 1840. Like all missionaries, he wanted to convert the Arabs and believed that his Protestant faith was intrinsically superior to other religions. But he demonstrated a natural facility with Arabic, a language with which most of his peers struggled, and an ease with Arab culture that few of them would contemplate. Van Dyck was also not educated in a religious seminary and thus was not as thoroughly immersed in evangelical orthodoxy as were many of his fellow laborers. Bilingual to begin with, Van Dyck engaged and socialized with Arab converts and repudiated what he saw as missionary arrogance.

Van Dyck's openness to Arab people, and not simply to the Arabic language, was exceptional. So too was his awareness of the damage to the goal of winning Arab hearts and minds caused by American missionary prejudice. Yet together with Thomson and Smith, Van Dyck represented an important shift in American thinking about the Arab world. Opposition to Islam remained utterly central to how the missionaries viewed this world. But their years of contact with individual Arabs and with Arab culture began inevitably to make subtle changes in their perceptions in a manner unimaginable to American evangelicals who had never had sustained interaction with Arabs. The best missionaries did not simply read the Bible and expect the world to conform to it. Rather, they gained a deeper sense of the Bible through a prolonged encounter with different people and through a marked willingness to travel—in every sense of the word—into foreign worlds. The missionaries began to develop a considerable appreciation for the Arab "race."

Thomson confided to Anderson in Beirut that there was a foundation among Arabs "for taking care of themselves" that was greater than what was to be found in Africa or Hawaii.[42] The *Missionary Herald*, in turn, boasted in 1844 that the "Arabs are a wonderful people. They have the elements of a noble character."[43] Eli Smith rounded out this description by explaining to an American audience six years later why the "Arab race is my favorite." Arabs had literature and poetry, "the soul of sublimity," a record of achievement in science, mathematics, philosophy, and history, and a language that made English sink "into insignificance before its beauty and force."[44] The attitude adopted by Smith amounted to a romantic view of history: The people of the West had adopted several centuries ago their religion, arts, and sciences from the East; the Arabs had preserved the Western heritage during the Western Dark Ages—Granada in particular had been a center of learning that had preserved for the West its own glorious heritage—and now the missionaries were simply repaying to the Arabs a long overdue debt.

Such romantic views were not addressed to Americans alone. Rather, they were presented publicly to Arabs. The missionaries believed that national cooperation between Americans and Arabs was inevitable if the American presence was to bear its full fruit. Not content to be simply shepherds of a small and as yet insignificant Protestant community, and unable to convert most Arabs through direct evangelism, the missionaries increasingly emphasized a more pragmatic and less evangelical approach. Smith, Thomson, and Van Dyck regarded and presented themselves to Arab assistants, congregations, and audiences as avatars of modern science, technology, and spirituality. They became apostles of progress as well as of Protestantism, although in their minds the two were firmly linked together.

That very few of the Arabic-speaking inhabitants of the region considered themselves "Arabs" in any national sense was hardly the point. The missionaries did not advance a notion of self-determination. They advocated instead a notion of gradual racial improvement and progress in a manner that attracted rather than repelled Arabs to their point of view. They continued to hold and publicly promote to American audiences a fundamentally anti-Ottoman doctrine, but increasingly they believed that they had arrived at their views through an objective and scientific lens, not simply through evangelical conviction. Islam, they declared, was not simply wrong and hateful; it was backward.

Perhaps no missionary exemplified this promotion of the Arab race with an excoriation of Islam more than the bellicose Presbyterian Henry Harris Jessup. A Yale undergraduate and holder of a degree in divinity from New York's Union Theological Seminary, Jessup's early descriptions of "Mohammedanism" were marked by an intense and raw hostility that was clearly less tempered by experience than was Thomson's imagery of Islam. In a long exposé published by the *Missionary Herald*, a journal unread by Arabs in this period, Jessup describes a stock figure of a "Mohammedan boy"—one whom he follows into a school, onto the streets, and into his home. This boy sees Greek, Maronite, Druze, and Jewish boys playing sports, but he walks by them "in sullen contempt" because, he adds, "it is the duty of the true Moslem to hate and curse all infidels."[45]

Like the Amherst-graduated Daniel Bliss, whom he had accompanied to the Levant in 1855, Jessup was energetically committed to the triumph of Protestantism. In this respect, his outlook was similar to that of the pioneer generation of Fisk, Parsons, and King. But his was a generation of foreign missionaries who were decidedly cooler to the idea of millennialism and also clearly more enamored with the idea of American manifest destiny.

In Jessup's understanding of the struggle of races, the Arabs unquestionably enjoyed a higher level of civilization than native Americans. And yet like the early missionaries, Jessup and his fellow missionaries were frustrated by the undeniable fact that the majority of Arabs refused to convert. When Eli Smith succumbed to cancer in January 1857, the Americans of this new generation found themselves bereft of their leader, just as the pioneer generation had found itself robbed of Pliny Fisk. Once more reinforcements were called for. The missionaries had more schools and stations than ever; they had more female students than ever; missionary wives were more active than ever; America was more powerful and known than ever; and yet the number of converts remained paltry relative to the other religious communities. In all of Syria the American mission could count only 317 Arab congregants in 1857.[46]

Exactly as the generation before them had done, so too did these men put a hopeful gloss on a great evangelical failure in the Syria mission; just as their predecessors had pleaded for more time to accomplish their task, so now was patience the watchword of the day. The pruned vine was about to flower in these "sin-darkened plains and mountains," the new missionaries said.[47] Just as it was with Parsons and Fisk, the religiously diverse Arab society stubbornly refused to conform to a narrow and zealous missionary reading of the world. William Eddy, whose grandson would translate for President Franklin Delano Roosevelt and Ibn Saud on an American destroyer eighty-seven years later, even let slip a desperate note of alarm. Noting the ruins of Crusader castles that crowned the mountain summits around him, Eddy pleaded for more help to sustain the faltering spiritual crusade. Wholesale technological and ideological changes in the Ottoman Empire had not—and would not—herald wholesale religious change.

It would take an extraordinary upheaval in Mount Lebanon and the Civil War in America to give the missionaries the impetus they needed to fully appreciate the new secular horizon before them. For at least a decade the missionaries who knew the most about the land they worked and were the most fluent in Arabic—Smith, Van Dyck, and Thomson—had flirted with a new direction for the mission: Without acknowledging it, they had moved perilously close to a decisive break between being Americans and being missionaries. Two powerful elements of their identity that to them seemed entirely intertwined, the evangelical and the national, were actually working at cross-purposes in their efforts to win Arab hearts and minds. The small, dedicated community of converts, beginning with As'ad Shidyaq and continuing with Raheel and Butrus al-Bustani, was a testament to the real but limited power of evangelicalism. These converts admired the missionaries, but an immensely greater power lay in the idea of a modern America that appeared to shun any material interest in the Arab world and that inspired Arab Muslims and Christians without demanding that they abandon the faiths of their fathers or their standing in society. Four decades of trial and error and of dashed expectations were about to be radically transformed into an unanticipated bounty of converts—not to evangelicalism but to the idea of America.

The missionary Henry Harris Jessup's feverish dispatches from the summer of 1860 captured the intensity of the conflagration around him. "Civil war," Jessup wrote at the beginning of June, "has actually commenced in all its fury. The Druzes and Maronites have plunged into deadly strife, with a savage ferocity which seems inspired by Satan himself."[48] Like all wars, the conflict between the Maronites and Druzes had arisen for complex reasons, and as with most wars, the stories told about it were not. Amid conflicting interpretations of Ottoman reforms, Maronites sought to liberate coreligionists from Druze control; they also fought among themselves. The Druzes feared that the Maronites were going to eradicate them. British and French agents actively intervened in the area, while local Ottoman authorities lost control of the situation. The result was that the Maronites were comprehensively defeated in Mount Lebanon, and several large Christian towns were sacked. The missionaries' version of events was ultimately reduced to a tale of Muslim perfidy, especially after a Muslim mob in Damascus fell on a Christian quarter and slaughtered several hundred—some sources claimed several thousand—Christians there.[49] The riot in Damascus was an urban affair, not a rural civil war such as the one that had raged between the Maronites and Druzes; its Christian, mostly Orthodox victims had very little in common with the Maronite peasants who had played a key role in instigating the violence in Mount Lebanon. But Christians had been slaughtered in both locales, adding to the atmosphere of dread that surrounded the missionaries in Beirut. They were not attacked, but Jessup was convinced that the violence he had witnessed was nothing less than a Turkish conspiracy to efface Christianity and civilization from the region.

The upshot was that the American missionaries and the native Protestants such as Bustani struggled to cope with the flood of refugees who poured into Beirut—more than eight thousand depended on missionary rations. By the end of August, Ottoman and French armies had landed in Beirut to restore order to the region. European outrage at the massacres of Christians and sympathy for the survivors produced a remarkable humanitarian movement, the very first of its kind in which Europeans and Americans mobilized on behalf of refugees in the Arab world. European missionary organizations took the lead in promoting the welfare of refugees. They acted, they said, out of a sense of impartial compassion and civilization, but their solicitude undoubtedly originated in the fact that the victims were Christian and the perpetrators Muslim.

At this very moment, when English, Prussian, and French missionaries were flooding into Beirut, the American Board demanded drastic cutbacks from its own mission there. The United States was also on the brink of civil war. The American mission in Beirut risked both bankruptcy and marginalization in the face of stiff foreign competition. When its mission schools, which had been closed as a result of the sectarian tumult, reopened, students were reluctant to return. They wanted, as they always had, education without conversion. They understood that foreign languages, medicine, and accounting skills served them far more immediately than religious sermons. Now, in a city that had become the object of intense European concern, there were other missionary organizations, and some were willing to teach science, including the Jesuits. As America plunged into its own debilitating conflict, the missionaries in Beirut took a momentous decision. They decided to open a college that would appeal directly to the aspirations of Arabs for change.

This turning point in the history of the mission also marked a profound moment for the meaning of America in the Arab world. Already in Constantinople, Cyrus Hamlin had opened an institution called Robert College (after its principal benefactor, Christopher Rheinlander Robert), in defiance of Rufus Anderson. But now in Beirut a much grander experiment was launched by Daniel Bliss and William Thomson. Anderson, predictably, was unhappy and only reluctantly agreed to give it his blessing. He called it a "necessary choice of evils" because he felt, correctly, that this new institution would take the missionaries in new and ultimately secular directions.[50]

The name of the new institution, the Syrian Protestant College, reassuringly signaled a continuity with the mission that had given it birth. From the beginning, however, the college was formally independent of the American Board, and from the beginning it was clear that it represented a new kind of secular American presence in the region. "The world is moving fast," Bliss wrote to his brother.[51] Americans, he intimated, were determined to consolidate a leading position in the scientific enlightenment of the Arabs, and from this position they hoped to inspire a belief in a Protestant God.

Following a frenetic fund-raising campaign in America and England, Bliss opened the college in 1866 on makeshift premises. Its first class had only sixteen students. Within a decade and a half, a new campus on the outskirts of town had been designed, and several imposing stone buildings were constructed; a medical school was opened, and Bliss moved into a new residence with a stunning view of the Mediterranean. The new college was no seminary; in its decidedly modern literary and scientific orientation, it was the first institution of its kind in the Arab region. The Jesuits, never far behind, were quick to open their own rival university in 1875, called St. Joseph University. Although successful, it could not match the Syrian Protestant College in either scale or beauty.

On December 7, 1871, Daniel Bliss watched William E. Dodge, treasurer of the college's board of trustees, founder of one of America's largest mining companies, and an evangelical philanthropist, lay the cornerstone of the massive stone building that would be known as College Hall, the clock tower of which would dominate the surrounding landscape of Beirut for at least one hundred years. Dodge hoped that this new edifice would be a "city on a hill"—a beacon of hope, he thought, in a land that needed it. Bliss, in turn, declared proudly that "this College is for all conditions and classes of men without regard to colour, nationality, race or religion. A man white, black, or yellow; Christian, Jew, Mohammedan or heathen, may enter and enjoy all the advantages of this institution for three, four or eight years; and go out believing in one God, in many Gods, or in no God. But," Bliss insisted, "it will be impossible for anyone to continue with us long without knowing what we believe to be the truth and our reasons for that belief."[52]

It was a revolutionary statement calculated not to offend the evangelical spirit that sustained his enterprise. In a single utterance, however, the founder of the college had turned the history of the American mission on its head. There was very little that connected what he said with Levi Parsons and Pliny Fisk, who had first set foot in the Ottoman Empire fifty-one years earlier. Rather than zealous exhortation, persuasion would now be used; rather than spiritual belligerence, tolerance would be emphasized; rather than unrealistic expectations, there was measured aspiration. Rather than searching out Arabs, it was Arabs who would discover the Americans on a new terrain that, while still clearly Protestant, was marked by a commitment to secular science and literature. It was now the turn of Arabs to have expectations of Americans. It was now their turn to discover in America a promised land. It was now their turn to dream.

2

THE ARAB DISCOVERY OF AMERICA

In his massive nineteenth-century encyclopedia *Da'irat al-Ma'arif* or *The Circle of Knowledge*, the eminent Protestant convert Butrus al-Bustani offered one of the first Arab views of the United States and its people. In a typeface originally brought to Beirut by the missionary Eli Smith, and hence known as "American Arabic," Bustani explained to his Arabic readers the geography, zoology, topography, and basic history of North and South America in ten succinct pages. He noted that the continents were discovered by Christopher Columbus and named after Amerigo Vespucci. About the United States itself Bustani said simply that it "extended from the Atlantic Ocean to the Pacific Ocean, and is bordered by English America [Canada] to the north, Mexico to the south, the Atlantic to the east and the Pacific to the west." The country, he wrote, encompassed over 3,600,000 square miles and its population was around 38,558,371, of whom he noted 33,589,377 were "white," 4,880,009 were "black," 63,254 were "Chinese," and 25,721 were "civilized American Indians."[1]

Bustani's description of the United States was schematic, but his precise enumeration of the country's population represented the beginnings of a modern Arab understanding of America. If inherited notions and prejudices about the Orient and Islam pervaded the initial American missionary expectations of the Arab world, nineteenth-century Arabs approached America with a far more open perspective. Bustani worked with a tabula rasa. America was simply not known in any significant manner. As early as the seventeenth century a Chaldean Christian priest by the name of Ilyas al-Mosuli from what is today Iraq had braved the Atlantic Ocean and traveled to the New World. He left an Arabic account of his extraordinary travels across Spanish America, but he did not visit any of the English colonies. When the Egyptian Muslim shaykh Rifa'a al-Tahtawi was sent to Europe in 1826 by the ruler of Egypt to discover the secrets of Western progress, he wrote extensively about France, where he resided for several years. But of America Tahtawi said simply that "in Arabic, 'America' is also called the West Indies and 'Aja'ib al-makhluqat ('the wonders of creation'). It first became known to the Franks after the Christians conquered al-Andalus and drove the Arabs from it." Tahtawi added that the continent of America "lies on six seas" and that there was in it a country called "the land of *Itazuniya* [a corruption of the French *États Unis*]."[2]

For most Arabs of the nineteenth century, "the West" was defined primarily by Europe—by its science, its arts, its armies, its cities, and its imperialism. For Bustani and every other educated man and woman of his generation who interacted with American missionaries but did not actually travel to the United States, America remained an abstraction. Unlike ideas of Europe, which were forged across centuries of trade and conflict between Muslim and Christian empires, the idea of America among Arabs was built squarely on the back of the very recent missionary encounter.

It was of great significance that the Arab perception of America would initially and most comprehensively be created by ardent missionaries and their descendants, not by sailors, merchants, or soldiers. From the very beginning the idea of a benevolent America was most powerfully felt and propagated by those who had the closest association with American missionaries and their institutions, particularly the Syrian Protestant College. Also from the very beginning, the impetus for the earliest repudiation of America came from either those who were threatened by the missionary message or those who were disenchanted by the profound gap they experienced between their idealization of "America" and its vastly more complex reality.

The small native Arab Protestant community and the other Eastern Christians who worked closely with the missionaries were the most intimately familiar with the Americans. Many came from rural Mount Lebanon, others from the coastal towns of Syria. In Egypt those who were converted from the Coptic community by the Presbyterian mission there were also the ones who were closest to the missionaries. As teachers, missionary assistants, students, or translators, they helped build a bridge over the chasm of ignorance and indifference that separated Americans from Arabs. Just as the missionaries began to build and cross the bridge from one side, Arab men and women energetically set out from the other.

But they worked at a different pace and with different intent than their missionary patrons. The men and women who made up the first generation of Arab Protestants believed in the missionaries in a manner that was rarely reciprocated; their lives revolved around powerful personal bonds and material relationships that they established with their patrons. But they never accepted or used the pejorative term "native" to describe themselves. Instead, they routinely used the term *wataniyyun*, or "nationals," which, like "native," indicated local rootedness and distinguished them from the American Protestants but possessed none of the former's condescension. Tannus Haddad, for instance, one of the very first Arabs to work with the early mission, took tremendous pride in his position as a teacher in mission schools. He even named his daughter Sarah Smith Haddad after the missionary Eli Smith's first wife. In his Arabic letters to Isaac Bird, he shared a language of respect that was entirely contradictory to the harsh missionary judgments of the "natives" in their English-language books and letters.

For the most part, the relationship between Americans and Arabs was unequal. The missionaries hid from their native converts their disdain for their culture, but they valued men such as Tannus Haddad because they were indispensable to the functioning of the mission. The Americans routinely paid these individuals less for the same kind of work that they themselves undertook, but at the same time they offered salaries, medicines, and educational opportunities that were readily seized by increasing numbers of Arabs. Both Americans and Arab converts criticized local culture—especially Eastern ecclesiastical traditions, such as the veneration of saints and icons and, in the case of Maronites and Greek Catholics, the primacy of the pope—but their starting points were very different. The missionaries found it very hard to abandon their idea that Eastern Christians were "bad specimens of Christianity," as Eli Smith put it; their private correspondence betrayed their frustration with their failure to build an army of converts.[3] They ultimately upheld the difference between their ideal (for that is what it was) of a "Christian America" and a benighted native society. It was as if there were two faces to the missionaries: the benevolent, paternalistic face that encouraged the natives, that spoke Arabic with them, that sincerely engaged with and fitted into an Arabic-speaking world, and the condescending face of the missionary who, unseen and unheard by his local colleagues, continued to caricature Islam and "Orientals" and "nominal" Christians to American audiences.

There was no denying, however, that the presence of American missionaries had helped carve out a space for individual Arabs to reflect on their own society. As'ad Shidyaq's youngest brother, Faris, was perhaps the most gifted of these nineteenth-century Arab Protestants. Appalled by his brother's persecution, he fled to Malta with the missionaries. He converted to Protestantism, thus disproving the Maronite patriarch's pronouncement that the missionaries had been vanquished and their message had fallen on the deaf ears of a perpetually faithful and Catholic nation. Possessing a stinging sense of irony, Faris used his experience of exile in Europe to unleash an extraordinary repudiation of traditional society.

Faris was an individual in a world of communities. Tannus Haddad was a devoted teacher who stayed with the missionaries until his death in 1864; Faris proved to be a far more rebellious spirit. He was a man who took up writing and worked extensively with the missionary press in

Malta; he also worked on an Arabic translation of the Bible, experimented with the Arabic language, traveled to England and France, and wrote a witty travelogue of his time in Malta. He pioneered a new Arabic literary form as well, the allegorical autobiography. In it, he extolled the American missionaries' commitment to the advance of knowledge, comparing it to the Maronite Church's defensive and oppressive mentality.

Faris Shidyaq praised the "English priests"—the American missionaries—for they have "spared no effort to do good for our community."[4] However, he ultimately tired of the evangelicalism of the missionaries. He recognized that the ills of his own society could not obscure those of the West. He concluded that the West, by which he meant France and England, preached civilization but practiced colonialism. Eventually, he converted yet again, this time to Islam, and he became known as Ahmad Faris Shidyaq. He settled in Constantinople, where he pioneered the first Arab newspaper that was distributed throughout the empire. Mercurial, opportunistic perhaps, Faris Shidyaq was a brilliant yet orphaned child of the first encounter between Americans and the Arab world.

Another figure who was indelibly impressed by his introduction to the missionaries was a Greek Catholic by the name of Mikhayil Mishaqa. Like As'ad and Faris Shidyaq, he forsook his fathers' faith. From an established merchant family that had long enjoyed the patronage of powerful local families, Mishaqa became evangelical in 1848. He became a pamphleteer and a polemicist. Condemned by the Greek Catholic patriarch for his conversion, Mishaqa responded vigorously and in kind. "He anathematized me with his word and that of his congregations, so I anathematized him with God's word and that of His Prophets and apostles."[5] Despite the Greek Catholic patriarch's desperate pleas to the Ottoman government, Mishaqa was appointed as the vice consul of the United States in Damascus in 1859. That a non-U.S. citizen could hold such a post indicates the insignificance of the official American presence in much of the empire at this point. Mishaqa also worked as a medical doctor, and toward the end of his life he wrote an autobiography that very clearly captured the influence on him of the modernizing Ottoman age and the possibilities that it offered for a new relationship of equality among men of different faiths.

Very few of the Arab converts, of course, were like Faris Shidyaq or Mikhail Mishaqa. Most were rather ordinary individuals who turned to Protestantism or to Protestant schools because of the educational opportunities they afforded. These Arabs were often acting out of frustration with their own traditional clergy, who had been reluctant to provide them with the schools they wanted, although in the second half of the century the educational gap was closed considerably. In 1869 Beirut, a center of learning in Syria, boasted forty-five boys' schools, one of which was run by the Americans.[6] The Ottoman state belatedly sought to provide modern higher education for its subjects, but in the Arab provinces it remained one crucial step behind the Western missionaries and unable to provide an adequate substitute for the various parochial and missionary institutions that served its Christian population.

So new was the Arab Protestant community, and so well did it reflect the age of reform that had given it birth, that the leading Protestants of the day were inevitably marked by an optimism that was not as easily discerned in the leaders of other communities. The Protestants alone had no religious investments in the past. Unlike Muslim or Maronite clerics, they had no orthodoxies to defend; they had literally made change foundational for their self-consciously modern and, in cities like Beirut, bourgeois lives. They took the lead in the education of women, and after 1850 they successfully transformed the stigma of being associated with "English" heretics into an open Arab connection with American missionaries, mission schools, and, especially, the Syrian Protestant College.

They became, not surprisingly, the Arab avatars of modern education. The story of Youssef Badr, the first Arab pastor of the first native Protestant church of Beirut, began with a search for education. His daughter Munira proudly embraced the "civilized" habits of domesticity taught her at mission schools, ranging from needlework to the manner in which houses were furnished, to the manner in which children, including girls, were expected to be raised, dressed, and educated. She also taught at a mission school in the town of Marjyoun before she married Shukri Musa, who would make his way to Texas and there become a Baptist and be ordained; on returning to Palestine, he would be a representative of the first mission of the Southern Baptist Convention in Palestine, establishing himself at Nazareth. Youssef Badr's niece Emelia Badr would go on to help found in 1901 a school that would become the American College for Girls in Cairo.[7]

Because of their intimate connection with the missionaries, Arab Protestants took the lead in filling in a portrait of Americans and America that, if not ebullient, was certainly positive in its broad strokes. In almost all their sermons, lectures, and writings, they made either an implicit or explicit connection between the work of American missionaries and American missionary institutions, on the one hand, and their own individual and national advancement, on the other. Men such as Bustani acknowledged that through their descriptions of Arab culture and history American missionaries played a role in the revitalization of Arabic culture that would be retrospectively called the *nahda*, or "the renaissance."

When Bustani, Faris Shidyaq, and Mishaqa were born, religious clerics dominated education. They offered a parochial and communal worldview. The Arabic language was not written in a grammatically proper manner in many parts of Syria, especially among the Christian elites; there was neither a press nor an educational system that spoke of or inculcated a sense of Arab history. The dizzying pace of imperial reform and modernization in the nineteenth century saw telegraphs, steamers, printing presses, universities, and railways transform life in the Arab cities of the Ottoman Empire. The emergence of Arabic literary and scientific societies, newspapers, and journals in Beirut and Cairo, many of which were founded by men who had worked with or taught alongside missionaries, helped create a feeling of being Syrian, Arab, or Egyptian in a national sense that could unite Muslim and Christian Arabic speakers.

The new Arabic press not only presumed the existence of an educated Arab readership but helped create one—and with it, a notion of a modern and civilized public. Virtually overnight the Arabic press dramatically expanded the horizons of literate men and women in cities and towns across the Ottoman Empire. It stripped Christian and Muslim clerics of their long-held monopoly on defining morality and challenged their notions of what constituted useful or heretical knowledge. It also prompted imperial statesmen, functionaries, and bureaucrats to censor what would appear, to Ottoman eyes at least, to be potentially seditious information about the state of the empire and the world.

This Arab "awakening" was but one of several still inchoate national identifications that competed for the hearts and minds of the Arab population of the Ottoman Empire. The rise of Greek, Serbian, Bulgarian, Turkish, and Armenian nationalisms, to say nothing of incessant European interventions in the internal affairs of the Ottomans and other invasions, was proof that the diverse empire was beginning to fray at its seams, but the determined attempt of imperial officials to inculcate a sense of a secular Ottoman citizenship was proof of a countervailing influence. Bustani, at different points in his life, declared himself to be an evangelical Protestant, a Syrian, an Arab, and an Ottoman citizen. For Muslim reformers of this period, Islam offered the basis for a revivified national community. Regional, urban, sectarian, class, and tribal affiliations added to the complexity of how nineteenth-century Arabic speakers identified themselves.

The decisive cultural shift from an age of political and legal discrimination toward a belief in progress and the desirability of uniting citizens regardless of religious affiliation was the hallmark of the Ottoman reformation. It manifested itself in both Egypt and Syria, but it was most noticeable among the Protestant Arabs and in the circles that associated intellectually with the American missionaries in Beirut. The main difference between the manner in which Arab Protestant converts and their missionary patrons represented progress was centered on the vital question of agency. The missionaries firmly believed that progress was something they as Americans would have to inculcate carefully and patiently among "natives" who were culturally inferior. However, for many Arab Protestants and other Christian Arabs who were influenced by the American missionaries but did not convert—such as the Greek Orthodox Christian As'ad Khayyat, who, in 1847, was the first Arab to write an English-language autobiography, entitled *A Voice from Lebanon*—progress was a project of self-improvement.

Bustani himself was the clearest example of this difference. Because of his intimate and formative experience with American missionaries, Bustani was open to the idea of borrowing from Western cultures. His contempt for those whom he described as intoxicated with all things Western was as forceful as was his contempt for those who rejected out of hand everything Western simply because it came from the West. He was the very first subject of the Ottoman Empire to call publicly for the emancipation of women. He called as well for a complete secularization of politics and public life, in a manner that rendered faith a matter of private conscience but that also upheld the religious pluralism of Syria. The former call reflected his full acceptance of an American Protestant missionary ethos that consistently spoke about the elevation and liberation of "heathen" women from spiritual, physical, and moral darkness; the latter signaled his fundamental break with his missionary peers who still believed in subverting Islam and in converting all peoples eventually to their evangelical form of Christianity.

In reaction to the sectarian massacres of 1860 that devastated his native Mount Lebanon, Bustani abandoned narrow evangelical work for a much broader secular outlook. Like other men of his generation drawn to the allure of the burgeoning city of Beirut, he donned the *fez*, a red felt hat that the Ottoman state had encouraged as a form of secular national dress. He became an immensely influential educator, encyclopedist, publisher, and reformer. Bustani, above all, turned an often harsh and chauvinistic American Protestant criticism of stultified Eastern religious traditions into a usable language of self-criticism. He became an apostle for a dialogue across cultures. Most of his countrymen, like most American missionaries, regarded the events of 1860 as a grim reminder of the allegedly age-old hold of sectarianism. Bustani, however, believed firmly that sectarianism was a malaise that could be overcome through the secular education of Muslims and Christians and through a proper appreciation of what he regarded as a shared Arab history.

Therefore, when Bustani opened the first secular school in the Ottoman Empire in 1863, he called it the National School. He also published several important newspapers and journals, and writing his massive encyclopedia *Da'irat al-Ma'arif*—whose fourth volume contained the physical description of "America" and the "civilized American Indians"—was part of a broad didactic effort to persuade his Arab compatriots to widen their intellectual, cultural, social, and, above all, political horizons and to take advantage of what the nineteenth century had brought in its wake.

Bustani could not have guessed the nature of the tragic history of American missionary work concealed within the phrase "civilized American Indians"—he did not know of either the great hope that had accompanied the initial American missionary enterprise to "civilize" the Indians or its terrible disappointment. Bustani could not have appreciated the degree to which his history was bound to that of the American Indians: Both Arabs and Indians had been objects of the solicitude of American missionaries in their attempt to evangelize the world, and both had been shaped by a powerful and unsolicited American impulse to remake their worlds. Still less did Bustani recognize that the American missionaries' celebration of the "undying race" of the Arabs went hand in hand with their abandonment of the Indians.[8]

Like so much else in Bustani's writings about the wider world, many of his references to foreign cultures were borrowed directly from his American missionary patrons. Their Arabic missionary journal entitled the *Monthly Bulletin* featured articles about America and other places across the world, such as India, China, and Africa, in which the Anglo-American evangelicals worked. They described America glowingly, as a place of "freedom of conscience, freedom of the press and schools so that the country has become a shelter for those deprived of hope, the poor, and the oppressed from every realm and tribe; and for years, the American government has called on all peoples of the world to settle in her own vast territories."[9] The missionaries painted an understandably positive picture of their country; they depicted American Indians as heathen savages (many of whom, they said, had ultimately been Christianized) and African Zulus as fearsome warriors, creating in Bustani's imagination a vivid picture of the hierarchy of races.

Bustani and most Arabs of this period readily acknowledged that Europe, and by extension America, represented the height of material progress. They positioned themselves in an intermediate scale of civilization—not yet as advanced as the West, but far superior to Africans or American Indians. As invidious as such comparisons were, and as much as they drew on Arab stereotypes of Africa that predated the arrival of American missionaries, they nevertheless served a positive purpose for Bustani. They located the Arabs as a nation in a hierarchy of nations and identified two urgent imperatives. The first was to transcend the religious differences that separated Christian from Muslim Arabs. The second was to catch up to the West.

The new Arabic press gave the widest currency yet to a new understanding of America, and the West more generally, in the second half of the nineteenth century. The most famous of the Arabic nineteenth-century journals was *Al-Muqtataf*, founded in 1876 by Faris Nimr and Yaqub Sarruf. Both were Christians who had been heavily influenced by the American evangelical presence in Syria. Sarruf was born in the same town as As'ad Shidyaq and was part of the first graduating class of the Syrian Protestant College. Nimr was also educated at the SPC. He came originally from the town of Habsayya, in what is today southern Lebanon, where his father had been killed during the war of 1860. Like so many of their compatriots of the late Ottoman era, they were imbued with a tremendous optimism. They believed that their own personal transformation from natives of parochial small towns and villages into cosmopolitan citizens of the world and men speaking a universal language of science and knowledge indicated an Eastern social and cultural revolution in the making. Like Bustani's encyclopedia, *Al-Muqtataf* was initially published in "American Arabic," that is, using the fonts that the missionary Eli Smith had developed specifically for the American press in Beirut. The journal's name, which meant "Digest," had been suggested to them by Cornelius Van Dyck, whom both men admired. Its purpose was to present a nineteenth-century Arab elite with the knowledge to create a new kind of literate, scientific, and secular modern citizen. It described itself as an "Arabic Scientific Review." The thrust of *Al-Muqtataf* was unmistakable: It introduced the concepts of Darwinism to an Arab readership, and it highlighted the role of American missionary figures and American educators at the Syrian Protestant College.

When Edwin Lewis, a young American teacher in the Syrian Protestant College, gave a lecture outlining the principles of Charles Darwin in 1882, he ignited a furor within the American missionary community. Senior American members of the faculty were scandalized. In New York, where the college's board of trustees sat, powerful members of the board, including David Stuart Dodge, the son of William E. Dodge, who laid College Hall's cornerstone in 1871, demanded Lewis's dismissal for expounding allegedly heretical beliefs. The controversy continued to swirl, and the pages of *Al-Muqtataf* hosted an unprecedented exchange of letters in Arabic between Americans. A conservative American missionary, James Dennis, who would go on to publish a series of books celebrating American missionary work across the world, was highly critical of Darwin. He asserted that the native audience was hopelessly confused by the lecture. Lewis and one of his former students, Yusuf Hayek, who was then living in Alexandria, Egypt, strongly defended Lewis's speech.[10]

College president Daniel Bliss soon pressured Lewis to resign. Almost all the students in the school of medicine petitioned for Lewis's reinstatement. The administration, however, rejected their petition and suspended the students from the college for a month for their insubordination. Bliss informed them that they would not be allowed to return unless they formally retracted their petition and apologized. Many refused. Instead, they submitted additional Arabic petitions in which they implored the American administration to take note of the irony of its stand. "Dear Honorable Sirs," they began. "May God inspire you to be just. We appeal to your wisdom. . . . Sirs, it never occurred to the minds in Syria or in the Syrian Protestant College that noble people like you who belong to the American land of freedom would issue judgments without considering the related evidence." The students naively elaborated their appeal. "Sirs," they said, "we thought that presenting our requests to noble, pious American people who came to serve our countries in the name of the good and the right would assure us about all that we were struggling for."[11]

Cornelius Van Dyck waded into the controversy. From his earliest association with Butrus al-Bustani in the 1840s and his many condemnations of missionary chauvinism toward the people of Syria, Van Dyck had consistently marked himself as the man most able to break with American prejudice. Now he broke with Bliss over the student protest. He threatened to teach in his own house those who might be expelled from the college. Bliss was outraged by what he considered Van Dyck's misplaced sympathy for the natives. "Gentlemen," he declared to the assembled American and English board of managers who ran the daily affairs of the college in Beirut, "Anglo-Saxons, English, and Americans. I ask you if this was not abetting rebellion."[12]

Van Dyck resigned and was followed in his action by all but one of the medical faculty. He carried through with his promise to teach several students of the graduating class at his home. He even reached an agreement with the Christian Orthodox Hospital of St. George in Beirut to allow these students the practical training now denied them at the American college. Through his mediation, the expelled students were allowed to sit for the imperial licensing exam in Constantinople.

The Darwin affair revealed radically different understandings of the meaning and implications of nineteenth-century American missionary work toward the Arab world. In a vindictive but revealing backlash, the college, under the stewardship of Daniel Bliss and with the approval of the board of trustees in New York, instituted an official policy that required faculty to sign a written declaration of evangelical principles and to commit themselves formally to promote the missionary character of the college. More startling was their decision in 1883 to exclude Arabs from the professorial ranks, a blatantly racist policy that seemed to strike at the very heart of the altruistic image of the American missionary that the college president had tried so hard to project. Both Nimr and Sarruf were dismissed as a result of the new policy.

American benevolence, then, had obvious limits. In Bliss's mind and in those of most of his compatriots, altruism was not to be confused with equality. Nor was missionary work in the Arab world to be confused with liberalism or any other manifestation of spiritual degeneracy that a stalwart evangelical such as David Stuart Dodge believed haunted

America and might infect what he took to be spiritually and civilizationally immature native Syrians. "Unhappily, if the recent troubles indicate what may occur even with trusted men from America," Dodge confided to Bliss, "what might not be our position with several natives in the Faculty?"[13]

If anything, the reaction among the students and "native" tutors such as Sarruf and Nimr, who publicized Darwin's views in Arabic, revealed to Bliss and Dodge the need to strengthen and oversee a proper racial hierarchy; to guard against overweening native ambition, which was how American missionaries routinely viewed Arab and Armenian demands for equitable treatment; and to ward off liberal threats to their cherished institution that operated in one of the few corners of the world not yet under direct Western colonial control or direct influence. For Bliss, as for so many other Americans of this period, Anglo-Saxons were destined to lead less civilized—if not to say inferior—races, including the Arabs, toward civilization and ultimately Christianity.

The dissenting students and Sarruf and Nimr obviously saw things differently—and so too did Cornelius Van Dyck, his son William Van Dyck, and Edwin Lewis. The issue for them was not about maintaining an unambiguous racial hierarchy in which Americans who believed themselves to be compassionate tutored natives whom they unquestionably regarded as politically, religiously, culturally, and intellectually inferior. It was far simpler. It was about reconciling basic noble American claims with a corresponding reality, and without prevarication.

Nursing their wounds, Sarruf and Nimr published a scathing article about the college in *Al-Muqtataf* in 1885, three years after the Darwin affair. In it, they were uncharacteristically blunt. The college, they insisted, had established its excellent reputation on account of the good intentions of its founders. It had also gained its standing because it was a "national school": With Arabic as its language of instruction, its express intention was to turn over the college to local hands as soon as the nationals of the country had proved themselves qualified. Sarruf and Nimr wrote acerbically that, unlike during the first years of the college, now the American faculty monopolized "the benefits of the college for themselves, their children, and their descendants." They lamented that the most reactionary American professors who remained at the college after the Darwin affair had decided that the college "was American through and through, and that it would remain as such indefinitely, and thus they have placed a limit on [our] compatriots' advancement in the faculty ranks."[14]

Compounding their disenchantment was the pejorative representation of Syria and Syrians that Sarruf and Nimr discerned in the American missionary press. By what right, they wondered, did Americans who lived several thousand miles away and had never been to Syria or met with Syrians speak so arrogantly about the college, about the Darwin affair, or about the nature and motives of the dissenting students and their supporters? They also specifically took issue with the manner in which Henry Harris Jessup, one of the leading and most respected missionaries in American evangelical circles, represented to American readers what constituted true faith among Syrians. They found it unacceptable for a missionary such as Jessup to pass judgment on them any longer, or to characterize their dissent in the Darwin affair as heresy or as a lack of gratitude for missionary benevolence. Syrians, however, could speak for themselves. And it was time, they made it clear, that an American such as Jessup should take heed of this.

They disputed the language and assumptions of the missionaries not by rejecting them outright—as had the Maronite patriarch who oversaw the persecution of As'ad Shidyaq in the 1820s, or as the imperial Ottoman authorities had done subsequently—but rather, they called for American missionaries to speak a consistent language, not one for Arab consumption and another for the American audience. It was an exceptionally important moment. Sarruf and Nimr were the first Arabs to realize the extent to which what was being said about them in America and what was being said to their faces were fundamentally contradictory in both tone and content.

Despite this realization, Sarruf and Nimr stepped back from a total repudiation of the missionaries and their institutions. Instead, they contented themselves with the notion that the Americans had betrayed an original benevolent mission that genuinely put the interests of Arabs first. For men who had staked their reputations on their position as liberal cultural interlocutors between a modern West and a modernizing Middle East, Sarruf and Nimr wanted desperately to believe in the halcyon days of the American mission. The truly remarkable aspect of the Darwin affair and its aftermath was therefore not so much Bliss's or Dodge's prejudice, which passed for conventional Western wisdom at that time, but the degree to which Arab students and men like Sarruf and Nimr continued to believe in an idea of American benevolence even when they had already run afoul of it. To call the entire missionary enterprise pernicious from its outset was to repeat the anathema first leveled against the Americans by the Maronite patriarch in 1823; it was also to find common cause with reactionary elements of local society who felt threatened by the intellectual challenge embodied in the American evangelical message. But fear was manifestly not what animated Sarruf and Nimr; they were not afraid of missionary evangelism, they were not afraid of cultural interaction, and they were not against the American presence. They had counted themselves among its most enthusiastic and energetic supporters.

Yet in stepping back from the precipice, they exposed their own inability—or perhaps their refusal—to recognize or accept what was plainly apparent to men such as Daniel Bliss and Henry Jessup. American racism was not a complete rupture from the original mission, as Nimr and Sarruf wanted to believe; it followed logically from the impulse of the first mission, although it had a distinctly harder edge to it than did the paternalism of Pliny Fisk and Jonas King. Sarruf and Nimr extolled scientific modernity as a vehicle for Arab emancipation without realizing that it was the same historic force that had given rise to powerful Western, including American, ideas about the fundamental superiority of the white Anglo-Saxons over all other races. Like most philanthropy, American solicitude for Arabs came with strings attached. As the prestige of the Syrian college increased, so too did the stakes in its control. Missionaries were not creating a beautiful campus, erecting imposing stone buildings, and equipping scientific laboratories simply to turn things over to the "natives."

Part of Sarruf and Nimr's appeal to an original benign American mission was incontrovertibly tactical: They were attempting to shame the conservative American administrators by suggesting to them that the pioneers in mission were men of integrity whose words matched their deeds. Part of their despondency was in the nature of self-deception. Part of it reflected their naïveté. But the greatest part of their disappointment was palpable and sincere.

For Sarruf and Nimr, disillusion was augmented by the final decision at the college to make English the official language of instruction. In truth, the decision had been years in the making; its express justification was both the belief among the Americans, including the college president, that English was *the* language of modern civilization and the inefficiency and costs of translating English texts into Arabic. From the perspective of Sarruf and Nimr, who believed firmly in the possibility and desirability of an Arab renaissance through Arabic scientific knowledge—which was the very purpose of their journal—the decision was a signal blow.

In the event, the decision to teach in English was far less controversial to the wider Arabic-speaking public than it was to Sarruf and Nimr; it actually cemented the college's advantage over all other rival institutions at a time of growing British imperial power and presence in the Middle East. After resettling in Egypt, which Britain had occupied in 1882, Sarruf and Nimr relocated *Al-Muqtataf* there as well. Despite their criticism of the racial policy adopted by the college administration, Sarruf and Nimr continued to believe in the importance of the Syrian Protestant College, and the pages of *Al-Muqtataf* continued to extol America as an exemplary case of rapid modernization and education, a country that not only cherished and offered great educational opportunities but enjoyed unbounded wealth and prosperity.

These sentiments were echoed in another major Arabic journal established in Cairo in 1892 and called *Al-Hilal.* Its founder, Jurji Zaydan, was a Greek Orthodox native of Beirut. Zaydan, like Sarruf and Nimr, had been enrolled at the SPC but left the college as a result of the Darwin affair. Like many other Syrians of his day, he made his way from Beirut to Cairo, which was rapidly establishing itself as the vibrant center of intellectual life in the region. He worked for Sarruf and Nimr and then taught Arabic at a Greek Orthodox school in Cairo before eventually devoting himself to working as a journalist, publisher, and novelist. Zaydan pioneered the genre of historical novels in Arabic and wrote more than twenty novels by the time of his death in 1914.

In *Al-Hilal*, which he described as a "Scientific and Literary Arabic Review," Zaydan adopted a more historical approach than the editors of *Al-Muqtataf*. As an Arabic-speaking Christian, Zaydan embraced an ecumenical view of Islamic history in which Islam was an important part of a modern Arab identity that could bring together Christians and Muslims. Given the secularizing reforms of the Ottoman state and the tremendous expansion of education across the empire, Zaydan optimistically believed that the nineteenth century provided a unique opportunity to build a new political culture of equality between Muslims and Christians.

Al-Hilal published biographical sketches of famous Islamic leaders, including Ottoman sultans such as the eponymous founder of the empire, Osman Ghazi, and Suleyman the Magnificent, as well as such legendary figures as Hannibal, Confucius, and Peter the Great. Zaydan described George Washington as the "liberator of America" and one of the "greatest men of freedom."[15] Zaydan's sketch of Washington included an account of the American Revolution that emphasized Washington's heroic leadership. He provided Arab readers with possibly the first published Arabic narrative of the establishment of the United States. "Washington was an important example for zeal, vigor, judiciousness, and sincerity," waxed Zaydan lyrically. "He was very pious and extremely reliant on God, careful with his time, and Americans still mourn him till now for men like him deserve to be mourned because he liberated a country and sacrificed himself for his compatriots. May God have mercy on him."[16]

Zaydan told an unabashedly positive story of America, although he had been scarred by the Darwin affair. The American desire for freedom and independence from an oppressive England and Washington's sacrifices for his fellow citizens were points that were translated easily into Arabic. The British, after all, were occupying Egypt, and the modern ideas of patriotism and nationalism were finding fertile ground there, as well as elsewhere in the Ottoman Empire.

The Egyptian writer Qasim Amin, in turn, grounded a famous, if controversial, argument for the necessity of the liberation of Muslim women by pointing to what he regarded as the advanced and liberated state of Western women, particularly American women. It was in female education—and in education more generally—that the idea of America took on its brightest hue. In the East, Amin wrote, "one finds that a woman is man's slave, and the man is the slave of his ruler." In Europe governments were based on "freedom and respect for personal rights," and the status of women was accordingly higher. But it was in America that women's liberation was greatest because, Amin argued, it was there that general freedom was strongest and government regulation of the private affairs of citizens weakest. "As a consequence, women's freedom in the United States in America," wrote Amin admiringly, "is much greater than that of European women."[17] Amin did not have to look far to appreciate the connection between women, education, and liberation. Although American missionary schools formed only a fraction of the foreign schools in Cairo and Beirut—the French in this period had more schools than any other Western power—they were very prominent in female higher education in the Ottoman Empire.

In Beirut, of course, the American Board missionaries had established the first school for girls in the Ottoman Empire in 1834; in Constantinople the American missionary Mary Mills Patrick set up the important Constantinople Women's College in 1890, which was followed in 1909 by the founding in Cairo of the American College for Girls. In Arabic journals and newspaper articles, graduates of American women's schools lauded the advances in female education. When one such graduate, Rujina Shukri, spoke in Beirut at the commencement ceremony at the American School for Girls in 1899, she evoked the same theme that Butrus al-Bustani had evoked exactly fifty years before—female education was the key to national regeneration, and American missionaries were owed a debt of gratitude for taking the first, crucial step in inspiring an entire generation of Arab women and men to improve themselves and for contributing so benevolently to "the benefit of the nation."[18]

Many Syrians and Egyptians directly influenced by Protestant missionaries were prepared to see in "America" what they wanted to see. Some were students who were unaware of or unconcerned about the racism that barred natives from becoming faculty members at places such as the Syrian Protestant College or from becoming head teachers in missionary schools; others were those who accepted the logic of American missionary paternalism in an era of manifest Western technological superiority. Some were pragmatic and unwilling to bite the hand that fed them; others were simply more charitable. Christian Arabs for the most part, they were also shaped by a knowledge, even experience, of Islamic discrimination and by their own intimate knowledge of ecclesiastical corruption. This personal history made them appreciate the transformations wrought by their modernizing age, transformations that they experienced most intensely through their association with American missionary institutions.

Tellingly, Sarruf and Nimr themselves amplified Zaydan's and Amin's simple abstractions about American freedom in a lengthy essay published in 1893 on the "Progress of America in a Century." Against the backdrop of the World's Fair in Chicago, their article celebrated the "incredible" rate of American development in various economic and social fields since the founding of the country. The article held up America as an example for the East to follow, but it also noted that this progress was confined to the white population because of their industry and purpose; as for the Indians, "the native population are almost extinct, and the blacks who were originally slaves increase numerically but not in terms of progress, and the Asians who emigrate do not settle there but return just as soon as they make enough money." Sarruf and Nimr believed that blacks and Indians were inferior and doomed to a subordinate status in the United States.[19]

A decade after the Darwin affair, which had left them so sensitive to American prejudice against natives, Sarruf and Nimr were now willing to partake openly in the discourse of social Darwinism. Like Bustani before them, they were positioning themselves as "civilized" natives who occupied a midpoint on a ladder of progress that separated them from those on its highest and lowest rungs. They had both been awarded honorary doctorates by the Syrian Protestant College in 1890, making them the first Arabs to be so recognized.

For them, racial progress was first and foremost a metaphor for modernization. It was not, as it was for many Western leaders and imperialists, a justification for the pacification and extermination of natives and the conquest of their lands. Nevertheless, Sarruf and Nimr's essay revealed the degree to which self-consciously "civilized" Arabs were willing to deal in a dehumanizing language of racial progress and civilization without realizing the extent to which it could easily be turned against them. The journal *Al-Muqtabas*, edited by the Damascene Muhammad Kurd Ali, upheld an Arab belief in a dynamic America. Its pages also deprecated the Indians. A contributor from Nebraska wrote to laud U.S. efforts to "uplift" the Indians, but noted that those efforts had failed because Indians were an "indolent" and "incorrigible" race. He wrote that "thousands of years have passed by whilst they remain in the same state of savagery and ignorance." He added that American charity toward them had persisted and in this persistence America had set an "example" for all other nations.[20] Syrian reformers believed that Arabs were somehow a people of a different order—ones at whom the bayonet and the Maxim gun ought not be pointed.

Like their reforming Ottoman masters, many Westernizing Arabs of the nineteenth century were initially dazzled by the spectacle of the West. They believed that with enough effort, Western powers would recognize them as equal. Putting great faith in a secular language of modern civilization, they hoped that East and West could be made two equal parts of a coherent and symbiotic whole. Meanwhile, several graduates of the American college in Beirut found work with the British as they expanded into Africa and the Middle East. Zaydan, for example, joined another Syrian, Jabr Dumit, to work as a translator with General Garnet Joseph Wolseley's British expeditionary force in the Sudan. For most of these men, employment entangled them directly in Western colonialism. Their ability to move between Arabic and English, after all, qualified them to work for various British enterprises across the Middle East and Africa, but there was an undeniable aspect of chauvinism and innocence at work. Arabs had long felt themselves superior to Africans, and so long as they could maintain their belief that the most sordid aspects of Western colonialism were not going to be directed at them, nineteenth-century Westernizing Arabs enthusiastically embraced Western progress.

When the American missionary and medical doctor Cornelius Van Dyck died in 1895, a genuine, almost palpable sense of grief could be discerned in the major Arabic journals and newspapers of the day. The editors of *Al-Muqtataf* wrote "that we woke up on the 13th of this month (November) and found a telegraph announcing the death of our great teacher, Dr. Cornelius Van Dyck." They—together with most major papers in Syria and Egypt—eulogized Van Dyck as the single most important and noble of the many good men who had come from abroad, an individual who more than anyone else had led Syria "in its scientific and literary renaissance."[21] What was so impressive about Van Dyck to Sarruf and Nimr was the degree to which he made himself one of the very few men of the age who came to know and love Syria—"I have left my heart in Syria," Zaydan quoted him as saying when he declined an offer from Union Theological Seminary in 1867.[22] He was a foreigner who went native. To many of his American contemporaries, such a tight embrace of Arab language and culture was quaint but ultimately inexplicable. The point for them was not to love Syria but to evangelize it. For his many admirers in the Arab provinces, Van Dyck's Arab turn and his promotion of ecumenical science as opposed to divisive sectarianism was the highest sign of respect that he or any American had paid their culture.

Sarruf and Nimr did not dwell on the Darwin affair in their eulogy of Van Dyck—to them, Van Dyck, not Bliss or Dodge or Jessup, embodied America. Across Syria, Egypt, and even into Baghdad, the fame of Cornelius Van Dyck had grown enormously in his fifty years as a missionary, educator, scientist, and doctor. He was a Bible translator who defended the teaching of Darwin. His output of scientific tracts in Arabic was prolific. *Al-Muqtataf* regularly featured stories about him or even extracts of articles by him or by his son, William, who, like his father, had been a medical doctor at the SPC. Zaydan memorialized him in *Al-Hilal* and included Van Dyck in his important account of the famous individuals of the "East." The key point for Zaydan was that the American Van Dyck was a pillar of the American mission and yet was careful not to offend or insult the faiths of others around him; as Zaydan put it pointedly, Van Dyck espoused "freedom of conscience in word and deed." The Ottoman sultan awarded Van Dyck an imperial medal in 1890 on the fiftieth anniversary of his arrival in Syria, the patriarch of the Orthodox Church also praised him fulsomely, and the Muslim Hasan Beyhum and Syrians from other faiths lauded his "humanitarian" work and his "service to the nation."[23]

The sympathetic portrait of Van Dyck painted in the Arabic press was a metaphor for U.S.-Arab relations of the nineteenth century. An American, then, more than any other foreigner, came to embody a cultural revolution for a small but influential group of Christian and Muslim Arabs in Syria and Egypt. They trusted him not because he was an American per se, but because he showed that it was possible to embrace modern life without imperialism or sectarianism.

In an era when Egypt was ruled by Lord Cromer—who declared that "reformed Islam is Islam no more," who was opposed to the higher education of Egyptians, and who held forth about the differences between "subject" races and "civilised" nations—Van Dyck's love of Arabic and Syria marked him as an extraordinary man.[24] Yet despite the British occupation of Egypt, and despite Cromer's racism, the notables of late Ottoman Syria and Egypt who celebrated Cornelius Van Dyck—shaykhs, priests, doctors, and journalists—were imbued with confidence about how the century might yet unfold; like Bustani before them, who died in 1883, they took their own experience as a portent for how the Arabic-speaking world as a whole might yet be transformed into something greater than the sum of its different religious and geographic parts. The "enlightened" Arabs were willing to accept the notion that they were "behind" the West, but they were not willing to accept indefinite servitude to it.

The first missionary conference "on behalf of the Mohammedan World" was held in Cairo in April 1906. Protestant missionaries gathered from all corners of the Muslim world to take stock of their evangelical enterprise. They were determined, as had been two generations of Protestant missionaries before them, to replace the crescent with the cross. That the gathering occurred in an illustrious Islamic city now firmly under British occupation was replete with significance. The scope of the meeting was unprecedented: it covered mission work among Muslims from west Africa to China, from Morocco to Java. Not a single Arab or Muslim was asked to present native views on Islam, and it is not known whether any attended. It scarcely mattered to the assembled Christian men who pored over numerous maps, studied surveys, and considered the extent of the worldwide "Mohammedan" problem and the best means to combat it. Collectively, they reflected just how profoundly the missionary crusade had changed in the course of a century. From the hopeful, rather naive spiritual assault launched in 1819 by Levi Parsons and Pliny Fisk, a much more widespread and modern Protestant army was now in place. Americans figured more prominently than ever in its ranks.

The introductory paper was read by none other than the revered missionary to Syria Henry Harris Jessup. Drawing on his vast half-century-long experience in the field, Jessup summed up the Muslim world and the prospects for its conversion. The topic was one that the missionary had addressed many times before. Jessup was pithy. He conceded that Islam was capable of expressing sublime magnificence, and yet, he said, it was also rooted in unmitigated horror. Insofar as it approximated the great truths inherent in the Bible, it expressed "God's existence and unity." And insofar as it departed from the Bible, it represented "the sloughs of polygamy and the oppression and degradation of women."[25] Jessup quoted from historical Muslim figures, including the first caliphs who had done so much to spread Islam in its first century. He made it a point, as did most of the other missionaries present at the conference, to demonstrate that his hostility to Islam was a function not only of evangelical conviction but of dispassionate observation.

In holding to this belief, Jessup was indeed different from the first American missionaries to the Levant, whose knowledge of Islam had been rudimentary. The initial forays made by Fisk and Parsons had grown into a thick web of American missionary societies operating in the Middle East. The pride of American evangelical work across the Arabic-speaking world remained Beirut, which by the turn of the century had become the center of a new Ottoman province. The American Presbyterian Missionary Board, for which Jessup worked and which had taken over from the American Board, ran four main stations in Syria and Palestine and 102 outposts in rural communities or villages that were classified as substations. It employed 14 ordained and lay male missionaries, 3 medical missionaries, 13 wives, and 10 unmarried female teachers or assistants; American women by this date were taking the lead in American missionary work, although they had not been granted the title "missionary."

In Egypt, the other center of American mission work, the American United Presbyterian Mission dominated the scene. It presided over 12 stations and 125 substations, which were occupied by 48 ordained and lay missionaries, 12 medical missionaries, 29 wives, and 35 unmarried female teachers or assistants. In Palestine, which American evangelicals had largely ceded to British missionary societies, Quakers had established a number of small schools for girls in the vicinity of the town of Ramallah as well as two larger ones for girls and boys in the town itself. Exploratory missions into Arabia itself had commenced in 1889. Missionaries of the Reformed Church in America dedicated their Mason Memorial Hospital in Bahrain to "God and Arabia" in 1903. There was also significant work in Persia.

The American Board of Commissioners for Foreign Missions still held sway in Constantinople and Anatolia. Its labor, however, was focused not on Arabic-speaking communities, but on the Armenian Christian community, whose towns and villages spread out across eastern Anatolia. In Turkey the ABCFM deployed 42 ordained and lay missionaries, 12 medical missionaries, 63 wives, and 68 unmarried female teachers and assistants across 20 main stations and 269 substations. These figures accounted only for the large American missions. There were also Dutch, German, English, Scottish, and Irish missions at work. The total number of native congregations overseen by all Protestant missions in the Middle East was 395, including 34,606 communicants and 94,428 adherents. They ran, in addition, 975 primary and secondary schools and

15 colleges, educating over 64,000 students in all grades. They also administered 49 hospitals and 63 dispensaries that cared for over 650,000 patients.[26]

There was, in short, great progress from a missionary point of view. The sheer scope and scale of Protestant institutions molded tens of thousands in the Arabic-speaking world. Christian missionary ecumenism, however, stopped short of Islam. The liberal spirit of Cornelius Van Dyck was mostly overshadowed by the militant enthusiasm of new Protestant missionaries who worked in the shadow of the greatest Western imperial expansion in history. Their watchword was to convert the world in "this generation."[27]

Samuel Zwemer was the most aggressive of these late-century spiritual warriors. Born in Michigan in 1867, he graduated from the New Brunswick Theological Seminary in 1890. A member of the Reformed Church ministry, Zwemer would go on to found an important missionary journal out of Hartford Seminary called *The Moslem World* (today still in circulation as *The Muslim World*). He built his reputation in American (and wider Protestant) missionary circles through his uncompromising view of Islam and his pioneering missionary work among Muslims in Arabia. "We always coveted the whole of the promised land and our eyes were beyond its coasts," he admitted.[28] He wrote a series of books outlining his thoughts about Arabs and Muslims, all of which took a predictably negative view of Islam. One of these, entitled *The Nearer and Farther East*, was published in 1908. The study was the eighth textbook issued by the American-based Central Committee on the United Study of Missions, a women's group founded just after the turn of the century to help "liberate"—in other words, Christianize—women in other, allegedly darker, parts of the world. In his account of the "Mohammedan world," Zwemer outlined the "social evils of Islam," the "deficiency of the Moslem character," the oppression of women, and the certainty of evangelical success if only the Western patrons of the missions would do their part.

Above all, Zwemer assured his American evangelical readers, the modern colonial era was not only a blessing for missionary prospects but facilitated those prospects more than any previous age. A clear majority of Muslims, he said, echoing almost word for word what Jessup had said at the Cairo conference two years before, lived under Christian colonial rule. This was "startling evidence of the finger of God in history and a wonderful challenge of opportunity."[29] American missionaries such as Zwemer and Jessup, then, took hope in empire, but denied that they were imperialists.

When Theodore Roosevelt visited the Sudan and Egypt in 1910, the former president of the United States gave several public lectures. The situation on the ground in Egypt at the time was particularly tense. The British occupation had grown increasingly unpopular, a nationalist movement had arisen, and the British were harshly stifling dissent—in one infamous case an entire village was forced by the occupying authorities to witness the flogging and hanging of Egyptian peasants who had insulted and beat British officers who had been shooting pigeons on their land. The first Egyptian Coptic Christian prime minister, Butrus Ghali, who had worked closely with Lord Cromer, signed the Anglo-Egyptian Condominium Agreement that cemented Britain's occupation of Egypt and Sudan, and overseen the tribunal that led to the hangings of the Egyptian peasants, was assassinated in February 1910 by a nationalist, Ibrahim al-Wardani.

Roosevelt, having spent the months prior to his speeches hunting big game with his son Kermit in Africa, entered this seething cauldron oblivious to the depth of nationalist sentiment. In the Sudan, he praised British "civilization" work and strongly commended American missionary work. At a speech at Cairo University, he lauded the great work of the university and urged the Egyptians to be patient in their quest for freedom from the British—he even quoted a proverb in Arabic: "God is with the patient, if they know how to wait"—and to understand that a constitution in and of itself was worthless unless the people for whom it was intended were sufficiently developed to be able to appreciate and utilize it. "With any people," he said, "the essential quality to show is, not haste in grasping after a power which it is only too easy to misuse, but a slow, steady, resolute development of those substantial qualities . . . which alone enable a people to govern themselves." The former president believed that Egyptians would have to wait for "generations" before they would be ready for responsible self-rule, a conceit that the British themselves had aired time and again to justify their unrelenting grip on the country. This sentiment, in addition to Roosevelt's unequivocal condemnation of what he would call the "anti-foreign movement, led, as it is, by a band of reckless, foolish, and sometimes murderous agitators"—nationalists—led many in the Egyptian press to criticize Roosevelt's speech.[30]

Al-Muqtataf strongly defended Roosevelt. It pointed out that whatever one liked to think or say about the English, it was undeniable that they had introduced more "civilization" into the Sudan (and by extension neighboring Egypt) than had previous rulers. Although they felt that Roosevelt was at fault for appearing to dismiss the importance of a constitution for Egypt, Sarruf and Nimr gave the U.S. president the benefit of the doubt. They pointed out that he had praised the Arabs extensively in his speech and that "Americans are the most generous people" in regard to charitable giving—far more, they said, than were Arabs.[31]

But in their defense of Roosevelt, Sarruf and Nimr exposed an important tension in the Arab renaissance of the nineteenth century. They were Syrians in Egypt and Christians in an overwhelmingly Muslim country. They had both been on good terms with Lord Cromer, and both had ingratiated themselves with the British. Nimr also oversaw the pro-British Arabic daily *Al-Muqattam*, which he had established with Sarruf. That they were far more willing to see what was positive in the speech than dwell on what was negative in it was a testament to their optimism, but their view also stemmed from the fact that they were not the target of Roosevelt's patronizing attitude. Roosevelt, moreover, appeared unaware that the British themselves had opposed the establishment of Cairo University. And in making out the nationalists to be mere Muslim fanatics, he disregarded what nationalists took most seriously about themselves: their ability to rule themselves and to rise above sectarian tensions that discriminated between Egypt's Coptic Christian minority and its Muslim majority. As if to dispel any doubt about what he truly thought, Roosevelt confided to an English journalist that his speech in Cairo was "a crackery jack. You should have seen the Fuzzy Wuzzies' faces as I told them off. They expected candy, but I gave them the big stick. And they squirmed, Sir; they squirmed."[32]

The students of the university were sorely disappointed with Roosevelt's speech. Hundreds of young Egyptian men demonstrated outside his hotel. "Down with Roosevelt!" they cried, and "Down with the Occupation and long live the Constitution!"[33] The Egyptian Muslim journalist and nationalist Ali Yusuf, who was trained at Al-Azhar University and was himself the founder of an important nationalist newspaper, published an article in the *North American Review* in an attempt to make Americans understand the degree to which Roosevelt had unnecessarily antagonized Egyptians by his speech. The local Egyptian Muslim outrage, he insisted, was not anti-American. Egyptians had believed in America but were shocked by Roosevelt's un-American support for British imperialism. "We Egyptians," he wrote,

> anticipated the arrival of the ex-President of the United States with great pleasure and impatience, for all Egyptians believed him to be the best representative of the great American nation, and they still consider that the Americans are the greatest nation in civilization of the present time, and that they are the best friends of liberty of nations, inasmuch as in that country constitutional principles have received their widest development.[34]

As with all such articles calculated to appeal to an American public, Yusuf's article was replete with rehearsed phrases about the goodness of America. It also included what was then becoming a standard Muslim apologetic about the "perfect tolerance" of Islam. The substance of his argument, however, was built upon basic common sense: Roosevelt ought to have educated himself about foreign cultures and nations before lecturing to them; he ought to have understood that foreign occupation was not something that people suffered patiently; and he would have discovered, had he taken the time to conduct serious conversations with leading Egyptians, that nationalism in Egypt was a vital force, not just a facade for Muslim fanaticism. Above all, he might have appreciated the degree to which the positive idea of America among educated Arabs rested on its anti-imperialist mantra. Yusuf continued by noting that "Egyptians have a greater liking for Americans than for Europeans, because they consider they have not been harmed by the Americans."[35] In a tone that recalled Sarruf and Nimr's 1884 essay against American nepotism at the Syrian Protestant College, Yusuf expressed his belief that an American ideal of "civilization" had been betrayed by unrepresentative American action. The solution was therefore simple: Roosevelt should act as an American, not as an imperialist European.

Like Sarruf and Nimr before him, Yusuf wanted to see in America only what was convenient for his argument. He seemed unaware that Roosevelt himself was one of the most energetic imperialists in the United States, which had amassed by 1909 considerable overseas territories. As much as he wanted to believe that Americans were "friends of freedom," as he put it, most of them would have agreed with Roosevelt's instinct to judge the darker Egyptians as inferior and civilizationally immature. The United States had recently occupied and brutally pacified the Philippines, and although there was a significant anti-imperialist movement within the United States, much of it was motivated by a desire not to mix with or rule over "mongrel" races.

Ali Yusuf was making a heartfelt argument that was bound to fall on deaf ears. Freedom, which appeared to be so simple and obvious a matter when observed from the standpoint of the colonized, appeared far more complicated when examined from the standpoint of those colonizing. In the case of Americans in the Middle East, especially the missionaries whom Roosevelt supported, Egyptian self-rule was an ominous proposition. As much as the American missionaries had consistently and loudly proclaimed that they had no imperial intentions and that they were citizens of a nation that had no territorial designs on the Ottoman Empire, they had equally supported the idea of British colonial rule in Egypt and were overwhelmingly opposed to equality with Arabs. Like all foreigners of the great powers, they were not subject to local law. They had also, as a matter of course, institutionalized structures of discrimination in their various institutions of learning even as these institutions had become in local eyes important locations of reformation and civilization.

Muslim Arabs, like their coreligionists across the empire, had by the time of Roosevelt's speech grown far more apprehensive about Western imperialism than had Christian Arabs. The French conquest of Tunisia in 1881 and the British occupation of Egypt in 1882 put paid to any idea that Westernizing reforms, which the Ottoman elite had been diligently pursuing since the 1840s, might lead to a relationship of equality with the West. As if to add insult to injury, the secular French philologist Ernest Renan gave a major lecture in 1883 at the Sorbonne in which he compounded an already acute sense of Muslim apprehension.[36] In his address, Renan stated that no matter how much it might reform itself, Islam was essentially incompatible with modern civilization. His suggestion was scandalous to Muslim ears, not only because it was laced with openly racist dogma, but because it revealed to them very clearly an intensely intolerant, bigoted, and dangerous West. Renan's lecture elicited a storm of protest and dismay in intellectual circles across the Ottoman Empire.

In the first half of the nineteenth century, it was Eastern Christian patriarchs who had been most vehemently opposed to American missionaries: Now Muslims became more anxious about the work of these foreigners, including the Americans. Ottoman authorities had initially underestimated what they believed was a small group of evangelicals whose conversion work was focused almost exclusively on Eastern Christian communities. In the second half of the century, however, the Ottoman government and Muslim religious leaders grew thoroughly alarmed by the danger posed to Muslim and Ottoman identity by missionary education. In 1869 the Ottoman government passed an education regulation to control and harmonize education across the empire, a regulation that missionaries of all stripes invariably attempted to evade or ignore. In 1881 the minister of education warned that foreign schools could have the corrosive effect of sapping loyalty to the Ottoman state, and in 1893 another minister of education lamented the success of Protestant schools in the empire. Students at these foreign schools, he said, "remain subjects in name only, their minds having been changed."[37] This assertion was an exaggeration, but it was not devoid of truth.

For all the evident advances in education, in urbanization, and in reform that had revolutionized the Ottoman landscape, the empire was under huge strain. A series of Ottoman defeats in the Balkans against both Russia and the Austro-Hungarian Empire in the 1870s and 1880s had led to an enormous loss of Ottoman territory. Massacres of Christians in these wars occurred frequently—epitomized by the "Balkan horrors" decried by the English prime minister William Gladstone—but in these struggles Muslim subjects also had been murdered, expelled, or forced to flee from their homes. Unlike the Christian victims, the Muslim victims of the fragmenting Ottoman Empire were mostly ignored by Western public opinion. Sultan Abdülhamid II, who ascended the imperial throne in 1876, responded to the crisis in his empire by appealing directly to Muslim pride and loyalty. He worked feverishly and autocratically to promote a thoroughly modern and civilized pan-Islamic Ottoman identity to hold together what was left of his domains.

And what Abdülhamid sought to do at a political level, Arab Muslim reformers such as Muhammad Abduh and Rashid Rida sought to do at an intellectual level. They argued passionately and incessantly for the urgent need of Muslims to modernize and adapt to the times and yet at the same time to maintain what they described as the integrity of the Islamic tradition. If Christian, and especially Protestant, Arabs saw themselves as cultural mediators between Americans and the Arab world, Muslim Arabs regarded themselves as its undisputed core. Some among them were remarkable in their openness to the American missionaries, such as the Al-Azhar–trained Shaykh Yusuf al-Asir, who worked extensively with Cornelius Van Dyck and corrected his final Arabic translation of the Bible. He even composed several Arabic hymns for the Protestant church.

Others were simply reactionary and recalled directly the example of the Maronite patriarch who fought against Pliny Fisk and Jonas King. The Syrian shaykh Yusuf al-Nabhani fulminated that "the greatest catastrophe in this age for Muslims" were the Christian schools opened across the region.[38] His position was as bigoted as it was ignorant—and it was directed as much at Jesuit as at Protestant institutions. When Muslims felt the full weight of European racism and colonialism, defensiveness became heightened and, in its worst moments, expressed itself as xenophobia. Jurji Zaydan himself fell victim to precisely this form of Muslim prejudice when he was denied a position to teach Islamic history at the newly established Cairo University in 1910 because he was Christian. For Zaydan, this was a terrible blow. He had devoted himself to reviving and promoting Arab and Islamic history and sought to reconcile the two elements in a manner that genuinely included Christian Arabs. His rejection made him realize that the ecumenical national solidarity he advocated (and advocated by others before him such as Bustani and Sarruf and Nimr) contended with more than Western chauvinism and Eastern Christian intolerance. It vied with another, inherently more exclusionary and defensive notion of nationalism that was not nearly as open in spirit as was theirs. This was Islamic nationalism, which conflated rather than simply connected (as Bustani and Zaydan had done) Arabs with Islam.

But it was not Nabhani or the rectors of the newly established Cairo University who commanded the respect of Muslims across the Arab provinces—it was Rashid Rida. More so than any other figure, Rida, an imam, writer, and reformer, expressed the genuine ambivalence that Muslim Arabs felt toward the missionaries. Rida was born near the Syrian city of Tripoli in 1865, a time when Muslim thinkers across the empire were grappling with the evident problem of Ottoman decline. He became a disciple of the reformist Egyptian Azharite shaykh Muhammad Abduh. Like Sarruf, Nimr, and Zaydan, Rida had settled in Cairo, where in 1898 he founded *Al-Manar*, the leading Arab Muslim reformist newspaper of the era.

Like many others of his generation, Rida struggled to separate his repugnance for missionary proselytizing from his respect for the vital work of modern education offered at missionary schools, especially the American ones. Rida insisted in 1903 that the American college in Beirut—as opposed to Jesuit schools—did not deliberately attack Islam. Of all the foreign schools, the Syrian Protestant College was the "most suitable" for Muslims because it was imbued with the "spirit of freedom and independence." More so than any other school in Europe, Constantinople, Egypt, or Syria, it raised "men."[39] Six years later, Rida admitted that all foreign Christian schools established in the empire were missionary by nature, "but the American schools," he said, "are better than others in terms of education, more disciplined, and more independent and less fanatical to those who espouse different faiths and politics, for America has no political ambitions in these lands, although these schools might support English policy."[40]

Rida came to embody the modern Arab Muslim search for reform that struck a balance between the emulation of foreign knowledge and the preservation of Muslim independence. It was not an easy task, especially since Rida perceived that Westerners routinely acted and spoke fanatically against Islam, yet perversely and consistently accused Muslims of fanaticism. Like the Protestant Bustani before him, he deplored those Arabs whom he described as deracinated, overly Europeanized, and intoxicated with Western ways; at the same time, he had to answer the many in his community who sought refuge in empty traditions and who rejected Western education when they had no suitable alternative and when Ottoman Muslims had not yet put money into higher education institutions of their own.

Like the Maronite patriarch's own original encyclicals that called the American missionaries "ravening wolves," this late-nineteenth-century intellectual Muslim anxiety about the "dangers" of mission schools could not staunch a general Muslim interest in foreign schools. In 1878 Beiruti Muslims founded a benevolent society and opened a school for girls that would become the first of several Muslim Maqasid schools. These schools were modeled on missionary institutions but explicitly promoted their Islamic nature. The first headmistress of the girls' school, however, was Julia Tohmeh, who was herself both Protestant and educated by missionaries.

When Muslims did begin to attend foreign schools in increasing numbers, the Syrian Protestant College found itself once more at the center of a maelstrom. The July 1908 Young Turk Revolution had ousted the despotic Sultan Abdülhamid and ushered in a constitutional government across the empire. The Muslim and Jewish students, although only a minority of the student body (128 out of 876 scholars in 1908), were emboldened by the political upheaval around them. They decried the evangelical stipulation that all students had to attend compulsory daily chapel and Bible classes as contrary to their own religious beliefs. "This is a Christian college," replied the faculty defensively.[41] The board in New York concurred. In a reprise of the Darwin affair, the college dug in its heels. Chairman of the board David Stuart Dodge wondered if socialist agitators were behind the student protests in Egypt and Syria, filling young men, he said, with "false conceptions of liberty."[42] Just as Roosevelt would prove to be a year later in Cairo, Dodge in New York seemed purposefully ignorant of the true nature of Arab discontent.

The president of the Syrian Protestant College at the time was Howard Bliss, who had succeeded his father Daniel in 1902. The younger Bliss was born in Mount Lebanon and raised in Beirut. He had more than a passing acquaintance with Arabs. He was also of a decidedly more liberal frame of mind than his father, having worked with the noted liberal American theologian Lyman Abbott, who was open to both biblical criticism and Darwinism. At the beginning of the crisis, Bliss was on leave in America. Accompanied by David Stuart Dodge, he met with Theodore Roosevelt, who was then president. Roosevelt assured both men that the American navy would protect the American property.

But the issue was not one of violence, nor one of impending native fanaticism. Quite the opposite. There was consensus that the striking Muslim and Jewish students had conducted themselves properly even as they violated the religious policy of the college. The Ottoman government urged the Americans to change course on their religious policy. The U.S. ambassador in Constantinople also urged the college authorities not to be shortsighted. Bliss therefore urged the American faculty and the board to accept the need to adapt to the circumstances. "Our horizon must be broader," he pleaded. He was right. The situation on the ground was ironic. Arabs and Muslims—the leaders of the student protest were in fact two Indian Muslim students—were upholding the principle of freedom of conscience, and for the second time in living memory the American board of trustees in New York and most of the college's American faculty on the ground were militating in an opposite direction. They were defending what Bliss warned had become a "cold, arid, dead" system of evangelical education.[43]

Bliss understood, in a manner that few of his American colleagues did, that the nepotism, evangelical fundamentalism, and racial hierarchy of the college undermined the ability of Americans to inspire and to lead. He moved to rescind policies that had been instituted in the aftermath of the debilitating Darwin affair of 1882, such as the Declaration of Principles, which had mandated a religious test for faculty. He also confided to David Stuart Dodge, during the 1909 Muslim and Jewish student rebellion against compulsory chapel service, that "we have been looked upon too long as *an oligarchy of good intentions* but with harsh manners."[44]

Bliss oversaw the promotion of the Arabic teacher Jabr Dumit to full professor—an event that sat very well with men such as Rashid Rida. Dumit became the first Arab to achieve such a position, although he was still paid less than his American colleagues and was not allowed to participate in the local administration of the college. Bliss's relative moderation stemmed not simply from his liberal outlook. He sensed that the 1908 revolution had heightened expectations around him in Beirut and across the Arab provinces of the empire. He also recognized that the revolution had not succeeded in abolishing Western imperialism; it had only managed to depose an Ottoman sultan.

Howard Bliss, more than any of his peers since Van Dyck, appreciated the degree to which the positive idea of America and the success of the college he led depended on gaining and maintaining the trust of the Muslim majority of the Arab provinces and not simply that of their Christian minorities. "The first task is the task of putting ourselves in the place of our non-Christian students, our Moslems, our Tartars, our Jews, our Druses, our Behais. We must remember the whole Moslem world. We must remember Arabia," he said.[45] And well Bliss might have fretted. The American missionaries faced becoming an anachronism in a rapidly changing world. Through their obdurate embrace of evangelical principles and their overt disregard of educated Muslim opinion, the Americans risked turning their greatest cultural asset in the region—the Syrian Protestant College—into a mere sectarian school. By forcing Muslims to attend Christian prayers at a time when religious liberty was the watchword of the day, they risked confirming everything that xenophobic religious scholars such as the shaykh Yusuf al-Nabhani said about them. By praising Lord Cromer, as Theodore Roosevelt had done, they also risked tainting the hitherto insulated idea of America with the stain of Western imperialism.

The idea of America in the Arab world, Bliss instinctively knew, could not and should not rest on a minority at the expense of the overwhelming majority. As he nudged his American colleagues to adapt their evangelical beliefs to the multi-religious world that surrounded them, his Muslim contemporary Rashid Rida published a speech he had given to the striking Muslim students. Rida said that he understood their frustration and knew that the college's ultimate aim was to propagate Protestantism. He urged them, however, to be patient and to appreciate the modern education that the American college had given them.

Thus, two influential men, one an American missionary and the other an Arab Muslim scholar, counseled moderation while working from very different intellectual positions. They drew on their own long experience of interacting with those who did not share their inherited beliefs. They had come to recognize that simply denying legitimacy to others of different faiths and cultures was not only wrongheaded but also self-defeating. The choice at the Syrian college, Rida insisted in 1909, was ultimately an American missionary choice. They could either show forbearance and toleration of their Muslim students and thus win their hearts and minds, and those of the wider Muslim community, or, he said, they could unnecessarily alienate Muslims from their institutions by insisting on compulsory Christian education. The first choice would illuminate the shared goal of both modern Islam and Christianity to work for the betterment of humanity; the second choice would simply fire the embers of fanaticism and mutual alienation, although it would also teach Muslims of the need to depend on none but themselves.[46]

The American missionaries chose to continue the compulsory religious education. Presented with the opportunity to demonstrate their understanding of local society, the American missionaries decided instead to defy it. It was the straw that broke the camel's back; henceforth, even Rida would admit that there was an undeniable Western "hatred" and "fanaticism" at work in the very American missionary institutions that he had previously lauded.[47] The missionaries for the most part appeared out of step with the nationalist mood of the late empire. Fearful and mistrustful of the very Muslim Arab environment they sought to convert, they risked opening an irreparable breach with it. But for all the evident Muslim alarm at missionary activity, there was virtually no hostility to America itself to be found anywhere in the Arab world.

The opposite, in fact, was unfolding. As Bliss and Rida struggled to define the nature of an American presence in the Arab world, thousands of Arabs were drawn to what one immigrant described as the "gold-swept shores of distant lands, to the generous cities and bounteous fields of the West, to the Paradise of the World—to America."[48] They joined the hundreds of thousands of European emigrants in redefining the face of an expanding country. The new world beckoned Arab immigrants in a manner that Europe never did.

In the early 1890s, America offered hope for a new life at a time when the silk trade in Mount Lebanon, which had grown into a vital industry by the 1870s, employing thousands at its peak, had all but collapsed. Population pressure, land scarcity, unemployment, heavy taxation, fear of conscription, and stories about the untold wealth of America made the expensive and extremely arduous voyage to distant America in steerage a viable option for thousands of impoverished subjects of the Ottoman Empire.

The very first Arab immigrant to the United States appears to have been Antun Bishalani, who landed in New York in 1854.[49] Like the vast majority of immigrants from the Arab provinces, Bishalani was a Christian from Syria. He had worked as a dragoman, or translator, for Western tourists in the Holy Land. He followed the promise of prosperity to be found across the Atlantic. He died of tuberculosis, however, within two years of his arrival. The first Syrian family arrived in 1878, led by Dr. Joseph Arbeely, who later recalled that he emigrated "for the progress of my children."[50] A trickle of Arab immigrants to the United States became a stream in the 1890s. Between 1896 and 1914, several thousand Syrian immigrants entered America annually.[51] In the United States, Arabs settled mostly around New York, creating a Syrian colony in Brooklyn on Washington Street. From there, they fanned out across the country. They worked as peddlers, selling trinkets, baubles, and supposed relics from the Holy Land; they also labored as seamstresses in sweatshops, as workers in textile mills, as autoworkers in Ford plants, and as merchants and shopkeepers. Most were uneducated and, like other immigrants, struggled to adapt to an unfamiliar climate, language, and country.

With this influx came an inevitable sharpening of the Arab idea of America—the texture of everyday immigrant life, the struggle to assimilate or simply to earn enough money to return home to Syria filled out what had been until then a schematic and anodyne Arab idea of America. The Syrian Mikha'il As'ad Rustum provided one of the first detailed Arabic accounts of America and the nature of Arab immigrant life in it. Rustum was blunt and had an eye for detail. Originally from the Lebanese mountain village of Shwayr, where a Scottish Presbyterian medical missionary, William Carslaw, had established and ran a church, a manse, and two schools, Rustum had lived in Baalbek and taught at an American missionary school in the nearby town of Zahle. He visited Chicago for the World's Fair in 1893 and spent nine years in America. He traveled from Chicago to Cincinnati, and from there to Richmond and Washington, then on to Philadelphia and New York. Not surprisingly, he praised American education as an example for all peoples to emulate and said of the Americans that they were "the most industrious people in the world in every task they undertake."[52] Like most other immigrants, he was astonished by the majestic skyscrapers, public buildings, and bridges of American cities. Before these edifices of modern civilization, Rustum confessed that he gazed upon a new wonder of the world.

And yet for all his praise of America, and especially Washington, D.C.—whose landscape struck him as "one of the gardens of paradise"—and Philadelphia, where he took in the sight of the Liberty Bell, Rustum described himself as a man out of place, a stranger in a strange West. He criticized what he described as exotic American habits. He was appalled by the excessive drinking he witnessed during his tour and was disgusted by the American habit of chewing and spitting tobacco. He frowned as well on the unnatural freedom Americans "gave" their women. He tut-tutted that in America women ruled over their men—though he confessed they were also very generous—whereas in the East women were more naturally subordinate to their men. He included in his book two pages on the "Superstitions of the Americans" and ridiculed the ubiquity of "Santa Clauses" across the country during Christmas.

Rustum typified the simultaneous sensations of wonder and alienation that defined the Arab discovery of America. He noted that Americans were not well versed in geography and had imbibed so many stereotypes about Arabs that they "believed that we were demons out to eat them." He wrote that when "you say to them you are from Syria, they reply 'where is that?' And when you say it is in Turkey [the Ottoman Empire], they say, 'we thought it was in India.'" One of them even believed that Damascus was in Armenia. "Still," Rustum concluded, "we must not say about them that they are 'at the level of donkeys in their dull-wittedness' as Doctor Jessup described some of the simpletons in Syria in his . . . book." Rustum's swipe at the American missionary Henry Harris Jessup was intentional. He had stumbled across books by Jessup in Virginia, where he had been visiting the home of the "hero" of American independence, George Washington, and in Philadelphia. He was horrified by what he described as the bad faith of the missionary for his extreme bias in portraying Syria in the negative light that he did.[53]

Rustum objected not simply to the misrepresentation of Arab women in Jessup's writing but to the flawed nature of Jessup's comparison between America and Syria. He asserted that there was neither balance nor humility in the American's perspective. Rather than compare history to history, experience to experience, anecdote to anecdote, Jessup had highlighted the failings of the East but ignored those of America. Rustum was defensive. He denied that women were oppressed in Syria; if there was an occasional instance of oppression there, he said, there were also cases of oppression of women in America. And if American tourists in Syria habitually complained that boys in Syria pestered them with the phrase "baksheesh Mister," so in America, he said defiantly, he was routinely accosted by boys asking for "one cent, Mister."[54] Rustum categorically refused Jessup's logic, and in his refusal there is a larger point to be made.

Both Americans and Arabs stereotyped each other, and both did so freely and without hesitation. But they wrote from very different positions of power and therefore with very different consequences. Rustum's simplification of American culture may have missed the mark every bit as much as Jessup's caricature of Arab culture. But his perspective carried no weight in shaping American attitudes. Jessup's influential writings, on the other hand, reflected mainstream American beliefs about the backwardness of Islam and the Orient.

As much as Rustum proudly celebrated his Syrian heritage, and as strongly as he denounced Jessup's willful "defamation" of Syrian culture, most Syrian immigrants felt far less confident in defending their culture. They had neither the interest nor the energy nor the need to challenge American assumptions about them—they simply wanted to earn a living. They either parried or shrugged off white American notions about the uncivilized and uncouth "Syrians"—or as the *New York Times* described them in 1888, the "dirty, ragged, shiftless Arabs" (as opposed to the "earnest, honest faces" of Swedish immigrants), those "most filthy of immigrants" who were intent upon "invading" and "infesting" American cities.[55]

Rustum's defense of Syria notwithstanding, some immigrants internalized American ideas about the wretched and uncivilized unassimilated Syrian. This was especially evident in the new Arabic press that was established in the United States. Arabic-language newspapers such as *Al-Huda* and *Mir'at al-Gharb*, like Rustum's travel memoir, sought to explain to their immigrant readers how to navigate the hierarchy of races that made up America. They identified themselves as "Syrian," not as "Arab" or "Turk." They also sought self-consciously to inculcate among Syrian immigrants a modern, middle-class (white) "American" sensibility that would determine how Syrian women should raise their children, how Syrian men should work productively in accordance with American notions of discipline and punctuality, and so on.

Unlike *Al-Muqtataf* and other journals that discussed "America" from afar, the editors of the America-based press grappled with the very real fear of being stigmatized by their host society. In a white Anglo-Saxon–dominated republic, the Syrians desperately wanted to be included as "white," and to this end they deliberately parlayed their Christian origins into acceptance by an often mistrustful white public. Until well into the twentieth century, acquiring American citizenship depended on Arab immigrants being legally classified as white. Some U.S. courts balked at such a view: They deemed Syrians to be "Asiatic"—or at any rate not white like Anglo-Saxon American whites—and therefore not eligible for naturalization under American law. Salloum Mokarzal, who was the brother of the founder of an important Arabic newspaper in America, *Al-Huda*, and who would himself establish the English-language *Syrian World*, defiantly proclaimed that he belonged to a community of "full blooded white Syrians."[56]

The Mokarzal brothers seized upon a prevalent American image of the rapacious and conquering Muslim Turk who oppressed Christians to press their claim for inclusion. Throughout the 1890s and until the 1920s, the sufferings of the Armenian Christians became the major foreign humanitarian cause of evangelical circles in America. The Syrian immigrants jumped on the bandwagon. They pleaded for an American appreciation of the deep scars that Turkish oppression had left on the empire's Arabic-speaking Christian population. It became commonplace among immigrants to emphasize stories—and for the most part they were apocryphal, though passionately recounted, stories—of the terrible persecution they had endured at the hands of Muslim Turks.

The immigrant Protestant Leah Barakat was typical in this regard. She was originally a Maronite and came from the same village as As'ad Shidyaq. Barakat ingratiated herself with her evangelical patrons in her 1912 memoir *A Message from Mount Lebanon* by describing America from the perspective she knew would strike a responsive chord. For the helpless Eastern Christian immigrant, she said, America was "a land of liberty, where no more cannons would deafen their ears, no more persecution follow their fleeing footsteps, where there would be no more cursing of the name of Jesus, since here His name was loved and honored."[57]

Barakat, however, recognized that most Americans could not tell the difference between a "Syrian" and an "Arab." She was taunted by children who called her a gypsy, an Indian, and an Arab. She insisted, therefore, that just as there was a distinction to be made between native Americans and the evangelical American people, so too must a distinction be made between Muslim Arabs—the real Arabs who conquered others and spread their language and religion by the sword—and her own "Phoenician" ancestors, who received their Christianity directly from the apostles.

In their Arabic newspapers, meanwhile, Syrian immigrant editors zealously berated, cajoled, and exhorted their first-generation immigrant readers to act more "civilized" and less "Syrian." Rustum himself intimated that a certain hierarchy of races was at work in America—with those he referred to as "Yankees" at the top. Then came the Germans, the Poles and the Irish, who were followed by the Italians, the Greeks, the Jews, and the Chinese, who in turn, were to be differentiated from the blacks and the native American Indians. For all his defense of Syria and Syrians, or perhaps as a result of it, Rustum indulged in clearly racist descriptions of blacks and Indians. To him, the former were as uncouth as the latter were uncivilized, and both were worlds apart from what he regarded as the unfairly disparaged Syrian. Like most other immigrant communities, the Syrians understood that there was a powerful and apparently unshakeable racial orthodoxy at work in America. Their job was not to criticize it. It was simply to fit in.

If a simple desire for a better life drove most of the thousands of Syrians who emigrated to America, the country also provided the setting for the rise of a new kind of exuberant Arabic self-expression. This was known as the *mahjar* literature, or the literature of exile in America. Among its founders was the novelist, poet, and essayist Ameen Rihani, who arrived in New York as a twelve-year-old in 1888. Rihani was the first modern Arab writer to express himself fluently in both Arabic and English. He was also the first Arab immigrant to the United States to pursue a literary career. Rihani shocked his father by abandoning bookkeeping in the family store in Brooklyn; he joined a theater group, playing Hamlet and Macbeth, and after it failed he pursued a writing career that appeared at first extravagant for a humble immigrant. Unlike most Syrians, Rihani plunged into Western literature and poetry and was especially taken by the transcendentalist poetry of Ralph Waldo Emerson, Walt Whitman, and Henry Thoreau. Naturalized as a U.S. citizen in 1903, he did not, at first, search for the roots and origins of Arab history, as did Bustani or Zaydan; nor did he defend Syrian culture in the patriotic manner of Rustum. Rather than history, he embraced his intermediary situation between Arab and American cultures to explore both in relation to each another.

His most important English-language work, *The Book of Khalid*, was published in New York in 1911. The dense allegorical tale revolves around the journey of two Syrians, Shakib and Khalid, who illegally enter the United States. More than any other Arab of his era, Rihani demystified America. He adopted the vantage point of the daily immigrant experience. From the "Juhannam [hell] of Ellis Island" to "Tammany Land," Rihani described the extraordinary fusion of cultures that made up New York City. He wrote about power, love, and corruption, not as Eastern or Western vices or virtues but as issues that transcended particular cultures. "Yes, even Shakib, who knew only a few English monosyllables, could here make himself understood. For money," he wrote about one of his protagonists bribing his way out of the purgatory of the examinations enforced by grumpy immigration authorities, "is one of the two universal languages of the world, the other being love. Indeed, money and love are as eloquent in Turkey and Dahomey as they are in Paris or New York."[58]

Inevitably, the image of America comes off tarnished by the end of Rihani's work—not because Rihani was anti-American in any political sense, but because his intimate emigrant's recounting of so dynamic a city as New York could not but contradict purely idealistic descriptions of America. When Khalid tires of his immigrant's life, he announces to Shakib that he is overcome with nostalgia for his native country. "O, my greatest enemy and benefactor in the whole world is this dumb-hearted mother, this America, in whose iron loins I have been spiritually conceived." Summing up this paradox of a country whose very materialism has allowed him to discover a transcendent, universal spirituality, Khalid offers his sharpest assessment of the country that launched him back into the world.

> O America, equally hated and beloved of Khalid, O Mother of prosperity and spiritual misery, the time will come when you shall see that your gold is but pinchbeck, your gilt-edge bonds but death decrees, and your god of wealth a carcase enthroned upon a dung-hill. But you can not see this now; for you are yet in the false dawn, floundering tumultuously, worshiping your own mammoth carcase on a dung-hill—and devouring your spiritual children. Yes, America is now in the false dawn, and as sure as America lives, the true dawn must follow.[59]

Remarkably, for Khalid as for Rihani, America's overseas conquest of the Philippines, its occupation of Cuba and Haiti, and its treatment of blacks and Indians went almost entirely unnoticed. Occasionally someone, like the Syrian socialist Farah Antun, who lived in New York between 1905 and 1909, would express thorough disillusionment with the poverty he witnessed in America. Antun lashed out at the ruthless white treatment of Indians and the veneer of civilization that had but the "beauty of a painted woman."[60] But he was an exception. For the vast majority of immigrants, the materialism of U.S. society was the other face of the great monuments and buildings that so routinely filled them with wonder. American prosperity, not American imperialism, emerged as the first great, enduring Arab stereotype of fin-de-siècle America; money was what drew Syrians to America in the first place, and money was what they sent back to their families. Although most immigrants sought to assimilate as best they could, others began returning home to Mount Lebanon bearing newfound wealth and regaling villagers with tales of the riches to be amassed in the United States. They sought wives and plied money back into their homes in their villages. Probably more than any other factor, the material prosperity of returning immigrants consolidated an image of America as a bountiful land of opportunity. But the idea of the materialism of America—as opposed to the far more prosaic idea of it simply being an available destination for desperate emigrants, a place to make money and strike it rich—also became a literary conceit. It allowed immigrant writers to exploit American motifs about the dreamy and ancient Orient and to turn them to their advantage by casting themselves as representatives of a mystical, authentic spirituality of the East.[61]

This is how the Syrian émigré writer Mikhail Naimy made his name. He had first joined his two elder brothers in Walla Walla, Washington, in 1911, then enlisted in the U.S. army at the very end of the First World War before moving to the center of Arab intellectual life in New York. In 1925 he wrote a short story, called "The Cuckoo Clock," in which the simple pastoral life of Mount Lebanon is ruined by the false promise heralded by a returning migrant from America. The well-heeled returnee dazzles the simple villagers with the wondrous mechanical objects he has brought with him, including a cuckoo clock. Through it he is able to enchant and steal the heart of a young girl on the eve of her marriage. She elopes with him to America, leaving her broken-hearted lover embittered and lacking any option but to emigrate himself to the land of the "dollar." There he becomes rich. He comes across the girl he was meant to marry, but finds her long since abandoned by the man who lured her away and in a pitiable state. He himself is unable to find solace, despite his wealth. He decides, at the end, to leave America and return to the simplicity and beauty of his native land. He finds peace and exhorts his countrymen to forsake emigration. America, for Naimy, constituted the antonym for an idealized home. Naimy returned to Lebanon in 1932 and lived through World War II, the partition of Palestine, and the outbreak of the Lebanese Civil War in 1975. He died in 1988 at the age of ninety-eight, having grown increasingly disillusioned with Western civilization.

Of all the Syrian immigrant writers in America, the most famous was Kahlil Gibran, a close friend of Naimy, who was at Gibran's side when he died in a New York hospital in 1931. The attitudes of the two men toward the West were fundamentally different. Whereas Naimy had been ill at ease in his exile from Mount Lebanon, Gibran flourished in

America. Gibran, who died at the age of forty-six, did not live long enough to see the most intractable conflicts in the Middle East develop. He spent most of his adult life in the United States. A precocious young boy, Gibran emigrated to Boston in 1894 with his mother and two sisters. His father, a drunkard with a violent temper, remained behind in Mount Lebanon. In Boston the impoverished Gibran was fortunate to have a social worker recognize his artistic talent; she connected him with a wealthy American patron, who, in turn, decided to introduce the young Syrian from the South End slums into the bohemian circles of Boston. Gibran later befriended the older Rihani and was commissioned for $50 to draw the illustrations for *The Book of Khalid*. Gibran's most celebrated work, *The Prophet*, which would become the first best-selling English-language book by an Arabic author in the modern era, bore the unmistakable mark of Rihani's influence. Both Rihani and Gibran directed their most penetrating criticism toward their own native society.

Both Maronites, they were appalled by the corruption of their native church and the sectarianism that permeated Syria; they became committed anticlericalists and explicitly championed religious toleration. As a consequence, Rihani suffered excommunication from the church; Gibran was threatened with it. Each in his own way evoked the spirit of As'ad Shidyaq. Their writings depicted hypocritical priests, misled commoners, tyrannical emirs, and unjustly accused heretics. They admired aspects of American society and recognized their own debt to it. But unlike the missionaries, neither Rihani nor Gibran venerated American culture or held it up as a model to be embraced simplistically by their own native society. They criticized, instead, specific facets of their culture without indicting the whole of it. They purposefully refrained from lashing out at Islam, leaving it to Muslim compatriots to take on their own religious authorities. In place of exclusionary religions, they proposed a more diffuse and universal spiritualism. "The truly religious man," Gibran would write, "does not embrace a religion; and he who embraces one has no religion."[62]

The Arab discovery of America came full circle. The country that had sent out missionaries to convert all the peoples of the East into Protestants now provided the setting for visionaries of a new kind—individuals who called for a more productive relationship between America and the

Arab world that could harness the strengths of each to the common cause of human betterment. Rihani described his vision of a synthesis between West and East through the voice of his heroic and mystical Khalid: "Give me, America, thy hand; and thou, too, Asia. Thou land of origination, where Light and Spirit first arose, disdain not the gifts which the nations of the West bring thee; and thou Land of organization and power, where Science and Freedom reign supreme, disdain not the bounties of the sunrise."[63]

This was a dream, but that Rihani could dream, and that America itself would figure so prominently in his vision of a union of East and West, testified to how far the Arab idea of America had progressed in a single century. From nothing, sustained interaction and mutual transformation had created an Arab imagination of America as a major Western power that was not imperialist. By the turn of the new century, however, the fate of the Armenian Christians in the Ottoman Empire moved American missionaries to clamor for a political intervention in Ottoman affairs. And by 1914, Ottomans plunged themselves and their vulnerable Arab provinces ill prepared into the great debacle of the First World War. Disease, war, genocide, and famine took their immense toll. The British and the French seized the opportunity to defeat and carve up, once and for all, the sick man of Europe. Yet alongside this great crucible, giving great hope to the Arabs, was the revelation of the American president Woodrow Wilson as a prophet of self-determination. A new, more overtly political chapter in U.S.-Arab relations had dawned.

3

BENEVOLENT AMERICA

"They are such an anachronism, so foreign to the spirit of the age, as to seem unreal—in fact, impossible under any European Government," wrote the recently resigned missionary Frederick Davis Greene about the Ottoman massacres of the Armenians in Anatolia between 1894 and 1896. "But it must be remembered," he added, "that Turkey herself is an anachronism, and that she is not simply foreign, but hostile to the spirit of the age."[1] More than any single event in the nineteenth century, the tragedy that befell the Armenian Christians of the Ottoman Empire in the late nineteenth century crystallized American missionary antipathy to Muslim rule.

Among the Armenian Christian community of Constantinople and Anatolia, unlike their Arabic-speaking Christian counterparts in Syria and Egypt, revolutionary organizations had spearheaded the emergence of a separatist national movement. In their bid for independence, Armenians sought to emulate the Greeks, Serbs, and Bulgarians who had already waged successful revolts against Ottoman rule. These earlier battles had been won after terrible struggles and resulted in the loss of huge swaths of Ottoman territory. They had also been accompanied by the massacre and rape of thousands of Muslim, Christian, and Jewish villagers and townspeople throughout the Balkans and had culminated in the expulsion or flight of hundreds of thousands of Ottoman Muslims from their homes and properties. Western public opinion, including American public opinion, scarcely noticed the ordeal of Muslim civilians—their plight did not prick American or European consciences, just as the oppression of Christian civilians made no obvious impact on Muslim writers of the day.

The Ottoman rulers grew increasingly bitter at the West for its incessant encroachment into their domains. While the rulers sought to hold their failing empire together by embracing Islamic nationalism, Armenian separatists worked in fits and starts, openly outside the empire and clandestinely within it, to transform a distinct Armenian religious identity into a nationalist movement. Capitalizing on the glaring weakness of the Ottoman state, they hoped for Western military intervention on their behalf. The Armenians, however, were deceived. They failed to predict the ferocity of the Ottoman response: the bloody refusal on the part of the sultan and his imperial councilors—let alone the rural, often irregular, soldiers, bigoted religious students, and urban mobs—to accept one more humiliation at the hands of rebellious Christians. They also failed to understand that Western sympathy was not going to translate into Western action unless there was a direct imperial interest at stake. Armenian civilians therefore bore the brunt of Muslim resentment and Ottoman imperial fury. Tens of thousands of them perished in the ensuing battles and massacres between 1894 and 1896.

It was left to American missionaries such as Frederick Greene to take the lead in publicizing the plight of the Armenians. Scattered across Armenian villages and towns in Anatolia and centered in Constantinople itself, Americans dominated evangelical work among the Armenians. They proudly presided over an Armenian evangelical community of 125 churches, 12,000 members, 423 schools, and several acclaimed colleges throughout their field of work in the imperial capital and, in Anatolia, around the provincial towns of Tarsus, Van, Harput, Bitlis, and Erzerum.[2] The Armenian Protestant community dwarfed its Arab counterpart. During the terrible events of 1895, several missionary schools were destroyed and missionary properties were vandalized. Just as the massacres of Arab Christians in 1860 had outraged and terrified the Syrian missionaries, so now those most settled in Turkey took the lead in raising the cry in America on behalf of the Armenians.

American missionary compassion for the Armenians created the first genuine humanitarian movement for a foreign people in the United States. It far exceeded the efforts made on behalf of the Greeks during their war of independence in the 1820s or the Syrian Christians in 1860. The movement on behalf of the Armenians also far exceeded the sporadic expressions of official U.S. concern for the Jewish inhabitants of the Ottoman Empire. Across evangelical circles in the United States, churches took up collections on behalf of Armenian victims and prayed for them. Sunday schools, societies, and colleges took up their cause, and mass meetings were held for them. Relief subscriptions were channeled through the American Board and the Red Cross. Together they helped raise approximately $175,000 for the Armenians.[3] The reports that circulated in the United States of the rape of women, the massacre of Armenian children, and the forced induction of girls into Turkish harems furnished the basis for an extraordinary outpouring of American charity.

The antidote to the "brutal sensuality" of "Mohammedanism" was what one American missionary described as a display of the healing power of "American Christianity."[4] Americans set up the National Armenian Relief Committee, headed by Associate Justice David J. Brewer of the U.S. Supreme Court. Clara Barton of the American Red Cross traveled to the Ottoman Empire to oversee the distribution of relief. Although the American missionaries often exasperated American ministers in Constantinople with their propensity to instigate religious controversies with Ottoman authorities, the evangelists were confident of their standing in America. The influence of the American Board and the evangelists reached into high places in the United States. John Hay, the secretary of state during President McKinley's term, was a cousin of George Washburn, the head of Robert College, the important American missionary institution in Constantinople, and the next president, Teddy Roosevelt, was on good terms with Howard Bliss.

American missionaries in Anatolia and Constantinople repeatedly cried out for American gunboats. They wanted their damaged properties indemnified. Their swelling national pride, moreover, pushed them to call for a show of American force to cow the Ottoman sultan. Their pleas were echoed by missionaries in Beirut, although there was no threat to their properties in Syria. Upon the repeated recommendations of one particularly zealous American minister in Constantinople, himself a former president of the University of Michigan, "to rattle the sultan's windows," an American warship was eventually dispatched in 1900.[5] In Egypt, of course, the British gunboats had already made their presence felt.

But American military engagement in the region remained symbolic. For all of President McKinley's contemplation of the use of U.S. gunboats, and for all of President Roosevelt's subsequent bluster about carrying a "big stick," they nevertheless regarded the Ottoman Empire as a strategically less important part of the world. The U.S. government was simply not going to intervene to save Armenians. Precisely for this reason, Edwin Munsell Bliss, whose father was the Constantinople agent for the American Bible Society, took it upon himself to describe the terrible fate of the Armenians. Through his account, entitled *Turkey and the Armenian Atrocities*, Bliss wanted to shame the American government into action. The book was introduced by the famous suffragist and head of the Woman's Christian Temperance Union, Frances W. Willard, who bewailed the Turkish crimes against wives, mothers, and "babe unborn."[6] One of several books that took up the Armenian cause, its tone was unmistakable in its outrage; its design was to "SHOCK THE ENTIRE CHRISTIAN WORLD."[7] Bliss and Willard immediately homed in on two significant facts: The perpetrators were Muslim, and the victims were Christian.

Their anger stemmed primarily from genuine horror at the spectacle of human cruelty played out in the twilight of the Ottoman Empire. The combination of sectarianism and nationalism, in the context of aggressive Western imperialism and obvious Ottoman military decline, had unraveled Ottoman coexistence with remarkable speed. A Christian minority that had previously been favored by Ottoman authorities now found its existence imperiled in different parts of Anatolia. Though the story of the tens of thousands of Armenian victims in the 1890s would be effaced by an even more cataclysmic, more systematic—and certainly more planned—assault on the Armenians in the empire during the First World War, at the time it outraged American evangelicals. Bliss could easily imagine the tragedy that befell the Armenians, for the regions in which the massacres took place had long been evangelical hunting grounds. His and Frances Willard's moralizing, however, reflected not simply Christian concern but also the racial disgust with the Turks that characterized so much of the American, and indeed Western, press at the time. Their underlying presumption was categorical: What the Ottoman Turks perpetrated against the Armenians was something "civilized" peoples, especially Anglo-Saxons, did not do. Americans were civilized; so too, by virtue of their ancient Christianity, were the Armenians. The Muslim Turks were not. It was, to most Americans who concerned themselves with the Armenian question, that simple.

The Christian Ottoman minister in America, Mavroyeni Bey, repeatedly disputed this description of the uncivilized Turk, although the massacres themselves could not be denied. He condemned instead, as would his successor during the First World War, what he saw as sensational, biased, and bigoted American reporting on the Ottoman Empire. Ottoman hostility to the missionaries reached its peak at this time. The sultan's officials were convinced that the Americans were aiding and abetting the Armenian cause. The missionaries vehemently denied that this was the case. As Americans, wrote Edwin Bliss, "we have no political ends to serve; we want not a square foot of the Sultan's domains."[8]

That the Indians of America were being persecuted in the American West at the exact same time—the culmination of a century of expropriation, forced removals, killings, and innumerable treaty violations all dressed up as the inevitable march of civilization—and that Jim Crow laws made a mockery of the post–U.S. Civil War Reconstruction amendments were facts ignored by every American who commented on the Armenian crisis; so too was the fate of the Aboriginals being hunted down in Tasmania. From an American point of view, Western brutality was fundamentally irrelevant to judging the "awful fanaticism" of the Turks.[9] What transpired in Anatolia, Bliss insisted, and Willard heartily concurred, was something that had no parallel in history. To compare the

Ottoman treatment of its minorities with the white American treatment of blacks or Indians would have struck them as an impertinent outrage.

In the Arab provinces, this standoff between missionary and Muslim was less overtly charged. Arabs were not Turks. There was no significant Christian national movement among the Arabic-speaking Christians, with the possible exception of the Maronites of Mount Lebanon. Arabs held at this point no powerful feelings, such as those harbored by influential Turkish Muslims, about their inability to live with Christians. The dean of American missionaries to Syria, Henry Harris Jessup, was on leave in the United States when the Armenian massacres took place. Jessup found it uncharacteristically difficult to instill his experience of the mission field into the simplistic formulations of the American press. Perhaps because Arabs, not Armenians, were his principal concern, Jessup avoided speaking publicly on the issue. In his memoirs, however, he squarely blamed "Armenian revolutionists" for provoking the conflict with the Ottomans and thus bringing catastrophe upon the Armenian population of the empire.[10] The Armenian massacres, so frightful in their scale, coincided with the flourishing of Arabic-speaking Christian communities in Beirut and Cairo. Jessup knew that the Christians of the empire were a kaleidoscope of communities and that what occurred in one corner of the empire might barely register in another.

The American missionaries in Syria, Egypt, and Arabia therefore read closely what their counterparts in Anatolia and their press in America were saying about the "Turk." They shared similar fears of Muslim fanaticism, and yet, at the Syrian Protestant College, students were taught that Arabs were the "Semitic" branch of the white race and that though inferior to the Anglo-Saxons, they were inherently more cultured and civilized than the warlike Turks.[11]

At the close of his career, none other than Jessup even confessed to admiring certain traits of the "Syrian people of the Arab race." He praised their hospitality, their fondness of children, their aptness to learn, their natural religiosity, their "very extensive and beautiful" Arabic literature, their educated men and the fact that they had "caught the enterprising spirit of Western civilization," and the successful, if small, evangelical community, some of whose members "have been an honour to the Church of Christ."[12] Still, such high praise did not conceal his desire to see the end of Islam. Even Edwin Bliss warned against the folly of a vindictive partition of Turkey and recognized some of the noble aspects of the Turks at the same time as he accused them of committing the most terrible massacres in recorded history. American missionaries' militancy against Islam fit perfectly with the general prejudice of American culture regarding the Ottoman East, yet their intimate knowledge of the language and their personal relationships with individual converts, scholars, teachers, and provincial officials occasionally pulled them in a different direction.

The upshot was that missionaries as a whole did little to alter negative American stereotypes about the Orient. Their positive knowledge of the region and its inhabitants was constantly being filtered by their own negative impulse to overthrow, to occupy, to tear down, to reject, to condemn, and to proselytize. Samuel Zwemer, for instance, was not interested in bridge-building. Instead, he wanted to level and rebuild Arab culture on evangelical foundations, ideally with an American cultural and social cast. The American missionaries' modus vivendi with the late Ottoman Empire was strictly tactical, and they awaited the first opportunity to revolutionize it. "The instinct of the Crusaders was right, although their method was wrong," said Zwemer.[13] Such was a savior of the Arabs.

By the dawn of the new century, the full ambiguity of the American missionary position was revealed. The advent of American tourism to the Holy Land and Egypt, archaeological interest there and in Mesopotamia, and above all the rise of a new breed of American millennialists who advocated the restoration of the Jews to Palestine challenged half a century of missionary domination of descriptions of the Middle East. The demise of Pastor George T. Adams's Palestine settlement in 1867 was a portent of the future. The evangelical's scheme was extraordinary. He had decided to lead 156 members of his Church of the Messiah in Maine to the Holy Land and there to found a colony near Jaffa. Adams was as enthusiastic as any of the American evangelicals who preceded him to the region. But he was also radically different. He was motivated not by a desire to convert Palestine's inhabitants. Rather, he aimed, quite simply, to regenerate the land and to precipitate an influx of Jews whose arrival into Palestine would herald the Second Coming of Christ.

Adams's scheme failed for the reasons that such schemes often do. It was fantastical; it not only ignored but flew in the face of the Arab reality of Palestine. Within months of arriving to establish their colony, for which they had no formal Ottoman permission, the settlers found themselves riven by disease and dissension. Totally out of place, the colony rapidly foundered. Members accused Adams of having misled them; others maintained their belief in him. But the effort failed. The American agricultural techniques and equipment brought over from Maine did not work in the soil of Palestine; the colonists' lack of Arabic and foreign manners, their self-styled isolation from the native environment, and their lack of money or support doomed their quixotic enterprise. Within a year Adams was desperate; he was reported by the American consul in Jerusalem to have been found "in the most degrading drunkenness."[14] He was soon forced to return to the United States.

The fiasco and its author would have been forgotten had not Adams represented one of the earliest attempts to put Christian Zionism into practice, and had Zionism itself—the European Jewish movement to create a Jewish state in Palestine—not eventually succeeded. The idea of "restoring" the Jews to their biblical homeland was not new; long before the first American missionaries had set foot in the Ottoman Empire the idea had circulated among notable Protestant theologians. Levi Parsons himself had flirted with the idea. In the face of the diversity of the land, and in recognition of the huge majority of Muslims and Christians who inhabited the Ottoman Empire, however, the American missionaries chose to focus their limited resources elsewhere. Beirut, Constantinople, and Cairo, Syria, Egypt, and Anatolia, all had good prospects for conversion, and so they became central to American mission work. Palestine did not.

Christian Zionists were different, for they embraced the notion that the Scriptures prophesied not simply the "restoration" of the Jews to the Holy Land but their control of it as a prelude to the apocalyptic Second Coming of Christ. In their view, the world was not improving but hurtling toward a "coming doom."[15] Their beliefs defied centuries of Christian tradition that spoke of the Church as the new covenant to replace the old covenant that God had made with the Jews. They also ran counter to a prevailing belief among American evangelical circles that American Protestants and America itself were God's most favored nation, the New Zion in a New World. For Christian Zionists, Jews, not Americans, remained the chosen people.

Such radical arguments originated not with the Jews of the Ottoman Empire, nor even with European Jews. They had absolutely nothing to do with local Jewish, Christian, or Muslim sentiment. They did not stem from the religious figures who walked the land, knew its terrain, or spoke its languages. They were the ideas of an Irish dispensationalist, John Nelson Darby, whose own notion of prophetic trajectory centered on a series of dispensations, or eras, that would culminate with a terrifying end to human history and the advent of the purifying reign of Jesus Christ. The "restoration" of the Jews to Palestine was a crucial step on the road to the so-called Rapture in which Jesus Christ would save the true believers while millions of others, including most Jews, would perish.

Darby's belief inspired more than one adventure in Palestine as Americans, even more than British evangelicals, took up what Herman Melville described as "this preposterous Jew mania."[16] Christian Zionists themselves were not then a cohesive group. Their interpretation of the mechanics of a Jewish return to Palestine remained inchoate. They were a marginal force in U.S. politics. Most American millennialists, let alone most American Christians, were not Christian Zionists.

In 1881, in the wake of the disintegration of the Jaffa colony, another group of Americans also possessing beliefs about the imminent approach of the millennium set out for Palestine. They were known as the Spaffordites, after their leader, Horatio Spafford, who had been expelled from the Presbyterian Church for his peculiar messianic beliefs. The Spaffordites set up the American Colony in Jerusalem. So convinced were they that the signs of the times portended Jesus Christ's impending return that they did not at first work in any organized manner or send their children to school, nor did they believe in medical care. Guided by Spafford's wife Anna following Horatio's death in 1888, they did charity work among the local population, including impoverished Yemeni Jews recently arrived in Jerusalem. Reinforced by a contingent of millennialist Swedes in 1896, the American Colony became a fixture in Jerusalem. Time, however, took its predictable toll. The millennial fervor of the group dwindled, its divisions increased, and its communal basis began to disintegrate. The Spaffordites would become, in time, defenders of the rights of the native Arab Palestinians.

Religious enthusiasm had once more been tempered by local reality. The problem was that American Christian Zionism, although not an organized political movement at this time, was churning out many ambitious individuals in the United States. Its men and women enjoyed considerable material resources and seemingly unshakeable messianic convictions. Palestine, in a sense, was the playground for their imaginations. Most did not live there, although some adherents toured Palestine, as did thousands of other American and Western tourists in the late nineteenth century. Because the consequences of their ideology were not primarily borne by them, they concocted ever bolder projects to transform Palestine's landscape. While the Spaffordites were content initially to wait for the Messiah and to interact charitably with the Arab and Jewish population of the Holy Land, another millennialist, the Christian Zionist William Blackstone, proposed a far more political and interventionist project.

Like Horatio Spafford, Blackstone was a businessman from Chicago. And like Spafford, he was a friend of Dwight L. Moody, the charismatic and influential Chicago-based evangelist who established the Moody Bible Institute and laid the basis for the modern American fundamentalist movement. Moody harangued, preached, and touched the lives of millions in America and Britain. He believed that he taught God's unvarnished truths. Blackstone wrote and petitioned to achieve the same goal. Both were gifted in the art of simplification. Both opposed liberal theology. Blackstone published an immensely popular tract in 1878 entitled *Jesus Is Coming*, which went through several editions and was translated into over thirty languages. In it, Blackstone summarized Christian Zionist convictions. The corrupt human world was on the verge of expiration; Jesus was coming at any moment; there would be a Rapture, a millennium, and finally Judgment. Before this happened, the Jews would—indeed were—returning to their divinely sanctioned land of Palestine. This movement of Jews had to be strongly encouraged; it was destined to happen.

The contrast between a missionary with intimate knowledge of the Holy Land, such as William Thomson, and Blackstone was revealing. Thomson, who spent over forty years working for the American Board mission in Beirut, wrote the immensely popular biblical travelogue entitled *The Land and the Book* (see Chapter 1). Although it was typical of most missionary writings in its harsh judgments of Muslims and Islam, it nevertheless exposed the gap between evangelical expectations and the hard realities of the contemporary Holy Land. Blackstone was far more successful in covering up the contradiction. Not having been to the Ottoman Empire when he wrote *Jesus Is Coming*, Blackstone called for Jewish political control of Palestine. Israel was "God's sun-dial," he declared.[17] The land, he insisted, belonged to the Jews because the Bible said it did.

For Blackstone, and virtually every Christian Zionist since, the Holy Land was all text and no life. He rendered irrelevant the presence of hundreds of thousands of Muslim and Christian inhabitants. There could be no stronger contrast to American missionary work. In spite of their great myopia, the American missionaries who worked the Ottoman Empire were not willfully blind. Though their evangelicalism was worrisome to Eastern Christian religious leaders and Muslims such as Rashid Rida, most American missionaries in the region were not Christian Zionist.

They knew that the Middle East went beyond Palestine. The New Testament was always far more important to them than the Old. People, not prophesy, lay at the heart of missionary work.

Although Jessup was harsh and judgmental of Arabs, he at least knew Arabic and spent decades of his life learning about Syrian culture and communicating with Syrians. He and his peers who represented America abroad through leading educational institutions such as the Syrian Protestant College sought to reconcile faith and science. They wanted to represent modernity to the Arabs. In many respects, they waged a difficult, and ultimately unsuccessful, battle. As the 1882 Darwin affair at the college illustrated, many missionaries were often defensive. But once the debacle over Darwin had died down in the college, even the conservative missionaries accepted that the battle for science was worth waging. Had they withdrawn from the secular community altogether, the missionary institutions would have abandoned their greatest advantage. They would have withered away as surely as an abundant fruit tree suddenly replanted in unsuitable soil.

Forgoing missionary work among the diverse peoples of the Middle East, Christian Zionism's most famous advocates focused instead on a transcendent, divinely promised Jewish title to the Holy Land. A natural, almost inevitable gulf separated Americans who interacted with the Arabic-speaking populations of Syria, Egypt, and Palestine and the Christian Zionists. Both claimed to be concerned with the Holy Land, but only one set of Americans was concerned with its real inhabitants. Not surprisingly, the resident missionaries often scoffed at the messianic message brought over by this new wave of American zealots. "This Holy Land," Jessup noted wryly, "is the happy hunting-ground of cranks and visionaries of all stripes, Oriental and Occidental."[18] There was more than humbug in the missionary disdain for other, less conventional kinds of American enthusiasts. The issue that fundamentally divided the missionaries and Christian Zionists was not so much theological—although it was that too. The issue was one of audience and perspective. Both groups believed that they—and they alone—possessed the only correct interpretation of the Bible. Both were hostile to Islam. But one recognized the Arabs, and the other ignored them;

one included Arabs on certain terms, while the other excluded them entirely; one was optimistic in spirit, but the other was pessimistic; one embraced science, while the other did not. Most crucially for the story being told here, one knew the Arab world, and the other did not.

In 1891, after having hidden away thousands of copies of *Jesus Is Coming* in a cave at Petra for Jews to read following what Blackstone believed was to be their imminent persecution from the Antichrist, Blackstone initiated his signal contribution to Zionism. It was a petition, or a "Memorial," entitled "Palestine for the Jews," and it was addressed to the president of the United States, Benjamin Harrison. Blackstone wrote it with a sense of urgency. He knew that the Jewish population of Russia was suffering following a series of dreadful pogroms. Blackstone reckoned that this presented an opportunity for action. He opened his Memorial with the question: "What shall be done for the Russian Jews?" Insisting that Europe was too "crowded" and that it was too costly to bring the Russian Jews to America, Blackstone hit upon what struck him as the righteous, humanitarian, and obvious solution. The answer he gave to his own question defined Zionism itself:

> Why not give Palestine back to them again? According to God's distribution of nations it is their home—an inalienable possession, from which they were expelled by force. Under their cultivation it was a remarkably fruitful land, sustaining millions of Israelites, who industriously tilled its hillsides and valleys. They were agriculturists and producers as well as a nation of great commercial importance—the center of civilization and religion.[19]

"Turkey," he said, could be compensated, but he did not mention the Muslim and Christian inhabitants of Palestine. Many Reform Jews in the United States at the time were deeply opposed to Zionism, in both its Jewish and Christian variants, because of their fear that it was simply anti-Semitism disguised as humanitarianism. Blackstone took the time to dismiss them in his cover letter to the president. But so categorical was his judgment that Palestine's inhabitants were not native and that, regardless of where or how they lived, the Jews were native, that he did not even bother to consider what claims the Arabs might have to Palestine. Their history was fundamentally irrelevant to Blackstone. Muslim claims to Palestine were to him, as to most other Christian Zionists, by definition null and void. The Bible, instead, was the sole source of what he recognized as reality to a degree that the resident American missionaries who had to navigate and circumvent Ottoman laws and societies could never dare contemplate.

In the case of the Memorial, however, the Christian Zionist perspective was deliberately muted. In its place was a powerful, largely secular, Zionist argument. Although the Jewish claim to the land of Palestine was justified by the Bible, the urgency to save the Jews derived not from the Scriptures or from prophecies, but from an explicit humanitarianism and a need for atonement that Christians felt they owed the Jewish people for centuries of persecution. For this reason perhaps, Blackstone was able to garner the signature of 413 religious, business, judicial, press, philanthropic, and government figures, including major newspaper owners in Chicago, Boston, New York, Baltimore, Philadelphia, and Washington; Chief Justice of the U.S. Supreme Court Melville W. Fuller; John D. Rockefeller, Cyrus Hamlin, and Dwight Moody; the mayors of New York, Baltimore, Philadelphia, Boston, and Chicago; the Boston-based leaders of the ABCFM; and Baptists, Orthodox Jews, Congregationalists, and Presbyterians.

Each of these signatories saw in the Memorial what they wanted to. Blackstone and Moody thought that it would further a Christian Zionist schema; Hamlin and the American Board leaders were motivated perhaps by a sense of traditional missionary and humanitarian concern. Either way, although the Memorial failed to achieve anything concrete, it announced the birth of American Zionism. The Memorial bespoke power. As Blackstone noted, the petition was signed by "representative Americans"[20]—a truly impressive list. But not a single individual among the signers, including Hamlin, had lived for any considerable period among the Arabs. Without most of them even realizing it, they were proposing to ruin the lives of hundreds of thousands of people in the region by advocating the "return" of Jews from Europe to Palestine. They were advocating yet another ruinous national contest in a region already rife with them. They were taking a wrecking ball to the edifice of American benevolence that American missionaries had worked so hard to construct. It was a signal of things to come.

If there were differences between the American missionaries in the Arab world and the Christian Zionists such as Blackstone, what brought them together was almost as important: a common belief, with radically different implications, about the illegitimacy of Islam and a fervent desire to see an end to Muslim Ottoman rule. As long as Zionism remained a marginal force and American imperialism was unseen and unfelt by Arabs, American missionaries who worked among the Arabs or the other people of the Middle East were not called to account. They could continue their uneasy, nearly century-long adaptation to a multi-religious world, emphasizing to the local people their humanitarian and charitable sensibility, while always reminding their domestic audiences of their unbridled missionary desire. They could have it both ways. Arabs, meanwhile, could go on thinking of the United States as a great, but not imperialist, power, even as the Ottoman Empire grew increasingly agitated by what it regarded as subversive American missionary work.

The picture of American and Arab relations was colored with contradiction, but there was enough ambiguity in it to allow for a constructive and mutually beneficial relationship to flourish. Trade between the United States and the Ottoman Empire had expanded significantly over the past fifty years, with the Ottomans sending 23 percent of their exports to the United States by 1913, mostly tobacco, licorice root, dates, figs, and raisins. In return, although the empire remained a modest market for American goods (less than 2 percent of Ottoman imports came from the United States by 1913), it did receive chiefly American kerosene products and Singer sewing machines.[21]

The First World War ruined the Ottoman Empire. Many more civilian lives were lost in the region than on either European front. Famine stalked Mount Lebanon and coastal Syria. A British and French naval embargo, Ottoman military requisitions, and a locust plague devastated the population there. Genocidal Ottoman policies toward the Armenians of the empire wrought further horror on an already victimized people, but so too did Russian and Armenian massacres of Muslims in eastern Anatolia. Disease, especially cholera and typhus, further reduced the population. And then, of course, there were the actual military campaigns that took the lives of thousands of young conscripts.

Ottoman military defeat opened the door to a new round of European imperialism. Russia temporarily removed itself from contention because of the Bolshevik Revolution, but neither London nor Paris hesitated in pressing their vision for a new, subservient Middle East. During the war itself, Britain and France secretly carved up the Ottoman Empire. The British wanted what is today called Iraq, while the French coveted Lebanon and Syria. For the British, oil and the route to India were at stake. For the French, there was imperial pride and an alleged solicitude for Mount Lebanon's Christian population. For both, however, local nationalism presented an obstacle. Neither the Turks nor the Arabs were going to passively watch imperial powers carve up their lands without a struggle. Under the leadership of the hero of Gallipoli, Mustafa Kemal, later known as Ataturk, the Turks fought back hard and won independence for Turkey. In the Arab provinces, however, the nationalists, shorn of military leadership and even a semblance of an army, lost decisively.

The aftermath of the war saw the creation of "mandates"—a Western euphemism for nominally sovereign states under European tutelage—in Syria, Lebanon, Iraq, Jordan, and Palestine. An English-dominated but ostensibly independent kingdom was created in Egypt. In the shadow of this thinly disguised European colonialism, Arabs looked toward President Woodrow Wilson's vision of a new world order. Because of Wilsonian principles—which became associated with the idea of self-determination—and the American relief work in Syria, the benevolent image of America among Arabs reached its zenith. But because of the war itself and the beginning of the conflict in Palestine that Great Britain created, that image was soon to be tarnished.

From an American viewpoint, the First World War in the Ottoman Empire witnessed immense tragedy but offered great hope. The specter of human catastrophe surrounded the missionaries in virtually all their stations except those in Egypt. The United States did not declare war on the Ottomans, who sided with Germany in an attempt to stifle the relentless Russian, British, French, and Italian encroachment on their territories.

Once more the Armenian question became a burning one for American evangelicals and diplomats as Ottoman imperial fury and fear turned on the Armenian Christians in 1915. The scale of massacres and deportations was far greater than what had occurred two decades earlier. This time the existential anxieties that animated and justified their actions, the Turks believed, led them to commit genocide. Russia had invaded Ottoman territories, and Armenian revolutionaries had explicitly sided with the Russians. The empire was on the verge of collapse. The Ottoman response was both brutal and sustained. The goal was to depopulate eastern Anatolia of any significant Armenian presence and therefore to extinguish the Armenian question once and for all.

The Ottoman interior minister, Talaat Bey, allegedly told the American ambassador Henry Morgenthau in 1915 that Turkey was dealing with the Armenians as the Americans had dealt with the Indians.[22] The comparison, however flawed it may have been, was entirely lost on the Americans. Ambassador Morgenthau himself took the lead in reporting harrowing stories about the fate of the Armenians. Muslim Turks, he related in his account of the genocide, extracted fingernails or applied red-hot irons to the breast and then poured boiling butter on the wounds. They crucified their Armenian victims or nailed horseshoes to their feet.[23] The American press and evangelical societies mobilized.

The upshot in America was the revival of the image of the fiendish Muslim who killed not for national purpose or interest, however monstrously conceived, but to satisfy a primal Mohammedan bloodlust. The Muslim Turk was, in Ambassador Morgenthau's view, "unspeakable." The Armenian Christians were entirely innocent. Based upon this dualism, another extraordinary movement of American humanitarianism on behalf of the Armenians and other victims of the war commenced. The American Board foreign secretary, James Barton, who had himself served as a missionary in Anatolia, took the lead in organizing a national American relief campaign. He described it as a "narrative of American philanthropy."[24]

And an outpouring of American generosity it certainly was. By 1917 an organization called the American Committee for Armenian and Syrian Relief (ACASR) had raised over $2 million. By the time Barton wrote his *Story of Near East Relief* just over a decade later, Americans had collected and administered over $116 million.[25] People from all walks of life gave freely and quickly. But as with the earlier outpouring on behalf of the Armenians in 1895, the political situation in the Middle East was far more complex than most benevolent Americans could either fathom or accept. The Ottoman ambassador in Washington protested the simplistic depiction of his country in a public representation. When, to remind Americans of their own crimes, he referred to lynchings in the U.S. South and a history of white American cruelty toward blacks and Filipinos, he was declared persona non grata. Barton, meanwhile, abandoned an early idea to get the U.S. government to allow for increased Armenian immigration to America. He also played a delicate balancing act: On the one hand, he encouraged American outrage at Turkish perfidy to underscore the urgency of donations, and on the other hand, he maintained to the Ottoman government (and to the American public) that American missionaries played no politics.

Barton was disingenuous. From the Presbyterian station in Urmia among the Nestorian Christians to the Congregationalist stations across Anatolia, American missionaries inevitably intruded in politics to a degree they never had before. In Urmia, the missionary William Shedd attempted to reconcile Muslims and Nestorian Christians, and following his failure to do so, he took to supplying weapons to the Nestorians. For his part, Barton firmly believed that what politics he did play served a righteous cause. He and his supporter Cleveland Dodge, a classmate and friend of Woodrow Wilson and an industrial magnate and philanthropist whose grandfather William had been instrumental in establishing the Syrian Protestant College and whose son Bayard would become its third president, convinced President Wilson not to declare war on Turkey to protect missionary interests.

As reports of thousands, and then tens of thousands, and finally hundreds of thousands of Armenian victims of massacre and deportation and of Syrian victims of famine arrived, the American missionaries knew that so long as the Ottoman Empire existed they needed at least its tacit consent to carry on relief work. Outright American belligerence would only hamper their work and further threaten the vast American missionary network already in place. Barton found himself fighting a rearguard action against those in the United States, such as former president Theodore Roosevelt, who clamored for immediate American military intervention against the Turks. "Let us realize," Roosevelt thundered, "that the words of the weakling and the coward, of the pacifist and the poltroon, are worthless to stop wrongdoing."[26]

Barton and his fellow relief workers were caught in a bind. They instinctively agreed with Roosevelt's characterization of the Ottomans as uncivilized—for far longer than the former president, American missionaries had worked and prayed for the destruction of the empire—but they also knew that such destruction had consequences and entailed obligations. They became increasingly infatuated, and soon intoxicated, with the idea of an American mandate over the Armenians. They worked to convince President Wilson of its feasibility, necessity, and justice. In September 1917, Albert H. Lybyer, a professor of Near Eastern history at the University of Illinois, urged an American naval landing at the Gulf of Alexandretta on the southern coast of Turkey. In March 1918, Barton himself recommended putting ashore at the same place fifty thousand American troops to cut the Berlin-to-Baghdad railway. For both men, the goal was to secure the remnants of the Armenian population and to establish an American presence in the region.

Far more so than Roosevelt, they understood that Ottoman defeat had not ended national struggles and that European imperialism threatened to provoke renewed fighting. It was urgent that a solution be found. Barton in particular became like a man possessed. He wanted to believe that it was in America's capacity to set aside its own ambitions, its own chauvinism, and its own "isolationist" tradition to save another people. He wanted to believe that the United States could seize the opportunity to embody what he described as "disinterested Christian internationalism."[27] In his perseverance, he evoked the spirit of the original American Board foreign secretary, Jeremiah Evarts, who had fought so hard and so unsuccessfully to save the Indians from white American avarice.

As Barton single-mindedly marshaled American resources on behalf of the Armenians, another American, Howard Bliss, moved to influence American policy toward the Arabs. Bliss was far more perspicacious than the American Board secretary. Whereas Barton was deaf to Turkish Muslim concerns and plunged into politics to convince American and British statesmen of the necessity of a U.S. mandate over Armenia, Bliss was alert to Arab Muslim concerns. The son of the founder of the Syrian Protestant College betrayed none of the crusading evangelism of his contemporary Samuel Zwemer, nor the philo-Armenianism displayed by Barton. Bliss was not afraid of Islam. He published a famous essay in 1920 just before he died on the nature of the "modern missionary." Bliss urged his fellow Americans and evangelicals to appreciate the prerequisites of the "modern missionary," abjuring harsh words to describe others of different faiths. The modern missionary accepts "ungrudgingly and gratefully" that Christianity is not "the sole channel through which divine and saving truth has been conveyed." Such a missionary, most importantly, "comes to supplement, not solely to create. He prays for all men with a new sympathy—for all mosques and temples and synagogues as well as for all churches."[28]

These were remarkable words. They were not only the outgrowth of Bliss's intellectual embrace of a liberal Protestant theology but equally, if not more obviously, a product of his life in Syria. Bliss had been tested severely at the outbreak of the First World War. The Ottoman government had immediately abrogated the hated "Capitulations," the legal and tax immunities that had granted foreigners enormous privileges over imperial subjects and that had become a symbol of discrimination in the eyes of the Ottomans. They had also insisted in 1915 that the Syrian Protestant College be subject to all Ottoman laws, including new education regulations, which included compulsory Turkish-language education and Ottoman history and geography, passed in the aftermath of the abolition of the Capitulations. And they had demanded that obligatory chapel service for non-Christians be ended once and for all. Despite his strident protests against the new regulations, Bliss had had no choice but to comply.

As famine raged in Beirut and Syria, Bliss developed a working relationship with the wartime Ottoman military governor of Syria, Jamal Pasha, who instituted martial law and hanged leading Muslim and Christian dissidents as traitors who had collaborated with the French enemy during the war. Syrians in both Damascus and Beirut were shocked by the severity of Jamal Pasha, and the hangings more than any other act helped galvanize Arab discontent with oppressive Ottoman rule. The governor, however, was also a firm modernizer. He supported an orphanage for Armenian children in the village of Ayntura and invited Halide Edip, the famous Turkish writer and graduate of the American Constantinople Women's College, to run it. He wanted Ottoman women to assume the role that Western women played in their societies; he shook hands with them and urged them to unveil. Jamal Pasha insisted that the college was an "Ottoman" institution. Bliss, in turn, demonstrated that the college, "commonly known as the American University of Beirut," had a vital role to play even in the darkest of times.[29]

From the protected forty-acre campus of the college west of the city overlooking the Mediterranean, relief operations were set up to cope with the famine, a locust plague, the Allied blockade, and vast poverty. In 1915 the American Red Cross established a large office near the college to oversee aid distribution. Led by Dr. St. John Ward, sixteen students from the college worked with four German nurses to set up a rudimentary hospital in southern Palestine, where they treated two hundred wounded Ottoman soldiers. Syrians and Americans worked together to do what they could to relieve the suffering around them.

Faculty member Edward Nickoley wrote in his diary in 1917: "Did you ever see a starving person? I hope you never may. No matter how emaciated a person may be from disease he never looks exactly like the person suffering from pangs of hunger. It is indefinable but when you have once seen it you can never mistake it, nor ever forget it."[30] A single British doctor had been allowed to operate a soup kitchen in the village of Brumanna in Mount Lebanon. American educators and missionaries opened up their own soup kitchens in the cities of Sidon and Tripoli, and the mountain villages of Suq al-Gharb, Ainab, and Abeih. They took in starving children and provided work—spinning, weaving, and shoemaking—for their parents. They set up orphanages for Arab children and for Armenians who had survived deportation from Anatolia. Doctors and nurses went out to minister to the ill, while Syrian immigrants in America raised and sent (until 1917 when America entered the war and such aid was suspended) over $1 million to aid their relatives and compatriots. Bayard Dodge concluded his report on American relief work in Syria by saying that "America has done a wonderful service. In all of Syria the people bless the very name 'American.' Only those of us who have talked and lived and worked with the poor mothers and sick fathers can realize what the American relief has meant."[31]

Through the looking glass of relief work, Dodge's pride in America was justified. But it also sharply narrowed his perspective. By no means did "all of Syria" bless the American name, nor could relief work obscure the fact that there remained real questions among leading Muslim figures about the intentions and integrity of American missionaries. Racial discrimination within their institutions continued. Yet in their eagerness to craft an American Protestant diplomacy, Dodge, Bliss, and Barton regarded America from an angle that obscured its undeniable blemishes. Their emphasis on American innocence and lack of imperial ambition in the region obscured the fact that the United States was, in its own right, an expansionist power that had trampled many nations and many peoples whose lives and dreams were inconsistent with its own. And missionaries, for the most part, had cheered this expansion along.

More than any single act of American charity, it was President Wilson's dramatic vision of a new world order that confirmed America's ascendance on the world stage. Before a joint session of Congress on January 8, 1918, Wilson employed the finest and most inspiring American rhetoric. From a dispassionate beginning to the speech in which he discussed negotiations between Germany and Russia, Wilson went on to insist that "the day of conquest and aggrandizement is gone by; so is also the day of secret covenants entered into in the interest of particular governments and likely at some unlooked-for moment to upset the peace of the world." The American president then laid out fourteen points that would serve for him as the basis for lasting peace.

The first of these points rejected secret treaties. The twelfth took up the question of the Ottoman Empire. Wilson declared that the "Turkish portion" of the empire should be "assured a secure sovereignty." The "other nationalities" of the empire, however, "had to be assured an undoubted security of life and an absolutely unmolested opportunity of autonomous development." The Dardanelles, Wilson added, had to remain open "to ships and commerce of all nations." The twelfth point was discordant: It combined a concrete commercial interest with loftier, but nevertheless vague, political principles. Although he did not actually use the term "self-determination" in his speech—that was the Communist Vladimir Lenin's contribution to the modern political vocabulary—the president conveyed an inspiring new template for the world. "An evident principle runs through the whole program I have outlined," he said. "It is the principle of justice to all peoples and nationalities, and their right to live on equal terms of liberty and safety with one another, whether they be strong or weak." Wilson concluded prophetically. "Unless this principle be made its foundation," he insisted, "no part of the structure of international justice can stand. The people of the United States could act upon no other principle; and to the vindication of this principle they are ready to devote their lives, their honor, and everything they possess."[32]

Wilson's speech inspired millions of men and women around the world. The importance of the speech lay not so much in what Wilson actually said or intended, but in the association that was made between the idea of America and freedom in the minds of contemporary Arabs, Koreans, Chinese, Indians, and other peoples. Hopes had suddenly been raised. Owing largely to the indefatigable Barton, President Wilson was sympathetic to the Armenians. He understood their plight and was convinced of America's Christian obligation to them. But of the Arabs he knew very little other than the fact that there were significant American missionary stations and that the most prestigious overseas American college was in their midst. Wilson was not opposed to Arab self-determination. He was aware, however, that both he and American wartime propaganda, which relentlessly and globally publicized his message of freedom, had raised enormous expectations among Egyptian, Iraqi, Syrian, and Arab nationalists that he had no hope or real intention of fulfilling.

Arabs had a highly embellished sense of the American president. Muslim and Christian, they followed his speeches. Like so many other people around the world, they saw in Wilson's words an unprecedented commitment of a major power to their freedom. They took the president at his word. Rashid Rida's *Al-Manar*, which had made it a practice to criticize European imperialism, waxed eloquent about a speech given by President Wilson in New York in 1918 outlining his vision for a League of Nations. What stood out for Rida was Wilson's insistence that strong nations must not be allowed to subjugate weaker nations, that secret imperialist treaties must be rejected, and that a single standard of justice must apply to all people. "Justice must not distinguish between people," *Al-Manar* quoted Wilson, "or discriminate or accept any standard but that of the equality in rights between the different peoples of the world." Faris Nimr's pro-British *Al-Muqattam* praised Wilson for being the "prophet of truth and the advocate of justice and compassion in this age."[33] The Egyptian nationalist leader Saad Zaghlul took English lessons in anticipation of meeting Wilson in person. "We do not believe," he wrote to Wilson in 1919, "you wish Egypt to be condemned unheard."[34] So too did Syrian nationalists laud the "lofty principles proclaimed by President Wilson."[35] And Iraqi nationalists, reacting to the British conquest of their land, also seized upon Wilsonian ideas and urged the U.S. government to help push for their immediate application in their country. The British, who had proclaimed to the Iraqis in 1917 that they had come not "as conquerors or enemies, but as liberators," worried about the extent to which "extreme" nationalists—their word for those who called for actual independence as opposed to the gussied-up version of colonialism that the British and French were proposing—embraced Wilsonian ideas.[36]

The problem with Wilsonian idealism ran deep. The American president had held aloft noble ideals without paying enough attention to the details. The British and the French cherished the details and dismissed the noble ideals. As Wilson spoke, the British and the French readied themselves to seize whatever parts of the Middle East they desired. The British under General Edmund Allenby had already defeated the Ottomans and occupied Jerusalem in December 1917. Through their high commissioner in Egypt, Henry McMahon, they had prior to that encouraged an Arab emir from Mecca, the Hashemite sharif Husayn, to throw in his lot with them in return for a general promise of Arab independence. The British had hedged when Husayn pushed them for details. Eventually, however, they agreed to put in writing their commitment to an independent Arab state. The sharif's vision for a grand Arab state was vitiated by British evasiveness; his pompous claims were whittled down by the conception the British had of what the Arabs deserved. They told the would-be "King of the Arabs" that they had to exclude from his kingdom "portions of Syria lying to the west of the districts of Damascus, Homs, Hama and Aleppo"—essentially Lebanon today and Alexandretta—because they were not "purely Arab"; they told him that he had to accept the treaties they had already signed with other Arab chiefs; and they told him that they could not act against the interests of France. Subject to these reservations, the British declared that they were prepared "to recognize and uphold the independence of the Arabs in all the regions lying within the frontiers proposed by the Sharif of Mecca."[37]

For all intents and purposes, the British deceived the Arabs. They were never serious about providing Husayn with so large or important a kingdom. His claim was extravagant not because the allure of Arab nationalism was superficial, or because there were not legitimate differences that pulled Arab and Turk apart, but because Hashemite lordship over the independence movement was so novel and so untested. The British told Husayn directly that Britain was bound to respect "the interest of her ally, France." But they did not tell him that they were in the midst of negotiating with the French a secret partition of the Arab provinces. The British-French pact became known as the Sykes-Picot Agreement, after the English negotiator Sir Mark Sykes, a self-styled expert on the Arabs, and the French representative Georges Picot, an ardent proponent of French imperialism. With cynicism born of contempt for the Arabs, they agreed that Arab unity was detrimental to Arab national interests. They also agreed to place Jerusalem and the areas surrounding it under an international administration; the British would be granted control of the ports of Acre and Haifa, as well as the right to build a railway for commercial and military purposes to Iraq, which they would also control. France was to take Lebanon and Syria and control areas as far east as Mosul.

This secret agreement was concluded in May 1916. In June the Arab revolt against the Ottomans began under the leadership of Husayn's son, Faysal. The British dispatched a young Oxford-educated captain named T. E. Lawrence, an archaeologist by training who was drawn to the architecture of Crusader castles, to Arabia. Romantic and ambitious, Lawrence was enamored with those whom he regarded as the "pure" Arabs of the desert. They represented for him the essence of manliness. The modern Arabs who lived in Syrian cities he regarded as corrupt and emasculated. Lawrence was thrilled to play with the destiny of other men. He knew that the British had no intention of fulfilling their pledges to the Arabs. But he also knew his duty as a loyal servant of the British Empire.

While the Hashemites put their faith in Lawrence, Rashid Rida saw right through British pledges to the Arabs. "Only an enemy of the Arabs," he bluntly told a British official who informed him of the agreement between Sharif Husayn and the British, "will be satisfied by such an agreement or a donkey who doesn't understand its [real] meaning."[38] Nevertheless, the tragic Faysal wanted to create an independent Arab kingdom, and he hoped to be in a position through his alliance with the British to turn his dream into a reality. He assured the British, and anyone else who would listen, that there would be no distinction in this kingdom between Christians, Jews, and Muslims. All were to be treated as equal citizens of the new state. Even before Faysal and his Arab army raced to capture Damascus in 1918 and there tried to set up an Arab government that claimed all of Syria as its own, the British government made a dramatic declaration that reverberated around the world.

Issued on the second day of November in 1917, a single paragraph in a letter from the British foreign secretary, Arthur Balfour, to the wealthy Jewish banker Lord Rothschild—which came to be known as the Balfour Declaration—proclaimed that "His Majesty's government view with favor the establishment in Palestine of a National Home for the Jewish people." Lord Balfour was a creature of the old school of empire. As prime minister in 1905, he had overseen legislation to prevent Eastern European Jews from emigrating to England. He characterized Jews then as "a people apart."[39] Now, twelve years on, Balfour announced the British government's endorsement of Zionism, the movement to create a Jewish state in Palestine. He added, mindful of being accused of anti-Semitism, a crucial qualification: that it should be "clearly understood that nothing shall be done which may prejudice the civil and religious rights of existing non-Jewish communities in Palestine, or the rights and political status enjoyed by Jews in any other country."[40]

The caveat did not deter the Zionist movement or its Christian supporters. They knew they had gained a powerful ally. Balfour acted out of imperial interest that sought Palestine for the British. He wanted to win the war, secure the Suez Canal, and gain what he regarded as powerful Jewish support for the Allies. But like Blackstone, he also believed that the Jews had a right to "return" to their ancient "homeland." However, according to the only Jewish member of the British Cabinet, Edwin Montagu, Balfour acted out of anti-Semitism, for his declaration, which Montagu desperately opposed, suggested that Jews really belonged in Palestine and not in Britain. Moreover, Balfour denied that the Arab majority had any *political* rights or historic claims to Palestine. But most of all, Balfour acted because he could—it did not matter to him what the "natives" had to say. They were to him irrelevant and dispensable. At their expense, the West would solve its Jewish "problem."

From the outset, the conflicting British promises to Arabs and Zionists were irreconcilable, but the British sought to convince the Arabs that they were in fact reconcilable. They insisted that the Balfour Declaration would never result in Palestinian Arabs being ruled over by Jews and that a Zionist homeland in Palestine would prove beneficial to the Arabs. When the Bolshevik revolutionaries revealed the secret Sykes-Picot Agreement in November 1917, the embarrassed British sought again to calm Arab fears. They said that there was no contradiction between the Sykes-Picot Agreement and Arab national aspirations. Sharif Husayn and his son were by now too steeped in revolt to turn back to the Ottomans, and too dependent on the British to break with them. They clung, therefore, to vague British assurances and to Zionist pledges that the Arabs would benefit from Jewish colonization. They continued to put their faith in Western promises, seeing in them the only way to achieve their ambitions.

In Egypt several Arabs, including Faris Nimr, the editor of *Al-Muqattam*, even tried to convince Rashid Rida that there was room within the Sykes-Picot Agreement for Arab independence. Rida dismissed this is as delusion and mocked Nimr for his gullibility. "Freedom and independence have but one meaning, the opposite of which is enslavement."[41] The British, he said, were selling the Arabs a false bill of goods. Colonialism was masquerading as liberation. And, he added bitterly, there were Arabs such as Sharif Husayn and Faris Nimr who were only too willing to play along with this charade. In Cairo in November 1918, the British and the French jointly upheld the notion that they were working only for the freedom of the region. Once more their aim was to mollify the Arabs, especially their fear of Sykes-Picot. They also sought to assuage President Wilson's concern regarding an old-style colonial partition of the Arab world. They pledged that they would create "national governments and administrations drawing their authority from the initiative and free choice of the native population."[42] The ink on the public declaration was not yet dry when the British prime minister, David Lloyd George, and the French premier, Georges Clemenceau, met in London to confirm their respective shares of the Arab provinces. By mutual interest, they altered the initial allocation of territory of the original Sykes-Picot Agreement; they also reconfirmed its main imperialist thrust: France was to get what would become Syria and Lebanon, and the British were to get Palestine and Iraq.

Of all the conflicting pledges made by the British, the most dangerous related to Palestine. For unlike the rest of the Arab world that the British were to divide and rule, only in Palestine were they committing themselves to introducing a foreign settler population in an age of self-determination. Arabs saw their case for Palestine in the simplest of terms: The native population had an inalienable right to its own land. Their case was built from that simple supposition. In their own minds, the facts spoke for themselves. There was no need for eloquence or argument because their case was so obvious. The Zionists built their case with an extraordinary diligence and dexterity, and with passion and politics. But no matter how hard they worked to make their case appear rational, religious, positive, civilized, and just, it not only directly contradicted what the natives wanted but aimed to transform a multi-religious Arab reality into an exclusively Jewish state.

Although sympathetic to the Jews, President Wilson refused at first to publicly endorse the Balfour Declaration. Instead, contending with his evangelical solicitude for the Jews and his friendship with American Jewish Zionists such as Louis Brandeis and Felix Frankfurter, he privately endorsed it. There were American missionary interests in the Ottoman Empire to consider. An Arab-American surgeon of Palestinian origin and a member of the Palestine Antizionism Society, Fuad Shatara, pleaded with Secretary of State Robert Lansing to understand the broader Arab concern with the Balfour Declaration, namely, how flagrantly Zionism in Palestine contradicted Wilson's own principle of self-determination. "We do not claim what does not belong to us," he wrote. "We merely demand the right to our homeland. We beseach [*sic*] you to come to our defense as a champion of right and justice."[43]

When Wilson went to the Paris Peace Conference in January 1919 he hoped he could put an end to all imperial wars. The British and French went simply to divide the spoils. Faysal also went to Paris, as did the Zionists. They were joined by delegations from many parts of the world. Greeks, Armenians, Chinese, Koreans, Japanese, and Indians made their way to the French capital. The British would not allow independent Egyptian, Syrian, or Palestinian delegations to participate, but the French made sure that a pro-French Lebanese delegation attended. Those without independent states shared a common purpose: to see what they believed were Wilsonian principles put into effect. The British and, even more, the French stood resolutely against this.

From the beginning of the Paris Peace Conference, it was evident that the Middle East required urgent attention. The defeat of the Ottoman Empire had not ended the war. It had merely kindled rival national ambitions among its former subjects and emboldened contending imperial plans. As the victorious allied powers assembled at Paris, the struggle over the remains of the empire was already well begun. Mustafa Kemal was rallying Turkish nationalists to his banner. Faysal's Arab nationalists were attempting to consolidate their grip on Syria. Lebanese Maronites dreamed of a separate Lebanon. The Greeks eyed Izmir, and the Zionists coveted Palestine.

The American delegation to the peace conference was overwhelmed by the magnitude of its task. It was inundated by contradictory reports and claims emanating from the Middle East. It was also stymied by how precisely to go about applying Wilsonian principles without alienating the British and the French. The Armenian question was the most serious for the American delegation. The calls for an American mandate over Armenia were persistent, but so too were American anxieties about how large would be the responsibility and how little the material reward. Wilson hesitated, not sure whether to press for an American mandate over all of Anatolia or simply its Armenian regions.

When it came to the Arab provinces, the question of Wilsonian principles in its most basic form was raised. Was the principle of self-determination to apply to Syria, including Palestine, or not? And were secret treaties such as Sykes-Picot to stand or not?

Emir Faysal submitted on January 1 and January 29 two memoranda to the peace conference. In the first, he confessed that the ideal he sought was "Arab unity," but acknowledged that each Arab country had distinct characteristics. Sensing French imperial designs, he was far more concerned with securing his own claim to Syria than he was in defending the Arab nature of Palestine. To him this point seemed obvious and in no need of elaboration. He was also desperate not to alienate the British. He insisted that the Jews "are very close to the Arabs in blood, and there is no conflict of character between the two races." In a concession that revealed the extent of Lawrence's influence as much as it betrayed Faysal's own attempt to ingratiate himself with the British, the emir added that the Arabs there wished to ally themselves with a great power, or a "great trustee, so long as a representative local administration commended itself by actively promoting the material prosperity of the country." One of Faysal's senior Arab advisers insisted subsequently that Lawrence simply forged this section in order to bring Faysal's views closer to the British position. The key, either way, was a "representative" administration that reflected the fact that "the enormous majority of the people are Arabs."[44] Anxious Muslim and Christian Palestinian Arabs underscored this point by petitioning the great powers at the peace conference to live up to Wilsonian principles, to maintain the unity of Syria, and to reject Zionism.[45]

In his memorandum of January 29, Faysal was more forceful than he had been in his earlier communication. He declared, "I have come to ask that the Arabic-speaking peoples of Asia, from the line Alexandretta-Diarbekr southward to the Indian Ocean, be recognized as independent sovereign peoples under the guarantee of the League of Nations." Faysal stressed that "I base my request on the principles enunciated by President Wilson, and am confident that the Powers will attach more importance to the bodies and souls of the Arabic-speaking peoples than to their own material interests."[46]

Faysal finally appeared in person before the great powers in Paris to plead his case on February 6. Secretary of State Lansing imagined Faysal to be the "reincarnation of Haroun al Raschid."[47] President Wilson's adviser, Colonel Edward Mandell House, recalled that "he looked not unlike the accepted picture of the Christ."[48] Faysal's own adviser, Rustum

Haydar, recorded in his diary that as Faysal spoke in Arabic, "amazement" was evident on the faces of Wilson and other leaders.[49] Faysal was not permitted by the French to represent Syria, which he claimed on behalf of the Arab nationalist movement. He appeared instead on behalf of his father, the self-styled "King of the Arabs" whom the British and the French insisted was merely the "King of the Hijaz." He knew no English, and none of the men listening to him knew Arabic. With Lawrence translating into English and a Moroccan transcribing what he said into French, Faysal again indicated that Palestine had a "universal character" that should be set aside for the "mutual consideration of all parties interested"—phrases that reflected Lawrence's continuing hold on him, for they implied a willingness to work with the Balfour Declaration and Faysal's desperate need to placate the great powers.[50] However, he reminded the Allies that the Arabs had fought and died on their behalf, and he asked that they now fulfill their pledges to honor Arab independence. The lamb was pleading with the wolves and offering them not very much in return.

The Zionists, led by the tireless, Russian-born Jewish chemist Chaim Weizmann, presented their own view on Palestine in late February 1919. Weizmann, who taught in Manchester and dominated the European Zionist movement at this time, was on excellent terms with Lord Balfour. The Zionists were more organized than Faysal and better prepared, knew English and French, and were far more confident of their standing among the imperial powers. They enjoyed one additional advantage: The representatives of both the United States and Britain were sympathetic to their cause.

Like Faysal, the Zionists presented a written statement to the peace conference before they appeared in person to make their case. In it, they called for the "historic title of the Jewish people to Palestine" to be recognized in conformity with the Balfour Declaration. Weizmann and his fellow Zionists, however, went far beyond the Declaration by outlining how a tiny Jewish minority in Palestine were to become a majority through immigration and settlement activity. In their statement, they were careful not to use the term "majority" when referring to the Arabs or the term "minority" for Jews; they were equally careful not to ask for self-determination or any form of democratic governance that might jeopardize the Zionist goal of a Jewish state. Instead, they asked for a British mandate in Palestine, with borders encompassing what is today southern Lebanon and reaching into the west along the Hijaz railway to include what is today Jordan.

The Zionists justified these expansive territorial claims through religion, race, empire, and civilization—everything, in short, but democratic self-determination. In an era when most colonized peoples were advancing claims on the basis of Wilsonian principles, the Zionists in Paris did not. Weizmann had confided to Balfour nearly a year earlier that "the brutal numbers operate against us." To trump native self-determination the Zionists in Paris fell back upon racial stereotype. The Jews, they said, were not only far wealthier, more modern, and more energetic than the "present population," but they were also more intelligent and civilized. This assessment echoed a similar, but even more vitriolic, judgment that Weizmann had privately shared with Balfour. The "Arab," he wrote from Tel-Aviv, was "superficially clever." He was insensible to justice, revealed a "treacherous nature," and would be likely to "stab the [British] Army in the back." He "screams as often as he can and blackmails as much as he can."[51] The Jews therefore deserved Palestine. However more circumspect Weizmann and his fellow Zionists were in Paris, they were no less adamant in claiming the land. In addition to emphasizing the historic and humanitarian aspect of Jewish suffering, they emphasized the quid pro quo at the heart of their ambition. In return for gaining Palestine, the Jews would no longer form a "congested population" in Europe or press to emigrate to the United States.[52]

Compared to Faysal and his naive presentation, Weizmann was polished and astute. The Arab leader pleaded the Arab cause in a manner that totally denied French imperial ambitions and fit only awkwardly, at best, within a British view of the region. The Zionists, meanwhile, pushed for their ultimate goal of a Jewish state in Palestine in a manner that accepted French imperial ambitions in Syria and derived its authority explicitly from the Balfour Declaration. But there remained the obstacle of President Wilson and his American advisers, who had little vested interest in the region. For the most part they were not unsympathetic to

Zionism. On the contrary, President Wilson was predisposed in its favor. Yet the struggle for Arab independence was the first question at the conference that brought into the open the contradiction between aspiring Asian nationalism and European colonialism.[53]

Whether the American president wished it or not, he was being asked to take a stand and to say, now that theory had come into conflict with reality, whether his principles were relevant or not. For the French, the answer was immediately and obviously no. For the British, the answer was also no. For the American missionary Howard Bliss, president of the Syrian Protestant College, the answer had to be yes or else American prestige, which had risen so high among Arabs because of Wilson, would inevitably be diminished. At the urging of Cleveland Dodge, whose son Bayard was married to Bliss's daughter, Bliss traveled to Paris. Fitted between Faysal and the Zionist presentations of their respective cases, Bliss brought with him a wealth of experience about Syria that Wilson could intuitively trust. The American president could relate to Bliss in a manner that he could not to the exotic Faysal.

Appearing on the afternoon of February 13 before Wilson, Lloyd George, Clemenceau, and Italian prime minister Vittorio Orlando, Bliss stood with a missionary sympathy for the Arabs. Like almost all missionaries in the region, he did not actively champion Arab independence, nor did he embrace Zionism. But he did represent one strand of the legacy of one hundred years of mission work among the peoples of the Middle East, a century that had changed profoundly both Arabs and the Americans among them. Bliss knew that he had a precious opportunity to demonstrate the purpose of the modern American missionary. He was brief and to the point. "Mr. President, Gentlemen," Bliss began, "I shall not detain you long. My deep interest in the people of Syria, irrespective of race, creed or condition, bred from a long residence among them—in fact I was born on Mt. Lebanon—is my only excuse for detaining you at all."

Drawing on Wilsonian language and Allied promises to the Arabs, Bliss pleaded "on behalf of the people of Syria"—they, after all, were not allowed to represent themselves formally at the conference. He criticized Turkish policies that had long oppressed the region, undoubtedly to the unanimous approval of all the powerful men in the chamber. His deep paternalism regarding the Syrians, whom he claimed were a "loveable" but defective "race" and who had to be treated with "sympathy, firmness, and patience" and guided "into a capacity for self-determination," fit perfectly with Wilson's own attitude toward Mexicans, Haitians, and Filipinos. Bliss spoke also about the need for an "absolute separation between religion and the state" and about how the Allies and the United States had worked together "for the establishment of freedom of the world." These sentiments too would not have caused any consternation among either the British or the French. But far more significantly, he asked that "an Inter-Allied or a Neutral Commission, or a Mixed Commission, be sent to Syria—including Lebanon—to express in a perfectly untrammeled way their political wishes and aspirations, viz: as to what form of government they desire and as to what Power, if any, should be their Mandatory Protecting Power."[54]

This was a revolutionary proposal. It defied the imperial nature of both Sykes-Picot and the Balfour Declaration. It sparked the hostility of the French, who feared it was directed at stripping them of Syria, and it produced British reservations, if not outright resistance. Balfour was contemptuous of the idea, although Allenby, who was the supreme military commander in Palestine and Syria, favored it. Lawrence was opposed to a commission of inquiry.[55] The Zionists were deeply opposed as well. None of these groups actually wanted to know what people in the region thought. For the same reason that it worried Zionists, Balfour, and the French expansionists, the idea of a commission of inquiry was embraced by the Arabs. Faysal himself had earlier proposed a similar commission to ascertain the wishes of the people in Syria.[56]

Wilson concurred with Bliss's suggestion. This was enough to see the Inter-Allied Commission created in March 1919. Its scope was laid out by Article 22 of the covenant of the League of Nations that called for mandates "to form a sacred trust of civilization" in which "peoples not yet able to stand by themselves under the strenuous conditions of the modern world" were to be tutored by Western powers. "Certain communities formerly belonging to the Turkish Empire," the article continued, "have reached a stage of development where their existence as independent nations can be provisionally recognized subject to the rendering of administrative advice and assistance by a Mandatory until such time as they are able to stand alone. The wishes of these communities must be a principal consideration in the selection of the Mandatory." Their task defined at last, the American commissioners prepared to embark on an extraordinary tour of Palestine, Syria, Lebanon, and Anatolia and from there, if possible, to make their way to Mesopotamia.

For the first time in history, Western powers were contemplating listening to what natives had to say about how they wanted to determine their political future. From the beginning there was resistance; doubts emerged, and myriad proposals and formulations were suggested for how the commission should be organized. The French tried to dissuade the Americans from going to Syria, suggesting, on the one hand, that American missionaries would have bribed the population and, on the other hand, that the Americans were too inexperienced and honest to understand the East.[57] The British dragged their feet. Several American advisers to the president had second thoughts, for they realized that in the face of concerted French and British resistance there was little point in raising Arab hopes. Colonel House, however, believed that the commission should go. The American Zionist and Harvard Law School professor Felix Frankfurter desperately sought to exclude Palestine from any investigation. But still Wilson gave the commission his personal blessing. Eventually, only the American Section of the International Commission on Mandates in Turkey was sent out. Informally, it was known as the King-Crane Commission because it was headed by two Americans, Henry Churchill King and Charles Crane.

King was precisely the kind of man who embodied what was most inspiring to Arabs about America. He was the president of Oberlin College. He was as idealistic as he was straightforward. He was appalled by the colonial intrigue of the French and the British and dismayed by Turkish "misrule," and as he took up his task, he genuinely wanted to know how the people of the Arab provinces envisioned their own political future. Charles Crane was more of a maverick. From Chicago, he was the wealthy heir to the Crane plumbing fixtures company and had contributed generously to Wilson's election campaign. Crane shared in the prejudices of his era. Even more, he doubted that most American Jews—with a few exceptions such as his friend the Supreme Court justice and American Zionist Louis Brandeis—were truly loyal to America. Perhaps because of these sentiments, Crane, before his arrival in Palestine, had thought that Jews might serve as a "natural bridge between Europe and Asia."[58] Crane was also enamored of China and, above all, with Russia, although he was horrified by Bolshevism. When it came to the Middle East, Muslim Turks unquestionably bore the brunt of Crane's animus in 1919 because of the Ottoman genocide of the Armenians, which he had strongly denounced. An eccentric philanthropist, Crane thought of himself as a cosmopolitan humanitarian.

Crane was more familiar than King with the Middle East, for he served on the board of Robert College and Constantinople Women's College. He also served as the treasurer for the American Committee for Armenian and Syrian Relief. Well connected, well traveled, and with easy access to Wilson, Crane declined any salary. The two commissioners took with them Professor Albert Lybyer and two technical experts, Captain William Yale, who had worked for the U.S. army as a military observer to the Egyptian Expeditionary Force in Palestine, and Dr. George Montgomery, a clergyman who had worked as a special assistant for Ambassador Morgenthau in Constantinople. They also had a small support staff that included Dr. Sami Haddad, who was an instructor in the school of medicine at the Syrian Protestant College and who served as their interpreter.

At the dawn of a new colonial age, Americans plunged themselves into the Arab world. King and Crane believed they represented Wilsonian principles. They were not so much naive as hopeful. King knew before his departure that as far as Great Britain and therefore Wilson were concerned, the Mesopotamian and Zionist questions were "virtually" closed. But he also understood from the president that the inquiry was not bound by any preexisting agreement.[59] The commissioners were assisted in their work by British and French occupation authorities as well as by Faysal's provisional Arab government in Damascus. From the beginning, they were aware that competing interests sought to influence testimony in opposing directions, but they maintained full control over the interview processes, the data collection, and the drafting of their report.

Using several rented Ford automobiles from the Near East Relief organization, rail, and General Allenby's own yacht *Maid of Honor*, the commissioners crossed thousands of miles in forty-two days between June 10 and July 21, 1919. They began at Jaffa, went on to Jerusalem, then traveled northward through Nazareth, Haifa, Acre, and across to Damascus; then, cutting across Baalbek, they made their way to Beirut. From there they set out again up and down the Lebanese coast, visiting several cities before they finally reached Alexandretta, Homs, and Aleppo. Their final stretch saw them in Adana, Tarsus, and Mersina, where they finally boarded an American destroyer, the *Hazelwood*, to return to Constantinople. They were not ultimately able to travel to Mesopotamia. In all, they received 1,863 petitions, visited 36 major towns and cities in Syria, and also heard from representatives of 1,520 villages. They interviewed Muslims, Maronites, Armenians, Chaldeans, Orthodox, Catholics, Copts, Jews, Circassians, and Druzes. They met with British officers, American and European Zionists, Arab nationalists, and Lebanese nationalists, each of these groups presenting a different picture of the situation in Syria. The American commission was nothing if not comprehensive.

Everywhere they went the commissioners repeated that the American people had no political ambitions in the region and that their job was to get as "accurate and definite information as possible . . . in order that President Wilson and the American people may act with full knowledge of the facts in any policy they may be called upon hereafter to adopt concerning the problems of the Near East."[60] Following their grueling tour, the American commissioners presented their report to President Wilson on August 28, 1919. It laid out in extraordinary detail precisely what the people of Syria, including Lebanon and Palestine, desired in their overwhelming majority: independence, a unified Syria, a single democratic government, an American mandatory—if absolutely necessary because people had more faith in the United States than in Britain and France—and an immediate end to the settlement in Palestine of Zionists, whose "title" over Palestine they rejected. But the report also noted the aspirations of various minority groups, including the Zionist settlers who wanted to build up in Palestine a Jewish commonwealth and secure unfettered Jewish immigration from Europe as a prelude to eventual Jewish sovereignty over Palestine.

King and Crane believed that they demonstrated the sincerity and impartiality of the American people. They flattered themselves and their compatriots when they proudly reported that both the Turkish and Syrian people revered America, for they saw that it "had a passion for democracy, for the common man everywhere, in spite of inconsistencies at home and abroad." They revealed their anti-Turkish bias when they described "the hideous mis-government of Turkey for centuries." Like most other Americans of this period who took an interest in the region, they believed firmly that the Armenians deserved a separate mandate because they had been subjected to terrible Ottoman persecution. As much as they tried to draw a distinction between the Turkish people and the Ottoman government, they merely reiterated the conventional Anglo-American belief that the Turks were peculiarly wicked because of their historic mistreatment of minorities. They noted as well Turkey's "utter unfitness for the strategic world position in which she is placed." They celebrated the end of "Oriental domination" of the East and indulged in hackneyed sayings about the "quietism" of the East and the "pragmatism" of the West. In all this, the King-Crane report was thoroughly unoriginal.[61]

In their specific recommendations for Palestine and Syria, however, the commissioners struck new ground. Defying the Sykes-Picot Agreement, they strongly recommended that the unity of Syria, including Lebanon and Palestine, be maintained because its population shared basic economic, geographic, and racial characteristics and spoke a common language. Although they recognized that the Syrians were strongly in favor of independence, the commissioners, "in strict harmony with our instructions," felt compelled to call for a mandatory power.[62]

In the spirit of Wilson, they emphatically noted that whatever mandatory was chosen over Syria, it could not be "as a colonizing Power in the old sense of that term." They suggested only one mandatory, for much the same reason as they advocated the unity of Syria. If popular sentiment was to be the chief consideration in the selection of the mandatory, then

America, they said, was the fitting choice given the abundant testimony in favor of America that they heard on their tour. France they described as being widely feared, except in Lebanon, and therefore a poor choice as a mandatory power. They noted with satisfaction that the United States was perceived by the Arabs of Syria to have "no territorial or colonial ambitions." And they suggested that Faysal be made head of the new unified Syrian state.

King and Crane were clearly impressed by Faysal, whose forces in Damascus had organized a national Congress in July 1919 while the Americans were still in Syria. The Congress had called for independence, opposed Zionism, rejected French colonial claims on Syria, and declared in favor of a democratic state under a constitutional monarchy headed by Faysal. The Congress had also lauded America and President Wilson. King and Crane accepted at face value Faysal's ascendancy at the head of the Arab national movement and also badly misjudged the influence of his father, Sharif Husayn, whose lordship over the Hijaz would soon be overthrown. They also underestimated the centrifugal forces at work in Syria and the popular and national mobilizations that were antithetical to Faysal's politics. But the commissioners also knew that Faysal was a figure palatable to Britain, the power they recommended in case America declined a Syrian mandate.

Most importantly, the commissioners called for a "serious modification of the extreme Zionist program for Palestine of unlimited immigration of Jews, looking finally to making Palestine distinctly a Jewish State." It was this recommendation, more than any other, that stemmed from basic realities that Lord Balfour, Chaim Weizmann, and William Blackstone either ignored, denied, or dismissed. Henry King and Charles Crane admitted that they had begun their mission "predisposed" in favor of Zionism. They recognized the passion, the devotion, and the success of Zionist settlers. But "actual facts" on the ground in Palestine, they said, "coupled with the force of the general principles proclaimed by the Allies," drove them to their recommendation. They stated the obvious: There was no way to reconcile honestly the principle of self-determination with Zionist colonization of Palestine. And they stated it bluntly: "If that principle [of self-determination] is to rule, and so the wishes of Palestine's population are to be decisive as to what is to be done with Palestine, then it is to be remembered that the non-Jewish population of Palestine—nearly nine-tenths of the whole—are emphatically against the entire Zionist program." They said, moreover, that it was not just the Arab inhabitants of Palestine who were concerned but those across Syria who voiced strong opposition to foreign colonization.

Most prophetically, they foretold the course of events should the West choose Zionism over the Arabs. "The Peace Conference," they warned,

> should not shut its eyes to the fact that anti-Zionist feeling in Palestine and Syria is intense and not lightly to be flouted. No British officer, consulted by the Commissioners, believed that the Zionist program could be carried out except by force of arms. The officers generally thought that a force of not less than 50,000 soldiers would be required even to initiate the program. That of itself is evidence of a strong sense of the injustice of the Zionist program, on the part of the non-Jewish populations of Palestine and Syria.

By the end of their journey in Syria, King and Crane were totally disenchanted with Zionist colonization. Their recommendation amounted to a revelation of the bitter realities glossed over by the romantic, religious, and racial idea of building a Jewish state in a land inhabited overwhelmingly by Muslims and Christians. They gave their verdict. "Decisions, requiring armies to carry out, are sometimes necessary, but they are surely not gratuitously to be taken in the interests of a serious injustice. For the initial claim, often submitted by Zionist representatives, that they have a 'right' to Palestine, based on an occupation of 2,000 years ago, can hardly be seriously considered."

From a Zionist point of view, this was unquestionably harsh, but it had the merit of being candid. King and Crane refused to engage in the evasions that characterized British policy in Palestine, which was to deny what was glaringly obvious to Arabs, to Zionists, and to most, if not all, British officers on the ground. But they also underestimated the degree to which most Western officials and the general publics of America and Britain could not, or would not, equate Arab history with Jewish history, especially its religious history. They had not far to look. Although Lybyer supported King and Crane, Montgomery and Yale dissented.

Montgomery believed that Islam was incapable of reformation and was incompatible with the modern world. The American, furthermore, refused to put any trust in Faysal or his government, for, he maintained, Muslims could not work with Christians on an equal footing. He insisted that the question of Palestine could not be viewed simply through Palestinian eyes. He urged not only that Syria should be broken up, but that in Palestine "the standpoint of history, of racial considerations, of Jewish persecution and of anti-semitism" must trump self-determination.[63] Palestine itself was not, he intimated, the place to properly judge what should become of it. Once more, "history" was understood axiomatically to exclude the native, Islamic, or Eastern Christian history. There was an advantage, Montgomery thought, in having a non-Muslim state wedged between Egypt and Syria. As with Blackstone's Memorial, a sense of obligation to the Jewish people rendered Montgomery insensible to Arab aspirations and their fears about Zionism. But unlike Blackstone, Montgomery had before him their unequivocal testimony. He chose to dismiss it.

Yale also dissented. From the outset he had belonged to the American group at Paris unconvinced of the utility of asking Arabs how it was that they wanted to determine their own future. He was no different at the end. He thought Arab nationalism was artificial, although, when he had met with Faysal's senior advisers at Paris, he had assured them of his support for their cause.[64] He thought that most Muslims, even educated Muslims, were "profoundly fanatical," and like Montgomery, he urged that self-determination not be applied to Palestine. Jews, he said, had a national history; Arabs did not. Jews were modern and civilized, he said. Arabs were not. For Yale, the Zionist movement was turning a dream into a reality. A Jewish state, he added, would become an outpost of Americanism because of the role that American Jews would take in its creation. Yale believed, as did Balfour and Weizmann, that when it came to Palestine, native wishes were ultimately inconsequential. There was a higher purpose at hand.[65]

The King-Crane report was presented to the American delegation in Paris at the end of August 1919. Crane cabled the report's basic conclusions to Wilson on August 30. Captain Donald Broadie, on the staff of the commission, personally delivered the original copy to the White House in September. The facts then were before the American president and his senior staff. They were also before the British and the French. The real question about the King-Crane report was raised by Ameen Rihani, the author of *The Book of Khalid* and a Syrian immigrant to the United States. As the American commission was traveling to Syria, Rihani wrote, "it will have no trouble in finding out what the people really want; but, having found out," he wondered, "will it prevail upon the Allies to act upon its report?"[66] It was a most pertinent question.

The answer from Lord Balfour was straightforward. The American King-Crane Commission, he said in a memorandum in 1919, has been "going through the form" of consulting the natives. Concerning Syria, he admitted that there was a basic contradiction between the letter of the covenant of the League of Nations and the policy of the Allies. Britain and France were going to impose their view regardless of what the Syrians wanted. Concerning Palestine, he admitted that the contradiction between proclamations and policy was even "more flagrant" than in the case of Syria. On Palestine, he said, "the Powers have made no statement of fact which is not admittedly wrong, and no declaration of policy which, at least in the letter, they have not always intended to violate."[67]

President Wilson did not give an answer to the King-Crane recommendations or even acknowledge receipt of the report—whether owing to illness, exhaustion, disinterest, or despair is unknown. By the time the final report was submitted, the situation in Anatolia had descended into full-scale war between Turkish nationalists and a Greek army that the Allies had authorized to occupy Izmir. As fighting there raged, the American president lost his credibility at home, where the Senate moved to destroy his vision of a League of Nations. The French, meanwhile, began to close in on Syria, with British acquiescence. By July 1920, a French army had marched on Damascus to unseat Faysal's government. The Arab king of the United Kingdom of Syria—for that is what Faysal had been proclaimed in March 1920—appealed to the "civilized world," including the United States, to prevent so brazen a colonial intervention.

A discouraged and ill President Wilson, however, had already washed his hands of the Middle East. At the end of the day, the British and the French, not America, and least of all the Arabs themselves, were going to determine the future of the new Arab world.

As many American officials in Paris had foreseen, the King-Crane Commission was doomed before it began. The commissioners had raised Arab hopes, only to dash them. They acted not in the deliberately misleading manner of the British, but out of a self-regarding conviction of what it meant to be "American." At Jaffa, they were asked directly by Palestinian Arabs whether Wilson had changed his principles. He had not and would not, they replied.[68] Politically speaking, the commission was a failure, except in one respect. Henry King and Charles Crane had accomplished their principal objective: to furnish Wilson, and the Western powers, with the information they needed to make an informed decision. They had witnessed and recorded the sentiments of Arabs against foreign colonialism and Zionism, and for national freedom. For this reason, their report was suppressed—or at any rate, deliberately ignored. So too were the Arabs of Palestine and Syria.

A new colonial age had dawned.

4

BETRAYAL

When the Arab nationalists met in Damascus in July 1919 to press for an independent Arab nation, they carried within them great expectations—of themselves, of their leader Faysal, and of America. As they hastily drew up their program for a constitutional monarchy, seeking to impress the King-Crane Commission, they appealed directly to the United States. They looked, they said, toward "President Wilson and the liberal American nation, who are known for their sincere and generous sympathy with the aspirations of weak nations, for help in the fulfillment of our hopes."[1]

The Arabs had been swept along in the current of revolution and great-power politics and in the extraordinary upheaval that defined their time. Their familiar world was fading before their eyes. As the Ottoman Empire lay defeated, nationalists believed that they would have a strong hand in shaping their own future. Faysal's father Husayn ruled the small kingdom of the Hijaz on the western coast of Arabia and harbored ambitions to rule a far larger territory. Husayn was unable, however, to deflect the growing influence of a rival Arab chieftain, the austere Abdul Aziz Al Saud from Najd in central Arabia. Even inside Syria, Faysal's hold was tenuous at best at the end of the First World War. The core of his support came from former Ottoman military officers, many of whom were Iraqi and from middle-class families. Older, established Syrian landowning families resented his authority. As the events at the Paris Peace Conference confirmed, Faysal could not parlay his wartime alliance with the British, or his friendship with T. E. Lawrence, into significant British support for his rule in Syria. The expectations of the Arab nationalists in Damascus were therefore grossly inflated. Unlike the Zionists, the Arab nationalists could neither insinuate themselves into imperial schemes nor rely on a romantic Anglo-American predisposition in their favor. Unlike the Turkish Mustafa Kemal, they possessed no real army able to resist colonialism.

But for all their failings, Arab hopes had a basis in reality. There was no reason why Arabs in Syria, who spoke a common language and shared a common culture, could not be molded into a unified nation. Certainly there was as deep a foundation in their national dream as there was in Turkish nationalism, which had still to overcome a Greek army in Izmir. Arab nationalism was also far less implausible than was the Zionist dream of encouraging Jewish inhabitants of nations around the world who spoke different languages to emigrate to an unfamiliar, distant land.

Faysal and his followers knew that Maronite Christians from Lebanon advocated a pro-French Lebanese nationalism that opposed their Arab project. Yet Faysal, despite his failure to navigate the imperial waters in which he sailed, was able to inspire many Syrians, both Christians and Muslims, and especially members of the educated class, to rally around the new idea of an Arab state of Syria. For the first time in hundreds of years, an Arab sought to rule from what had once been the great Arab capital of Damascus. There was genuine enthusiasm for Faysal upon his initial entry into the city in the fall of 1918, even as Faysal's adviser Rustum Haydar noted in his diary "how quickly men transform words of disparagement into those of flattery."[2] Mustafa Kurd Ali, the editor of the journal *Al-Muqtabas*, which the Ottomans had shut down during the war, insisted that people "built their hopes on him and longed for an Arab government."[3] Even Rashid Rida, who criticized the Hashemites severely for their continuing faith in the British even after they found out about the Sykes-Picot Agreement and the Balfour Declaration, opted to work with Faysal in an attempt to unify Syrians. The

Sunni Muslim Anbara Salam, a woman born to one of the leading families of Beirut, recalled her joy at seeing the Arab flag raised for the first time in Beirut by Fatima Mahmasani, the sister of two Syrians hanged by the Ottomans during the war for sedition. Christian Arab nationalists were heartened as well by Faysal's repeated calls for coexistence and equality between the citizens of his Arab kingdom. After meeting Faysal in Beirut, where the Arab leader pledged freedom, democracy, and equality, Anis Khuri Makdisi, then a young Protestant adjunct professor at the Syrian Protestant College, recalled that "truth be told, he who listens to Faysal's words and speaks with him feels drawn to his logic, sincerity, and devotion to the Arab cause."[4]

Proclaimed king of a united and completely independent Syria on March 8, 1920, Faysal was soon to find himself a king without a kingdom. The French dismissed out of hand the nationalist pretensions of the Syrian Arab Congress that was presided over by Rashid Rida. Like the British and the Zionists, the French saw that Arab aspirations ran far ahead of Arab military strength and that nationalist sentiments on their own did not constitute a viable movement. The French military governor of Syria, General Henri Gouraud, instead transformed Mount Lebanon into "Grand Liban," thus creating Lebanon as an independent country. He privileged the Maronites because he saw in their community, whose leaders did not consider themselves Arab as much as Phoenician, the most fervent supporters of French rule, but he also attached to the new country Muslim-dominated coastal cities—including Beirut—the fertile Bekaa Valley, and the southern foothills that extended into Palestine, giving Lebanon a large Muslim population, many of whom yearned to join Faysal's Arab kingdom. Gouraud gave Faysal an ultimatum to either submit to French domination or abdicate. The British reacted to Faysal's presumptive independence by losing patience with their former subordinate, feeling, as the new foreign secretary, Lord Curzon, put it, rather put off because the Arabs were trying to decide the future of the Arab world "behind [our] backs."[5]

Buffeted, on the one hand, by nationalist hopes he could not satisfy and by Western imperialism he could not appease, on the other, Faysal found himself and his kingdom in an untenable position. He had attempted to compromise with the Zionists, but they were not interested in any plan that did not secure their ultimate goal of transforming Palestine into a Jewish state, regardless of native Arab opinion. The imperial powers were not interested in any plan that did not give them their colonies. The more Faysal compromised, the less popular he became at home. For the first time, but not for the last, an Arab leader was being forced to choose between growing nationalist sentiment and a West that scoffed at the very idea of Arab sentiment. Faysal sought desperately to interpose himself between one and the other, but to no avail. William Linn Westermann, who advised the American delegation to the Paris conference, summed up Faysal's predicament: "He made the impression of a loveable and high-minded personality," Westermann said, "too little ruthless to carry through to success against western diplomacy, western desires for commercial privilege, and western arms the wishes of the Arab people for real independence."[6]

The British and the French proceeded to carve up the Arab world. They disregarded the King-Crane recommendations one by one. Instead of an American or British mandate over Syria, a French one was granted. Instead of a united Syria, Lebanon and Palestine were both torn away from it, and Syria itself was dismembered along sectarian lines. Instead of curtailing Zionism, the British created a mandate in Palestine that explicitly took the Balfour Declaration as its *only* frame of reference. Instead of fulfilling Wilsonian self-determination, an old-style colonial division of spoils was begun. Whereas Africa had been partitioned openly at Berlin in 1884 by European powers, forty years on, the Arabs were now being segregated into new and newly colonized nations. To add insult to injury, the Europeans pretended that Arab self-determination was enshrined in their respective mandates. Balfour, at least, was to the point. "They may freely choose," he said of the Arabs in Syria, "but it is Hobson's choice after all."[7]

This new colonial reality was legitimated by the West in April 1920 in the Italian coastal town of San Remo. The upshot of two years of Wilsonian rhetoric was as ironic as it was cruel to Faysal's aspiration for an Arab kingdom in Syria. The victorious powers agreed to issue an invitation to the Ottomans to sign a humiliating treaty at Sèvres. Anatolia was to be partitioned among different European spheres of influence; the Turks were to be left with roughly half their territory in Asia Minor, and they had to renounce all claims to their former Arab provinces. That was the penalty for defeat. The Arab allies of the British during the war, however, were treated the same way as the defeated Ottoman Turkish enemy. The most advanced, and certainly the most important, urban centers and populations of the Arab world were placed under direct British and French colonial rule, and Palestine was opened up to foreign European Jewish settlers. The less developed Hijaz, in which Mecca and Medina were located, was granted independence.

From a British and French perspective, the logic of their deal was obvious: Britain and France were to keep all important strategic areas of the Arab world under their control, and they showed munificence by not occupying the Arabian peninsula. Muslim opinion, they presumed, would be content. The secular nationalists would not, but they, in any case, were to be crushed. The British and the French also signed a separate oil agreement at San Remo. The French gave up their claim to Mosul, but they were to receive a 25 percent share in oil exploitation in the mandate of Mesopotamia. Syria was sold to the French for oil. The British, in turn, were to construct an oil pipeline to a Mediterranean port through the French-controlled mandates. The vast oil wealth of the Arabian Peninsula itself had not yet been discovered.

Having gained what they wanted at San Remo, the French turned to deliver the coup de grâce to the upstart Arab kingdom. Faysal's small army, with virtually no ammunition, was overwhelmed by a massive French expeditionary force made up of Senegalese, Moroccan, Algerian, and French troops, tanks, and planes near the Syrian town of Maysalun on July 24, 1920. Within six hours, the Arabs were crushed. The "civilized" world to which Faysal had appealed looked on. His defense minister lay dead on the field of battle, illustrating the gulf that separated Arab nationalist aspirations from the cold calculus of power that actually made nations. The next day Damascus capitulated to the French.

Faysal's residence was looted, and he was exiled and eventually remade by the British (and by himself) into the king of a new country called Iraq.[8] The secular Arab national dream was strangled at birth.

The United States did not directly partake in the colonial feast of San Remo. Rather, it observed. American diplomats and policymakers, however, quickly acquiesced to the British and the French in their imperial remaking of the Arab world. They recognized the mandates. In return, they asked not for self-determination or any such grand scruple attributed to Wilson, but for a grant of equal access for American companies, especially oil companies, to potentially lucrative commodities and markets. The British at first sought to keep American oil interests at bay. Under U.S. pressure, however, they allowed by 1928 an American petroleum consortium a 23.75 percent stake in what would become the British-dominated Iraq Petroleum Company. American archaeological excavations in Egypt and Iraq, Singer sewing machines, licorice and date exporting firms, and automobile and truck companies all made gradual inroads into the mandates.

While the Arab world fell under the shadow of colonialism, the Turks, through force of arms and brilliant leadership, rendered null and void the draconian terms that the British and the French had foisted upon them in 1920. Through war, not words, they forced a major revision of the terms of peace in their favor at Lausanne in July 1923. The ranking American diplomat in Constantinople, Admiral William Bristol, and a former member of his staff, a young Allen Dulles, pushed, accordingly, for productive relations that would safeguard American missionary institutions and allow American businesses to compete on an equal footing with European powers. They sought to diminish the negative stereotype of the "Turk" that had colored Western, and especially Anglo-American, views of the Middle East during and in the immediate aftermath of the war.

For a century the American Board missionaries and American educators had been hoping to undermine the Ottomans, but they had not reckoned with its successor state. They found themselves in an unfamiliar landscape. In place of the Ottoman Empire, whose vastness and diversity American missionaries had long exploited, American Board secretary James Barton and Robert College president Caleb Gates contended with a victorious Turkish nationalism. Having defeated the Greek army and repossessed Izmir, the nationalist Turks negotiated a population exchange with Greece. Over one million Orthodox Christians living in Turkey were expelled to Greece; likewise, hundreds of thousands of Muslims in Greece were uprooted and resettled in Turkey.

Accompanying this tragedy was the dawning realization among leading American evangelicals such as Barton that the Armenian question appeared hopeless. No matter how sympathetic Americans were toward the fate of the Christian Armenians, and no matter how relentlessly the missionaries had excoriated the "unspeakable Turk" during the war, the Turks had stymied Western imperialism. They had lost their empire, but won their independence. Not only was there no American mandate over the Armenians; there was to be no independent Armenian state at all. A pall of denial was to overcome the fate of the Armenians in Turkey. Americans slowly but inevitably accommodated themselves to a new reality.

In the Arab provinces the story was more straightforward. There was no Arab nationalist victory to reckon with. The kind of Western sympathy that had existed for the Armenians was not extended to the Arabs. Syrians had suffered terribly during the First World War, but they had not been the victims of genocide. Perhaps more to the point, despite the fact that the overwhelming majority of Arab immigrants to America were Christian, Arabs were thought to be uniformly Muslim. The best that could be said about them in America, other than sporadic missionary praise for their Arabic language and medieval history, was that they were the denizens of an exotic and enchanted land. For most Americans, Arabs remained a people without significant history. If Jews elicited both American prejudice and sympathy (and often both at the same time), Christian and Muslim Arabs were subject to popular American indifference, if not total ignorance.

The British and the French thus enjoyed a free hand to repress uprisings against their colonial rule in Syria and Iraq. Long before the infamous

Nazi aerial bombardment of the Spanish city of Guernica in 1937, the overlords of the new Middle East exhibited the power of airplanes to terrorize and cow recalcitrant Arabs. The British bombed Iraqis at will to crush an uprising in 1920. "Many of them jumped into a lake," one British report noted, "making a good target for the machine guns."[9] The French heavily bombarded Damascus in 1925 to quell another major revolt against European rule. Without giving warning, French authorities shelled the city for two days in October, killing more than one thousand civilians.[10]

In Egypt a similar story unfolded. Although not a mandate but a "protectorate," the country had been under British occupation since 1882. Saad Zaghlul, the undisputed leader of the Egyptian nationalist movement, mobilized Egyptians to challenge British hegemony. Like many other nationalist leaders across the world, he admired Wilson—not the man as much as the idea he believed that Wilson embodied. Like Faysal, Zaghlul was deceived, or deceived himself, into believing that there was an American democratic card to be played against European imperial designs. But when he attempted to lead a delegation to France in 1919, British authorities arrested and deported him to Malta, together with several of his colleagues. The popular revolution that ensued was repressed by the British. Women and men, Christians and Muslims, marched to demand Egyptian independence. The American legation in Cairo was bombarded with letters and telegrams from Egyptians who pleaded for America to stand up for President Wilson's principles. Eight hundred Egyptian dead later, the Wilson administration recognized the English "protectorate" over Egypt.

Zaghlul's appeals to the U.S. government for self-determination and democracy were ignored as thoroughly as were Faysal's pleas for American and British aid against French imperialism. In Palestine, meanwhile, the British shepherded Zionism in the face of universal Arab opposition. No matter what the Arabs said or did, and no matter how often they pleaded with the West, the British and the French were determined not to allow their colonies, newly won or old, to slip from their grasp. The U.S. government policy toward the region was as cautious as it was conservative. Ultimately, America had little interest in or sympathy for Arab nationalist aspirations, the King-Crane Commission's recommendations notwithstanding. In a remarkably short span of time, the gloss of Wilsonianism had grown dull; all that was left in the aftermath of San Remo was the hard edge of American interests.

Charles Crane returned to a colonized Syria in April 1922. He stayed at the Damascus Palace Hotel. As soon as his arrival was made known, over forty Damascene merchants, religious figures, physicians, lawyers, and other prominent men invited him to lunch with them Eastern-style in one of the city's parks. They regarded him, said an Arab account of Crane's visit, as "a prophet who had descended from the kingdom of freedom to save them" from their fate. They lamented Faysal's downfall and told Crane about the censorship they faced and the oppression they endured at the hands of the French. They begged him to tell their story to the world, including to America. Before Crane's departure for Beirut, Abd al-Rahman Shahbandar, formerly a minister in Faysal's short-lived Arab government, told the American that a throng of people had come to see him off. Shahbandar saluted America, and the crowd repeated his salute. Crane was touched. He turned to the crowd and thanked them for their sentiments. "Demand your independence in a modern and civilized manner," he was recorded as saying, "and you will achieve it with your Arab heads held high."[11]

There was undoubtedly a desperate quality to this Arab embrace of Crane, for the context that brought them together was so glaringly unequal. The Syrians who celebrated Crane saw in him the embodiment of the very principles that his country had, in effect, betrayed. They were willing to lionize the individual American as a palliative to a depressing tale of European perfidy and U.S. indifference. The same occurred in Iraq, where nationalists sought to underscore what they regarded as a contradiction between the British mandate and Wilsonian principles. The other option, increasingly seized by men such as Rashid Rida, was to articulate a powerful sense of anti-Western nationalism and to mock those who had heeded the false promises of the West. "We discovered," he wrote in *Al-Manar*, "that the covenant of League of Nations by which President Wilson considers he has changed the international system of states and nations and has moved humanity from a low stage to a higher stage of freedom and peace has actually permitted the partition among the powerful of weak peoples' countries on condition that the actions of each power is called a mandate, a trust, and not a protectorate, a possession, or a colony."[12]

Shahbandar and those who cheered Crane recognized in him a man—a white man—who had tried to help them sincerely in their cause. Shahbandar noted that Crane had belonged to the "historic" King-Crane Commission that had worked "in the service of freedom."[13] Although he did not speak Arabic, Crane appeared to be a figure from the same liberal mold as Cornelius Van Dyck. The Syrians who appreciated Crane did so because, patronizing as he may have been, the man did not insult their intelligence by pretending that colonialism was liberation. Unlike Lawrence, Crane left no bitter taste in their mouths. The identification with Crane personally, as with President Wilson more abstractly, underscored the resiliency of the Arab notion of an anti-imperialist America that had been decades in the making. The notion endured mostly because America, though it had sanctioned empire in the Arab world, was still not an imperialist power as far as most Arabs could see.

Crane capitalized on this theme of American innocence when he insisted, improbably, in an article addressed to the American public that even the Bedouin of the desert knew and appreciated what America had done for Cuba and the Philippines.[14] If Faysal's tragedy was that he had put his faith in Britain and America without realizing how low he lay in the imperial scheme of things, Crane's tragedy was that he had a positive message about the Arabs for an America that was fundamentally uninterested in them as a modern people. Crane's assessment of Arabs was based on his personal interaction with them, and like Howard Bliss, he tried to parlay that experience into policy that dealt with Arabs as deserving of political rights and independence.

Crane's embrace of the Arabs was, in part perhaps, related to his prejudice against Jews and his antipathy toward what he considered the pushiness of the Jewish Zionists. A deeply held conviction about a Jewish conspiracy would fester in him over subsequent years.

The Arabs, meanwhile, contended with two deeply ingrained Western assumptions about them that undermined their goal of political freedom. The first assumption built upon an active and general Western view of Islam; the dominant religion of the Arabs was widely regarded as uniquely unsuited to modern civilization.[15] The second assumption was that the Arabs were a quaint, quintessentially medieval desert people. Faysal may have cut a noble figure at Paris with his flowing white robes, but he knew that his dream of an Arab state encompassed many people, including urban, educated professors, doctors, lawyers, and soldiers. For Secretary of State Robert Lansing, Arabs were basically Bedouin. Symptomatic of this view, the popular American writer Lowell Thomas wrote an account of the Arab revolt entitled *With Lawrence in Arabia* in 1924. The book created the legend of "Lawrence of Arabia." Thomas was a master at romantic oversimplification. He described the Englishman who worked as an agent for British empire as a "modern Arabian knight" who understood better than any other Westerner the "art of handling Arabs." Lawrence was the hero of Lowell's story of the Arab revolt, which featured the blond romantic adventurer leading "wild nomad peoples" into the modern world. Thomas was also sympathetic to Faysal, but as Lansing had done in Paris, he portrayed the Arab leader as a modern-day Haroun al-Rashid.[16]

As Americans such as Crane and Thomas dabbled in myths of their own making about American innocence and Arab nobility, the missionary age in the Arab world entered its twilight. Once more, the flagship American cultural institution in the Arab world was a microcosm of what was most hopeful and most fraught in U.S.-Arab relations. As Arabs sought to make their way in a new colonial order bequeathed to them by Sykes-Picot and San Remo, American missionaries wrestled with the implications of Arab nationalism. They were confronted by an increasingly obvious gap that separated their paternalistic, gradualist understanding of Arab self-determination from the Arabs' own more urgent view of the matter.

When Howard Bliss died in May 1920 of tuberculosis, he was still unable to accept in practice the equality of American and Arab. Nevertheless, telegrams and letters poured into Beirut from across the world, mostly from former students of the college, eulogizing Bliss as a "martyr" for Syria. The Greek Orthodox patriarch of Damascus offered his condolences. The head of the Arab Club in Damascus, a center of Arab nationalist expression during Faysal's brief reign, wrote the faculty of the college to share the sense of loss the Arab Club felt at the passing of "the benefactor and true friend of the Syrian Cause." The letter-writer described "the high esteem the American Nation and her noble Principles have in the hearts of the Syrians" without realizing that neither Wilson nor Bliss were proponents of immediate Arab liberation.[17]

Bliss's successors at the Syrian Protestant College reached a fairly quick modus vivendi with the new French rulers of Syria and Lebanon, just as their colleagues in Egypt had previously come to terms with the British. As if to mark this new era, the Beirut municipality in 1920 renamed the wide street running alongside the campus Rue Bliss, in honor of Howard's father Daniel, which, after the medical gate that marked the southeastern edge of the campus, turned into a street aptly renamed Clemenceau. In that same year the college renamed itself the American University of Beirut (AUB).

At the same time the American faculty and administration finally gave in to the idea of equality between Anglo-Saxon and Arab, and then only reluctantly and conditionally. At leading American universities such as Princeton, Yale, and Harvard, for example, Jewish professors were not hired in significant numbers until after World War II. The request from Arabs in far-off Syria for higher pay and more recognition struck the university's board members in New York as distinctly ungrateful and even arrogant. It was not the way things were done—or at least, not the way the American evangelical patrons believed civilization ought to be manifested. The president of the board even considered establishing a chair in the school of medicine in honor of the British conqueror of the Middle East, Edmund Allenby.

Howard Bliss's temporary replacement, Edward Nickoley, warned against such a move given the nationalist climate in the region. He also recognized that it would no longer do to discriminate on the basis of either religion or race. "We must get rid of the color line," he admitted in August 1920. Nickoley confessed that he was saddened to see the end of what he referred to as Anglo-Saxon "fellowship," which had long conspired to exclude Arabs from the senior faculty. He added, however, that "the change that we are about to make is momentous and epoch-making."[18]

Recognizing how controversial was the idea of equality between white Anglo-Saxon Americans and natives, Nickoley put on a brave face to the university's board of trustees. He was quick to emphasize that the principle of parity he advocated should not be translated into actual equality of pay. As an example, he compared a young Lebanese instructor with another American faculty member. Nickoley explained that both were about to be married; both would require houses and would need to furnish them. The Lebanese would furnish his house locally, but the American, said Nickoley, would naturally require American furniture. Arabs should be encouraged to take their academic furlough abroad to further their education, but "the obvious thing," he added, "is for them to leave their families here, taking them would be distinctly in the nature of a luxury. On the other hand, we from abroad, expect to take our furloughs regularly and we can hardly think of doing so without taking our families."[19] The Lebanese professor, said Nickoley, would educate his children locally, but Americans would have to educate their children in America. All these considerations demanded supplemental allocations that once again gave Anglo-Saxons a far higher salary than Arabs. Racial inequality was formally abolished, but in reality it continued to govern.

The fitful transformation of the American University of Beirut reflected a more general American attitude in the region. Rather than fight nationalism actively, as the French and British sought to do at their institutions in the area, the Americans sought to parry it. They wanted to protect their own interests as much as possible and conceded to natives on general principles such as equality of pay only when further resistance appeared futile and self-defeating. In Egypt, the other location in the Arab world where an American missionary presence flourished, Charles R. Watson founded the American University in Cairo (AUC) in 1920. Like Howard Bliss, Watson was born to missionary parents, and also like Bliss, he demonstrated a more liberal and ecumenical spirit than his predecessors who convened the famous Cairo missionary conference on "Mohammedans." Even more so than Bliss, Watson struggled to adapt his missionary sensibility to the rising tide of nationalism. Watson saw AUC as an opportunity to build on the many American schools already in Egypt. He dreamed of founding a university that could offer professional and not simply rudimentary or ecclesiastical training, one that emphasized an American Christian commitment to modern life.[20]

Like AUB, AUC had a missionary provenance, it operated along racial lines, and it took on an increasingly secular orientation. In 1924 the famous Egyptian politician Saad Zaghlul attended the fledgling university's commencement exercises. His presence symbolized a nationalism that Americans such as Watson could simply no longer ignore. In the space of two decades, the aggressive Cairo conference and the crusading dreams of Samuel Zwemer had given way to a far more tempered evangelical approach to the Muslim and Arab world. Watson still wanted to convert Muslims—he was paternalistic—but he also acknowledged "the titanic force" that nationalism had become. "Nationalism and secularism," he admitted, "are dominating the life of Moslem peoples increasingly; traditional orthodoxy is on the wane. In some ways our freedom of action is becoming limited. We are made to feel more and more that missionaries have no natural rights that will be recognized. We are only guests in the lands in which we labor. At any moment and in any respect we may be asked to cease our activities."[21]

Fundamentally, Arab, Syrian, and Egyptian nationalism still frightened missionaries. The Presbyterian missionaries in Egypt had long taken refuge in British rule. Precisely as their compatriots in Syria did, they rationalized the unequal American educational and evangelical system they painstakingly built in Egypt. On the one hand, their more perceptive members recognized that Egyptian nationalism was a natural response to foreign occupation; the Inter-Mission Council of United Presbyterians, a body founded in 1920 that included British and American Protestant organizations and groups, called for a declaration of principles that disapproved scornful references to other religious beliefs, including Islam. On the other hand, the Americans as a whole were loath to abandon their inherited privileges. They clung to the Capitulations that sheltered them from the reach of Egyptian law, and they cherished the British presence in Egypt.

In Egypt even more so than in Syria, missionaries faced a torrent of criticism in the interwar years. The Muslim Brotherhood organization was one of several Islamist groups founded in the interwar period that sought to end the foreign missionary "corruption" of Egypt's youth and to ban Christian evangelical work altogether. Muslim activists identified AUC as the nerve center of an insidious "Christianization" campaign in Egypt and pointed to several controversies involving Americans. Although Watson and AUC had self-consciously dampened their own missionary enthusiasm, the American missionary Samuel Zwemer remained an anachronistic and unrepentant proselytizer. He was simply unable to set aside his deep contempt for Islam as a religious and social system. In 1928 Zwemer strode into Al-Azhar, the ancient Islamic university and the seat of orthodox Sunni Muslim opinion in the Arab world, and distributed missionary pamphlets to its students, provoking an uproar that forced him to leave the country for his own safety. In 1930 a Coptic Catholic medical doctor gave a lecture at AUC about women's rights and was understood by Muslim students to have directly defamed Islam. Finally, Kamil Mansur, an Egyptian convert from Islam to Christianity, was discovered giving lectures about the life of Jesus, allegedly with the purpose of converting Muslims, in an American mission building in Cairo. Al-Azhar students went on strike and Shaykh Muhammad Ahmad al-Zawahari, head of Al-Azhar, petitioned the government to arrest the "apostate." Bloody riots against the missionaries occurred across the country. Rumors about the kidnapping of Egyptian Muslim girls and their forced "Christianization," and a perverse determination on the part of some American (and other foreign) missionaries to persist in their ways led to a major backlash against missionary work. In 1933 the Society to

Resist Christianization was founded in Egypt by al-Zawahari and another Muslim cleric.

Reactionary piety and nationalist zeal joined together to overturn the missionary legacy in Egypt. The American evangelical presence that had flourished under British colonialism was destined to end with its demise. Islamists emphasized the religious aspects of their grievances; the nationalists underscored the need to secure Egypt's secular sovereignty. No matter how ideologically removed the two groups were from each other, their interests coincided in wanting to see the end of unregulated missionary work in Egypt. The government finally responded by passing a law in 1934 requiring missionary schools to be inspected by the state. By 1937 the Egyptian government had signed the Montreux Convention, which phased out the hated legal immunities of foreigners—the Capitulations—that Americans had long enjoyed in Egypt. "It does not require a drunk king to see or a prophet to interpret the handwriting on the wall," acknowledged an American missionary in 1939.[22]

The twilight of the missionary age did not, however, substantially alter the positive Arab reckoning of America. Far more so than in the nineteenth century, in fact, America's undisputed rise to prominence imbued the thousands of graduates of American institutions with prestige. As in the nineteenth century, praise of American society, government, and technology was evident in the Arabic press. The Egyptian Amir Boktor was a graduate of the missionary Assiut College in Upper Egypt who received his master's degree from Columbia University in 1923 and was one of the most prominent Egyptian teachers at AUC, heading its Arabic and government section. He wrote an account of his visit to America during the 1920s that he called *Al-Dunya fi Amrika* (The World in America). Boktor dedicated his book to his American teacher, the missionary Robert S. McClenahan, who, he said, had inspired him profoundly. Boktor, accordingly, enthused about America's brilliance, its advancement, its buildings, its liberation, and its democracy. The United States, for Boktor, constituted "the cradle of freedom, and the birthplace of democracy."[23] Unlike Rihani's *Book of Khalid*, there was no hint of dissonance in Boktor's belief in America. Instead, Boktor mythologized America. For him, America provided Egyptians with a blueprint of their own possible future. He believed that, as an Americanized Egyptian, he represented the spirit of the *Mayflower* in reverse: an apostle from the new world to the old bearing tidings of democracy and freedom.

Uncommented on by Boktor was the gulf that separated his own charmed experience of America and American educational institutions from the racial reality of the United States, let alone Egypt's subjugation to the British and the U.S. role in legitimating it. For Boktor, however, Wilson's politics were superfluous and American imperialism around the world irrelevant to his belief. His devotion to the idea of America was not like Faysal's or Zaghlul's, nor like that of the Syrians who surrounded Crane at Damascus. Boktor was not seeking U.S. political assistance. He relied instead on a generalization of his own successful individual trajectory. Boktor preached, therefore, not the imperative of religious conversion, but secular conversion to the idea of an "astonishing" America. He wanted Egyptians to imbibe what he hailed as America's spirit of industry and its genius manifested in its public schools, its universities, its democracy, its freedom of thought and conscience, and its liberation of women.[24] For Boktor, America, regardless of American policy, remained the foundation for genuine self-determination.

Even more so than Boktor, the Maronite Christian Philip Hitti represented a genuine Arab embrace of America that grew directly out of the missionary age. Born in the small Lebanese village of Shimlan in 1886, Hitti struggled to educate himself. His mother was illiterate, but a broken arm at the age of eight, gangrene, and a series of operations by the American missionary George Post set Hitti down his American path. He became the first Maronite from Shimlan to enroll in the American high school in the nearby village of Suq al-Gharb. As was the case with Boktor, Hitti was inspired and encouraged by American missionaries to pursue higher education. He graduated from the Syrian Protestant College in 1908 and went on to Columbia University, where he received his PhD in Oriental history in 1915. Hitti was the first Arab to receive a doctorate from Columbia and rapidly established himself as the leading authority in Arab and Oriental studies of his generation.

Though Hitti, like Boktor, did not consider himself to be an Arab in any nationalist sense, he grappled firsthand with American discrimination and witnessed American racism. Howard Bliss had personally encouraged Hitti to attend Columbia, but just before his death he balked at Hitti's request that he be appointed professor of Oriental history at the Syrian Protestant College. Professorships were for Americans, and though Hitti was married to an American and was exceedingly well qualified for his post, he was, according to Bliss, a Syrian and thus entitled to be appointed, initially at least, only as an adjunct professor. Bliss conceded that Hitti was not an "extremist"—that is, he was an Arab who did not call for a wholesale change in the racial policies of the institution or demand Syrian "control" over the academic affairs of the college situated in Syria (none actually did). Hitti was finally appointed a professor of Oriental history that same year, albeit at a salary well below that offered to an American associate professor, Arthur E. Hurt, hired at the same time.[25]

For Hitti, the discrimination he faced was a distraction from the overarching theme of his life—that he was the beneficiary of the "American dream." He wrote, therefore, an Arabic account of America that was published in the Egyptian journal *Al-Hilal* in 1924. Like Boktor's account, it was brimming with praise for the United States. Hitti sought to capture that sense of wonder that overwhelmed him when he first set foot in America.

> You will feel as though you have arrived in a country whose inhabitants are giants among men. . . . You will then realize that you are not in a country like others, and you are not among a people like others, but rather among a people superior in their qualities, distinguished in their vitality, and unique in their abundance of energy. The matchless skyscrapers, the quick pace of life, the ability to focus on one's work, are none other than the manifestations of the dynamism of a nation that is full of youth and pulsating with tremendous energy.[26]

In English, however, rather than extol America as he did for an Arab audience, he desperately sought to explain Syrians to Americans. Hitti knew full well that America in the early 1920s was in the grip of an anti-immigrant feeling. The eugenicist Madison Grant had published in 1916 a widely read book, entitled *The Passing of the Great Race*, that gloomily prophesied that the so-called pure, unadulterated "Anglo-Saxon" stock that made America great was threatened with annihilation by the massive influx of inferior races, including the "Slovak, the Italian, the Syrian, and the Jew." Hitti may not have known that a Columbia University professor of zoology and eugenicist, Henry Fairfield Osborn, enthusiastically endorsed Grant's racist book, but he certainly knew that Syrians were considered dirty and that they and other immigrants from the Mediterranean were regarded as undesirable; moreover, he knew that in a country overflowing with colleges and universities, there existed a paradoxical, but nevertheless pervasive, ignorance about the Arab world. When Hitti arrived in America, neither Harvard, Yale, nor Princeton taught Arabic at the undergraduate level, and across the country there was scant interest in the modern Middle East. Above all, Hitti feared that the gate into America, through which he and Boktor and Rihani and thousands of others had passed, was on the verge of being slammed shut.

To this end, two years before he moved to Princeton in 1926 to take up an assistant professorship in Semitic literature, he published a small book, *Syrians in America*. In it, he pleaded with Americans to understand that he and his compatriots—not Arabs exactly, he insisted, but an Arabic-speaking, racially mixed people who originated with the Phoenicians—were a civilized community. Hitti emphasized the Christian faith of most Syrian immigrants. Syrians, he stressed, were religious, family-oriented, and industrious; therefore, they could and would easily assimilate into the United States.

If Shahbandar did not know American racism and Boktor did not see it, Hitti knew it full well but made a calculated decision not to acknowledge it in his repeated tributes to America. Even after the United States confirmed the exclusion of Asians and curtailed the immigration of other "undesirable" races in 1924 with the passage of the Immigration Act, the country remained for Hitti a great land of opportunity. It was all the more great compared to the wreckage of the Ottoman Empire and to what Hitti believed was the empire's endemic corruption and Turkish misrule. Indeed, in his eyes and in his own experience, American missionaries were among the few bright spots in the war-ravaged East. Hitti was not so much naive as indelibly stamped by his radical and uplifting American experience. "Americanization, at its best," he wrote, "is the substitution of the law of right for the law of might . . . and the cultivation of fair play, justice, and good-will."[27] Like many, if not most, of the thousands of Ottoman subjects who had been immersed in American education and had passed through missionary institutions, he believed in America. The small boy from an insignificant mountain village overlooking Beirut had, through American intercession, American education, and American employment, become the most significant scholar of Islam and the Arabs in the United States of his day. Philip Hitti was the perfect advertisement for America in the Arab world.

But neither the Princeton professor nor his American missionary benefactors had counted on the question of Palestine. No single issue dramatized more clearly the fault lines in the unequal relationship that bound Arabs and Americans together or exemplified more generally the subordination of the Arabs to the West. No single issue revealed more sharply the ambiguity within the American missionary view of the Arabs, nor shed light as powerfully on how damaging was a Western Christian and Jewish Zionist view that separated the Holy Land from its historic and contemporary living Arab environment. No single issue exposed more obviously the naïveté at the heart of the foundational Arab view of America.

The U.S. Congress officially endorsed the Balfour Declaration in 1922. As House of Representatives members deliberated a resolution in favor of Zionism, they spoke overwhelmingly in favor of the establishment of a Jewish national home in Palestine. American congressmen recollected the Bible stories they had heard as children, praised Hebraic civilization, expressed sympathy for the Jewish people, condemned their persecution in Europe, and voiced admiration for modern and scientific Zionist colonization of the Holy Land. They cited the Old Testament, ancient philosophers, the Crusades, and Lord Balfour. But on a matter that was of such vital importance to the Arabs, there was scarcely an Arab perspective to be considered. The Palestinian surgeon Fuad Shatara and a Palestinian law student, Selim Totah, appeared nonetheless before the congressional committee. Shatara had appealed several times to President Wilson and to his secretary of state, Robert Lansing, in favor of Palestinian self-determination (see Chapter 3). Although his appeals were ignored, he tried again to open the eyes of American congressmen to the native reality of Palestine. Totah, making a similar plea, tried to put the Arab case in terms that he thought might make sense to the congressmen before him.

"Would you stand for things like that in California if the Japanese should come in and after 20 or 30 years become a majority and establish a republic of their own?" he asked incredulously. "Not for a moment. How would you expect the 93 percent of the people in Palestine to stand for that?" Congressman Ambrose Kennedy from Rhode Island retorted that the Jews simply "want to get a home. You do not want to let them. Is not that the idea?"[28]

The two men were confounded in their attempt to draw attention to the existence of a living society that existed on its own historical, political, religious, and cultural terms, not simply as a negation of Zionist aspirations. Well over 650,000 Arabs lived in towns, villages, and cities across the breadth of mandatory Palestine, densely inhabiting and cultivating the fertile land of the country. Extensive trade networks had long linked its labor-intensive citrus-, tobacco-, and olive-based agricultural economy to that of other cities across Syria. Palestine was not simply a "desert" waiting to be made to bloom, nor was it a primitive society waiting to be modernized, as American supporters of Zionism consistently claimed. It was very much like other former Arab provinces of the Ottoman empire. To have to state, therefore, that Palestine was inhabited by artisans, teachers, lawyers, judges, teachers, traditional notables, religious scholars (often drawn from long-established families such as the Husaynis and Khalidis in Jerusalem), and myriad clerics and government functionaries in addition to peasants was absurd. Such, however, was the peculiar burden of the Arabs of Palestine, who were compelled to prove their existence in the face of a Zionist movement that claimed a "land without a people for a people without a land."

Like every other contemporary society in the region, the local inhabitants contended with local, Ottomanist, religious, and increasingly Arab nationalist affiliations. Although higher education had been the preserve of Constantinople, Beirut, and Cairo, the inhabitants of Palestine had otherwise had the same kinds of primary and secondary schools that existed elsewhere in the empire. The American missionary presence was more muted in Palestine than in Syria or Egypt, the exception being the (Quaker) Friends School in Ramallah. Arab deputies from Jerusalem and other towns in Palestine had been sent to the Ottoman Parliament, and one of them warned his Ottoman colleagues of the dangers of Zionism at length in 1911. Also, an Arabic press was, finally, flourishing in Palestine. Palestinian society was not, therefore, any more or less cohesive than neighboring Syria or Lebanon in the aftermath of the sudden disintegration of the Ottoman Empire. But with the advent of Zionist colonization, it was now being exposed to a fundamentally different kind of stress. Not surprisingly, Palestinian Arabs made the most urgent and explicit remonstrations against Zionism, thus laying the basis for a modern nationalist Palestinian identity that is inextricably tied to Jewish Zionism.[29]

Both Shatara and Totah nevertheless found themselves caught in a surreal exchange—the native inhabitants were being cast in the role of the villains, the spoilers of a romantic story of American benevolence and Jewish rebirth. What they were actually pleading for was a state in Palestine based on the people living there. Shatara's and Totah's were voices in the wilderness.[30]

When House members later debated the resolution, several speakers acknowledged plainly that there was a great Arab majority in Palestine.

Yet each congressman, having raised what was to Arabs such as Shatara and Totah the heart of their objection to Zionism, cavalierly dismissed its significance. Congressman Walter Chandler from New York was typical in his praise of the genius of the Jewish people. He waxed lyrical about the contributions of Jewish people throughout the ages. Turning briefly to the Arabs, he admitted that their presence in Palestine raised a theoretical objection to Zionism. Chandler chastised the American government's inconsistency in supporting the idea of self-determination abroad. However, rather than support the Arabs, he immediately, and disconcertingly, thought of ways to deal with the "Arab problem": Ideally, the Palestinians would submit voluntarily to Jewish "government and domination," as he put it, or they would accept the mandatory sale of their lands to Jews ("at fair valuation") and emigrate to another Arab country; if they refused both these options, he declared that they should simply be expelled. For Chandler as for the other congressmen who went on record in 1922, the principle of self-determination was not to apply to the Arabs of Palestine. As far as he was concerned, they were in Palestine but they were not of it, although it was they, and not the Jews of Europe or America, who had lived on the land for centuries and whose claim to it required no circumlocution, no mystification, no religious mythology. The Arab argument for Palestine sprang first and foremost from the simple unvarnished reality of being there.

The lopsided debate within the U.S. Congress of 1922 illustrated a general rule on the question of Palestine. No matter how positive, sympathetic, understanding, or romantic its perception of the Jewish people, a favorable view of Zionism relied on a denial of the *meaningful* Arab presence in Palestine. The less one thought of Arabs, the more one could enthusiastically embrace Zionism. The more one thought of Arabs, the greater the obfuscation required to sustain a romantic Zionist argument. The converse of this attitude was equally true. The more one humanized and interacted with native Arabs, the less likely one was to be an ardent supporter of Zionism. It is a rule that still holds true today.

Predictably, the British mandatory policy of building up a Jewish homeland met from its outset with protracted Arab opposition. The townspeople and villagers of Palestine were loath to see their country transformed against their express wishes. They wrote petitions, protested, and rioted in a futile effort to get the British to alter their pro-Zionist policy. The Arabs of Palestine, however, were quite simply overwhelmed: Their own divisions, lack of a powerful nationalist movement, and weak leadership hindered their ability to overturn their fate as a people marked for colonization.

The persecution of Jews in Europe, and especially in Nazi Germany, increased mass Jewish immigration into Palestine. At the end of the First World War, there had been fewer than 60,000 Jews in the country; by 1939 the Jewish population of Palestine had swelled to 450,000, or approximately 30 percent of the mandate's total population.[31] For the persecuted of Europe, Palestine was indeed a refuge, one made all the more urgent by the refusal of the United States to relax its strict immigration quotas. But for many of the approximately 9,000 Jewish Americans who emigrated to Palestine, the mandate was something fundamentally more ideological. Because they had not been persecuted in the United States, Palestine for them was not a refuge in any immediate sense. Taking advantage of a British mandatory structure that encouraged the separation of Arab and Jew, most of the American Jewish immigrants segregated themselves from the Arab population.

The American Zion Commonwealth, like the Jewish National Fund that had been established at the turn of the century, purchased lands and established Jewish-only settlements, such as the aptly named Balfouria agricultural colony or Herzlia. It specifically prohibited the sale of lands to non-Jews and operated just as the Zionist leadership in Palestine did—to build up an autonomous Jewish reality with the ultimate aim of establishing an independent Jewish state.[32] From a Zionist perspective, Jewish settlers were bold, ambitious, and the leading proponents of "reclaiming" the land of Israel. From an Arab perspective, they were simply another expression of an imperial will that had opened up their country forcibly to outsiders—foreign men and women who were determined to build an exclusively Jewish state in an Arab land.

There were, however, some important exceptions among American Zionists to the general Zionist rule. Judah Magnes, founder of the American Jewish Committee and the first president of the Hebrew University, was among the most farsighted of them. Magnes emigrated to Palestine in 1922, but he worked tirelessly for a binational state. Like King and Crane before him, he recognized that because of an Arab desire for independence, a Jewish state could be erected only through coercion. He wrote that if it were only "upon the bayonets of some Empire" that the Zionist enterprise rested, then the project of creating a Jewish state ought to be fundamentally reconsidered.[33]

For American Zionists—indeed, for most Zionists—Magnes went too far. He acknowledged the central problem that they pretended either did not exist, was relatively minor, or could be overcome through sheer force. Vladimir Jabotinsky, the revisionist, Russian-born Zionist who would spawn some of the most violent and uncompromising Zionist organizations and leaders, candidly admitted that the Arabs were the natives and that, like natives everywhere, they would resist foreign colonization. Jabotinsky believed, however, in the righteousness of Zionism and therefore advocated building an impregnable "iron wall" to crush Arab hope and aspirations for an Arab Palestine. In his humanism, Magnes was utterly different from Jabotinsky.[34]

For Arabs, however, Magnes did not go far enough. His compassion notwithstanding, Magnes found himself unable to support simple democratic rule in Palestine. He remained a Zionist, trapped between his utopian vision of Arab-Jewish cooperation and a colonialist foundation for a Jewish political presence in Palestine that he dared not forsake.

British power created facts on the ground. By the 1930s, Jewish immigration was no longer the vague idea to which Faysal had conditionally given his approval, nor could the ultimate goal of Zionism to create a Jewish state be hidden any longer from the Arabs. Until the eve of the Second World War, the British administratively, politically, and militarily established the basis for a Jewish state in Palestine: They categorically refused constitutional or democratic rule; they gave Hebrew the same status as Arabic; they privileged European Jewish employees with higher salaries than their Arab counterparts; and they allowed Jews an autonomous administration. Crucially, the British segregated, in essence, the educational programs of the country: A chronically underfunded Arabic school system was reserved for the Arab majority, while a privately funded Hebrew school system served the mandate's Jewish population. Most crucially, the British kept the country open to Jewish immigration, and until 1939 they made no effort, as they had done in both Egypt and Iraq, to pretend that they were shepherding the existing population to independence.

Following a major Arab revolt in 1936, the British sent a royal commission led by Lord Peel to investigate the causes of Arab discontent. Lord Peel recognized what the Arabs had been saying all along and what the Zionists had desired all along: A Jewish state was being created. The Arab majority that existed, however, constituted an impossible contradiction. Lord Peel believed that the history of Palestine began with the Old Testament. He accepted that Jews more than any other people in the world had an intrinsic right, and not simply an unbroken connection, to Palestine. In his report to the British government, known popularly as the Peel Commission Report, he accepted therefore the premise that the Zionist claim to Palestine was as valid as the native Arab claim—hence the commission's equivocation that the struggle in Palestine was the result of British good faith to meet the "rights and aspirations" of both Arabs and Jews.

Aided by a self-defeating Arab boycott of most of the commission's proceedings, the Peel Commission Report recommended in 1937 the partition of Palestine into two states, one Jewish and the other Arab, although the Arabs were by far the larger of the two populations, and it was primarily their land that was being partitioned and their population that was going to suffer the consequences of partition. Palestinian Arabs would be compelled to give up their actual land and their homes. The Zionists would be compelled to relinquish a portion of their irredentist claims. It was hardly an equal exchange. Indeed, from a native perspective, the partition constituted a grotesque miscarriage of justice. From the first day of the mandate, Arabs had demanded that they be allowed to exercise their right of self-determination, and from the first day the British had refused this right and assured them instead—

despite the policies they were implementing to the contrary—that there would never be Jewish hegemony over the Arabs.

The Palestinian Arab population in the designated Jewish state numbered, according to the Peel Commission Report, some 225,000; the number of Jews in the proposed Arab state was only 1,250—such was the disparity of the population between the Arabs and the Jews in Palestine as late as 1937, and indeed as late as 1948. To make partition work, the Arabs would have to sell their lands and be "exchanged" for the Jewish population, just as the Greeks and the Turks had exchanged populations previously. To rationalize this injustice the Peel Commission Report turned to the question of Jewish suffering in Europe, making explicit what had been implicit in the Balfour Declaration. The Arabs of Palestine would be made to pay the price for historic and ongoing Western persecution of the Jews. "Considering what the possibility of finding a refuge in Palestine means to many thousands of suffering Jews, we cannot believe that the 'distress' occasioned by Partition, great as it would be, is more than Arab generosity can bear," declared Lord Peel and his fellow British commissioners.

> And in this, as in so much else connected with Palestine, it is not only the peoples of that country who have to be considered. The Jewish Problem is not the least of the many problems which are disturbing international relations at this critical time and obstructing the path to peace and prosperity. If the Arabs at some sacrifice could help to solve that problem, they would earn the gratitude not of the Jews alone but of all the Western World.[35]

Two decades of British evasions, false assurances, and prevarications to the Arab natives had led, after all, to the open call for a Jewish state in Palestine. In frustration and fury, the Arabs recommenced their rebellion against the British. But as happened with the Syrians, Iraqis, and Egyptians, their rebellion was crushed methodically by the colonial power. Many Palestinian leaders were hanged; others, such as the British-appointed mufti of Jerusalem, Hajj Amin al-Husayni, who was the scion of a venerable Jerusalemite family, fled the country. In Egypt, meanwhile, as in Syria and across the Arabian Peninsula, new radio broadcasts, newspapers, and most of all personal testimonies helped spread the word about the unfolding Arab tragedy in Palestine. Muslim fundamentalist and secular Arabs, liberals and conservatives, could all agree, almost instinctively, that the foreign Jewish colonization with foreign British imperial support was an injustice at the heart of the Arab world. Because there was no way to rationalize settler-colonialism from a native vantage point, and because the professed Zionist goal in Palestine was to create a "nationality which would be as Jewish as the French nation was French and the British nation British," as Weizmann had intimated to Lansing at Paris in 1919, Palestine became an Arab cause with a powerful and tragic tale at its heart.[36]

British policy created a national conflict between Jews and Arabs. It also undercut the very class of people who most identified with the West, whether because they were educated in its institutions, spoke its languages fluently, or were most under the spell of its culture and science and political forms of government. Zionism, and more specifically Western support for Zionism, put Arabs in an untenable position. Men like Ameen Rihani had emerged from the nineteenth century far stronger and more confident than xenophobic fundamentalists such as Yusuf al-Nahbani, who had fulminated against foreign missionary institutions in Syria, or the Maronite prelates, who had persecuted As'ad Shidyaq. And yet, as Palestine fell increasingly under Zionist domination, the eloquent Rihani and others like him who believed in the necessity and utility of a dialogue with the West were helpless to cure a myopic Anglo-American view that privileged Jewish history and aspirations over Arab. Liberal Arabs admired Western rationalism and science, but saw in Western support for Zionism a bigotry for which they could not account.

However much the British recognized that the mandate in Palestine antagonized the Arabs, and however much some of their officers and officials on the ground came to sympathize with Arabs, the British government nevertheless chose to proceed with its support for Zionism. It counted on the fact that Arab leaders in Egypt, Iraq, Jordan, and Arabia would act to preserve their own positions rather than mobilize on behalf of the Palestinian Arabs, and in this belief it was partially vindicated. Although the U.S. government was not the principal power involved and therefore played until 1946 a secondary role in the unfolding tragedy, it was also aware of the growing Arab discontent in Palestine. The issue at hand was not a question of oil. There was petroleum in Iraq, which the British had created as a single country under Arab rule; there was no petroleum in Palestine, which they turned over to Zionist colonization. The real issue was Western power and Palestinian powerlessness, as well as a mind-set nurtured by the West's own prejudice and superiority stemming from a colonial age. Even when the British acknowledged the human and economic costs of Zionism from the standpoint of the Arabs, they nevertheless rationalized these costs as inevitable. Against this hardened mentality, which had proved itself impervious to the sufferings of many "lesser" races, there was very little value in moral appeal. Words alone do not humble empires.

But the liberal, and not so liberal, Arabs did appeal to the West, even after Faysal's Arab kingdom in Syria, which had put so much stock in British pledges and American principles, had met its lonely end at the hands of the French. Rihani, for one, wrote repeatedly about the dangers of "political Zionism." Jews of Europe and America who espoused its tenets, Rihani insisted, were infatuated by dreams of conquest; if pursued under the protection of British "bayonets," Zionism would lead to the dispossession of the Arabs.[37] No opponent of Zionism, however, was more eloquent than the Arab Christian historian George Antonius. Born in 1891 in the Lebanese village of Dayr al-Qamar but raised in Alexandria, Antonius belonged to a tight-knit community of Syrians in Egypt known as the *shawam*. Coming from a well-off family, he was educated at the British school Victoria College in Egypt before continuing his education at King's College at Cambridge University. Enchanted with British parliamentary democracy and enamored of what he regarded as the educational renaissance initiated by the American missionaries in Syria, Antonius belonged to a generation of young Arab men who wanted a better, more tolerant, more liberal, more secular future for their people. After his graduation from Cambridge, he worked first in Egypt and then as a senior inspector of education in mandatory Palestine. He therefore witnessed firsthand what he regarded as a grotesque miscarriage of justice unfolding before his eyes, for he saw how British support for Zionist colonization ran roughshod over native Arab aspirations. He became, like many other Arabs at this time, consumed by the question of Palestine. But unlike most of them, for whom an appeal to a British or American public, even if contemplated, would have been complicated by a language barrier, Antonius was fluent in English.

He met the deposed Sharif Husayn and his son Abdullah in 1931, and they gave him access to hundreds of documents in Arabic in their possession, including the unpublished correspondence between the sharif and Henry McMahon, the British high commissioner in Egypt during World War I. Antonius recognized at once the opportunity to tell a history of the Arab nationalist movement that put Arabs front and center. Traveling from Cairo to Beirut to Jerusalem to Damascus to Baghdad, he interviewed Faysal, now king of Iraq, and dozens of other leading nationalist figures. He also scoured British and American sources, gaining access to confidential Department of State papers; he traveled to both London and Washington and met with men such as Albert Lybyer and William Linn Westermann, all in an attempt to get at what actually happened during and after the First World War.[38]

Antonius wanted to write a history that would not simply be read but would influence the debate about the future of Palestine. Published in 1938, his book was entitled *The Arab Awakening*. As much as he emphasized Arab agency, the story he recounted was essentially one of Western betrayal. Antonius included appendices in which he laid out the entire Husayn-McMahon correspondence, the recommendations on Syria and Palestine of the suppressed King-Crane report, and various British and French pledges and promises of independence to the Arabs. Having imbibed a general Arab nationalist prejudice against the Ottomans, Antonius portrayed their four-hundred-year rule over the Arabs as a period of "torpid passivity."[39] He glorified Faysal and the Hashemites and exaggerated both the strength and popularity of the Arab nationalists. He also accepted the American missionaries at their own word. For Antonius, these missionaries played a key role in the birth of the Arab national movement. In his own estimation, they had inspired an Arab educational and political renaissance. They were the Western heroes in a tragedy about the relationship between the West and the Arabs told for once by an Arab. The pivotal moment in this drama was the First World War, and the two documents that stood out for Antonius were the Sykes-Picot Agreement and the report of the King-Crane Commission. It is easy to understand why.

For Arabs, Sykes-Picot was a metaphor for Western imperialism. It represented a callous, dishonest way of dealing with the Arab world; King-Crane was a metaphor for American integrity. It lit the path for a more constructive relationship between the Arabs and the West because it captured without dissimulation the essence of the Arab position on Palestine—that it was obviously wrong to impose by force of arms a foreign settler population on a native one in an era whose watchword was self-determination. For this reason, Antonius dedicated his book to Charles Crane, not only because of his leadership of the famous commission of inquiry, and not simply because Antonius completed the manuscript thanks to Crane's generous support. (Antonius was employed by Crane's Institute of Current World Affairs.) Rather, Crane represented for Antonius the archetypical American, indeed Westerner, whom he firmly believed might yet contribute to a positive solution in Palestine if he only knew the simple facts of the story.

And for Antonius, the relationship between the Arab world and the West centered unquestionably on Palestine. He knew, of course—and wanted to relate to Western readers—that this small country, which Lord Peel hoped the Arabs might generously concede as if it were a trifle, lay at the heart of the Arab world. He knew that Jerusalem was of obvious religious importance to both Christian and Muslim Arabs, just as it was for Jews, and that in Palestine there existed an existential crisis not present in any other mandate. He also knew that the fate of this country lay no longer in Arab hands but in Western ones. The West, he believed, had a choice to make.

Antonius presented as persuasive a case as any Arab might have then made. He spoke from the heart and the mind. He recognized that there were Zionist arguments for Palestine that resonated powerfully in the West, but he also hoped that the presentation of a story in which the Arabs were portrayed not as an abstract problem but as dramatic actors, with the same kind of passion and history and aspirations and rights that Zionists were always assumed to have, might humanize Arabs in the eyes of his Western audience. Antonius recognized that in his day the most compelling argument in favor of Zionism rested less in the Bible than in the Nazi persecution of the Jews, the climax of centuries of European anti-Semitism.

Antonius saw right through Lord Peel's sleight-of-hand attempt to make the Arabs shoulder the responsibility for Western anti-Semitism. He ended his account with a prescient observation. "The treatment meted out to the Jews in Germany and other European countries," he wrote, "is a disgrace to its authors and to modern civilisation; but posterity will not exonerate any country that fails to bear its proper share of the sacrifices needed to alleviate Jewish suffering and distress." Antonius bluntly highlighted the hypocrisy at the heart of Western support for Zionism. "To place the brunt of the burden upon Arab Palestine," he argued,

> is a miserable evasion of the duty that lies upon the whole of the civilised world. It is also morally outrageous. No code of morals can justify the persecution of one people in an attempt to relieve the persecution of another. The cure for the eviction of the Jews from Germany is not to be sought in the eviction of the Arabs from their homeland; and the relief of Jewish distress may not be accomplished at the cost of inflicting a corresponding distress upon an innocent and peaceful population.[40]

On the eve of the Second World War, having overseen a train of events that were bound to lead to cataclysm, the British government stepped back from the brink. Anti-British sentiment across the Arab world had increased since the Palestinian revolt of 1936. Following a conference about the future of Palestine held in London in February 1939—to which they invited Palestinian Arabs, including Antonius and Zionist delegates as well as representatives from Saudi Arabia, Yemen, Egypt, Iraq, and Transjordan—the British declared that partition was, in fact, not British policy. Rather, in a so-called White Paper, they indicated that Palestine was to have an independent government in ten years' time and that the number of the Jewish immigrants to Palestine was to be drastically curtailed. This concession to Arab aspirations was too little too late.

The top Zionist leader in Palestine was now David Ben-Gurion, another European-born Jew; he had emigrated there in 1906 and had adopted his Hebrew surname in place of his original name, Green. Ben-Gurion was single-minded in his Zionism. He knew that the Arab Palestinians would resist Zionist colonization; therefore, he believed, it had to be imposed upon them militarily, precisely as the King-Crane report had foreseen in 1919. "We must expel Arabs and take their places," he concluded in 1937.[41] Ben-Gurion scoffed at British imperial backpedaling in 1939 and directed his energy instead at consolidating a Zionist grip on Palestine. He began to cultivate Washington, not London, in the hope that it would play the key role in the final disposition of Palestine. In May 1942, a week before the fifty-year-old George Antonius died of cancer in Jerusalem, Ben-Gurion played a key role in a conference at the Biltmore Hotel in New York City organized by the American Emergency Committee for Zionist Affairs. The occasion marked the political ascendancy of American Zionists and a decisive shift in Zionist strategy away from Britain toward America.

Galvanized by horrific German anti-Semitism and by the unfolding Holocaust of European Jewry, whose full dimensions were not yet known, Zionist organizations reiterated their long-standing demand for unrestricted Jewish immigration into Palestine. Inspired by Ben-Gurion, the Biltmore conferees openly came out in favor of transforming Palestine into a "Jewish commonwealth." American Zionists proclaimed their "unequivocal devotion to the cause of democratic freedom and international justice," although they refused, once again, the idea of one-man-one-vote in Palestine until a Jewish majority there had been achieved.

They renewed their vow to work with their Arab "neighbors," but once more they deliberately discounted the historical and political claims of the native Arab presence in Palestine.[42] Zionist dissenters such as Judah Magnes described the Biltmore program as the equivalent of a "declaration of war by the Jews on the Arabs," but he was outflanked by more militant Zionists who equated a Jewish state in Palestine with the end of anti-Semitism and the advent of a "new democratic world."[43]

Until 1946, American presidents had refused to become actively engaged in Palestinian affairs. Although Wilson had expressed sympathy for Zionism, he inadvertently did it a signal disservice by exposing its colonialist and antidemocratic underpinnings in mandatory Palestine by sending the King-Crane Commission. Congress endorsed the Balfour Declaration in a symbolic move in 1922, but the U.S. State Department had taken a more cautious position, neither advocating nor rejecting Zionism, just as it had not advocated Arab nationalism.

In 1944, however, a congressman from New York by the name of Sol Bloom oversaw hearings on a resolution submitted by fellow congressman James A. Wright from Pennsylvania. It called on the United States to "use its good offices and take appropriate measures to the end that the doors of Palestine shall be opened for free entry of Jews into that country, and that there shall be full opportunity for colonization, so that the Jewish people may ultimately reconstitute Palestine as a free and democratic Jewish commonwealth."[44]

Bloom was a self-made man with no experience of the Middle East beyond that which he had gained from his stint as a promoter and handler of the Algerian village at the Chicago World's Fair in 1893. But Bloom was committed to securing a Jewish state in Palestine. The hearings over which he presided, just like those of 1922, were lopsided in favor of Zionism. Bloom was Jewish, but he worked with the full confidence that almost all his Christian colleagues shared his sentiments and that the European persecution of Jews made the case for a Jewish state in Palestine virtually impossible to rebut in the United States. Anyone opposing it could be branded either callous, un-Christian, or anti-Semitic.

Bloom accordingly introduced into the record a compilation of documents relating to the question of Zionism in Palestine—it included the Balfour Declaration, the Zionist terms of the British mandate, and statements of various British ministers regarding a Jewish national home. The Committee on Foreign Affairs heard mostly from American Jewish and Christian witnesses sympathetic to the idea of a Jewish state in Palestine. The tone of these men was liberal, not fundamentalist. They stressed the urgency of the situation of the Jews of Europe and made clear that in their minds Palestine—not the United States—was the most appropriate final destination for the Jews. They also emphasized the democratic nature of the would-be Jewish commonwealth. The Arabs of Palestine were barely considered, and on the rare occasions when they were, their protests at the injustice of reconstituting their land as a state for European Jews, and not merely a refuge, were either dismissed as irrelevant to the great humanitarian cause at hand or found to be odious.

Amid a sea of pro-Zionist sentiment, a few American Jews testified against the idea of a "theocratic" Jewish state in Palestine, including Lessing J. Rosenwald, president of the American Council for Judaism, who insisted on the spiritual and religious but not political nature of the Jewish people. Instead of forcibly establishing an exclusively Jewish state in a religiously mixed land, Rosenwald advocated an independent, democratic state in Palestine in which all the inhabitants of the country had equal rights and obligations. Rosenwald asked that the King-Crane report be included in the record of the proceedings. Several of Bloom's colleagues on the committee had never heard of the report.

Almost as an afterthought, Edith Nourse Rogers, a congresswoman from Massachusetts and the longest-serving woman in congressional history, declared that she had "some Syrians around" and wanted to hear their testimony. Philip Hitti was apparently one of these, for he was duly asked for his views—one of only two Arabs to appear before Bloom's committee. Hardly predisposed to Arab nationalism, Hitti did at least know the Arab world. Between the time he left AUB in 1926 and his testimony before Congress in 1944, he had played a remarkable role in the promotion of the study of the modern Near East. At Princeton, he had virtually single-handedly turned the musty study of the Orient into a field of contemporary relevance. He would within two years establish the pioneering program for Near Eastern studies at the university. In the meantime, given the growing importance of oil and the strategic geography of the Middle East, he was working hard to convince the State Department and the army that a contemporary knowledge of Islam and Arabic was important to America's growing presence in the Arab world.

As he walked down the halls of Congress on February 15, 1944, Hitti sensed that America's heritage in the Arab world would be endangered by precipitous American action on Palestine. Standing to testify, he drew on all his professorial instinct to present what he must have known was a controversial perspective. Hitti foregrounded what he described as the "forgotten man"—the Palestinian Arab—in taking up the question of Palestine. For a historian from the region, this was basic common sense; in the House of Representatives it sounded as if it had come from Mars.

Hitti was blunt. He opposed U.S. support for the establishment of a Jewish state in Palestine on the grounds that the vast majority of the land's inhabitants were Muslim and Christian Arabs. A Jewish state could be imposed upon them only by force. In Hitti's view, this was unfair, unjust, and undemocratic. He also said that such a state would inflame wider Arab and Muslim passions and that it was utterly hypocritical to solve European anti-Semitism at the expense of Arabs. Above all, he warned, American support for the creation of a Jewish state would needlessly squander a century of goodwill that American missionaries had built up. The discovery of oil in Arabia and the deployment of American soldiers in North Africa and western Asia during the war gave impetus to Hitti's vision of American and Arab cooperation, but his notion of a mutual concern drew most of all from his own personal experience of American benevolence.

Hitti's dissenting perspective was clearly exceptional, and exception was quickly taken to it. He was interrupted frequently. Congressman

Bloom suggested that Hitti had been unduly influenced by Nazi propaganda; Congressman Joseph L. Pfeifer from New York asked Hitti whether he was an "American citizen" (he was) and whether he believed "in civilization" and "in the democratic way of life" (he did). He accused Hitti of misrepresenting the facts on Palestine. Congresswoman Rogers wanted to know what Hitti saw as an alternative "solution for the Jewish people" given their terrible persecution in Europe. She placed European anti-Semitism quite squarely in the professor's charge. Congressman Charles A. Eaton from New Jersey was also discomfited by Hitti's presentation; he pressed the professor to "locate himself a little more fully." Hitti replied that he was born in Mount Lebanon, was educated in American schools, attended the American University of Beirut, received his doctorate from Columbia, and was presently a professor of Semitic literature at Princeton. Eaton, however, got to the point: "If it is not too personal," he followed up, "are you an Arab?"

For Eaton, the question forced Hitti into a stereotype, reducing his scholarly credentials into mere "Arab" bias that had to be weighed against what was perceived as the more tangible narratives of European Jews. For the congressman, Palestine was simply the location for a Jewish national home; its Arab environment was alien and Muslim and of little interest or importance. Eaton thus ignored the larger point that Hitti was making: that there was a history of American involvement with this region.

For Hitti, understanding and accommodating Arab views was essential for a coherent American policy in the Middle East and for the stability of the region. Palestine, after all, was not simply a Holy Land for Christians and Jews, not simply the site of potential Western Christian atonement for the persecution of the Jews, and not simply an imaginary locale where scenes of the Bible could be reenacted by modern-day preachers. It was an actual place inhabited by real people. A Jewish home in Palestine therefore could never have been simply a question of looking at things from a Western perspective and with an eye fixed only on European history. From an Arab perspective, U.S. support for Zionism—and the Western belief in Christian righteousness, redemption for anti-Semitism, and humanitarian benevolence that undergirded it—looked radically different than it did from the elevated and isolated vantage point of the U.S. Congress.

Like Antonius before him, Hitti did not deny what was happening to the Jews of Europe, nor did he deny Jewish aspirations for security and a nation; by the same token, however, he could not pretend that the question of U.S. support for Jewish colonization of Palestine could or should ignore the Arab world upon which it so blatantly impinged. America's image and standing in the Arab world were at stake. "This is no time," he warned, "to turn old friends into potential enemies."[45]

Although the U.S. War Department under Henry Stimson urged Congress to delay its consideration of the resolution, owing to wartime exigencies, both President Franklin Roosevelt and his Republican opponent in the 1944 elections, Thomas Dewey, explicitly endorsed the Zionist program that called for unrestricted Jewish immigration and the "reconstitution" or "establishment" of Palestine "as a free and democratic Jewish commonwealth."[46]

As the United States took on an increasingly visible role in deciding the fate of Palestine, Arab politicians and leaders sought to convince the U.S. government and the American public of the reality on the ground in Palestine. Abdul Aziz Al Saud—or Ibn Saud, as he is known in the West—was the ambitious ruler of Saudi Arabia. He was also an adherent of the puritanical Wahabi Islam. Of far more consequence to the Americans, however, was the fact that Ibn Saud had swallowed up the hapless Husayn's kingdom of the Hijaz two decades earlier and established himself as the paramount Arab leader over much of the oil-rich Arabian Peninsula.

None other than Charles Crane had struck up a cordial relationship with the Saudi king following their meeting in Jidda in 1931. Ibn Saud's knowledge of America until that point derived mainly from the work of American physicians operating from the Mason Memorial Hospital in Bahrain. He had invited them to visit his own domains in 1917. The king did not tolerate Christian proselytizing, but he had welcomed the medical treatment offered to him and his son Prince Saud by Dr. Louis

Dame in the early 1920s. George Antonius, in any case, interpreted for Crane during his one-week visit to Jidda. Crane saw in the tall and imposing Saudi king a noble figure. The American philanthropist romanticized the Bedouins. More importantly for Crane, Ibn Saud's independent kingdom offered a new outlet for his determination to establish a constructive relationship with Arabs. He introduced the king to a mining engineer in his employ, Karl S. Twitchell, who, with Ibn Saud's blessing and Crane's financial support, embarked on a one-thousand-mile journey across Arabia to assess the country's agricultural and mineral wealth.[47]

Through Twitchell's mediation, Standard Oil of California was granted a concession by Ibn Saud. The king was eager to balance his long-standing dependency on the British with American support. American engineers and geologists scoured his land for petroleum. In 1938 they discovered a major field north of a sleepy town called Dhahran. A consortium of American oil companies, which by 1944 called itself the Arabian American Oil Company (ARAMCO), was the pivot around which U.S.-Saudi relations turned. Ibn Saud was clearly not someone who could be ignored, and now in 1945, fourteen years after his meeting with Charles Crane, who had tried and failed to promote the cause of Arab self-determination in the United States, the Arab king met the most powerful man in the world.

On February 14, 1945, the Saudi king sat with President Roosevelt for five hours aboard the USS *Quincy* at the Great Bitter Lake in Egypt. The sole translator of the meeting was Colonel William Eddy, the first U.S. minister plenipotentiary to Saudi Arabia. Born and raised in Sidon and the grandson and son of American missionaries to Lebanon, Eddy was the only man on the USS *Quincy* who was fluent in both Arabic and English. Although his parents had devoted themselves to missionary work, Eddy had joined the Marine Corps and had been wounded in France in 1918. Diverted from his study of English literature, in which he had received a doctorate from Princeton in 1922, Eddy became what one might call an Arabist—someone who was intimately familiar with the culture, geography, and politics of the region; who knew how to interact comfortably with Arab elites; and who, like Crane, expressed a paternalistic solicitude for the Arabs and tried to see the world through their eyes. He was therefore very familiar, and to a large extent sympathetic, with the extent of Arab frustration with the West over Palestine.

President Roosevelt quickly betrayed his ignorance about the depth of Arab feeling regarding Zionist colonization of Palestine. After an elaborate exchange of pleasantries and gifts—Roosevelt presented the Saudi king with one of his wheelchairs and, more importantly, with the promise of a DC-3—the two men got down to business. The American president pressed the Arab monarch to help resolve the plight of the persecuted Jews of Europe, assuming in the manner of so many other Western statesmen that Western anti-Semitism was a problem for which Arabs had to offer a solution.

According to Eddy, the king responded immediately. "Give them and their descendants the choicest lands and homes of the Germans who had oppressed them." But this was never an option. FDR later informed Congress that he had learned "more about that whole problem, the Moslem problem, the Jewish problem by talking with Ibn Saud for five minutes than I could have learned in the exchange of two or three dozen letters."[48] But he left the king only with a promise that he would never do anything hostile to the Arabs, nor would he change American policy regarding Palestine without fully consulting the Arabs as well as the Jews.

Ibn Saud was not prepared to sacrifice his relationship with the United States over Palestine (just as he had earlier refused to compromise his relationship with the British), but he felt strongly enough about the issue to press home his palpable concern in a lengthy dispatch to Roosevelt in March 1945. The king's utter disdain for the Jewish claim to historic title over Palestine was matched only by his incredulity that Western powers, including the United States, could speak of liberty, democracy, humanitarianism, justice, and Zionism as if indeed Palestine were a Jewish land inhabited by a Jewish majority.

Like many if not most other Arabs—and of course, like the Zionists themselves—the Saudi monarch often conflated Jews with Zionists. Ibn Saud, whose kingdom was harshly intolerant and whose own puritanical Wahabi ideology discriminated against Jews and Christians as well as Shi'a and other supposedly heretical or impious Muslims, decried the alleged villainy of "the Jews." Ibn Saud would not conceal his anti-Jewish prejudice. The embittered Palestinian mufti of Jerusalem, Hajj Amin al-Husayni, whose own country was being transformed into a homeland for European Jews and who had been exiled by the British following the Arab revolt of 1936, turned to Germany in desperation at British policy in Palestine. He promised the Axis powers that he would encourage an Arab revolt against the British in return for German and Italian recognition of an independent Arab nation and the abolition of the Jewish national home in Palestine. Consumed by his own hatred of Zionism and its British supporters, the mufti closed his eyes and his heart to Jewish suffering.

Prejudice and hatred, however, were not the reasons why Arabs of all backgrounds and faiths, including some Jewish Arabs, found Zionism so unacceptable. Rather, Arabs regarded the struggle for self-determination in Palestine as the crucible of their modern independence. Palestine was not the only Arab land colonized, but the form of Western coercion under which it labored was egregious—nowhere else was the indigenous Arabic-speaking population so obviously embroiled in a battle for the survival of its society. Like French Algeria, which had been colonized in 1830, the situation in Palestine was stark in its juxtaposition of foreigner settlers and native Arabs. Unlike French Algeria, where the painful process of ending French domination was just beginning, Palestine appeared to be headed in a direction entirely opposite to the decolonizing spirit of the age. To prevent the destruction of Arab Palestine became a rallying cry that reverberated across the Arab world; its greatest intensity was felt in Palestine and neighboring countries, but strong echoes were heard as far away as Bahrain, Kuwait, and Yemen. The first speech made by the representative of the newly independent state of Iraq at the League of Nations called for Palestine's independence. But as the lawyer Musa al-Alami told the Arab congress in Alexandria in 1944, the Palestinian Arabs had since 1919 sent nine delegations to London and the League of Nations, "but nobody listened to us." Bloody revolts had also been attempted, with similarly dismal results. Like a "cry from the grave," Alami declared that nothing the Arabs said or did seemed to prick the conscience of the West.[49]

Virtually every Arab protest lodged with Western and American observers, diplomats, prime ministers, and presidents emphasized the fundamental injustice of Zionism. Although Ibn Saud was an autocratic ruler with a tribal following and a man who, by his position, heritage, religion, and ambition, lived a world apart from the likes of the scholarly, urbane, and liberal Hitti, both men shared a fundamentally similar outlook on Palestine. They each expressed in plain language a sense of the seething Arab anger over Palestine that cut sharply across class, regional, sectarian, and national lines.

It was this point precisely that the Arab officials who appeared before the Anglo-American commission of inquiry sought to convey in 1946. The commission was dispatched to the Middle East to investigate the deteriorating mandate with an eye to resolving the crisis of Jewish refugees languishing in camps in Europe. The British government was beleaguered by the costs of maintaining its empire; ever since the White Paper of 1939, it had faced an increasingly violent Zionist insurgency that would culminate in July 1946 with the massive bombing of the King David Hotel in Jerusalem, undertaken by Menachim Begin's underground organization called the Irgun. The British were also coming under tremendous American pressure to scrap the White Paper. Financially dependent on the United States and exhausted by the war effort, the British could not easily dismiss President Harry Truman's explicit demand in 1945 for the immediate entry of one hundred thousand Jewish refugees into Palestine. The Anglo-American commission was an effort at compromise, not so much between Arabs and Jews as between divergent American and British positions on Palestine.

On the outskirts of Cairo, at the Mena House Hotel, on the morning of March 2, 1946, English and American committee members heard from the secretary general of the newly formed Arab League, Azzam Pasha, whose first urgent concern was the situation in Palestine. Azzam Pasha appeared before the committee flanked by representatives of several Arab states, including Syria, Saudi Arabia, and Yemen. Despite internal wrangling and infighting among the Arab states, and also among the Palestinians themselves, the representatives in Cairo sought to present the Anglo-American committee with a unanimous front on

Palestine. They rejected the idea of a Jewish state in Palestine, and they opposed mass Jewish immigration into it. Azzam Pasha pleaded, moreover, for genuinely democratic rule in Palestine that respected the will of the Arab majority but also safeguarded the equality of Jews, Muslims, and Christians. He contrasted the integrationist Arab nationalist ideal that brought together Muslim, Christian, and Jewish inhabitants of Palestine as equal citizens of a common state with the Zionist goal of creating an exclusively Jewish state.[50]

At the YMCA building in Jerusalem in March, the Anglo-American committee heard as well from the mild-mannered historian Albert Hourani. Born in Manchester to Lebanese parents, Hourani had received his degree from Oxford in 1936 and worked at AUB as a lecturer before joining British intelligence during the war. Hourani was a superb choice to represent the Arab position, for he laid out the Arab case methodically and logically before a committee that had already heard from Chaim Weizmann and David Ben-Gurion, who reminded committee members that anti-Semitism was "your baby, a Christian baby."[51] Unlike Ibn Saud, whose antipathy for the Jews undercut the strength of the Arab argument—"The Jews are our enemies everywhere," the king had told members of the committee in Riyadh[52]—Hourani was able to point out the obvious injustice of colonial Zionism without resorting to bigotry. He understood his audience far more than Ibn Saud had, and he had no illusions about where general Western sympathies lay. Like every other Arab, he pointed to the underlying hypocrisy of Western humanitarianism that sought to alleviate the suffering of European Jews at the expense of the Arabs. Hourani stressed the "injustice of turning a majority into a minority in its own country" and the "injustice of withholding self-government until the Zionists are in the majority and are able to profit by it." More pointedly, he reminded the commissioners that the Zionists were not aiming to solve a humanitarian crisis or a "refugee problem for its own sake, but to secure political dominion in Palestine, and that their demand for immigration is only a step towards dominating Palestine."

Most profoundly, however, Hourani repeated the warning given by Philip Hitti two years earlier. He feared that the relations between the Arabs and the West were at a crossroads. He said that the Arabs could either create a world that was liberal, tolerant, and open to the West, or withdraw into "spiritual isolation and hatred, taking nothing from the outside world except the material means with which to combat it." Hourani insisted that the Arab leaders wanted to follow the first course, but that the matter lay largely in the hands of the West and depended, above all, on how the Western powers resolved the question of Palestine. "And it is at this point that Zionism comes in," he testified.

> Zionism for the Arabs has become a test of Western intentions, and so long as the grievance, the intolerable grievance, of Zionism exists, it will be impossible for the Arabs to establish the relationship of tolerance and respect, of trust and cooperation, with the world and to live at peace with themselves and their neighbors. And it will be impossible for that Arab nation—progressive, tranquil, contented, and stable—to come into existence for which we all hope, and to which we are all trying to work.[53]

The Anglo-American committee recommended the immediate entry of one hundred thousand Jews into Palestine, despite strenuous Arab protests. In the larger political equation, the Arabs were not nearly as powerful as their unanimous public front on Palestine suggested. There were deep, often terrible, disagreements among them on the most appropriate strategy to pursue against Zionism; the Hashemite states of Jordan and Iraq competed with Ibn Saud and Egypt for leadership over the Arab world, and each Arab government suspected the others' approach to the Palestine question, not knowing what to fear more, popular anger in their own state against Zionism, the Zionists themselves, or rival Arab leaders. The kings of Egypt, Iraq, and Jordan still depended on Britain. Ibn Saud relied on the United States, in whose hands the fate of Palestine now rested, but in America the Zionists were far more powerful, politically speaking, than a far-off, exotic Arab king.

To its credit, the Anglo-American committee did at least acknowledge that the creation of a Jewish state in Palestine was impossible to reconcile with Arab aspirations and that the solution to the Jewish refugee problem was an international, and not simply an Arab, responsibility. It noted that "the period since the first World War has been marked by a rising wave of nationalism in all Arab countries. Palestinian Arabs share this sentiment, and they are strongly supported in their demand for independence and self-government by all the States of the Arab League. No other subject has occupied so much of the attention of the Arab League or has done so much to unite its membership as has the question of Palestine." It also corroborated Hourani's testimony and that provided by King-Crane two decades earlier by admitting that in neighboring Arab countries committee members "found that hostility to Zionism was as strong and widespread there as in Palestine itself."[54]

The Anglo-American committee nevertheless found itself unable to recommend democratic rule in Palestine. The Arab League secretariat strongly protested to the United States through its legation in Damascus. It warned of damage to U.S.-Arab relations as well as of the rise of anti-Semitism in the Arab world if the Arabs of Palestine were again denied their independence. President Truman was aware of Arab objections, but he wanted to believe that they were not insurmountable. The Arabs were a distant people, and their history foreign to him. Truman was far more preoccupied with trying to resolve the Jewish refugee crisis in Europe. Palestine appeared to him to be the one place in the world that could be made to accept the refugees. His interest in winning Jewish votes, his readings in the Bible, and his sympathy for the Jewish victims of Nazi persecution colored his view of Zionism. Egged on by some of his closest advisers, such as David Niles, who was a staunch Zionist, Truman made a mockery of FDR's promise to Ibn Saud in 1945 that he would not take actions that "might prove hostile to the Arab people."[55] In April 1946, he repeated his call for the immediate entry of one hundred thousand Jews into Palestine.

In May 1946, a general Arab strike in major Arab cities had been called to protest against the recommendations of the Anglo-American committee. In Cairo hundreds of students climbed atop the roof of the Al-Azhar mosque and hurled stones at the police, who responded violently, wounding forty and arresting more than two hundred protestors; in Lebanon two Jewish-owned stores were bombed. The first American diplomatic post in the Middle East to be bombed was in Beirut on the night of August 4. Ironically, the city in which the pioneering American missionaries Pliny Fisk, Cornelius Van Dyck, and Daniel Bliss were buried witnessed the birth of a new anti-American sentiment in the Arab world. Compared to the King David Hotel bombing in Jerusalem of July, in which more than ninety people died, most of them civilians, the Beirut bombing was, at first sight, a small affair. The nighttime attack heavily damaged the legation building, but there were no reported injuries. The Lebanese government quickly rounded up two suspects, expressed regret, and paid the U.S. government an indemnity.

But the significance of the bombing lay not in its immediate impact but as a portent of things to come. The assailants insisted that they were motivated by American policies on the question of Palestine. Though they had acted alone, their outrage was a manifestation of a more general Arab dismay at America. Across the Arab world, the question of Palestine became a cause around which Arabs of different faiths, classes, and outlooks could unite. Its adherents were no different in their clear-cut sense of right and wrong from those who had earlier fought against fascism in Spain or later for civil rights in America. Communists, nationalists, and Islamists each sought to define the cause in their particular vocabulary, but they collectively drew from the same sense of the need to do something about the grotesque miscarriage of justice for Palestine's Arabs. America suddenly found itself for the first time on the wrong side of Arab opinion.

The British government refused to implement the recommendations of the Anglo-American committee and turned over the question of Palestine to the United Nations in early 1947. That same year the majority report of the UN Special Committee on Palestine (UNSCOP) recommended the partition of Palestine, with Jerusalem to remain under UN trusteeship; a minority report recommended a single federal state. Although UNSCOP recognized that the Arabs were "for centuries the indigenous and preponderant" people in Palestine, Jewish "historical association" and the urgent situation of Jewish refugees in Europe made the committee decide that the "extreme solution" of a single democratic state was out of the question. Partition there had to be, though it would be the Arabs who would pay the principal price. UNSCOP conceded that the "Arab State will organize the substantial majority of Arabs in Palestine into a political body containing an insignificant minority of Jews; but in the Jewish State there will be a considerable minority of Arabs. That is the demerit of the scheme. But such a minority is inevitable in any feasible plan which does not place the whole of Palestine under the present majority of the Arabs."

Just as the Peel Commission had done ten years earlier, the UNSCOP majority report sacrificed democracy for expediency in the name of a one-sided humanitarianism. Whereas the proposed Arab state would have been overwhelmingly Arab, the proposed Jewish state would have had a very slight Jewish majority—498,000 Jews to 407,000 Arabs, although the report excluded 90,000 presumably Arab "Bedouins, cultivators, and stockowners who seek grazing further afield in dry seasons" from this Arab total. Partition, moreover, would be achieved only by cutting up mandatory Palestine in such a way that would bring together as many Jews as possible and grant them the richest agricultural lands. The fact that hundreds of thousands of Arabs would be forced overnight into a minority status was rationalized as a prerequisite for the eventual cooperation of the Semitic races. "The Jews," it said, "bring to the land the social dynamism and scientific method of the West; the Arabs confront them with individualism and intuitive understanding of life."[56]

The plan was unworkable. It drew on the experience of the past half-century—the massive upheavals, partitions, and population transfers that had occurred across Europe, Turkey, and South Asia. Tens of millions of European and colonial subjects had been moved across borders in the aftermath of both world wars; empires had collapsed, and new futures had begun. The plan was based on the hope that the immediate pain of partition would be overcome by the security of mutual statehood that was meant to be engendered in its aftermath. But at the heart of the Palestine partition lay the coercive idea that Palestine's Arab majority, whether they liked it or not, were bound to alleviate European Jewish suffering.

The actual UN partition plan voted on in November 1947 was a version of the UNSCOP plan. Although Jews owned less than 7 percent of the land, the proposed Jewish state constituted almost 56 percent of the Palestine mandate, and the Arabs in the proposed Jewish state still constituted just under half (46 percent) of its population.[57] From an Arab perspective, then, the plan was a travesty. King Abdullah of Jordan appealed directly to the American people on the eve of the United Nations partition of mandatory Palestine. The Jordanian king recognized that the United States was now indispensable for any peace in the dying days of British power, yet he believed that Zionist propaganda—or what Judah Magnes would refer to in 1948 as the "terror of the Zionist political machine" in America—precluded any serious public debate on the issue.[58] "I will be entirely frank with you," the king stated.

> There is one thing the Arab world simply cannot understand. Of all the nations of the earth, America is most insistent that something be done for these suffering Jews of Europe. This feeling does credit to the humanity for which America is famous, and to that glorious inscription on your Statue of Liberty. And yet this same America—the richest, greatest, most powerful nation the world has ever known—refuses to accept more than a token handful of these same Jews herself! I hope you will not think I am being bitter about this. I have tried hard to understand that mysterious paradox, and I confess I cannot. Nor can any other Arab.[59]

The eloquence of Abdullah's appeal masked his own double game. He was at that very moment involved in secret negotiations with the Zionists over a partition of Palestine. Impelled by his recognition of Zionist strength and influence (and the corresponding lack of strength and influence of the Arabs), by fears of rival Arab states, and by his own undiminished Hashemite dynastic ambition to extend his reach into Syria and Palestine, he recalled the tragic example of his brother's encounters with Chaim Weizmann. Abdullah was more Machiavellian than his brother, and far more willing to abandon the Palestinians to their fate than was his father. But for all his hypocrisy—or was his collusion with the Zionist leadership in Palestine a reflection of his pragmatism?—Abdullah expressed what he knew was a general Arab sentiment and a growing Arab frustration at the United States.

Truman, it is true, made a desultory effort at getting a nativist U.S. Congress to revisit America's rigid immigration quotas. He adamantly pushed, however, for the opening of Palestine to Jewish immigration. At various Arab conferences and at the UN, meanwhile, Arab delegates rehearsed familiar arguments even as they increasingly warned that they would resort to force to prevent the partition of Palestine. But against the most powerful nation in the world, and against a tide of Western public opinion preoccupied with the fate of the Jews, the weak Arab states had a poor hand to play. Their representatives fought a losing political battle in an arena designed by Western powers to safeguard Western hegemony in a new world order. They blustered and threatened but had no concrete alternative to offer that was acceptable to the Zionists or the West, and they had no real appetite for war. The Soviet Union, to which several Arab states would subsequently turn, was at this point firmly supportive of Zionism. The Arab states were playing a game of high-stakes poker, and their bluff was about to be called. The United States and Zionist representatives, meanwhile, put enormous pressure, through both moral appeals and outright intimidation, on wavering nations such as Haiti, Liberia, and the Philippines to vote for partition.

The West did not hate the Arabs, just as it did not suddenly love the Jews. But the momentum in favor of the Zionist position now overwhelmed the Arabs. This had been the case in 1917; this was the case even more so in 1947. Before the tangible fact of the persecution of Jews, the bleak fate of anonymous Arab villagers and townspeople in Palestine hardly registered in America and war-ravaged Europe.

Occasionally an American missionary or educator, such as William H. Hall or Charles R. Watson, raised his voice to remind the American public of the existence of the Arabs of Palestine. The tone of these missionary demurrals was generally defensive. Bayard Dodge, the president of the American University of Beirut and the son-in-law of Howard Bliss, recognized that Americans stood at a historic crossroads. Together he and Daniel Bliss, the grandson of the university's founder, and several other American citizens who had long experience in the Arab world published a long letter in the *New York Times* in which they urged their government not to go along with partition. These Americans made it clear that they understood the plight of the Jews, but they feared that American support for Zionism would undermine a century of goodwill built up by their forebears. "The spirit of the Crusades," they said prophetically, "will be revived again and it is inevitable that there will be a slow but sure lining-up of the people of Western Asia against the people of Europe and America."[60] Dodge perhaps grasped how little the missionary project had affected negative American Christian attitudes toward the Orient—or rather, how much missionary zealotry against Islam had played right into a Zionist determination to remake the Holy Land and thus, ironically, jeopardized American cultural institutions such as AUB. The patrician Dodge watched as the missionary community he embodied was stripped of its last pretensions to represent a benevolent America to the Arabs and the deserving Arabs to America.

Organizations such as the Christian Council on Palestine, led by the prominent theologian Reinhold Niebuhr, strongly advocated Zionism as the sign of a penitent, yet revitalized, Christianity. Niebuhr dismissed the significance of the Arabs of Palestine; they were inconsequential to his vision of a pioneering, liberal, modern, and redemptive Zionism. The council, as a result, lobbied far more strenuously for a Jewish state than the missionaries and educators living among Arabs fought for Arab rights. The council passionately embraced the figure of the unjustly persecuted Jew and was certain that the Nazi genocide of the Jews was an evil that required extensive liberal intellectual and spiritual self-criticism to ensure that it never happened again. The American missionaries and educators, who had been at the heart of the American encounter with the Arabs, found themselves impotent to stem the tide of Western conviction about the necessity of a Jewish state in Palestine.

The journalist and humanitarian activist Dorothy Thompson emerged, however, as another American critic of Zionism. Horrified by the Nazi persecution of the Jews, and motivated by a sense of Christian compassion, Thompson had been a vocal and staunch advocate for the establishment of a Jewish state in Palestine. When she traveled to Palestine in 1945, however, she came face to face with the reality that a Jewish state would have to be imposed upon the country's native population. Once she realized this crucial fact, she refused to equivocate. Like the

King-Crane Commission, she could not rationalize away what she regarded as the fundamental problem of Zionism in Palestine.

For her volte-face, Thompson was demonized as an anti-Semite, publicly smeared in what she called a "campaign of character assassination," and deprived of her regular column in the *New York Post*.[61] Undeterred, she repeatedly warned Americans about the costs of a blatantly pro-Israel position to America's moral standing and to its prestige in the Arab world. "The Zionists would like us all to believe," she would write in 1950, "that there is no such thing as an Arab."[62] The U.S. Congress, the executive branch, and public opinion, however, remained barely sensible to Arab opinion, no matter what its provenance. The major Western powers easily evaded what they regarded as abstract Arab arguments about justice and rights. By embracing the idea of a Jewish state and expressing deep sympathy for the plight of the Jews, these powers led by the United States regarded themselves as a moral and righteous civilization after the most brutal war in human history. They also pretended to turn a page on their own anti-Semitic past.

The senior leadership in the State Department's Office of Near Eastern and African Affairs, led by Loy Henderson, was more attuned to the kinds of arguments that Dodge was trying to make. Henderson, who had served as minister to Iraq and had traveled extensively in the Middle East but did not know Arabic, was wary of an American entanglement in the Palestine question. Others, such as Theodore Roosevelt's grandson Kermit Roosevelt, who would go on to play a critical role as a CIA operative in the 1953 coup against Iranian prime minister Muhammad Mossadegh, openly expressed suspicion that American Zionists had double loyalties. These men feared that the Soviets would exploit U.S. support for Zionism to create a bridgehead among Arabs. They also did not see how the creation of an anti-Arab Jewish state was a basic U.S. interest. America, Henderson wrote, was "forfeiting the friendship of the Arab world . . . [and] incurring long-term Arab hostility towards us."[63]

Henderson was bolstered by U.S. intelligence estimates of the consequences of U.S. support for partition. On the very eve of the partition vote, the newly created Central Intelligence Agency, in coordination with the intelligence organizations of the Departments of State, the

Army, the Navy, and the Air Force, issued a secret assessment in which it warned that armed hostilities were bound to occur in Palestine if the partition proposal was passed. The report insisted that the United States, "by supporting partition, has already lost much of its prestige in the Near East. In the event that partition is imposed on Palestine, the resulting conflict will seriously disturb the social, economic, and political stability of the Arab world, and U.S. commercial and strategic interests will be dangerously jeopardized." The report foresaw that most Arab governments would be subject to immense nationalist and religious pressure to act on behalf of the Palestinians because it correctly understood that popular sentiment across the region was fueled by a powerful sense of the injustice of Zionism. The "extremists" and "chauvinists," it predicted, would rise at the expense of those who advocated a friendly relationship with the United States and Great Britain.[64]

It was a sober warning and a reiteration of the more eloquent words of Albert Hourani on the cold calculus of U.S. interests. But such counsel—whether it came from Arab leaders, Arab intellectuals, American intelligence agencies, Near East experts at the Department of State—was ignored. Truman's close adviser Clark Clifford, who knew virtually nothing about the Arab world, contemptuously dismissed fears about an Arab reaction. He scoffed at the idea of "trembling before threats of a few nomadic desert tribes"—his shorthand for a vast region—and rejected out of hand "our shilly-shallying appeasement of the Arabs."[65] The Arabs, he believed, were paper tigers. He was not alone. Truman supported the partition.

On November 29, 1947, the United Nations voted for partition. The Soviet Union voted with the United States to divide Palestine. India, which understood the tragedy and turmoil of partition, voted against it. The majority of European states also voted to divide Palestine, whereas every state in or near the Middle East, including Greece, Turkey, and Iran, voted against the proposal.

In the wake of the vote to divide Palestine, Arab students and youths rioted and smashed the windows of the American legations in Syria and Lebanon and the American Information Office in Baghdad. In Aden the British authorities imposed martial law to curb Arab rioting caused by the Palestine partition decision. Libyans who had fought Italian colonialism in their own country volunteered to fight for Palestine. In an attempt to dissipate the anger of his compatriots, the Syrian president pleaded with demonstrators who had hauled down the U.S. flag, remonstrating that such acts were not becoming of the Arabs. But the Syrian president also promised that Palestine would be defended. Some seventy thousand protesters took to the streets of Baghdad; in Cairo, meanwhile, the Egyptian press denounced the "imperialism" of the United States, and the shaykh of Al-Azhar called for a jihad on behalf of Palestine. Students marched before the gates of the American University in Cairo and the Arab League offices in the city. They cried "Egypt for Palestine," emphasizing their sense of solidarity with and responsibility for their brethren in Palestine. Some students denounced the Jews, whose ancient communities scattered across much of the region, in Iraq especially, bore the brunt of Arab outrage at Zionism. Husayn Fakhri Khalidi, who was acting chairman of the Arab Higher Committee, warned of further violence, tragedy, and a "world disaster." Knowing precisely how Arabs felt about Palestine and about the U.S. role in ensuring partition, he admitted "that he was bitterly disappointed because he had always respected American fair play and democracy."[66]

In early December 1947, some fifteen thousand students poured into the streets of Cairo. The police again charged the crowd and beat it back with whips. The unpopular government banned further demonstrations, but it found itself under enormous pressure to do something about Palestine. The founder of the Muslim Brotherhood, Hasan al-Banna, announced that his organization had battalions of volunteers ready to fight for Palestine.[67] In mid-December, a massive political demonstration occurred. The protest was called by the Muslim Brotherhood. With more than one hundred thousand people crowding into Opera Square, the president of the Young Men's Muslim Association, Salih Harb Pasha, held aloft a Koran and a pistol. The throng heard defiant speeches by Prince Faysal of Saudi Arabia and the prime ministers of Lebanon and Syria. The leaders were playing catchup with the people.[68]

These were but the first sparks of what would in time become a smoldering Arab rage against Western, and especially American, arrogance and imperialism. After the partition vote, Truman flirted with the idea of a trusteeship over Palestine and still contended with conflicting advice from pro-Zionist advisers and those who counseled caution. Perhaps the most dispassionate analysis was provided by George F. Kennan, the archetypal Cold Warrior and then the director of the Policy Planning Staff at the Department of State. In March 1948, he wrote a top-secret assessment of the direction of U.S. national security for the U.S. secretary of State and the undersecretary. He made the point that still stands today. He understood that "domestic pressures" were uniquely at work in shaping U.S. policy toward Palestine. However, American support for Zionism was strategically unnecessary. He worried that the United States would become militarily involved. He noted, as well, that the U.S. approach toward the rest of the region was driven "solely by national interest." He perceived, therefore, a basic contradiction, or what he called a "duality of purpose" that was dangerous but not necessarily catastrophic. If the United States decided—and Kennan recognized clearly that there was a U.S. decision to be taken—to antagonize the Arabs by taking a "leading part in the enforcement in Palestine of any arrangement opposed by the great majority of the inhabitants of the Middle Eastern area," then the United States had to accept the "implications of this act by revising our general policy in that part of the world."[69]

The waning days of the British mandate, meanwhile, saw a savage war erupt. Jewish, Muslim, and Christian civilians were routinely murdered during this first phase of war. The Zionist forces under Ben-Gurion's leadership, however, were far better organized, trained, equipped, and commanded than the Palestinian Arabs, who had no effective fighting force and whose military leadership, such as it was, had been decimated earlier by the British. That many Palestinians resisted an unjust partition is certain, and that they also killed in defense of their land is also beyond doubt. Arab nationalist and Muslim Brotherhood volunteers came from Syria, Iraq, and Egypt to defend their brethren. But they could not significantly alter the course of events. A long-planned operation, called Plan Dalet, to secure Jewish control over large swaths of mandatory Palestine was begun in March 1948. Entire towns and villages were soon systematically emptied of their Muslim and Christian populations by the Haganah and the Palmach, the precursors to the Israeli army.[70]

The evictions and dispossession were relentless, but they had an undeniable logic: In order to create a Jewish state, the non-Jews, or at least a substantial majority of them, had to go. In April, the Irgun militia struck again, aided by Haganah and the Palmach, this time committing what would turn out to be the most infamous, but by no means the only, massacre of the war. Its fighters slaughtered men, women, and children in the village of Dayr Yassin near Jerusalem. Palestinian resistance, such as it was, crumbled as fear and bewilderment gripped villagers and townsfolk. A historic defeat turned into a catastrophic rout. About a quarter of a million Palestinians were uprooted. All this happened *before* the state of Israel had even come into being—or more precisely, as a necessary prelude to its coming into being. The following month, on May 14, 1948, Ben-Gurion announced the birth of Israel. Within minutes, Truman became the first leader in the world to recognize the new state of Israel. Once again he set aside the remonstrations of his own most senior staff in the State Department and his own secretary of state, George Marshall. He had made his choice.

Peering at Palestine through the looking glass of the Holocaust, the West celebrated the birth of Israel as a vindication of its own deep morality; the Arabs recoiled in disgust, but they had little in the way of a joint military plan to prevent partition, let alone to decisively defeat the Zionist forces in Palestine. Arab states reluctantly entered the conflict in May 1948 to prevent the establishment of what they regarded as an illegal and colonial state. Save for Jordan's British-led Arab Legion, their armies were poorly equipped and poorly led. The exiled and largely discredited mufti of Jerusalem, Hajj Amin al-Husayni, claimed to lead the Palestinians, but he had no independent army to speak of; full of bombast but short of bombs, he hated King Abdullah, who despised him in return, and they both distrusted the Egyptians. The Saudis refused to cut their relations with the United States, the Iraqis wanted to fight but were far from the field of battle, and the Lebanese were closer but desperate not to fight. None of the Arab states had really wanted war. They had hoped that Britain or the United States would intervene to impose a solution they could accept or that somehow the Arab guerrilla forces operating in Palestine could defeat the Jews. In their media, they greatly underestimated the strength of the Zionists and vastly overestimated their own. The Zionist military defeated the Arab armies one by one. The expulsion of the remaining Palestinian civilian population, meanwhile, continued to its inevitable end. Nearly eight hundred thousand were made into stateless refugees.[71]

The Arabs were humiliated. To an extent—but only to an extent—they brought catastrophe upon themselves because they had held out for the principle of self-determination without actually knowing what to do when the principle was repeatedly trampled underfoot by Western powers. They had no plan B. Yet the joy in the United States over the creation of a Jewish state was accompanied by an almost perverse blindness to the wreckage of an Arab society entailed by the creation of Israel. Most Americans who cherished Israel refused to see that in upholding their professed values regarding the Jews of Europe they had simultaneously betrayed them regarding the Arabs of Palestine. The minority that remained in what had once been their country were placed under martial law. The majority, who had been uprooted and expelled during the fighting, were prevented by the victorious Israelis from returning once the war ended. Their properties were confiscated. Many of their homes were taken over by new Jewish immigrants, including Holocaust survivors. The new Jewish state then systematically razed hundreds of Arab villages.[72]

Chaim Weizmann referred to these tragic scenes as a "miraculous simplification of Israel's task."[73] The Arabs came to refer to it for what it was, a *nakba*, or a catastrophe. Jews also suffered grievously in the war, but as the victorious party, their losses were partly made up for by the magnitude of their victory. There was, at the end of the day, no Arab state in Palestine at all. Abdullah staked his claim to what would become known as the West Bank (of the Jordan River); the Egyptian army occupied the tiny strip of land around Gaza. The Jewish state took all the rest for itself, refusing, as it has continued to do until this day, to delineate its final borders.

In their disarray, the Arab states took on a defiant attitude. They refused to recognize the legitimacy of Israel because they viewed it as an alien and belligerent state in the heart of the Arab world. Denial, however, did not preclude recrimination, and there was plenty of that to go around. Arabs blamed Israel, they blamed each other, but above all they blamed Western imperialism. The question of Palestine would remain at the center of Arab concern, both as an embodiment of collective Arab failure and as a spur to Arab unification. Resisting, indeed reversing, Zionism became the mantra of modern anti-imperialist Arab politics—one passionately believed in by millions of Arabs and one also relentlessly exploited by a bevy of competing leaders who sought to seize the mantle of pan-Arab leadership while struggling to consolidate their grip on power at home. Through its championing of partition and its immediate recognition of a Jewish state, America had drawn first blood. The Arab reaction was not long in coming.

5

PICKING UP THE PIECES

Philip Hitti retired from Princeton in 1954. At a reception and dinner held in his honor at the Tower Hall Club in New York City in November, Hitti was surrounded by colleagues, members of the Arab diplomatic corps, delegates to the United Nations, alumni and trustees of the American University of Beirut—his alma mater—and representatives of several educational and philanthropic agencies working in the Middle East. They had gathered at the behest of the North American alumni of the American University of Beirut. The celebration was fitting. Hitti, after all, was a great scholar and by far the best-known Arab historian of his age. He was the author of several important works, including the translation of the chronicle by Usama ibn Munqith (an "Arab-Syrian gentleman and warrior in the period of the Crusades,"[1] as Hitti called him) and wide-ranging histories of Lebanon, Syria, and the Arabs. More fundamentally, as Hitti himself told the assembly of well-wishers that evening, he was a man shaped by his exposure to American missionaries in Lebanon. Hitti waxed nostalgic about his childhood. He spoke about his enrollment at the Syrian Protestant College and his emigration to and subsequent success in the United States. Hitti exuded erudition. He belonged by heritage to the Arab and Muslim world and by circumstance to America, "a world leader to which other nations look for moral, economic, and intellectual support."[2]

Hitti's pro-Americanism echoed the sentiments expressed that evening by Charles Malik, the Lebanese ambassador to the United States. Malik lavishly praised Hitti as the product of cross-cultural cooperation between Americans and Arabs. Hitti exemplified for Malik the fruition of a history of American missionary benevolence toward the region. The two men were friends and shared much in common. Like Hitti, Malik was a Christian from Lebanon; he had graduated from AUB; he had earned his doctorate at Harvard (in philosophy, after initially studying with Martin Heidegger); and he had achieved international recognition following his participation in the UN committee that produced the Universal Declaration of Human Rights. Malik had also distinguished himself in his eloquent defense of Arab Palestine in the UN debates leading up to partition. Like Hitti, Malik embraced America.

Yet both men surely knew that their evocation of a golden age of American-Arab relations was itself an idea under siege. Palestine had changed matters. Truman's decision to play a leading part in the creation of Israel decisively interrupted the cultural trajectory embodied in long-standing American missionary and educational work. Henceforth, U.S. government policies, especially on the Arab-Israeli conflict, created their own powerful trajectory. Given the controversial circumstances of its birth and its location in the heart of the Arab world, Israel inevitably acted as a disturbing presence in the relationship between Arabs and America.

The irony is that American support for Israel was not, in the first instance, driven by any obvious U.S. military or strategic concern with the Middle East. Quite the contrary. As we have seen, domestic American politics and a genuine concern about displaced Jews in Europe clearly motivated Truman to embrace Zionism and to provoke a rupture with the Arabs. In all likelihood, as the United States became more invested in the oil-rich region during the Cold War, the nature of American involvement would have changed regardless of Israel. Interests, after all, are not necessarily compatible with missionary work, and even this work was being challenged at the time by nationalists in the Arab world. But how this transformation of the U.S. role in the Middle East was to affect U.S.-Arab relations was inseparable from how the Arabs viewed America. And this perception had taken a dramatic turn for the worse.

Malik understood this all too well. In 1949 he had sent a lengthy confidential dispatch to his government analyzing the state of U.S.-Arab relations. He admitted that the corollary of American official and political support for Zionism was an American "denial" of the Arabs. He also believed that it was foolish to assume that American economic interests in the Middle East, particularly oil, would in any way counteract what he regarded as Jewish influence in America. Israel's success on the battlefield had allowed its American supporters to triumph in the domestic battle to shape America's foreign policy toward the region. The Arab world, indeed, had been revealed "in its weakness, its impotence, its confusion, and in the disarray of its ranks." Far from rallying the Arabs, Palestine had simply exposed their insignificance. The Americans knew that they could support Israel and still extract oil from the region. Their overriding strategic objective was not cultivating the goodwill of the Arab world, but maintaining their control over, and excluding the Soviets from, the oil fields of the Middle East. The United States could count on Turkey, Iran, and Israel as allies.[3]

Hitti, meanwhile, had taken a different tack at a forum organized in 1951 by the Middle East Institute, based in Washington, D.C. Wanting Americans to understand the implications of their U.S. policy decisions in the Middle East, he had pointed out "a striking contrast between the humanitarian ideas professed by Western missionaries, teachers, and preachers, and the disregard of human values by European and American politicians and warriors; a disparity between word and deed." Hitti referred, in part, to the violence of the Second World War, and especially to the nuclear holocaust that now threatened humanity, but he returned inevitably to the question of Palestine, which had done more than anything else "to disillusion the man of the Near East who has been trying to establish an intellectual rapprochement with the West. . . . The influence in the Near East of this middle-of-the-road man educated at American institutions has been impaired; he has lost face. One of the results has been a revivification of Pan-Islamism."[4]

But all was not yet lost. The American University of Beirut remained the preeminent university in the Middle East. American technology, including automobiles, refrigerators, radio, American science, and American institutions were still held in high regard across the Arab world. American films were as popular then as they are today. The Egyptian journalist Mohamed Heikal recalled that the "whole picture of the United States at that time was a glamorous one."[5] The 1950s was an era when a Cadillac seemed a grand symbol of progress. Parts of the Arab world, such as Morocco and Algeria, were far more preoccupied with the struggle against French colonialism than with Israel. They still hoped for U.S. support in their effort to gain independence and were, for reasons of geography, history, and political context, more insulated from the fallout of the Arab-Israeli conflict than were Lebanon, Jordan, Syria, and Egypt. The degree and expression of the disillusionment with the United States varied across the diverse Arab world. Most Arabs understood that their relationship with the United States hinged on more than simply Palestine.

Most visibly, the far-flung operations of the American oil company ARAMCO, including oil exploration, drilling, and pipeline construction, and ancillary projects undertaken by the engineering firm Bechtel, were helping to modernize Saudi Arabia through the building of hospitals, government ministries, roads, and airports. All this activity helped cement the reputation of the United States as a leading force for modern development. As if to underscore this point, in 1952 giant U.S. C-54 planes averted a crisis in Lebanon by flying thousands of stranded Muslim pilgrims to Saudi Arabia in an impressive display of American logistical planning, organizational ability, and efficiency. The crisis had begun on the eve of the hajj, when far more pilgrims showed up at Beirut Airport than could possibly be flown to Saudi Arabia. Lebanese authorities turned in desperation to the U.S. ambassador, who in turn promptly cabled his government to request assistance. Soon U.S. military transports from Germany, Libya, and France were ferrying 3,763 pilgrims, each with a box lunch in hand, from Beirut to Jeddah. For four days the U.S. pilots shuttled back and forth in an operation—dubbed the "airlift for Allah"—that demonstrated, or so the U.S. ambassador hoped, American goodwill toward the Arab world. The pilgrims, of course, were grateful, and so too were the embarrassed Lebanese officials. A *Time* magazine correspondent wrote at the time that "it would take a lot before Arabs would forgive the U.S. for its help to Israel," but he added hopefully, "Operation Magic Carpet might well be the beginning."[6]

Such optimism, however, was badly misplaced. The predominant intellectual current in the Arab world was nationalist, and it was against this current that the United States found itself swimming. A CIA report on Iraq from 1951 had noted, for example, a rapid transformation of "admiration" for the United States "as the one world power which would abide by the principles of right and justice" into a new view of it as the "most hypocritical of nations" because of U.S. support for Zionism.[7] Another intelligence report about Egypt in 1953 reiterated the same point. "Egyptians," it said, "do not regard the U.S. as a colonial power, but U.S. support of Israel has made them profoundly suspicious and resentful of U.S. policy in the area."[8] The shock of Israel's colonization of Arab lands went directly against the decolonizing spirit of the age. The United States no longer seemed radically different from older European colonial powers.

The anti-American street protests and the student riots following the partition of Palestine were directed primarily at the obvious symbols of foreign presence, such as American consulates, information centers, and educational institutions. Anger, however, was also directed inward. King Abdullah of Jordan, who had annexed the West Bank, was shot dead in 1951 by a Palestinian for collaborating with the Zionist movement. In Syria, several coups took place in the immediate aftermath of the Palestine war. At the same time, and in reaction to Zionism, Jewish communities in the Arab world found themselves objects of suspicion and were sometimes attacked. Abruptly, coexistence was cast into severe doubt. In

Egypt young officers returning from the failed Palestine campaign set in motion the wheel of a revolution that would reverberate across the Arab world. The Israelis, meanwhile, continued building their Jewish state, absorbing Jewish immigrants from around the world, yet subjecting the remnants of the native Palestinian population they had not expelled to harsh military rule.

The Arab states had reluctantly agreed to an armistice with Israel by 1949, but refused to extend it diplomatic recognition. Rather than active military confrontation, they instituted an economic and political boycott of Israel and of companies that invested directly in the Jewish state. But Arabs also searched for reasons for their collective defeat in Palestine. There was a nearly unanimous belief in the need for a fundamental revolution in Arab affairs as a prerequisite to dealing with Israel, but there was also intense disagreement on what this revolution should be: secular nationalist or Islamist, democratic or authoritarian, pro-Western or anti-Western?

No figure expressed Arab self-criticism better than Constantine Zurayk, who coined the term "the *nakba*" to refer not only to the loss of Palestine but to the calamity this loss portended for modern Arab identity. Zurayk was born in 1909 in Damascus. He belonged to the small world of Christian Arab intellectuals who dominated secular Arab nationalist thinking of this era. He too was a friend of Malik's and overlapped with him in a diplomatic posting in the United States. Whereas Malik was a philosopher convinced of the superiority of Western Christianity over Islam, Zurayk was a historian clearly marked by the Arab nationalist current sweeping the land. He was also more interested in educational work than in seeking the limelight of the international stage.

Having studied history at AUB thanks to a fortuitous meeting in Damascus with Philip Hitti, whom he impressed, Zurayk went on to the United States to pursue doctoral work. He was captivated by the American universities he visited, including Chicago and Princeton, from which he received his PhD in history under Hitti in 1930. Yet he was also taken aback by how many American Christians believed that the Jews had an intrinsic right to Palestine, yet knew little of the rights or history of the native Arab population of Palestine. Zurayk returned to AUB to take up a professorship, determined to participate in the building of a modern secular society. In December 1947, he spoke openly about what he saw as the media, financial, and political strength of Zionists in the United States that, he said, represented an "appalling danger" to Arab Palestine.[9] As the extent of the Arab defeat became clear in the fall of 1948, however, he despaired at the magnitude of the gap between the ideology of secular Arab nationalism and its realization.

In reaction, Zurayk wrote what would be recognized as a classic essay—part analysis and part exhortation—entitled *The Meaning of the Nakba.*[10] The thirty-nine-year-old Arab nationalist was less interested in condemning America (or Europe or the Soviet Union) for having had a role in facilitating the Zionist conquest of Palestine than in urging his fellow Arabs to understand the depth and nature of the defeat they had just suffered. He did not simply blame the West or America, nor by the same token did he simply castigate the Arabs.

Zurayk believed that the Arabs had to undergo a wholesale revolution in their internal affairs. The Zionists triumphed not because one people was superior to another, but because one system had distinguished itself from another. "The reason [for their triumph] lay in the roots of Zionism that are firmly established in modern Western life, whereas we, for the most part, remain distant from it, turning our back on it. The reason lies in that they live in the present and for the future, whereas we still dream the dreams of the past and stupefy ourselves in its bygone glory."[11]

Zurayk was as unsparingly severe as Malik had been in his diagnosis. He admitted that the Arabs lacked strategic thinking, mobilization, preparation, and national bonds that tied rulers to their people. In their current condition, they were unfit to partake in modern politics and thus simply reacted to events rather than shaping them. Zurayk pointed out that although brave and heroic Arab individuals had fought colonization in Palestine, the Arabs lacked modern institutions and organization. The Zionists, in contrast, were superbly organized and mobilized and could count on the support of Jews around the world. They had dreams and passions and resources and leaders who were able to make out of the radical diversity of the Jewish communities of the world and the babel of languages they spoke a singular state and a unified community.

In Zurayk's view, the Zionists had achieved the unnatural and improbable, in sharp contrast to the Arabs, who enjoyed the natural bonds of a common language, culture, and geography and yet had been unable to save Palestine or to unite. The Arabs needed to change the manner in which they related to the modern world. They needed to industrialize, to separate completely religion from politics, to have an enlightened and dynamic leadership, to build alliances with Latin America and Asia, and to turn toward objective and accurate scientific thought and away from what he regarded as "torpid imagination and vague and ruinous romanticism."[12]

Zurayk was clearly steeped in the assumptions of modernist Arab nationalism, and in this he diverged decisively from Malik, who had no faith in the efficacy of Arab resistance to Israel, feared that Arab nationalism could not be dissociated from Islam, and believed that a Christian-dominated Lebanon was destined to mediate between the West and the Muslim-majority Arab world. Indeed, Malik's enthusiasm for what he regarded as the genius and science of the West was counterbalanced by what he saw as the "irresponsible imagination" that he felt now threatened Asia. "The one new fact in the history of the East," he warned Western audiences, "is the awakening of the masses, whereby governments must—as never before—take into account the wishes of their people."[13]

Malik understood that the Arab states, which had been ill prepared for conflict in Palestine, had been pushed by their own people to do something for their Arab brethren. Yet in the aftermath of defeat, he worried that the prevailing deprivation, backwardness, and authoritarianism of Arab societies and governments prepared "fertile ground" for "anarchic" and extremist, impulsive, and ultimately doomed ideologies to overtake the Arab world. Having initially called for accountability and reformation, Malik, in his subsequent writings, took to shining a light on what he thought was the "socio-religious medievalism" that weighed heavily on the Arab world.[14] He became, in essence, a Cold Warrior. He represented Lebanon, but he appeared to fight America's cause in the Middle East. He imagined huge existential conflicts: East versus West, the Greco-Christian tradition versus Islam, the modern versus the medieval, the spiritual versus the atheistic, freedom versus communism. Malik's philosophical speculations were crude and tainted by Christian chauvinism, but having been confronted with apparently insuperable Western hegemony and what he saw as a fearful rise of Soviet Communism, he decided there was only one rational, acceptable path for Arabs to pursue. Rather than fight the West, the Arabs had to ally with it.

Zurayk thought differently. He refused to concede, as Malik apparently did, that reform and self-criticism went hand in hand with the abandonment of Palestine. He insisted that there could be no compromise with Zionism, for he saw that it had delivered a massive blow to the very idea of a unified, secular, modern Arab nation that could overcome sectarianism, tribalism, and imperialism. The liberation of Palestine remained for him a "sacred jihad," although his use of the term reflected not a religious orientation but rather a secular national struggle incumbent upon all believers in the Arab nation.[15] Zurayk recalled the figure of Butrus al-Bustani, the nineteenth-century avatar of Arab secularism who had worked intimately with American missionaries, but between them lay not only the wreckage of the Ottoman Empire, two world wars, and the loss of Palestine, but also the emergence of the United States as a decisive power in the Middle East. Zurayk therefore had few illusions left about America's enlightened role in the Middle East. He admired America for its science and education, its culture in broad terms, its government, its democracy, economy, and power, and yet he was repulsed at its policies toward the Arabs. It was a contradiction that was soon to grow into a chasm.

Zurayk was one of Hitti's "middle-of-the-road" men—liberal and secular Arabs who admired Western science and many facets of the United States. As individual Arabs, they had made enormous strides in learning about and understanding American society; they sincerely believed that they could serve as a bridge between cultures. And yet they were repeatedly rebuffed on the central Arab question of their day.

The contradiction between a liberal Arab faith in America and its antithesis represented by U.S. policy on Palestine was pounced upon by other Arabs who were far less enamored of the West. One of these was Sayyid Qutb, an Egyptian Muslim who shared none of Hitti's or Zurayk's indoctrination into American missionary institutions but who, like them, was remade in the aftermath of Palestine.

Sayyid Qutb was born three years before Zurayk and a world away from Damascus. He came from a small village a couple hundred miles south of Cairo. Qutb was a pious Muslim raised in the fervently nationalist atmosphere of interwar Egypt, an era when the British dominated a subservient monarchy, and their presence inspired a raging debate within Egypt about the nature of its people and society. Secularists, Islamists, nationalists, Communists, and monarchists battled with one another to mold Egypt after their specific ideology. Qutb was inevitably influenced by this ferment. At first, he tried his hand at poetry and literary criticism in Cairo; eventually he became a teacher of Arabic in government schools. Although he admired facets of Western literature and music and recognized Western superiority in science, he also worried about, and was increasingly consumed by, the damage to Egyptian society caused by the alleged wholesale adoption of Western culture. Qutb therefore denounced what he considered immoral and vulgar radio songs and cinema; he lashed out in particular at what he insisted was the loose nature of Westernized Egyptian women. Qutb was a self-righteous moralizer. He saw no contradiction between his attack on feudalism and imperialism in Egypt and his defense of patriarchy.

His criticism of the West sharpened as events around him spiraled toward a final confrontation between the British and the nationalists. Like most of his compatriots, Qutb felt humiliated when he heard that British tanks had surrounded the king's palace in 1942, and that the British ambassador had marched into the king's chamber to demand a change of the Egyptian government. He grew disenchanted with Arab politicians who were unable to confront their oppressors and disgusted by the inequality that permeated Egyptian society, in which "feudalism and serfdom" ensnared millions of his countrymen in a web of poverty and degradation.[16] Although the Communist Party in Egypt was prohibited, Qutb perceived the growing allure of leftist ideas among a generation of Arab intellectuals and trade unionists. He rejected, however, communism as an alternative to Western capitalism. Arguing that both systems were devoted to a ruinous materialism, he instead advocated a return to the precepts of the Koran to ensure justice and produce a truly legitimate government. Qutb wrote that in the great struggle between East and West, Islam alone offered a comprehensive and universal way forward, for it provided a social system that satisfied both the heart and the mind, both faith and intellect.

As he contemplated the state of the Muslim world, Qutb developed a consciousness of what he regarded as Western persecution of Muslims. Inevitably, this consciousness grew to encompass the United States because of its role in Palestine in 1947. Qutb expressed bitter disillusionment with America. "How I hate and despise those Westerners! All without exception: the British, the French, the Dutch and now the Americans who were at one time trusted by many. . . . And I do not hate or despise these alone. I hate and despise just as much those Egyptians and Arabs who continue to trust Western conscience."[17] Fundamentally, Qutb's outrage at Western hypocrisy and imperialism stemmed from a common sense of violation shared by fellow Arabs such as Zurayk, Hitti, and George Antonius. He perceived the same problem of injustice in Palestine that they had perceived. His reaction to injustice, however, categorically rejected their secular outlook. His defensiveness tarnished Westernized Arabs of all faiths with the charge of cultural treachery, just as the Maronite patriarch had condemned the first Arab convert to American Protestantism a century and a half earlier. Qutb's insistence on Muslim cultural and religious superiority exposed a fault line in modern Arab nationalism. Zurayk's answer to Arab defeat was complete secularism; Qutb's was total Islamicization.

A brief sojourn to the United States between 1948 and 1950 to learn about U.S. educational methods added little nuance to Qutb's harsh views. As he walked through the streets of New York and then in the rural community of Greeley, Colorado, Qutb was astonished at America's vastness, its technology, and its organization, but equally appalled by

American mores. He felt alienated by his exposure to unfamiliar customs—dating, dancing, and a consumerism that had no equivalent in Egypt. "How much do I need someone to talk to about topics other than money, movie stars, and car models," he wrote to the playwright Tawfiq al-Hakim.[18] In his alienation, the Egyptian fell back upon well-worn Arab stereotypes about the materialism of America and its lack of spirituality, but infused them with the urgency of an existential struggle that he believed defined Islam's antagonistic relationship to the West.

In an account entitled "The America I Have Seen," which he published upon his return to Egypt in 1950, Qutb declared war on Arab infatuation with America. He recognized that the nearly universal political opposition to U.S. policy on Palestine did not necessarily reduce the attraction of American cultural or educational models across the Arab world. Qutb conceded that America "has a principal role in this world, in the realm of practical matters and scientific research." He even extolled "American genius" in all that required "mind power and muscle." But he condemned American sexual and cultural "primitiveness" and emphasized the racism in American society. He commented on how Anglo-Saxons had enslaved blacks and oppressed Mexicans and pushed them out of their own lands; Malik, Zurayk, and Hitti never addressed this subject. The more Qutb saw of America the more he expressed his shock at how "the strange illusion that Americans love peace took root in the world, especially in the East."[19]

Qutb spurned the possibility of a middle ground between Americans and Arabs—indeed, he rejected a middle ground among Arabs themselves. He called instead for a radical rupture with the West, as well as with secularists, and sought shelter in a mythic world of Islamic purity. What was novel and dangerous about Qutb's condemnation of America was its encompassing and unforgiving nature. Disillusionment with American policy was widespread in this period, but it had not suggested hatred of America. If anything, it reflected Arab anger at the gap that separated American rhetoric from American action. Qutb was different. He did not expect that the Americans would close the gap, and he scorned those who still believed that they might ever do so.

Like Malik, Qutb acknowledged an American political hostility to Arabs, but he interpreted this hostility in a very different way. Malik clung to his belief that as individuals Americans were characterized by "a love of peace, justice, respect of the individual and of others."[20] He distinguished between the tiny minority of urbanized American Jews who, in his estimation, exerted an extraordinary influence on American policy regarding the Arab-Israeli conflict, on the one hand, and on the other hand, the vast majority of America's population in the country's heartland, who he insisted were simple, upstanding, and good. Malik's ambivalence toward American Jews—in his mind they were brilliant, motivated, organized, industrious, Western, and yet at the same time domineering, manipulative, and not genuine Americans—was mirrored by his romanticization of America's majority-Christian population and their values. It was a view that took some truths, stripped them of all their complexities and contradictions, and then venerated them as the pure essence of national character. Qutb did the same, but rather than venerate the American national character, he demonized it.

The irony is that neither view of the Arab world or America could compete at the time with that put forward by a young Egyptian who would soon capture the imagination of the Arab world. Gamal Abdel Nasser was part of a group of army officers who overthrew the Egyptian monarchy in July 1952. Within three years, Nasser had emerged as the undisputed leader of these officers. He was a revolutionary who believed that he had his finger on the true pulse of the Arab world. He understood that Arabs, in general, were neither romantically pro-American like Malik nor vehemently anti-American like Qutb. They wanted the same things that Americans wanted, but had to contend with a legacy of colonial domination. The son of a postal clerk from upper Egypt, tall, handsome, deeply charismatic, and apparently incorruptible, Nasser appeared to be a leader who would finally be able to restore dignity to the peoples of the Arab world.

The Egyptian revolution was principally a revolt against the old colonial order and its compromised native auxiliaries. Britain had invaded and occupied Egypt in 1882; it had declared Egypt nominally independent in 1922 but continued to control the nation's affairs. The stigma of defeat at the hands of the Zionist forces and the evidence it provided of both incompetence and indifference at the highest levels of the Egyptian government convinced the self-styled "Free Officers" of the need to depose the corpulent King Faruq. In the months preceding the revolution, nationalists and Islamists battled British troops in the Suez Canal Zone. Gradually, the British began to relent, but they insisted on maintaining their military and commercial control of the Suez Canal. Egyptians wanted them out, however, and the Muslim Brotherhood took the lead in trying to pressure the British to leave, although they conducted nowhere nearly as violent or as successful an anti-British campaign as had Zionist groups in mandatory Palestine.

Following a British massacre of Egyptian police in the city of Ismailiyya in January 1952, an astonishingly intense bout of rioting devastated Cairo the next day. On "Black Saturday," mobs burned several hundred shops, cinemas, hotels, airline offices, restaurants, bars, and department stores associated with foreigners, including some of the main symbols of the hated British presence in the country as well as the Ford Motor Company and TWA offices. Six months after the rioting, the officers seized power.

Nasser recognized what Malik, Zurayk, and Qutb had all identified before him: The Arab world was in desperate need of reform. The overthrow of the Egyptian monarchy was only one expression of this need. But Nasser also understood that the people of the region craved bold leadership. He was eager to supply it uncontested. His revolution signaled the end of Egyptian parliamentary democracy, such as it was. Nasser banned political parties, censored the press, and cracked down on both the Communists and the Muslim Brothers. He placed General Muhammad Naguib, the nominal leader of the Free Officers, under house arrest. Under Nasser's watch, Qutb was jailed, tortured, and eventually hanged in 1966 after a summary trial. The Muslim Brotherhood attempted to assassinate Nasser in 1954; he, in turn, described the organization and its followers as reactionary and out of touch with the nationalist spirit of the age. He said that the Communists were simply Soviet tools, and he pointed out that the imperialists were still a present danger. Although the last British soldiers finally evacuated the Suez Canal Zone in June 1956, Israel constantly threatened Egyptian troops in Gaza. As Nasser consolidated his power, eliminated rivals, and positioned himself as the sole voice of his people and eventually of the Arabs as a whole, he made it clear that he had little faith in his compatriots. Democracy was not an Egyptian priority; strengthening the army was.

Nasser's regime, to be sure, had huge ambitions and several important accomplishments. It exiled the king, turned Egypt into a republic, however flawed, and redistributed land from the vastly wealthy landowners to the desperately poor peasants. Although Nasser was first and foremost an Egyptian leader, across the Arab world followers of rival secular nationalist pan-Arabist movements recognized Nasser's rising star. Among them was the Baath (renaissance) Party, which had been founded by a Damascene Christian, Michel Aflaq, in the 1940s and was particularly active in Syria and Iraq. King Saud, the Saudi ruler who succeeded his father, Ibn Saud, in 1953, and the Hashemite kings of Jordan and Iraq, who represented the conservative axis of the Arab world, also contended with the emergence of Nasser.

The revolution in July 1952 came at a crucial moment in U.S.-Arab relations. At the outset, Nasser believed that it was still possible to build constructive relations between the Arabs and America. Some of Nasser's fellow officers remained wary of American motives, but they acquiesced in his reaching out to the Americans. The incoming Eisenhower administration was initially supportive of the revolution. Khaled Mohi El Din, a member of the Revolutionary Command Council that ran Egypt, recalled that despite his own suspicion of American motives, the "United States . . . a big power, was making approaches and was not hostile, but indeed expressed signs of possibly assisting us."[21]

Both the U.S. and Egyptian governments understood that the British hold over Egypt was broken; both believed themselves to be anticolonial; both were anti-Communist; and neither believed deeply in democracy for Arabs—the Americans because they found it easier to deal with strongmen than an entire people, and Nasser because he believed that he embodied the destiny of his people. Nasser and the Free Officers therefore established cordial relations with U.S. representatives in Cairo. They sought military aid and diplomatic support that hastened the British exit from the Suez Canal. The widespread disillusionment with America's support for Israel notwithstanding, Nasser understood full well that most of his people, and most Arabs, could and did distinguish between American politics and American culture and were unwilling to go down the path of cultural isolation and chauvinism that Qutb advocated. Nasser admired facets of American history; indeed, it seemed as if the Egyptians had taken a leaf out of America's book by fighting the British.

America was not Britain, and Britain in any case was not the empire it had once been. Egypt, above all, wanted to cut itself off from British imperialism; it wanted to modernize and to deal quickly with the problem of its surging, largely rural population of 20 million in 1952. This was Nasser's point of departure for casting his regime's aspirations in terms that he hoped Americans could understand. In his one meeting with Secretary of State John Foster Dulles at the American embassy in Cairo on May 11, 1953, over a meal of soup, sole, and lamb, Nasser sought to convince Dulles, who had pressed the Egyptian leader to join an anti-Soviet alliance, that Egypt's problem was not communism but imperialism. There was, after all, no Arab predisposition in favor of the Soviet Union, which had itself rushed to recognize Israel in 1948. Soviet credibility rose in relation to how the Americans compromised their own standing. The appeal of Marxism rested on its ability to graft itself onto a much wider nationalist sentiment among Arabs and a demand among them for liberation from Western colonialism. Egypt needed weapons to defend itself against real enemies, not against the Communists of Washington's imagination. The Americans, however, refused to supply Nasser with heavy weaponry and were more interested in assuming Britain's leading role in the region (where it could not be preserved) than in allowing the Arabs to slip away from the Western grasp. This was a crucial and, in the event, critical divergence.

Nasser, however, persevered. In a lengthy article published in the prestigious policy journal *Foreign Affairs* in 1955, Nasser sought to justify his regime and educate Americans about Egypt's history and about the weight of British imperialism in his country. He said the revolution had removed an effete, corrupt monarchy and given the Egyptian people a "new deal." This new era would rest upon the building of the Aswan Dam, the massive hydroelectric project that promised to provide tremendous increases in electricity production and irrigation for millions of Egyptians, as well as much-needed flood control when the great Nile River periodically overflowed its banks.

For Nasser, U.S. aid was crucially important to Egypt. Although the Americans were considering financing the Aswan Dam, Nasser wanted immediate movement. He complained in one press conference of the "chicken aid" he had received from America, a sardonic reference to a poultry improvement program set up by American officials.[22] But equally important as substantial economic and military assistance for Nasser was U.S. acceptance of the region on its own terms. He refused, for example, to join the anti-Communist Baghdad Pact, which aligned royalist Iraq, Turkey, and Pakistan with Great Britain and the United States. "The defense of the Middle East must rest primarily with the inhabitants of the area," Nasser warned, and this in turn meant understanding that, in the Arab view, Israel, not communism, was the principal foreign threat Egypt faced.

"Egyptians feel," pleaded Nasser to the Americans, "that a great injustice was committed against the Arabs generally, and especially against the million or more Palestinian Arabs who are now refugees. Israel's policy is aggressive and expansionist, and Israel will continue her attempts to prevent any strengthening of the area."[23]

Egypt's leader threw down a challenge to the great power of the age. "Free men," he wrote, "are the most fanatical defenders of their liberty, nor do they lightly forget those who have championed their struggle for independence." It was a presumptuous declaration made for American consumption, but it also served as a public notice of Egyptian intentions.

Although the British had been, until their withdrawal from the Suez Canal Zone, Nasser's primary military concern, Israel proved itself by far his most dangerous and implacable adversary. In the summer of 1954, Israeli military intelligence and Egyptian Jewish agents initiated a bombing campaign targeting United States Information Agency (USIA) libraries in Alexandria and Cairo, as well as cinemas, a railway terminal, and the central post office in Cairo. Their goal was to disrupt U.S.-Egyptian relations. The spy ring was quickly caught, two of its agents were executed, and the rest were imprisoned. The so-called Lavon Affair, named after the Polish-born Israeli minister of defense, Pinhas Lavon, backfired.

Undeterred, Ben-Gurion, who had come out of retirement as a result of the Lavon Affair, ordered Israeli forces to stage a massive raid on Gaza in February 1955. The raid was led by a ruthless officer who had already distinguished himself in fighting Arabs—Ariel Sharon, Israel's version of Andrew Jackson. In this one episode, he left thirty-seven Egyptian soldiers dead and thirty more wounded. Eight Israelis also died in the raid, and nine were wounded.[24] Israelis claimed that they had operated out of self-defense and in retaliation for Palestinian attacks facilitated by Egyptian intelligence. On constant edge because they lived on land forcibly cleared of Arabs, who nevertheless still surrounded them, the Israelis existed in a state of acute paradox: They were extremely aggressive toward Arabs, and yet they believed themselves to be existentially vulnerable. They never tired of pointing out that the Arabs rejected them, but they also never tired of evading, obfuscating, and denying the obvious reasons why the Arabs rejected them. Their leaders knew full well that they had implanted themselves by force in mandatory Palestine, at first under the protection of British bayonets and subsequently using their own arms. Their Zionism was justified in their minds, and legalized by the Western-dominated UN of 1948, but it was through violence that they had thus far survived. Their outlook was shaped, moreover, by a long history of Western anti-Semitism and, of course, by the Nazi genocide of the Jews. Israelis were understandably adamant about their security, although it was not against the West as a whole or Germany as a nation that they vented their outrage, but against Arabs in general, and Palestinians in particular.

The scale of the Gaza assault and the Egyptian death toll, in any event, humiliated Nasser. It exposed his military impotence and, in Ben-Gurion's mind, affirmed Israel's superiority over the Arabs. Nasser turned to the Americans once more, hoping to secure weapons with which to defend Egypt from his enemy. In his escalating confrontation with Israel, however, Nasser walked a fine line. He understood that Palestine was one of the touchstones of the Arab world. He also clearly understood Arab internal divisions and military weakness regarding Israel. He had witnessed firsthand the disastrous state of affairs during the 1948 war when, as a young officer, he had to contend with defective ammunition and the tenacity of the Zionist forces. Nasser therefore followed in a pattern of Arab leadership that alternately believed in and exploited the metaphor of Palestine and proclaimed the ideal of Arab unity but acted on the assumption of Arab disunity.

Nasser had been approached by Dulles and several other American intermediaries about the possibility of making peace with Israel. Nasser indicated that he was not averse to a comprehensive, just settlement of the conflict. In the face of the ideological and political nationalist currents of defiance, denial, and anger that had seized the Arab world, the idea of peace with what Arabs regarded as the usurping state was heretical. Given the Israeli commitment to an aggressive "iron wall" strategy—forcing the Arabs, and the Palestinians in particular, to accept the finality of their defeat in 1948 as a prerequisite to any final settlement—the idea of seeking peace with Israel was also fraught with obvious dangers. Before any peace could be contemplated, Nasser had to be assured that the United States, as Israel's principal political patron, was willing to restrain Ben-Gurion; that it was going to restore rights to the Palestinians; and most urgently from his perspective, that it was going to provide Egypt with the means to defend itself. The ball, he felt, was very much in America's court.

The U.S. policy establishment was not sentimental about Israel. In the wake of 1948, American officials were fully aware of Arab alienation from the United States because of its support for the creation of Israel at the expense of the Palestinians—dispatches from U.S. embassies in the Middle East, national intelligence estimates, and national security documents consistently pointed this out. President Dwight D. Eisenhower did not ignore the Arabs so much as view them through the lens of the Cold War. Like every postwar U.S. president, he coveted control over the Middle East's vast oil reserves and therefore required Arab acquiescence, but his administration also plainly accepted what it confidentially assessed to be the "preponderance of Israel's military strength."[25] The region was an important piece in an elaborate global game played against both Soviet communism and the so-called radical Asian, African, and Latin American nationalism that threatened to redirect the unequal flows of resources that made the United States a superpower. Although Americans viewed it as regrettable that Palestinians had suffered because of Israel's creation, there was very little to be done for them beyond providing humanitarian assistance and pressing both the Arab states and Israel to reach some sort of compromise.

The United States had indeed voted in December 1948 in favor of UN Resolution 194, which legitimated the right of Palestinians to return to their homes and properties or, if they were so inclined, to seek compensation. It was also the major funder of the United Nations Relief and Works Agency (UNRWA), which cared for Palestinian refugees. From the outset, however, the Americans took the view that, whatever the letter of the law, to allow total repatriation was unrealistic. They urged Israel instead to take a limited number of refugees back, but mostly the United States pressed the Arab states to resettle the majority in their own countries. The U.S. Congress even appropriated several hundred million dollars for this purpose. Some Arab leaders were willing to consider the idea, including the Syrian dictators Husni al-Za'im and Adib Shishakli, each of whom had come to power in successive military coups that took place in the immediate aftermath of the Palestine debacle. Both men contemplated settling hundreds of thousands of Palestinians on their land in return for major infusions of U.S. aid.[26]

Eisenhower was convinced that a more evenhanded approach to the region than Truman's would dampen anti-Americanism and weaken the allure of the Soviets. Oil, not Israel, was for him America's priority in the region. His administration was solution-oriented; it envisaged and planned major water-sharing plans between Israel and the neighboring Arab states of Lebanon, Jordan, and Syria without fully appreciating that the idea of Israel remained anathema to most Arabs; it also underestimated how resistant Israel was to making any major territorial concessions, let alone taking back the Palestinians it had forced out in 1948.

A series of secret negotiations, proposals, and plans were nevertheless drawn up in Washington. The British actually took the lead with the most comprehensive of these, the so-called Project Alpha. The proposed deal failed, but it elaborated a quid pro quo that would become the basis of all further U.S. peacemaking activity: Arabs were to recognize Israel, which, in turn, would relinquish territory. The actual plan expected that Israel would limit its expansionism and even concede territory in the south to Egypt. According to Mohamed Heikal, Nasser's close confidant, Americans were absorbed in technical details such as building overpasses and underpasses to give Israelis and Egyptians separate roads to traverse. A bemused Nasser quipped: What would happen if an Arab on the overpass decided to answer a call of nature and accidentally urinated on an Israeli using the underpass? Heikal noted that Nasser subsequently irreverently referred to this as the "pee-pee discussion," but Nasser's substantial point was that Americans fundamentally misjudged the mood of the Arab world and thus deluded themselves about the prospects for peace between Arabs and Israel.[27] Alpha, in fact, assumed that the bulk of Palestinians would not be repatriated, but compensated. This plan was hardly in keeping with UN Resolution 194, but then again, the military reality stood clearly in Israel's favor. As far as the U.S. government was concerned, the Arabs had lost the decisive war of 1948, and Israel was here to stay.

The major Arab states understood full well the reality of their military defeat, but were bound by the public sentiment in their own countries that refused to submit again to Western imperialism so soon after achieving independence from their European masters. The cumulative wounds of colonialism and Zionism were far too deep for the Arabs to embark on any reconciliation with their unrepentant enemy, and the tide of nationalism was also too strong for any Arab leader to contemplate swimming against it. The Algerian war for liberation added to the conviction among Arabs that all forms of colonialism in the Middle East and North Africa were bound to fail.

The Arab leaders of Lebanon, Jordan, Syria, and Egypt were adamant that their resources were too meager to divert to the refugees; they also said that the situation of Palestinian refugees constituted not simply an economic and humanitarian crisis but a political problem. Israel had driven these people out; the legal and moral solution was therefore to allow the refugees to return to their homes. Israel, predictably, dismissed this option out of hand. The Arabs, it said, had rejected the UN partition plan of 1947; therefore, they alone were to blame for the plight of the refugees.

In the event, Jordan annexed the West Bank and granted Jordanian citizenship to the Palestinians there in the aftermath of the *nakba.* Every other Arab state refused to grant refugees citizenship in their country. The refugees themselves held on to their right of return, while slowly accommodating themselves to the new, harsh reality of their statelessness. The Palestinians would remain the collateral damage of Arab pride and principle just as they were the direct victims of Israeli colonialism.

In the early 1950s, the morass of the Korean War, China's embrace of communism, Soviet nuclear weapons, and the specter of "anti-American" communist activities within the United States conjured up by Wisconsin senator Joseph McCarthy preoccupied Americans far more than the distant troubles of the Middle East. The picture of cruel Islam, which had been the focus of so much of the animus of American missionaries in the Middle East throughout the nineteenth century, while still extant, appeared to have faded in intensity along with the missionary age that had done so much to propagate it. The anti-Turkish and pro-Armenian crusade of World War I had long since run its course. For most Americans of this era, the Arabs were not their bogeymen.

The American champions of Israel, both Jewish and Christian, however, laid the basis for a potent political equation that yoked American standing in the region to Israel. They spoke of the Jewish state in terms of a Western history of the persecution of the Jews. Mostly, however, they celebrated what they regarded as modern miracle work in a desolate landscape, very much as Americans of the era talked about the American conquest of the savage frontier. In the Maghreb, as in ARAMCO's Arabia, one set of Americans were filled with expectations about adventure in the timeless Arabian desert landscapes and encounters with supposedly primitive Arabs. In Palestine, now Israel, however, another set of Americans justified their disappearance.

Eleanor Roosevelt, for example, believed passionately in Israel.[28] Her belief stemmed from her own intense liberalism, her grappling with American anti-Semitism, her friendship with several Jewish individuals who introduced her to the idea of Zionism, and, above all, her revulsion at the German persecution of European Jews. Yet her belief in the justice of Israel's creation ultimately could be sustained only by overlooking the wreckage of Arab humanity left in its aftermath. When approached by a Palestinian woman by the name of Wadad Dabbagh with an account of the Arab displacement at the heart of the events of 1948, Eleanor Roosevelt rationalized Palestinian suffering as the inevitable, and therefore justified, consequence of the Arab rejection of Israel. She confessed that she was sorry about Arab suffering, but felt that the blame rested entirely with them; their "warlike attitude" had brought catastrophe upon themselves. When Dabbagh persisted in pleading for a fair hearing about the *nakba*, the former first lady wrote back curtly that "I regret there is nothing I can do to help in the situation about which you write."[29] She warned Truman that the Arabs, whom she viewed as backward, emotional, illogical, nomadic, and lacking in spirit or purpose, had to be "handled with strength."[30]

Leon Uris also refused to countenance the Arab viewpoint on Palestine. He was a young American Jewish writer and a former marine who decamped to Israel for two years in the early 1950s. Uris had been commissioned to write a story that would improve Israel's image in the United States. Faithful to his task, the novelist traveled across the new state, absorbing Zionist perspectives and understandings so thoroughly that his 1958 novel, *Exodus*, captured the imagination of an entire generation of Americans who came to identify with the new state. *Exodus* narrated the founding of Israel from a romantic, unapologetic Zionist perspective; its title was a reference to the former U.S. navy ship that was carrying Jewish refugees to Palestine in 1947 in open defiance of British mandatory authorities. The ensuing standoff over the refugees' fate constituted a major triumph for the Zionists, who were able to portray the struggle over Palestine decisively in their terms. The battle that Uris described was not therefore one of Arabs fighting their colonizers, but one of heroic and long-persecuted Zionist Jews, led by Ari Ben Canaan (played by the dashing Paul Newman in the blockbuster movie version of the novel), fighting for their homeland against the unprincipled, callous, and anti-Jewish British. The Holocaust loomed large over the entire story, whose principal witness was an American nurse who falls in love with Ben Canaan and joins the Zionist cause.

Far more stridently than had Eleanor Roosevelt, Uris dehumanized the Arabs. The novel's Palestinians, for instance, mutilate the bodies of Jews and laugh about it; they indulge in "primitive brutalities"; they are "thugs . . . slithering along the ground with knives between their teeth"; but they are also indecisive, cowardly, cringing, and ultimately no match for modern, manly Jews. As Uris portrayed them, Arabs were medieval in their beliefs, fanatical, ignorant, lustful, filthy, and greedy. Their leaders were deeply sinister, for they expressed an atavistic hatred of the Jews similar to that of the Nazis. Uris's depiction of the UN partition debate was memorable for the manner in which the "white-robed Arab screamed out against partition in a hate-filled voice."[31]

The overt racism of the book did not prevent it from becoming an extraordinary best-seller—an event in and of itself that set the stage for the movie version in 1960, which further erased the Arabs as a meaningful presence in the story of the founding of Israel. The irony was that Uris, and presumably the many Americans who derived their knowledge of the Arab-Israeli conflict from reading his book or watching the movie, readily accepted a portrayal of one of the great turning points in modern Arab history in which Arab humanity and history were thoroughly effaced. In this portrayal, the Palestinians were not victims of Zionist conquest, and they were not driven from their homes and lands. Instead, they were themselves the victimizers of Jews—or at best, the dupes of what Uris described as their malicious and deceitful "racist" leaders who "had implanted the idea of mass murder in their minds."[32] Just as Roosevelt had contended, Uris repeated the Zionist mantra that the Arabs had only themselves to blame.

The Arabs, it is true, had always resisted the notion that they should pay the price for German persecution of the Jews. It was also true that in the aftermath of defeat, a sharp increase in anti-Jewish prejudice and the circulation of Western anti-Semitic literature became one symptom of an overarching Arab rejection of Israel. Because they perceived how Israel's creation had been justified by the Holocaust, they reacted by either minimizing its significance or, more commonly, drawing direct parallels between what occurred to the Jews in Europe and what occurred to the Arabs of Palestine. More directly, Jews in Iraq and Yemen especially were discriminated against and generally scapegoated as a result of Zionism and the creation of Israel. But the European genocide that Arabs sometimes denied, no matter how crudely or how deplorably, was not of their own doing. American, European, and Israeli Zionists, by contrast, denied what was directly Israel's doing, and to cover up Israel's culpability for the massacres, evictions, and mass expropriation of hundreds of thousands of Palestinians, they resorted to a ceaseless propaganda campaign that transformed the natives of the land into the would-be destroyers of an epic, beautiful, historic tale of Jewish self-determination.

The cycle of denial was therefore mutual, but it was hardly commensurable. On the Lebanese coast an hour and a half north of Beirut, in one of the schools in a makeshift camp of seven thousand refugees run by UNRWA, set up in 1949 to care for the Palestinians who had fled or been evicted from their homes, maps of Palestine were hung. "We shall never forget Palestine" and "The Holy Land, which was lost cheaply, will not be restored without bloodshed of a new generation" were among the slogans that kept the memory of an extinguished country alive.[33] In distant America, a world removed from this pathetic, if defiant, reality, sat Uris, an American who had never been to the Arab world but who self-righteously indicted the Arabs because they had stood in the way of, and still actively resisted, Zionism.

The significance of Uris's story rested ultimately in its total reversal of cause and effect and in the upwelling indignation—moral outrage even—directed at Arabs. Quite simply, Uris equated their rejection of Zionism with another bout of historic Jew hatred. *Exodus* framed the Arabs for an entire generation of Americans who came to identify with Israeli Jews as "fighting people" (as Uris put it in the foreword to the second printing of the novel). Most tragically, this form of American Zionism demonized Arabs in order to rationalize a love of Israel. To oppose Israel was to be ipso facto an anti-Semite and therefore to stand outside of the fold of modern post-Holocaust Western civilization.

Uris was by no means alone in caricaturing Arabs. Inevitably, he drew on stereotypes of the primitive Arabs that existed in America, many of which had nothing to do with Zionism and long predated the struggle over Palestine. But the implication of his characterization of the conflict was clear: American Zionism sought to shore up support for Israel in the United States by making the Arabs enemies, not simply of Jewish Israelis, but of America and the West as a whole. The manufacture of a new language of a clash of civilizations was well under way—this time not between American missionary Protestantism and "Mohammedanism," or between freedom and communism, but between "Judeo-Christian" civilization, embodied by both Israel and the United States, and its fanatical Arab antithesis.

But there were also those Americans who knew something about Arabs, who lived among them, who interacted with them professionally, if not always socially, and who, despite their own prejudices, may well have recoiled at the depiction of Arabs in *Exodus*.

The romantic spirit of Lowell Thomas's "Lawrence of Arabia" mythology was evident in the story of ARAMCO's modernization of Saudi Arabia, except that now the narrative was centered less on any single Arabized agent of Western empire, and more on the dramatic person of Ibn Saud. Titles such as *Arabia Reborn* by George Kheirallah offered a typically panegyric view of Ibn Saud as a brave desert warrior who sought to develop his country by entrusting its modernization to pioneering American oilmen.

The oil company itself enthusiastically played its part in this tale of what it described as the "great proving ground for the ability of people of widely different cultures and backgrounds, of different personal and national allegiances, to work together harmoniously in projects of great mutual advantage."[34] When ARAMCO hosted a lavish dinner for Crown Prince Saud at the Waldorf Astoria in New York in January 1947, Saud and American executives, government officials, and publicists sat around a massive table complete with a model New England village in wintertime, a Texaco filling station, and an electric train whose controls were located at Saud's plate. ARAMCO went on to publish opulent volumes that expounded the story of Arabian nobility (and need) partnered with American ingenuity. The features of Wahabism that would so alarm Americans decades later appeared at this stage to be far more benign—a "return to a strict and simple message of the Koran and the teachings of the Prophet Muhammad," ARAMCO's handbook for its American employees advised.[35]

Knowledge of one group of Arabs continued to mix with paternalism, just as it had in the bygone missionary age. Saudis and other Arabs were described as politically and culturally immature, as "harping" (again according to the ARAMCO handbook) on past grievances, and also as "impatient" with the rate of progress natural to a people in their circumstances and with their abilities. But whether oilmen, former missionaries, diplomats, or educators, Americans with any experience of real Arabs—as opposed to the fanatic creatures of Leon Uris's imagination—tended to be sympathetic to the Arab viewpoint on Palestine. ARAMCO, for example, informed its employees straightforwardly that "current problems in the Middle East cannot be understood without a comprehension of how strongly the Arabs feel on this issue." It added that "the West's apparent indifference to the Arab viewpoint and to the plight of a million or so Arab refugees displaced from their homes in Palestine has been both disillusioning and frustrating to the Arabs."[36] Lydia Bacon, whose sister headed the girls' school in Ramallah in 1948 and whose husband taught at AUB, expressed her dismay at the unfairness of partition in a letter to Eleanor Roosevelt. "We know these Arabs as a people and love them," she wrote. "They have been there for 1,300 years and there is nothing right about the partition. . . . If we feel so badly for the Jews why do we not give them one of our own states?" Roosevelt ridiculed the notion in her syndicated column "My Day" and, without any apparent sense of irony, said that the idea of displacing people against their will was "somewhat funny."[37] Her reply was revealing. To the extent that Bacon or any other well-intentioned individual sought to inform fellow Americans about the reality of the Arab position toward Palestine, they fought an uphill battle in America.

William Eddy, however, thought the battle was worth fighting. The former marine, Princeton graduate, former OSS officer turned CIA man, ARAMCO consultant, and head of the U.S. diplomatic mission to Saudi Arabia in the 1940s knew the Arab world more than just about any other American then living. Given his missionary heritage, Eddy's turn to American diplomatic service, intelligence, and oil work represented the metamorphosis of the American presence in the region from religion to resources. Eddy, as we have seen, was comfortable and at ease with Arab men of power because of his background and because of his fluency in Arabic. He had served not only as a mediator and translator for FDR's meeting with Ibn Saud (see Chapter 4), but he had been on excellent terms with the latter, and with several other Arab leaders as well. He worked from Beirut in the late 1950s for the Trans-Arabian Pipeline Company (TAPLINE), which built and operated the great pipeline that sent ARAMCO oil from Saudi Arabia to a terminal just south of Sidon (it had initially been meant to transport oil to Haifa, but the conflict in Palestine undid the idea), whence it was shipped to the rebuilding, oil-dependent economies of Western Europe.

Eddy saw no massive impediment to U.S.-Arab relations other than the issue of Israel. He knew, and in fact had predicted and then lived to see firsthand, the damage that U.S. support for Israel had done to America's reputation in the region. Eddy resented Israel, and even more so, the American supporters of the Jewish state (presumably such as Uris), who he believed had subverted America's interests in the region by opening a wholly unnecessary chasm between Americans and Arabs. He did not conceal his antipathy toward those whom he called "traitors," who he felt promoted Israel's interests over what he felt were America's. Such hostility drew from his belonging to a white Protestant elite that held American Jews, and Jews more generally, in disdain. Privately, he speculated that there was "a very important conspiracy to keep the blinders on the American peoples' eyes."[38] Eddy clearly suspected American Zionists of harboring dual loyalties. But prejudice alone could hardly explain his position. The overriding truth was that, just as many Americans sincerely embraced the idea of Israel, so too did Eddy plainly believe that Israel was bad for America. He was convinced that if Americans only had known the Arabs and become acquainted with their perspective on the conflict, the United States would not have embarked on what he believed was a rash and immoral course over Palestine. America would not have made enemies out of a population that had been predisposed in its favor, especially not at the onset of the Cold War.

Because he had traveled and resided from one end of the Arab world to the other, from Tangier to Yemen, Eddy could confirm what U.S. embassy dispatches and national intelligence estimates of the Arab world had already diagnosed: that anti-Americanism as a problem was due almost entirely to American policy over Palestine. The obvious solution, it seemed to Eddy, was to fix the policy rather than to try and bend the Arab world to an unjust—and in his mind, ultimately unsustainable—pro-Israel stance. When he was invited to speak at the Naval War College in Newport, Rhode Island, in April 1953, the former marine did not hold back. He delivered an extraordinary speech that summed up not only his own attitude but also the missionary tradition that he had inherited.

Eddy began by sketching the history of the Arabs and their contributions to world civilization. It was a rushed primer for an audience that in all probability knew very little about Arabs. Eddy, however, took full advantage of his reputation as an Arabist to make his argument compelling. He said that Americans needed the 300 million Muslims of the world on their side during the Cold War just as they obviously needed the petroleum resources of the Middle East. The obvious conclusion was therefore to cultivate the people of the region, not to antagonize them. "Resentment at the rape of Palestine," for which Eddy held the United States responsible, was the direct cause of an "anti-American fever" running high in the Arab and Muslim world. U.S. taxpayer–funded aid for the Jewish state, which overtly discriminated against Palestinians and reserved first-class citizenship for Jews, added insult to injury, as did incessant statements of support for Israel expressed by both American political parties that ran roughshod over Arab sentiments.

Eddy could not have been blunter or less diplomatic. He suggested that Arab resentment had initially been directed at "the pro-Zionist Truman Administration with its self-admitted catering to Zionist votes"; it had now developed to include "the American people, the educators, businessmen, missionaries, and diplomats all of whom previously had been accepted for what they really are—friends of fair dealing and justice, who had no part in the pro-Israeli and anti-American Truman clique that consistently bypassed the Department of State and deluded the American public." Eddy's outburst expressed in equal measure uncontained bitterness at men such as David Niles (Truman's adviser on minority affairs, an ardent Zionist, and a key figure in the lead-up to U.S. lobbying for partition, which Eddy had vehemently opposed), real empathy for the Arab perspective on Palestine, and nostalgia for what he considered a far more innocent age of U.S.-Arab relations that Israel's creation had ruined.

Eddy sensed the same struggle over the orientation of the Arab world that Philip Hitti—and Albert Hourani before him—had also experienced. Whereas Hitti had bemoaned the eclipse of the "middle-of-the-road man," Eddy described an ongoing Arab war between "friends of the West" and "fanatical xenophobes" in which American support for Israel undercut the former and galvanized the latter. It was an overly simplistic portrayal, but Eddy maintained that a corrective course was urgently required. "The reservoir of goodwill for Americans, built up over one hundred years ago," he declared, "is low but it is not quite empty." American bribes, he said, would not guarantee stability; only a redress of the "deepest and most lasting wounds" would. He called attention, therefore, to UN resolutions that Israel continued to defy, including repatriation or compensation for Palestinian refugees and the return to the partition borders that Israel had overrun. Eddy urged, finally, a "crusade for three faiths" to rescue Jerusalem from the domination of any one side. The notion of a crusade recalled Eddy's missionary heritage, but his plea for shared control of the contested city also indicated how far removed he was from the initially uncompromising and self-defeating evangelical vision of the original American missionaries, Pliny Fisk and Levi Parsons.

The final words of his Naval War College speech were perhaps his most prophetic. He admitted that the Arabs and Muslims might now be "unimpressive" and "underdeveloped," but he insisted that to hastily dismiss their concerns and views was to trade long-term advantage for precarious present gains. "Three hundred million Muslims," he concluded, "not yet militarized, offer to the United States of America a potent friend, or a dangerous enemy. The choice is still ours on April 1, 1953. If we choose wrong, then may God have mercy on our souls."[39]

Eddy was prescient in foreshadowing the militarization of some Muslims, but he also obfuscated to himself as much as to his audience at the Naval War College some crucial points about post–World War II American policy toward the Arab world. No matter how ardently the Saudis felt about the violation of Arab Palestine, they were not going to jeopardize their relationship with their patron, the United States. Ibn Saud had spurned Iraqi efforts to cancel ARAMCO's concession to punish American support for Zionism. Whereas before 1944 Saudi Arabia was exporting less than twenty thousand barrels daily, by 1950 ARAMCO was producing over six hundred thousand barrels.[40] The government depended entirely on its oil export revenues to finance the modernization of the country, to buy the allegiance of its subjects, and to support the increasingly lavish lifestyles of its royal family. Although Ibn Saud's son Faysal, Saudi Arabia's foreign minister, felt betrayed by the U.S. role in partition and was genuinely attracted to Arab nationalism, he would not dare break with the United States. Instead, he sought to push up the price of Saudi acquiescence to a U.S. dominance by demanding, for example, larger lease payments for the American airbase at Dhahran, which had been established in 1945. His brother, who became King Saud in 1953, was even less willing to alienate America. As to the other Arab states such as Egypt and Syria, their nationalism could be contained, if not rolled back. Indeed, Eddy had maintained up to the moment of the Arab defeat in Palestine that the Arabs would soon crush the nascent Jewish state. Their failure to do so left men like Eddy badly exposed as false prophets.

By blaming a pro-Israel and anti-American "clique," Eddy magnified one aspect of the post-1948 dynamic that bound Arabs, Israel, and the United States together and overlooked others. Eddy knew full well that ARAMCO was hardly the model of "fair dealing and justice," its own glossy promotional literature on the subject notwithstanding. The American company and its many propagandists, employees, and directors had consistently portrayed their relationship with the Arabs as one built upon partnership. Eddy lionized Ibn Saud as a man who "possessed those epic qualities of the leader which Samuel recognized in Saul,"[41] at the same time as the company also glorified its dedication to modernizing Saudi Arabia, in contrast to the nefarious colonial-era British oil regimes that dominated Iran and Iraq.

In some very broad outlines, there was truth to these descriptions. Ibn Saud was obviously of a different mettle than his Hashemite rivals. Faysal and Abdullah were given control over their countries by the British; Ibn Saud conquered his, although he sought and received the patronage of the British and then the Americans. Also, the origin of the ARAMCO concession occurred before the age of American political imperialism in the Middle East. But the actual nature of ARAMCO's operation presented a very different picture than the image of "perfect co-operation" presented in public by its champions such as George Kheirallah in *Arabia Reborn* or Eddy in *FDR Meets Ibn Saud*.[42]

ARAMCO ran a segregated system of labor and conspired with Saudi authorities to crush labor unrest and strikes. Arabs were not allowed to live in the American camp, whose luxuries accentuated the rudimentary and unsanitary conditions in which most Saudi workers lived. The company, furthermore, routinely haggled over material improvements it made to the well-being of Saudi and other Arab workers; it often had to be forced by Saudi authorities into reforms that it subsequently claimed as its own. Just as the great missionary institutions such as AUB and AUC had been compelled to relent before the "tidal wave" of nationalism (as the missionary Charles Watson put it), so too had ARAMCO, but not before sporadic and localized anti-American sentiment had formed because of the company's haughtiness and racism. The U.S. cultural attaché in Riyadh noted that "remarks by all classes of Arabs expressed an antagonistic trend against the American methods of handling the Arab workers in the oil fields. There was much talk of injustice, of discrimination in wages, in housing and quality of food." One anonymous Arabic leaflet with a hammer and sickle found at Khobar in 1954 demanded that Arabs expel the "American pigs" and seize ARAMCO.[43] These hostile expressions were independent of U.S. support for Israel, and they pushed the Saudi government to redouble its efforts to prove its allegiance to a puritanical Wahabi Islam in return for its monopoly on power and its alliance with America.

Still, Eddy could at least take solace from the fact that despite ARAMCO's self-serving portrait of a benevolent force for modernization among the Arabs, oil production was very much a two-way street. The anti-American sentiment in parts of Saudi Arabia was undercut by the fact that the Saudi state and subjects and an entire class of Arab professionals, particularly Lebanese, Palestinian, Syrian, and Egyptian expatriates, benefited either from working with ARAMCO or from the oil revenues the company generated. Of the 20,400 ARAMCO employees in the early 1950s, nearly 13,400 were Saudis; 3,000 were African, Arab, or from other parts of the Mediterranean. There was something ARAMCO could do, and did, to mollify its Saudi critics: It could open the tills, divide the profits more equitably (as it did in 1950), and force its rhetoric to come closer to matching its reality without immediately overturning its raison d'être as a profit-seeking corporation.[44]

Eddy drew attention to a powerful dynamic at work. The incipient Arab rhetoric of American oil imperialism in the Arabian Peninsula drew much of its persuasive power from America's role in both creating and perpetuating the Jewish state. American support for Israel had created a foundation of anti-American antipathy in the region to which other anti-American discourses that were not immediately or necessarily tied to Israel could easily be added. Eddy nevertheless allowed his fury at Israel's spoiling role to cover up the fact that there was—whether he admitted it or not—an increasingly apparent American strategic decision to create a pro-American Middle East that relied not on the free will of its people but on the rule of conservative Arab monarchies, Israel, and the shah of Iran.

Anticommunism was at once a motive and a pretext for an assertion of U.S. power. The American embassy in Damascus had apparently helped Husni al-Za'im to overthrow the Syrian government in 1949, hoping that he would make peace with Israel, but more importantly hoping to gain his consent for the passage across Syrian territory of the American oil pipeline that nationalists had been holding up in the Parliament. Za'im gave his consent before he, in turn, was deposed. In 1953 the CIA went to even greater lengths to topple the populist-elected Iranian prime minister, Mohammed Mossadegh, who had nationalized Iranian oil during Operation Ajax. The very same people—Kermit Roosevelt and Loy Henderson—who had been very critical of Israel's creation because they had correctly seen that it would alienate the Arabs plunged headlong into regime change in Iran, despite the consequences of their actions in fostering anti-American sentiment in Iran. For them, the removal of Mossadegh, unlike the creation of Israel, was a basic U.S. interest. Kermit Roosevelt even tried to bribe Nasser, who promptly used the proffered funds to build a massive radio tower and panoramic restaurant in Cairo.[45]

Americans in the Arab world, including Eddy, ultimately resigned themselves to salvaging their relationship to the Arabs within new parameters that took Israel's existence for granted. They would not seek to return to the status quo ante. Nor would most of them acknowledge the nature of a new antidemocratic American hegemony in the region. Former missionaries or educators such as Bayard Dodge instead took the lead in overseeing the Palestine Refugee Relief Program, precursor to UNRWA, and worked with the Quakers' American Friends Service Committee (AFSC). They thus reprised a humanitarian role that American missionaries had played during and after World War I, except now without the evangelical fantasies of Protestant conversion. Dorothy Thompson, the erstwhile Zionist who had been disillusioned by Zionism, admired Nasser as a "patriotic idealist" and hoped that he presaged a genuine revolution in Egypt's affairs.[46] She worked as president of an organization called American Friends of the Middle East. AFME very much regarded itself as an organization that sought to redress a grievous imbalance in American attitudes toward the Arab-Israeli conflict. William Eddy sat on its national council. Lowell Thomas, Philip Hitti, and William Ernest Hocking were also members, as was Elmer Berger, a Jewish rabbi who in his book *The Jewish Dilemma* argued passionately that Zionism did not represent Jews and who was aghast at the racialism inherent in the state of Israel. Virginia Gildersleeve, the dean of Barnard College, friend of Charles Crane, and admirer of George Antonius, and the only woman appointed to work on the preamble of the UN charter, was also moved by the injustice of the situation in Palestine to join AFME. Gildersleeve refused to turn a blind eye to those victims of Europe's archetypal victims.

But AFME had another side to it. The organization was evidently funded by the CIA, several of whose agents sat prominently on its board. Genuine conviction, propaganda, and self-deception came imperceptibly together. From the outset, AFME was undermined by contradictory pulls. The U.S. government expected it to serve and subordinate itself to U.S. policy, even when this policy clashed with a leader such as Nasser, yet several prominent board members believed that U.S. policy on the Arab-Israeli conflict was fundamentally misguided and sympathized with Nasser. Dorothy Thompson believed, disingenuously perhaps, that she and her organization were not instruments of propaganda. They did not tell Arabs what to think but constituted, according to Thompson, a genuine medium for exchange and communication between Arabs and Americans. She presided over a major conference in 1953 under the theme of "Partnership in Meeting Needs in the Middle East." Under her direction, American civic, educational, and humanitarian organizations heavily involved in the Middle East came together in the hope of charting a new course for U.S.-Arab relations. Thompson confessed that her organization "exist[s] to communicate the Middle East to America, and to communicate at least part of America—that part we can justly claim to represent—to the Middle East."[47] Besides trying to alter perceptions on Palestine within the United States, AFME sought to convince Arabs that Soviet communism was their real enemy, while also emphasizing American sympathy for the Arab world and an American appreciation of Arab history and culture.

It was a thankless task. The U.S. ambassador to Baghdad, Burton Berry, pointedly reminded the State Department that Arab distrust of America was "a *political* distrust" based fundamentally on American support for Israel and identification with colonial powers. "It can only be met," he added, "by a political solution."[48] But the ambassador, Eddy, and Thompson all knew that no political solution acceptable to the Arab world was in the offing. Rather than abandon its support for Israel, the U.S. government embarked on a widespread, although not fully coordinated, campaign to create a positive image of America. The goal was not so much to win the hearts and minds of Arabs—impossible so long as America privileged Israel over them—but to diffuse political hostility aimed at the United States by emphasizing cultural cooperation and to convince Arabs that, American support for Israel notwithstanding, America was "impartial" when it came to the Middle East.

The United States professed its friendship with the Arab world and openly supported its most implacable enemy. It was an incongruous message. Undeterred, American officials went on a propaganda offensive. They planted stories in the Arab media, distributed Arabic pamphlets and posters, made anti-Communist films, broadcast radio programs and news, and fostered exchange programs in the 1950s. Many of these efforts were comical in their ineptitude: An American mobile unit traveling through Iraq, for instance, showed films involving the popular character Juha—the legendary satirical Sufi character around whom had developed a rich tradition of anecdotes, parables, and jokes—to illustrate the dangers of communism. Iraqis were unimpressed by the crude propaganda. American officials in Washington fretted about the need to redirect Arab energy away from Israel and the West and toward "internal" Arab problems, yet at the same time they paradoxically emphasized the dangers of foreign Soviet communism. They never seemed to appreciate, moreover, that Arabs saw Palestine as a quintessentially internal problem and that Arabs in any case had already immersed themselves in intense self-criticism.

The upshot for Americans on the ground was a balancing act between mollifying Arabs without doing anything to compromise U.S. interests, without being able to influence U.S. decision-making in the Middle East, and without being able to temper significantly the growing influence and confidence of American Zionism. If overt U.S. support for Israel embarrassed Americans in the Arab world, they were far more preoccupied with the Arab tide turning against colonialism during the Cold War. Every American institution in the region reacted to the surge of nationalism, anti-imperialism, and anti-Zionism in the Middle East with similar caution, almost always pleading that they were private organizations and therefore not responsible for American policy.

The American University of Beirut once again found itself at a crossroads. Nationalist currents swept through the campus and politicized the student body. Student demonstrations against imperialism and the Baghdad Pact and for Palestine, Algeria, and Arab nationalism became routine. The university president, Stephen Penrose, who had been appointed in October 1948, cracked down on suspected Iraqi and Palestinian Communist students. In March 1954, in response to a protest called by Arab nationalist students, Lebanese internal security forces used water cannons and fired at the demonstrators, killing one and wounding forty. The administration (which included Zurayk, who was severely criticized by nationalist students for being a lackey of the Americans) responded by dissolving the student group that organized the protest and expelling several students, who were welcomed in Nasser's Egypt. At the same time, the university administration also complained ineffectually to the authorities about the police violation of the university campus. The turmoil recalled the nineteenth-century Darwin affair, when the conservative president Daniel Bliss expelled medical students because they had embraced Darwinism, but now the context was far more radicalized and the American presence in the region far more controversial. The self-proclaimed "liberal" mission of the university, which itself had always functioned as a metaphor for America in the region, appeared to be in tatters.

Meanwhile, Penrose had admitted that he stood "directly at the firing line" in the war against communism. He identified with the U.S. government, was an ardent anti-Communist, and was known locally as a CIA man. He had in fact worked for the OSS in Cairo during the Second World War, but he was also a Congregational Church lay preacher who spoke out on behalf of Palestinian refugees. Penrose confessed that he, as an American, was convincingly depicted by students as an "imperialist," not a "democrat," because of the "political blunders of the Western Powers." He noted that "Arab bitterness toward Israel and particularly toward the powers which brought it into being is played upon continuously," and he warned that counterpropaganda would not work "unless our policies begin more closely and more consistently to coincide with our oft-repeated expressions of principle. We have heretofore been held in highest regard by the Arab peoples but we cannot continue to win or deserve their admiration unless our policies are inspired once more by the ideals so frequently publicized which the Arabs had come to admire."[49] Penrose used the past tense advisedly. Like Hitti and Eddy, Penrose evoked and glorified, in effect, a moment in U.S.-Arab relations that had receded, and one that events were soon to push even further into the distance.

The nationalization of the Suez Canal in July 1956 was a great watershed in modern Arab history and in U.S.-Arab relations. If Israel's creation had demoralized Arabs, Nasser's bold decision to nationalize the Suez Canal exhilarated them. Nasser served notice of an Arab determination to take their history into their own hands. The British from the outset had detested Nasser. He had removed a weak king and pressured them to abandon their base at Suez. They wanted pliant Arab chiefs, not defiant nationalists.

Although the United States was initially less hostile to Nasser than Britain was, the Egyptian leader's independent course had caused consternation in the Eisenhower administration. Nasser made it clear that he would not be America's man, at least not in the manner that America expected its men to be; he was willing to persecute Communists and crush the Muslim Brotherhood, but he would not sacrifice his ambition to turn a final page on Egypt's colonial past and chart his own course in foreign policy. His decision to seek arms from Czechoslovakia in 1955 directly after the Israeli raid on Gaza, because of America's refusal to supply him with adequate military weaponry, alienated the Americans. His recognition of Communist China in the same year sealed the breach. Dulles responded vindictively by pulling the promised American funding of the Aswan Dam.

Nasser decided to nationalize the Suez Canal. Plans were readied to prove that Egyptians could responsibly navigate ship traffic. He believed that he could avoid the fate of Mohammed Mossadegh. The British could not embargo the Suez Canal in the manner that they had successfully embargoed the sale of Iranian oil under Mossadegh. Moreover, they had already withdrawn their troops from Egypt. Any assault on Egypt would take time, but Nasser firmly believed that he could count on not only Arab support but the support of the world. Decolonization was the watchword of the day, not empire. He revealed his hand during a long speech in Alexandria marking the third anniversary of the exile of King Faruq on July 26, 1956. The code word he used to signal the Egyptian takeover of the Suez Canal Company headquarters was "De Lesseps," the name of the nineteenth-century French engineer who had convinced Egypt's Khedives to build the Suez Canal, which had brought with it ruinous debt and eventually a British occupation of the country.

The nationalization of the Suez Canal "in the name of the people" overwhelmed the Egyptians and Arabs with pride as much as it stunned the West.[50] Here was an Arab leader finally talking and acting back. His open defiance instantly put Egypt at the forefront of the Arab world, and

Nasser at the forefront of Arab leaders. "I do not know," he had reflected in his tract *The Philosophy of the Revolution*, "why I always imagine that in this region in which we live there is a role wandering aimlessly about seeking an actor to play it."[51] To play this role of Arab leader and to claim, as he also did in *The Philosophy of the Revolution*, that Arab oil was an "Arab" patrimony—as opposed to a Saudi or Kuwaiti or Iraqi resource—put him directly on a collision course not only with the Saudis and Iraqis but far more ominously with the Western powers, including the United States, who buttressed these monarchies.

Secretary of State Dulles wanted Nasser to "disgorge his theft." At a White House meeting at the end of July, Admiral Arleigh Burke had advised Eisenhower that the Joint Chiefs believed that "Nasser must be broken," with force if necessary. Eisenhower disagreed, for he understood that the man Nasser, in and of himself, was not the problem; rather, Nasser "embodies the emotional demands of the people of the area for independence and for 'slapping the white Man down.'"[52] From the beginning of the crisis, Eisenhower had made it clear to British prime minister Anthony Eden that he was opposed to any overt military operation against Egypt. He pushed for a negotiated settlement in Suez. Eisenhower had exhibited no qualms about the deposing of Iran's Mossadegh, but that operation had been done covertly and with Iranian collaboration. The eyes of the world were riveted now on Suez. Eisenhower knew that to side with Britain and France against a poor nation such as Egypt would undermine further America's already battered standing among Muslims and Arabs, and more tangibly, it would erode the position of its most important ally, King Saud.

Both Eisenhower and Dulles realized that their paramount position in Saudi Arabia was threatened by Nasser's influence. Arab nationalism was making inroads into the conservative kingdom. In May, Saudi demonstrators at ARAMCO had carried banners that read DOWN WITH AMERICAN IMPERIALISM; their protest had been (again) violently broken up by Saudi authorities.[53] Opposition to the American military presence continued, and by the summer a petition with hundreds of signatures openly circulated calling for the closure of the U.S. military base at Dhahran. Eisenhower's National Security Council had urged him two years before to take the sting out of Arab nationalism by giving the Arabs the impression that the United States could separate its interests from Israel's, and its actions from Britain's. The United States had to appear to sympathize with the "legitimate aspirations" of the Arab states. Suez was not to be America's war.

The British government, however, was determined to topple Nasser. Nearly two-thirds of the oil bound for Europe passed through Suez. Prime Minister Eden routinely compared Egypt's president to Hitler and felt that Nasser had crossed swords with England once too often. Britain's last imperialists demanded that the "Moslem Mussolini" (as Eden also feared Nasser would inevitably become) be cut down to size.[54] The French too hated Nasser, both for his nationalization and for his support of the ongoing Algerian revolution, which Nasser made—through Radio Cairo, his speeches, and his press—a pan-Arab issue. Egypt offered military, diplomatic, and moral support for the Algerian revolutionaries. The Israelis feared him for his potential to unify the Arabs and for his determination to build up Egyptian military strength.

As a result of all this, two waning European empires and Ben-Gurion's Israel conspired to attack Egypt. Their plan of attack was confirmed in October at Sèvres outside of Paris, the very same place that had lent its name to the harsh treaty that dismembered the Ottoman Empire in 1920. Israel was to launch the first strike; the British and the French were to intervene subsequently, ostensibly to maintain order and "protect" the canal—but the goal of the conspirators was to eliminate Nasser and cow the Arabs once more into submission. The Americans, who had no love for the Egyptian leader, were left unaware of the collusion between their allies.

The British, French, and Israelis unleashed their campaign in the afternoon of October 29, 1956. Arab fears of Israel appeared confirmed; their view of its colonial foundations were reinforced by what they described as the "tripartite aggression" on Egypt. Nasser's army was no match for Israel's, which within a week had occupied the entire Sinai Peninsula. British and French aerial bombardments of Cairo and Port Said and troop landings along the canal added to the precariousness of Nasser's position. The Egyptian leader had not foreseen that the British would collaborate so openly with the Israelis and thus undermine their position in the rest of the Arab world. He resorted to heroic declarations and misled his people about the extent of Egyptian losses and vastly exaggerated Israel's. But every blow absorbed by Nasser made him a greater Arab hero. Although Hashemite Iraq's prime minister, Nuri al-Said, had urged the British to strike Nasser hard and quickly, Iraq's population was solidly behind Nasser. The Syrians also rallied to Nasser's side. They cut a major pipeline running from Iraq to Lebanon that passed their territory. The Saudis refused to send oil to either Britain or France.

The Egyptians also blockaded the canal, further choking Europe off from a regular supply of Middle Eastern oil. With world opinion on his side, Nasser had simply to survive in order to win politically, no matter how many Egyptian soldiers were killed defending their country. Major American Zionist organizations waded into the fray, pleading with Eisenhower that Israeli and American interests were identical and therefore the "dictator" Nasser ought to be allowed to fall. The mayor of New York, Robert Wagner, launched a stinging rebuke of the president, who had tried, Wagner said, "to appease the Arabs" over Israel, "the only democracy in that area."[55] And the Israeli government, whose army had invaded Egypt and smashed its army, insisted that Israel was in fact mortally threatened by Nasser.

Nasser refused to capitulate. His fate now rested as much in American and Soviet hands as in his own. Eisenhower was outraged at the unprovoked Israeli attack and at the arrogance of the British for beginning a war despite American warnings against it. He demanded an immediate end to hostilities. The British prevaricated and, with the French, blocked a UN security council ceasefire resolution sponsored by the Americans, adding insult to injury. The United States turned to the General Assembly to gain a ceasefire resolution and admitted—to the surprise and genuine delight of a host of Third World countries—that it was there, and not with the Security Council where the great powers wielded veto power, that the voice of the world could truly be heard.

A major test of wills unfolded on the eve of the U.S. presidential election. Eden had misjudged Eisenhower's resolve as greatly as he had misjudged Britain's ability to break Egypt. Unlike Truman, Eisenhower confided to a friend that he would not allow concern for a domestic Jewish vote to influence U.S. foreign policy. He wanted Israel to know that it could not "take advantage" of the United States and that "we would handle our affairs exactly as though we didn't have a Jew in America."[56] Eisenhower was not bluffing. He understood that most Americans, including most congressional representatives, were not well versed in world affairs. But he had faith that if Americans were properly informed, they would make the right decision.

Appearing from the White House on American national television on October 31 at seven in the evening, Eisenhower explained the Suez war to the American people. His tone was earnest and his language diplomatic, but his point was utterly clear. The United States had been deceived by its allies. No matter how provocative Egyptians may have appeared to the aggressors, the latter's actions were wrong, "for we do not accept the use of force as a wise or proper instrument for the settlement of international disputes." Eisenhower stressed the importance of law. "There can be no peace—without law. And there can be no law—if we were to invoke one code of international conduct for those who oppose us—and another for our friends." He called for a strengthening of the UN and for a search for a real solution to the problems of the Middle East. "The peace we seek and need means much more than mere absence of war. It means the acceptance of law, and the fostering of justice, in all the world."[57]

On this one occasion, the American president was able to bridge the great gap that had hitherto separated American ideals from American actions in its Middle Eastern dealings. The British and the Israelis were both taken aback, perhaps by the sudden and selective turn to international law in a part of the world where for so long Western powers, often with American acquiescence, had been able to impose themselves through force alone. The United States, nevertheless, demanded that its will be respected, and its will this time at least coincided with that of the Arab, African, and Asian countries. A writer in the Lebanese daily *Al-Hayat* noted that Eisenhower's stand against the tripartite invasion of Egypt was unique in the annals of American diplomacy in the Middle East, for never before had an American president come out so unambiguously against colonialism.[58] The central question, declared the columnist, was whether the United States could maintain so bold and revolutionary a stand following the end of the immediate crisis.

For a moment, it seemed as if Eisenhower might be able to revive, almost single-handedly, America's flagging reputation among Arabs. Several Arab ambassadors expressed their governments' gratitude at the firmness of the U.S. position. The beleaguered Nasser made sure to express his appreciation as well. The Egyptian *Al-Ahram* praised the U.S. stand for helping to defend "the cause of truth and the cause of peace."[59] Although the Soviets put down an uprising in Hungary on November 4, they threatened to intervene on behalf of Egypt. The Americans threatened to cut support for the British pound.

Eden finally recognized that the way forward was blocked. The British and the French crumbled under sustained American pressure. They accepted a ceasefire on November 6. The Israelis proved the most recalcitrant, stubbornly resisting Eisenhower's demand for a rapid withdrawal. They pulled back from Suez but remained in Gaza and at the mouth of the Gulf of Aqaba.

Eisenhower threatened to place sanctions on Israel, including cutting off the considerable private aid that flowed to it—a rough estimate prepared for Eisenhower indicated that some $40 million annually went to Israel as private tax-deductible gifts and that about $60 million worth of Israeli bonds were also sold in America each year.[60] However, a senator from Texas, Lyndon Johnson, objected that Eisenhower was "cracking down" on Israel. American politicians refused to take a strong stand against Israel, although it had openly defied its major political patron.

Eisenhower found the situation intolerable. He appealed again directly to the American people, this time in February 1957. He began awkwardly, apologizing for a stubborn cough. "The United States," he said disingenuously, "has no ambitions or desires in this region." But when it came to the matter at hand, the continuing Israeli occupation of Gaza and Sharm el-Sheikh, the president was remarkably frank and concise. Israel not only continued to defy "the opinions of mankind" and law—in sharp contrast to its coconspirators, who had bowed to the will of the international community—but was trying to set preconditions for its withdrawal from Arab territory despite the fact that America had worked hard to ensure that Israeli concerns were assuaged. United Nations peacekeepers had been authorized to patrol the armistice lines, but Ben-Gurion continued to stall and to demand more guarantees before Israel withdrew.

"This raises a basic question of principle," Eisenhower reasoned. "Should a nation which attacks and occupies foreign territory in the face of the United Nations' disapproval be allowed to impose conditions on its own withdrawal?" Once again, his appeal to international law was selective; the covert role that his administration had played in Iran, and the Truman administration's role before that in Syria, went uncommented upon. Yet Eisenhower was by no objective measurement anti-Israel. If anything, he identified far more with it than with the Arab states. He referred to the shared values that he believed characterized Israelis and Americans. He had already, in fact, conceded a point to the Israelis when Dulles assured them formally that the United States would support the opening of the Straits of Tiran to Israeli shipping—a point that had disappointed the Egyptians, who felt that it was tantamount to appeasing Israel and exhibited American "weakness" when it came to Israel.[61] Eisenhower was explicit about the need for Israeli security and the need for recognition of "the right of Israel to national existence," and he would mention the Palestinians only abstractly. "The Arab refugee problem," he said weakly, "must be solved."[62] Still, he was administering a kind of pressure to which the Israelis and their many supporters in America were simply not accustomed. On March 1, 1957, the Israelis finally pulled back from Gaza and Sharm el-Sheikh. From an American perspective, Eisenhower's stand proved his impartiality to the Arabs.

In reality, America's posture toward the region had not fundamentally changed, despite Eisenhower's radical appeal to international law and his resort to the General Assembly as the real voice of the international community. Eisenhower himself never tired of repeating that his difference with Britain was tactical, not strategic. Both nations wanted to secure Middle Eastern oil; both wanted compliant Arab rulers; both were opposed to democratic rule in the region; both had involved themselves in coups to overturn "Communist" threats; and both wanted a divided and weak Arab world. The British, however, spoke and acted in a manner that constantly recalled their nineteenth-century colonial heritage. The Americans styled their interventions as a partnership and drew to the point of depletion on a benign legacy in the Arab world when their strategic interests were focused elsewhere. The United States, moreover, still talked of the Palestinians as "wards" of the UN rather than as a people with rights. Most ominously, the Eisenhower Doctrine enunciated by the president in January before Congress, with Israeli forces still occupying Egyptian territory and the Suez Canal still blockaded, had placed the abstract, theoretical threat from communism before the very real one of imperialism as the basis for U.S. policy toward the region, including military intervention and economic assistance to Arab states.

From an Arab perspective, the past five months had changed the political landscape of the Middle East considerably. Nasser had emerged from the Suez Canal crisis far stronger politically than he had been beforehand. He had entered into it an Egyptian leader, but emerged from it an Arab one. Despite Egypt's military defeat, there was a definite sense in the Arab world that Suez was a turning point in the quest for real self-determination. Nasser wanted to be treated like an equal. He also took the lead in criticizing the Eisenhower Doctrine. "We will not march behind the Great Powers," he informed a delegation of visiting Syrian students in February a week before Eisenhower's second televised address. "It is our Arab nationalism that protected us when the colonialists conspired against us and sent their soldiers against us."[63] Now that he had emerged as the undisputed Arab leader in the aftermath of Suez, Nasser's threat to U.S. oil-based hegemony in the region was that much more serious.

Eisenhower sought, therefore, to buttress King Saud as a rival Arab leader. The CIA had earlier searched to find a "Moslem Billy Graham," a charismatic leader who might fan religious fervor against communism and thus dampen anti-American sentiment.[64] Eisenhower hoped that Saudi Arabia would become the center of Arab politics. To marginalize

Nasser's secular Arab nationalism, Eisenhower promoted the explicitly fundamentalist Saudi alternative to it. He reminded King Saud that he was in a "special position . . . as Keeper of the Holy Places of Islam."[65] He opened the Islamic Center in Washington, D.C., in June 1957, stressing America's friendship with Islam and praising the past glory of Muslim civilization in a short speech that could have been written by William Eddy. In his effort to promote Islam over secularism, or at least the secular nationalism embodied by Nasser, the American president was supported by a host of American academics who stressed that Islam was a "way of life" for most Muslims who were, by definition, "pious."[66] The Saudis were recognized as an important asset in the fight against a Palestine-centered Arab nationalism and against the tremendous popularity of Nasser. King Saud had to be put in a position to lead what Eisenhower hoped would be a "holy war" against radical nationalism and communism.[67]

It was a fateful choice. Although neither the Saudi nor the Egyptian leader was democratic, and neither tolerated significant opposition, each state worked toward diametrically opposite visions of the future. Nasser's was modern and secular in orientation, while the Saudis were far more illiberal and religiously fundamentalist. In terms of values, there was no question as to which government more closely resembled professed American ideals. But the Saudis, despite various rumblings within the kingdom and pressures even from within the royal family to liberalize government, were far less of a threat to American dominance over the region. They were willing to play the game of politics by American rules. Nasser was not—at least not always. In American rhetoric, therefore, the Saudis were henceforth considered "moderate" and Nasser was "radical."

A confrontation between the United States and Nasser's Egypt soon became inevitable. There was no doubt as to which side most Arabs supported. Eisenhower recognized all too well that Nasser, despite his flaws and the cult of personality that surrounded him, constituted a "real leader" in a manner that King Saud did not—that is, he commanded the respect of people not simply through patronage or power, but because he embodied a universal Arab aspiration for freedom from Western rule. So great was the belief in Nasser, and so indispensable did he seem in the wake of Suez, that many Arab nationalists began to identify themselves as "Nasserists." The Baathists continued to organize in Syria and Iraq; so too did the Communists and the Muslim Brotherhood, but they were all now held hostage to the aura of invincibility that surrounded Egypt's leader. Many Saudis were enchanted by Nasser. Despite their rivalry, King Saud found himself publicly aligned with Nasser on several occasions, especially during Suez. He recognized Nasser's mass appeal and shared with him a common antipathy for Israel. There was very little Saud could do to stem the tide of adulation.

The Americans plunged, however, into Arab affairs as never before. Their confrontation with Nasser indicated a determination not only to safeguard the colonial Middle Eastern order that the United States was taking over from the British but equally to actively take sides in the great struggle to define the new face of the Arab world. An American-led plan to overthrow the Syrian government called Operation Straggle had already been uncovered in 1956, and the United States was denounced in the Syrian and Egyptian media for its imperialism. CIA officers persisted in trying to organize a coup in Syria the following year. Even Loy Henderson, who had participated in the overthrow of Mossadegh in Iran, was dispatched to the region to encourage Turkey and Iraq to invade Syria lest the country fall to "communism." Once more an exaggerated fear of communism served as both pretext and motive for American activity in the region. Amid rumors and real conspiracies that destabilized Syria, Syrian leaders begged Nasser for a political union with Egypt. In February 1958, the United Arab Republic (UAR) was created under his terms. All political parties were dissolved. Nasser now controlled not only Suez but the oil pipelines that crossed through Syrian territory.[68]

On July 14, 1958, Hashemite Iraq succumbed to a military coup. The royal family and Nuri al-Said were massacred. The revolutionaries insisted that they had swept aside the "corrupt crew that imperialism installed."[69] The violence of the uprising stood in stark contrast to Egypt's revolution. By nightfall in Baghdad, the statue of Faysal lay shattered and the British embassy was burned. Eisenhower was caught flat-footed. His response was to rush fourteen thousand American troops into Lebanon, where for over a year a small-scale civil war had been taking place following President Camille Chamoun's rigging of parliamentary elections in a bid to amend the country's constitution to stay in office. Opposition to Chamoun was also inspired by the creation of the UAR and by his refusal to break relations with Britain and France over Suez. However, Chamoun and Charles Malik, who was now Lebanon's foreign minister, had been pleading for months for U.S. troops, in line with the Eisenhower Doctrine. Malik consigned his protests on behalf of Palestine to the past. Nasser and Arab nationalism appeared to him to be the grave threats of the present.

Malik claimed that his country was being subverted by Nasser and pleaded for Western intervention. Eisenhower had rebuffed him until the Iraqi revolution forced the American president's hand. American marines and soldiers were now on the ground in the Middle East, albeit in a tiny, deeply divided country with no real army and no significant Communist movement. Lebanon was, however, the terminus for pipelines from both Iraq and Saudi Arabia. Realizing that Chamoun's presidency was not viable, the Americans would not support an extension of his rule. When his term expired, he was replaced by the head of the Lebanese army, General Fuad Shihab. The crisis was contained. American troops withdrew from Lebanon with scarcely a casualty. The British had also dispatched soldiers to Hashemite Jordan. The July landings were a show of force to prove to Saudi Arabia that the United States would back up its allies.

The Egyptian press fired a now-familiar fusillade against Western imperialism, this time setting America squarely in its sights. Eisenhower believed firmly that he had acted with different motives from those that drove the British invasion of Egypt. The United States had not outright invaded a foreign nation but had been invited to intervene, albeit under the terms of his own Eisenhower Doctrine. Israel was not involved. But these real differences, as well as the lofty rhetoric of defending "peace-loving" nations that Eisenhower used to justify his Lebanese intervention, obscured a fundamental turning point.[70]

The picture of America in the Arab world was now greatly transformed from where it had stood just over a decade before. Suez had initially suggested a major American break in its approach to the Arab world. Eisenhower's firm stand against British and French colonialism and Israeli expansionism appeared mindful of Arab aspirations. He was hailed for it. But when confronted with the implications of such a break for Western interests in the region—it might encourage Arab unification and a powerful Arab nation that had the power to reshape the colonial order of the Middle East and redirect the flow of oil—Eisenhower retreated. It was a decision rationalized by a Cold War logic. Rather than fighting imperialism, the United States became the new face of imperialism to many Arabs. American officials would protest the label of imperialism vociferously, but there was no denying that a new age of American power had dawned in the Middle East.

The ultimate lesson of Suez was deceptively simple. Any threat to America's newly acquired domination of the Middle East was to be repelled, whether it emanated from the British hubris and Israeli overreach manifested during the Suez war or from Nasser's secular pan-Arabism advocated in its aftermath. The United States demanded to know where Arab rulers stood in this pax Americana. The Saudis maintained their loyalty but were embarrassed by the fact that the United States, precisely as Charles Malik had foreseen in 1949, remained the principal political patron of Israel. As strategically important to the United States as they were, the Saudis were impotent to influence American policy on the Arab-Israeli conflict. They had no deep support in Congress, as Israel did; their military prowess paled in comparison to Israel's; and they appeared culturally as distant from America as Israel appeared close. In 1957, when King Saud visited New York, the city's mayor, Robert Wagner, denounced the Saudi ruler as anti-Israel, anti-Catholic, and proslavery. Wagner refused to acknowledge the king officially. At the same time, a leading Democratic city politician referred to Arab and other foreign diplomats as "monkeys." The spectacle of American-Arab friendship that ARAMCO had so carefully orchestrated ten years earlier now proved far more difficult to sustain. When 150 American teenagers picketed a dinner in honor of the Saudi king, ten boys held a mock "slave auction" of five girls chained together in "makeshift" Arab garb, shouting "Saud needs money for Nasser!"[71]

For Eisenhower, the episode was an embarrassment. For American Zionists, it was a demonstration of their clout in a major American city.

For Saud, it was a reminder of the degree to which American support for Israel was an unpalatable reality that had to be masked as much as possible from his own people. He and his brother Faysal, now the crown prince, could not therefore always play the role of obedient vassal in matters related to Israel, in part for the sake of appearances, but equally because, like Nasser, they genuinely hated the violation of the Arab world that Israel represented. "Except for Israel," Eisenhower lamented in July 1958, "we could form a viable policy in the area."[72] But by their deliberate subordination to America in its open battle with their era's most influential Arab leader, the Saudis also made it clear that they feared Nasser's leadership far more than they feared Israel. As much as Faysal in particular found Israel odious, he submitted to the fait accompli of American support for Zionism so long as the United States did not too brazenly flaunt it. He identified with many of Nasser's nationalist principles, but believed that the Saudi regime could not long survive with them.

In Nasser's open and apparently successful defiance of British colonialism, the Egyptian leader appeared to succeed where the romantic Hashemite Faysal had failed at the battle of Maysalun in 1920. But like many of his peers in the decolonizing world, Nasser also believed—and was encouraged to believe by a coterie of advisers and supporters—that he was destined to play an indispensable and historic role in Arab affairs. Millions of Arabs tied their aspirations to a single individual. They demanded unequivocal freedom from Western colonialism. Nasser understood this because he shared this basic sentiment that cut right across the Arab world.

The United States, Nasser felt, had a choice to make. It could choose to support an Arab aspiration for liberation or stand in its way. But it could not keep talking about freedom only to act against it. Palestine, of course, was the enduring example of American hypocrisy to the Arabs. But Algeria had become by 1960 a symbol of Arab and Islamic resistance to Western imperialism, just as Vietnam would become a Third World symbol by 1970. Eisenhower recognized perfectly the American quandary. His Joint Chiefs of Staff urged him in 1959 to adopt a pro-French position at the UN. Eisenhower refused. "The whole of our history," the President stated, "is anti-colonial and the French action in Algeria is interpreted by the rest of the world as militant colonialism."[73] There was no way to support the French openly as they waged a brutal pacification war against the Algerians; by the same token, Eisenhower could not stand too closely with the Algerians for fear of undermining a Cold War ally. The United States abstained from supporting Algerian and Arab calls at the UN for the recognition of Algerian self-determination.

Nasser exploited the ambivalence of American diplomacy. He could accept neither America's sustained efforts to deflate Arab nationalism nor its attempt to assume the mantle of leadership from the British, especially because both these endeavors marginalized his own ambitions and destroyed his own vision, however narcissistic, of a genuinely independent Arab world. At the UN in 1960, at the height of his prestige following Suez and the establishment of the UAR, Nasser warned the world of the "veiled colonization" that was taking the place of formal European rule. The Arabs would resist it, he said. He criticized the UN for its intervention in Congo, where the United States had encouraged the overthrow of the elected prime minister, Patrice Lumumba (who was subsequently tortured and murdered), by General Joseph Mobutu. Nasser reminded the world of the question of Palestine; later, in 1964, he would encourage the formation of the Palestine Liberation Organization (PLO) in Cairo. He called again for the liberation of the Algerians from French rule and spoke of the need for "economic freedom," not simply formal independence.[74]

On the international stage, he recalled Eisenhower at the peak of the Suez invasion when the U.S. president had admitted that the General Assembly, not the Security Council, was the world's true voice. But whereas Eisenhower had been discomfited by his appeal to the General Assembly in 1956, Nasser relished the idea that he represented something far greater than Egypt. His vision of Arab unity and economic independence clashed directly with the interests of the United States and its Saudi ally. Eisenhower had indicated that he would bend with the winds of nationalism, but that he would not allow them to change substantially the status quo of the oil-rich Middle East—regardless of what millions of Arabs (or Congolese, or Cubans, or Vietnamese) said or desired. In Port Said in the same year, Nasser thundered against the "hireling king" of Jordan and the Arab "stooges of imperialism."[75]

Nasser was confident, for America's continuing support for Israel—Eisenhower's extraordinary action to stem Israeli aggression in 1956 notwithstanding—gave him a political, emotional, and ideological advantage over all his Arab rivals. "Every bullet fired to kill an Arab," declared Nasser, "was paid for by America and all the Western imperialists because they give money to Israel."[76] There was very little either the Hashemites or the Saudis could say by way of answer. Nasser's demagoguery exploited the obvious weakness in America's position in the Middle East, for no Arab ally of America could be seen to openly stand with the nation that Arabs universally believed methodically usurped, and continued to usurp, Arab lands. There was no way for America to sell Israel to the Arabs, not while there remained Arab leaders and people who were determined to resist it.

The course of U.S.-Arab relations was determined at this moment. As Nasser chose the way of defiant, even hubristic, independence, Eisenhower took sides in an increasingly bitter inter-Arab rivalry that developed alongside, and intersected with, the Arab-Israeli conflict in which America played so pivotal a role. He had gone, moreover, as far as any American president would in trying to reconcile this basic contradiction in America's approach to the Arab world: expressing friendship with its peoples while continuing to aid its most obvious enemy. He would rein in Israel's expansionism, but not alter fundamental U.S. support for the Jewish state.

In the end, either U.S. policy would have to change substantially or the Arab world's secular nationalism, which was built on powerful notions of independence and anti-Zionism, would have to be tamed. The Americans were unwilling to give up on Israel; the Arabs were still unwilling to give up on the question of Palestine. The stage was set for widening confrontation.

6

RAISING THE RAG OF LIBERTY

Gamal Abdel Nasser built a regime in Egypt answerable to one man. He therefore bore ultimate responsibility for stumbling into a conflict with Israel for which he was ill prepared, and then watching helplessly as the Israelis destroyed his army and air force in just six days in June 1967. In the lead-up to the war, Nasser had been overtaken by a widespread Arab sentiment that the time of reckoning with Israel had finally arrived, a belief ironically bolstered by his own now-legendary defiance at Suez and by his nationalist speeches that consistently spoke of confronting, resisting, and defeating imperialism. He had also been provoked by the taunts of rival regimes, which accused him of avoiding conflict with the great enemy of the Arabs.

The 1960s had been, in truth, a decade of great frustration for Nasser. The union with Syria had been dissolved in 1961, thus breaking up the most serious Arab experiment in unification. Republican regimes in Syria and Iraq vied with Egypt for Arab leadership. Syrian Baathists, in particular, engaged in bitter recrimination against Nasser about the ill-fated United Arab Republic and harassed and imprisoned Nasserist sympathizers in Syria until, in a volte-face, they signed a mutual defense pact with

Egypt in 1966. The Saudis continued to cultivate their relationship with the United States. Nasser's open breach with President Lyndon Johnson—what Nasser's confidant and editor-in-chief of *Al-Ahram* Mohamed Heikal described in February 1967 as the "great clash" between Egypt and the "new colonialism" represented by America—was related centrally to his struggle with Israel, particularly his attempt to achieve military parity with it following the Gaza raid of 1955.[1] And the Palestine question continued to shape and dominate Arab perceptions of America.

Arab disunity was further exposed by an intra-Arab struggle in Yemen. The Egyptian army had bogged itself down in a protracted civil war in the country between 1962 and 1966; in this conflict, which Nasser would characterize as his "Vietnam," Egypt-supported republicans fought against Saudi-backed royalists.[2] The war in Yemen tied down tens of thousands of Egyptian troops and drained Egyptian resources at a time when the country was facing significant food shortages. In addition, the Johnson administration suspended wheat shipments to Egypt to signal its displeasure at Nasser's anti-imperialist rhetoric and Egypt's growing military dependence on the Soviets. Nasser retorted in a pique by saying that the Americans could "go drink up the sea."[3] With U.S. encouragement, the Saudi King Faysal, who succeeded his brother Saud in 1964, was determined to supplant Nasser as the fulcrum of the Arab world and to remake Nasser's secularist, Egypt-centered idea of Arab unity into an Islamic, Saudi-centered version.

The culmination in 1962 of the Algerian struggle for independence that Nasser had consistently championed provided scant solace. Ahmed Ben Bella, the hero of the Algerian revolution and Nasser's friend, was overthrown in 1965 in a military coup. Although the Algerian struggle was celebrated across the Arab world as the exemplar of armed struggle against Western colonialism, Algeria itself was peripheral to the main drama of the Arab-Israeli conflict. Israel proved to be a far more tenacious foe than the *pied-noirs* of Algeria; its brand of settler-colonialism also enjoyed far more extensive Western sympathy than did that of the French Algerians. In the decade following Suez, the Israelis had further strengthened their military and intensified their determination to be done with Nasser. In this period, with direct French assistance and despite American wishes, Israel became (and remains until today) the only nuclear power in the Middle East.

Nasser understood full well that Egypt could not defeat Israel militarily in the short term. He had worked for the better part of a decade to avoid military confrontations with his belligerent neighbor. Although he had overseen the creation of the Palestine Liberation Organization in 1964, he had tightly controlled the Palestinians in Gaza. As far as Palestine was concerned, "liberation" was to remain a slogan, a posture, or at best, a state of consciousness awaiting future realization rather than an effective, implementable plan for reclaiming Arab land and restoring Arab rights. Yet by virtue of being the most charismatic Arab leader, Nasser also found himself trying to manage pent-up Arab fear and anger toward Israel.

How one views the 1967 war depends almost entirely on how one views that of 1948. What for Israel was a war of independence and then a defensive struggle for survival, for the Arabs constituted a first great injustice followed by a blatant war of aggression. There was also the crucial matter of 1956, when Israel colluded with Britain and France to invade Egypt. Although there were fears and anxieties on both sides of the Arab-Israeli conflict, the military balance of power on the ground in favor of Israel was clear to Israeli and Western intelligence agencies and to the leaders, if not the people, who counted most: Nasser and Israeli prime minister Levi Eshkol. Eshkol feared an Arab *potential* to unite; he, like most other European-born Israelis of his generation, carried into their conflict with the Arabs the trauma of the Nazi genocide, and he was determined to stamp out sporadic Palestinian guerrilla attacks that Israelis feared in the same way, perhaps, that American settlers used to fear those of Indians. Nasser and the Arabs, however, feared the reality before them of a highly mobilized and militarized society that had displayed ruthless force in its dealings with them for nearly two decades. To the extent that Israel contemplated a final settlement, it was with the Arab states, but not with the Palestinians themselves. It prepared, in any case, for expansion. The Israeli general Yigal Allon, for example, wrote in the spring of 1967 that "in case of a new war, we must avoid the historic mistake of the War of Independence and, later, the Sinai Campaign. We must not cease fighting until we achieve the territorial fulfillment of the Land of Israel, and a peace agreement which will bring about normal relations between Israel and her neighbors."[4]

The West Bank Palestinians under Jordanian rule in particular had reason to fear Israel. Following the deaths of three Israeli soldiers killed by a land mine planted by Palestinian guerrillas, Israel launched a devastating reprisal attack against the tiny West Bank village of Samu in November 1966. Israeli soldiers razed most of the village, including its medical clinic and school. When Jordanian soldiers rushed to defend the village, the Israelis ambushed them, leaving eighteen Jordanian soldiers and civilians dead.[5] Israel collectively punished Palestinians in order to make them understand the exorbitant price they would pay if they aided guerrillas. The Hashemite government came under intense pressure to protect its nominal subjects. In April 1967, Israeli planes overflew the Syrian capital of Damascus; Israel's army operated essentially at will against the Jordanians and the Syrians. No matter how many Arabs it killed in the name of retaliation or deterrence, Israel presented itself as a tiny, besieged nation surrounded by a host of Arab enemies. In the words of Abba Eban, Israel's foreign minister in 1967, the Arab denial of Israel's "right to exist" constituted "the true origin of the tension which torments the Middle East."[6]

Nasser knew better, but he was both encouraged by his mistaken assessment of Egypt's ability to withstand an Israeli first strike and goaded on by Palestinian activists eager to transform words into deeds. The Jordanian government accused Nasser of hiding his army behind the UN forces in the Sinai rather than deterring Israeli aggression. In May 1967, he was warned by the Soviets that an Israeli invasion of Syria was imminent. Nasser acted. After seeking a limited withdrawal of a UN buffer force that operated on the Egyptian side of the border (the Israelis had never allowed UN troops to operate on their side of the border) and mobilizing his army, he blockaded the Straits of Tiran.

Nasser provided Israel with what it regarded as a casus belli at the same time as he encouraged a sense of anticipation on the part of many Arabs. Finally, there appeared to be an Arab leader willing to take on the Israelis. Radio Cairo lauded Nasser as a "new Saladin." From Lebanon to Iraq, the Arab press clamored for an Arab hero to finally do battle with their enemy who had time and again killed Arabs with impunity. Nasser obliged them. "If Western states brush us aside and disdain us, we will teach them to respect and value us," he insisted on the eve of a war he did not want. "Otherwise all our talk . . . [about Palestine] . . . and the rights of the Palestinian people will have been mere bombast."[7]

In the event, however, Nasser had merely provided the Israelis with a pretext to deliver a staggering blow to secular Arab nationalism and to the hopes of a generation of Arabs. Notwithstanding Egyptian propaganda, his Soviet-equipped army was no match for Israel's Western-supplied military. The Israelis seized their opportunity. They launched a surprise attack on June 5 and occupied huge swaths of Egyptian, Syrian, and yet more Palestinian territory. Sinai fell, the Golan Heights fell, East Jerusalem fell, Gaza fell, and so too did the West Bank. Once more hundreds of thousands of Palestinians fled or were expelled from their homes, this time from the West Bank; Syrian villagers were evicted from their homes in the Golan; East Jerusalem was annexed by Israel (the UN Security Council subsequently declared such action "invalid"), which also expelled the Arab inhabitants of an eight-hundred-year-old quarter adjacent to the Western Wall of the Haram al-Sharif and razed it to the ground in order to make way for what is today known as the Western Wall Plaza.[8]

Israel's evident military superiority greatly strengthened the pro-Israeli orientation of the United States policy. There no longer appeared to be any need to fear Arab nationalism or to take too seriously the disaffection among the Arabs about America's bias toward Israel. Lyndon Johnson was far more predisposed to Zionism than had been Eisenhower. He had staunch Zionist American Jewish friends, such as Abraham Feinberg, who ran American Bank & Trust Company and was a major Democratic Party fund-raiser, and Arthur Krim, head of United Artists Corporation, whose wife Mathilde was a former member of the Irgun organization that had carried out the bombing of the King David Hotel in 1946 and the infamous massacre of Palestinians at Deir Yassin in 1948. Both Feinberg and the Krims—who built a vacation home near Johnson's Texas ranch and had extraordinary access to the U.S. president—actively lobbied on behalf of Israel.

At a time of American quagmire in Vietnam, many of Johnson's key aides embraced what they regarded as Israeli boldness in beating back "radical" Arabs. One of them, Walt Rostow, the national security adviser, smugly referred to the "turkey shoot" of June 5.[9] The CIA had been aware of Israeli plans to demolish the Arab armies and predicted precisely how easily they could accomplish this task. Ten years earlier, during the Suez war, Eisenhower had forced Israel to abandon its conquest of the Sinai. Now, fatefully, Lyndon Johnson accepted the second Israeli conquest of the Sinai.

He also quickly accepted an Israeli apology after an Israeli air force and navy attack in international waters on an American intelligence-gathering ship, the USS *Liberty*, that went on for several hours on the morning of June 8 and left 34 U.S. sailors dead and 171 more wounded—the deadliest attack on Americans in the Middle East up until that point. Claiming that the American signals ship resembled an Egyptian transport ship less than half its size, the Israelis insisted that the strafing, napalming, and torpedoing of the ship was a tragic accident. Many of the American survivors and government officials at the time thought differently. The initial outrage and incomprehension in Washington over the attack turned, however, into official silence. Congress never held public hearings into the attack or formally investigated it.[10]

The widespread Arab revulsion at America's actions was also largely ignored. Throughout the Gulf region, where a large Palestinian community several hundred thousand strong had settled, and where Nasser's pan-Arab appeal was extensive, there was dismay at the Arab defeat and sporadic anti-American and anti-British rioting and acts of sabotage. More substantially, six Arab states, led by Egypt, cut their diplomatic relations with the United States. But these actions hardly moved the Johnson administration. Israel had become a useful stick with which to remind Arabs of their place in a U.S.-dominated Middle East. "The destruction of Nasser as an effective Pan-Arabist is fundamental to our hopes for gaining a reasonably quick settlement and for thus avoiding a protracted political impasse with all its dangers of further military action, polarization of the U.S. behind Israel, or both," reasoned the deputy assistant secretary of defense for international security affairs, Townsend Hoopes, in a memorandum to Secretary of Defense Robert McNamara written on June 8, 1967.[11]

Rather than becoming an impediment or embarrassment to U.S. policy toward the Arab world, Israeli militarism became one of its expressions. In 1962 President John F. Kennedy had authorized the sale of Hawk anti-aircraft missiles to Israel, but these were defensive weapons and were meant to have secured Israel's commitment to abandon its secret nuclear program. Israel took the Hawk missiles and developed nuclear weapons. Before the 1967 war, Johnson had authorized the sale of advanced U.S. weaponry to Israel, including M-48 tanks and A-4 Skyhawk fighter-bombers, seeking to supplant France as Israel's main weapon supplier. The American approach was premised, ultimately, on a wager that there was little the Arabs could do, individually or collectively, to alter America's growing relationship with the Jewish state.

The magnitude of the Israeli victory underscored the fact that only the United States, and not the Soviet Union, could be expected to restrain the Israelis. If the Arabs wanted even a partial return of territories seized by Israel, they would have to come to the White House and settle the Arab-Israeli conflict on American terms. The onus was on the Arabs to sue for peace, not on Israel to give up its newly occupied territories. U.S. officials hoped that the Arabs would now abandon their challenge to U.S. dominance in the region. They hoped, furthermore, that the Arabs would also abandon what Americans regarded as a fantasy of unification. "Stop talking about 'the Arab world,'" McGeorge Bundy admonished his colleagues on the National Security Council. "Help them come apart."[12] Most importantly, American officials hoped that the Arabs would accept the legitimacy of Israel by embracing the finality of their defeat in 1948. In return for normalizing their relationship with a country seen in the Arab world as aggressive and expansionist, the Arab rulers would be offered "peace," but one without justice as far as any Arab understood the term—a peace of the victors in which the Palestinian refugees would be permanently resettled outside their homeland.

This calculus of power was new in its boldness, but it was not, ultimately, a radical departure from the basic relationship that had already bound Arabs to the United States and that Charles Malik had outlined in his report to the Lebanese government in 1949. Malik had said then that American support for Israel was premised on both Arab military weakness and Israeli strength. He had also emphasized the virtual invisibility of Arabs, and the undeniable significance of Jews, in U.S. domestic politics. Finally, he had pointed to American religious and cultural identification with Israel.[13]

Little had changed since then. There was no Arab equivalent of the Krims in 1967. There was still no major Arab-American organization. Arab and Muslim Americans remained a negligible political force in the United States. Israel continued to defeat Arab armies in battle and therefore continued to define the terms of the Arab-Israeli-American relationship. Equally important, both Israel and its array of supporters in the United States strengthened their hold on how Americans perceived the Arab-Israeli conflict.

Major American Jewish organizations, including the American Israel Public Affairs Committee (AIPAC), which had been founded in 1953, were far more confident than American Zionists had been in 1948. They galvanized support for Israel and sought to stifle what little criticism of the Jewish state existed in the mainstream of America. They routinely and openly either accused American critics of Israel of anti-Semitism or imputed this motive to them. The Nazi Holocaust became even more of a central motif and served as a justification for both the idea of Zionism and Israel's belligerent approach to the Arabs. Genuine concern about the legacy of anti-Semitism thus intertwined with support for Israel. AIPAC accused the American Friends of the Middle East (AFME) of being an outlet for Arab propaganda. Just before the Six-Day War of 1967, AFME had its links to the CIA exposed. The organization was discredited as a front for U.S. intelligence and had to reconstitute itself as America-Mideast Educational and Training Services (AMIDEAST). In truth, the so-called Arabists had long been a spent force, if indeed they could ever have been considered a force at all. Israel and its allied American Jewish organizations reigned triumphant. In 1967 alone, the United Jewish Appeal raised more than $90 million for Israel, when Arab propaganda was turned on its head, and its bravado and hyperbole used to prove Israel's allegedly imperiled existence.[14]

American Jews were unquestionably proud and deeply attached to Israel. A few individuals, such as Rabbi Elmer Berger, who was one of the important leaders of the anti-Zionist American Council for Judaism and who had worked with AFME, reminded Jewish Americans of Zionism's meaning to Arabs, but Berger cut a lonely figure at the moment of Israel's success in 1967. American Jews did not want to hear about the hundreds of thousands of Arab victims of Israel. They were, in Berger's recollection, in a state of "intoxication" by Israel's lightning victory.[15] Indeed, the Zionist partisans among them went further.

Just as Uris had done in *Exodus*, AIPAC vehemently denied that the Palestinians had been uprooted at all in 1948. It blamed Arabs for rejecting partition without explaining the actual details of the partition plan or the nature of Zionist colonization of Palestine. American Zionists, furthermore, successfully framed for many Americans the origins of the Arab-Israeli conflict as essentially an Arab rejection of Jews and as rank anti-Semitism rather than as an Arab struggle for self-determination. AIPAC, for example, sent its *Near East Report* newsletter to members of Congress, journalists, congressional staffers, college students and professors. The publication highlighted anti-American or anti-Israeli comments made by Arab officials—invariably out of context—to illustrate what the lobby insisted was the fanatical and anti-Western nature of Arab opposition to Israel. It sought, moreover, to obscure the principal cost of America's relationship with Israel, which, aside from growing financial and military support for a foreign state, was the steady alienation of Arab and Muslim opinion from the United States.[16]

At a more general level, Jewish and non-Jewish liberal Americans continued to view the Arab-Israeli conflict from within a Zionist paradigm—or at the very least, from a perspective that fully accepted Zionist assumptions about the origins of the Arab-Israeli conflict and therefore about the 1967 war. By and large, Americans, with very limited access to

Arab perspectives, continued to remain ignorant of the history of Zionist colonization and Arab dispossession as completely as Algerians, Egyptians, Saudis, Lebanese, Syrians, and Iraqis took it for granted. With this key aspect of the Arab-Israeli conflict obscured, Israel's actions—especially its attack on various Arab states in June 1967—were sympathetically portrayed in the American media as matters of defense, security, and even "survival" in the face of an unreasonable and provocative Arab menace. According to this picture, the Arabs sought Jewish Israel's "destruction"; Israel was merely retaliating against a terrifying threat.[17]

On June 4, 3,742 American university professors signed a petition urging President Johnson to "safeguard the integrity of the state of Israel." They ignored the fact that a mere decade earlier Israel, together with Britain and France, had invaded Egypt. In addition, a "cross-section" of American Christians, "men of good faith" and "men of conscience," placed a full-page advertisement in the *New York Times* that called for the United States to stand by Israel. "Let us recall," the advertisement declared, "that Israel is a new nation whose people are still recovering from the horror and decimation of the European holocaust."[18] Signatories included the emeritus professor of Union Theological Seminary, the theologian Reinhold Niebuhr, and the leader of the struggle for civil rights in America, Martin Luther King Jr.

That a man like Martin Luther King could stand so openly with Israel, despite his own private qualms and criticism by younger, more radical, black Americans who had discovered the plight of the Palestinians, indicated the degree to which Zionism was embraced by the American mainstream. The tremendous social changes in America, the rise of both the counterculture and civil rights movements, and the growing protests against the Vietnam War did not impinge on an emerging consensus that placed America solidly behind Israel. Along with many other black ministers of his day, King's rhetoric was shaped not only by the black churches' traditional use of imagery and narrative based on the Old Testament, by the identification of black slavery with Jewish bondage to Pharaoh, and by the hope of freedom expressed in the "promised land"; it was shaped also by the parallels he drew between the modern Jewish struggle for statehood and contemporary black American attempts at liberation. And yet King would not tolerate what he believed were false analogies between the oppression of blacks in America and the fate of the Arabs at the hands of Israel. He genuinely deplored anti-Jewish prejudice among black American critics of Israel. One of the ways, however, that he reciprocated Jewish American support for desegregation in the United States was by turning a blind eye to the plight of the Palestinians.

The Arab historian George Antonius had anticipated as early as 1938 that the Western abjuration of anti-Semitism would rationalize the oppression of Arabs. Nearly thirty years on, his fears proved well founded. American Cold Warriors came to love Israel because it taught the Soviet-backed Arabs their place in the world, but American liberals continued to love Israel as they had in 1948. Israel's story, they still believed, was their story. The versatility and range of the meaning of Israel to Americans was impressive. It was liberal to American liberals, anti-Communist to Cold Warriors, Jewish to American Jews, and prophetic to a resurgent Christian Zionist movement that was itself a part of the wider white conservative political movement that would come to prominence in the 1970s. Christian Zionists drew strength from Israel's overwhelming victory in 1967, but imbued it with great eschatological, rather than secular liberal, significance.

For Christian Zionists, the fall of Jerusalem into Israeli hands was a portent of things to come, a prelude to the so-called tribulations, Armageddon, and Rapture that they believed were soon to engulf humanity. A Texan called Hal Lindsey expounded on these apocalyptic speculations in *The Late Great Planet Earth*. The book, which first appeared in 1970, was a publishing sensation. It became the best-selling nonfiction book of the decade, selling more than 35 million copies in over fifty languages.[19] Faith, self-congratulation, and obscurantism raged among dispensationalists, the vast majority of whom, like their nineteenth-century predecessor William Blackstone, disregarded Arab humanity, let alone the Arab perspective on the Arab-Israeli conflict.

If secular, liberal Americans marked the Arabs as backward and anti-Semitic, Christian Zionists depicted them as Satan's emissaries—as a people possessed by a "perpetual hatred" but destined for annihilation. The dean of Talbot Theological Seminary, Charles L. Feinberg, opined that Arabs would inevitably be "cast out" by God and replaced by the "sons of Isaac."[20] Feinberg used a more overtly religious language than the ostensibly objective mainstream American newspapers, but both Feinberg and the newspapers were enamored of the Israeli conquest of Jerusalem.

The multifaceted American embrace of Israel inevitably cast a pall over Americans resident in the Arab world. The ascendancy of Christian Zionism was paralleled by the final demise of the long-standing American mission to Egypt. The men and women whose predecessors sought to convert Muslims and Copts and in the process opened schools, orphanages, and clinics in Egypt had been losing ground steadily to the nationalists and Islamists in Egypt and the Arab world. A series of laws passed by Nasser's regime over two decades had effectively nationalized missionary institutions—the laws made it mandatory to teach students their own religion and also required Egyptian directorship of all schools. In 1964 the Sudanese government expelled all foreign missionaries.[21]

In the wake of the 1967 war, anti-American sentiment in Egypt had grown so extensive that most Americans left what had suddenly become an inhospitable country. Among them was Ellen Van Dyck, the eighty-two-year-old granddaughter of the legendary American missionary to Syria, Cornelius Van Dyck—one of the few missionaries to have truly won the affection of leading Syrians of his day. In Lebanon, meanwhile, the inheritors of the original American mission to the Middle East that had set out to the Ottoman Empire in 1820 reconstituted themselves as the United Presbyterian Commission in 1958; the few remaining American Christians were no longer referred to as missionaries but as "fraternal workers," and they worked under the authority of the local Arab Presbyterian Church.

Arab Protestants who had traditionally been at the forefront of American cultural engagement with the Arab world took a sharply different perspective on the meaning of Israel than did mainline American churches and evangelical Christian Zionists. The Coptic Evangelical Church, operating in the acutely nationalist environment of Nasser's

Egypt, was at pains to declare its solidarity with the Palestinians. Arab Protestant congregations were unable to relate to the Holocaust-driven paradigm that structured so much of liberal American Christian views of the Arab-Israeli conflict. They also refused to engage in the equivocation that made Arabs—including Palestinian Christians, whose existence was scarcely acknowledged in the United States—pay the penalty for Western guilt over European persecution of the Jews. The Near East Council of Churches, which had been founded in 1964, insisted on Christian witness, justice, and aid for the Palestinian refugees, setting up the Near East Council of Churches Committee for Refugee Work.[22]

The end of the American missions to Egypt and Lebanon, nevertheless, closed a significant chapter in U.S.-Arab relations. Although both the American University in Cairo and the American University of Beirut survived the near-total breakdown of U.S.-Egyptian relations, these institutions, operating as orphans of a different age, were torn between the past and present symbolism of America in the region. Their heritage pointed to an era when American prestige ran high and Wilsonian idealism was able to capture a crucial portion of educated Arab opinion; current U.S. foreign policy, however, continually diminished Arab faith in America.

As had been the case in 1948, Americans who lived in the Arab world and were familiar with Arabs were far less enamored of Israel and its conquest of Syrian, Egyptian, and Palestinian land in 1967, or with U.S. policy toward the region overall, than were those Christians and Jews who saw Arabs only as an abstraction, a problem, and a people without history. In Beirut several American citizens, mostly faculty members at AUB, created an organization called Americans for Justice in the Middle East (AJME). They were alarmed by what they regarded as the "lack of balance in the U.S. press coverage of the recent Israeli-Arab conflict. Whereas the Israeli point of view has received sympathetic coverage throughout the Western world, the Arab side of the story all too frequently has been inadequately presented." The refrain of AJME was almost identical to that of Hitti and Eddy: The prestige of the United States had been damaged and would continue to be damaged throughout the Arab Middle East as a result of America's pro-Israel policy, which was costing the country "friends, diplomatic support, and dollars." Once more, Americans on the ground believed firmly that if only the American public were presented with all sides of the story of the Arab-Israeli conflict, it would inevitably understand the nature of Arab "grievances" and the "validity" of the Arab position.[23] These Americans were also defending to themselves their own perceptions of an earlier, more idealistic United States betrayed by its foreign policy in the Middle East.

Israel, in short, appeared to many Americans living in the Arab world much as it appeared to Arabs. The Palestinian refugee camps, of course, were the greatest reminder of what Israel had done, but so too was the demonstration of Israeli military power during the 1967 war and in its aftermath. In December 1968, for example, soon after the United States announced that it was selling its most advanced military jet of the era, the F-4 Phantom fighter-bomber, to Israel, Israeli commandos landed in Beirut Airport. In less than an hour, they destroyed thirteen Lebanese civilian airliners, including two-thirds of the fleet of the national carrier, to avenge an attack by Palestinian guerillas on an Israeli airliner in Athens. But so great was the damage to a pro-Western Lebanese government, that an embarrassed United States found itself obliged to vote in favor of a UN resolution that chastised Israel for its vengeful raid. Overt U.S. military support for Israel, however, continued apace.

In vain would Americans in Lebanon and Saudi Arabia point out to Arabs that not all Americans supported the pro-Israeli bias of U.S. policy toward the region, and in vain would they urge an American policy that was more consistent with American professions of freedom. AJME, for example, put together a journal called the *Middle East Newsletter* that disseminated this viewpoint. The problem was that few people in the United States actually read or were influenced by so tiny an organization or its journal. At the same time, and to an even greater extent than "pro-Arab" missionaries and educators had been in 1948, AJME and the few other Americans who pleaded for a more evenhanded approach to the Arab-Israeli conflict were overwhelmed by the level of American government and mainstream support for Israel.

Arabs in America were also stunned by the overt identification of Americans with Israel in 1967. As far as any of them could tell, cause and effect, fact and fiction, were reversed. Goliath was portrayed as David, and David as Goliath. If the American Zionist commitment to Israel could be summed up in the word "security," "justice" was the mantra of those who supported Palestinian human and national rights. The two notions evoked entirely different ways of looking at the Arab-Israeli conflict: The Zionist way inevitably referred back to a history of Western anti-Semitism that culminated in the Holocaust and justified, in the name of security for the Jewish people, the dispossession of Arabs and an aggressive "iron wall" strategy toward them. The Palestinian way referred to a history of systematic imperialism and expropriation that began with the Balfour Declaration and culminated with the *nakba* of 1948.

In October 1967, in the wake of the June war, a group of young Arab graduates of American institutions, led by Rashid Bashshur, a Syrian sociologist at the University of Michigan's School of Public Health, Abdeen Jabara, an Arab-American lawyer from Detroit, and Ibrahim Abu-Lughod, a Palestinian professor who then taught at Smith College, founded an organization called the Association of Arab American University Graduates in Chicago. One of its principal aims was "promoting understanding of the Arab case" in the United States.[24]

Unlike earlier Syrian immigrants, who were mostly apolitical and who had been assimilated into American society, the men and women who joined AAUG were shaped by the nationalist age in which they had been immersed. They now called themselves Arab Americans, in part because of the consolidation of Arab political identity and in part because the new immigrants had arrived from many parts of the Arab world and thus could no longer properly be described as "Syrian." They had settled in the United States following the lifting of race-based immigration restrictions in 1952. Their political outlook was framed largely by the tragic history of Palestine and by their reaction to the crude stereotypes and ignorance they encountered on the subject in the United States. Many of the new immigrants were Muslim, although the Arab-American community remained predominantly Christian and did not identify easily with Arab nationalist causes.

The AAUG members were not the first Arabs to try to inform Americans about their history and culture, for they followed in the footsteps of Ameen Rihani and Philip Hitti. But as young Arab-American academics and professionals, they had witnessed the civil rights struggle and the anti-Vietnam marches and were inspired by the success of the Algerian war of independence. They were confident, therefore, that given enough objective information, most Americans could tell right from wrong and at least begin to see things from their perspective. They were idealistic and, in their own way, naive in their expectations. But they also comprehended far more than any of their predecessors that their success depended on breaking down the wall of denial around Palestine and the Palestinians that American Zionists had built.

Among this group was a professor of English and comparative literature at Columbia University. Edward Said was born in Jerusalem, raised in Cairo, and educated in America. Said's parents were Palestinian Christians, and his upbringing and heritage represented a merging of American and Arab traditions. His maternal great-grandfather was the first Arab pastor of the national evangelical Protestant church in Beirut. His maternal grandfather had traveled to America in 1908, ended up in Waco, Texas, converted from his Greek Catholic faith and become a Baptist, then returned in 1910 to the Ottoman Empire, where he became the first Arab Baptist pastor in Palestine and inaugurated the Southern Baptist Convention's mission to Palestine in Nazareth. Said's father served in the U.S. army during World War I in France and felt privileged to become an American citizen. He ran a stationery business, first in Jerusalem, and then expanded it to Cairo. The main store was burned down in the nationalist riot of January 1952, and the business was subsequently liquidated, so Said's parents moved to Lebanon.

Said himself was educated in the United States at Princeton University and then at Harvard, where he earned a doctorate in English literature in 1964. He was transformed by the negative stereotypes of Arabs in America during the 1967 war and used his passion for literary criticism to commence an urgent study of how such portrayals helped justify Western domination over the Arabs. He was not the first scholar to criticize Western depiction of Arabs. In their own way, George Antonius and Albert Hourani had earlier taken issue with what they saw as misleading or simply inaccurate descriptions of Arab history or political positions. However, Said's argument, which he developed over a decade and eventually published in 1978 in a seminal book entitled *Orientalism*, was neither a nationalist manifesto nor a defense of the "real" Arab world. Rather, Said insisted that the very idea of juxtaposing the "civilized West" with the "barbaric East" was an artifact of cultural and political imagination, or what he called Orientalism. This notion, he said, was advanced, in turn, by experts and specialists—the Orientalists—who spoke with great confidence about "the Orient" or "the Muslim" or "the Arab" as if such singular phenomena existed, but rarely allowed Arabs or Muslims to speak for themselves or to narrate their own histories. It was through this same process of representation that Israel could be celebrated so openly in the West as the pinnacle of morality despite what Zionism had entailed for Palestinians, and that Arabs themselves could be excoriated as Jewish Israel's immoral, dangerous antithesis. "Thus," Said wrote, "if the Arab occupies space enough for attention, it is a negative value. He is seen as the disrupter of Israel's and the West's existence, or in another view of the same thing, as a surmountable obstacle to Israel's creation in 1948."[25]

Because Said contended that ultimately neither the "East" nor the "West" existed as overarching, grand entities, he therefore insisted that there could also be no such thing as a clash between West and East. Rather, there were scholars, politicians, writers, and thinkers who were invested in totalizing ideas that inevitably justified political subjugation and served power rather than knowledge. It was the task of the community of "humanist" scholars, regardless of their faith or nationality, he said, to oppose these dangerous constructs that played on and perpetuated ignorance and injustice. His book presented a radical and, at the time, radically controversial argument, and as with all such arguments, it was not without its flaws, but *Orientalism* cemented Said's academic reputation as one of foremost intellectuals in the world.

Said rapidly emerged as the most articulate spokesman for the Palestinians in the West. He did not pretend to be a detached observer and instead came out as both a Palestinian shaped by the experience of exile and an American privileged by his formidable education. Said was singularly fluent in English and deeply versed in Western literature, music, and art. Positioned at the pinnacle of American university life at Columbia University, he was confident and insistent in his speeches on the question of Palestine—to the delight of Arab Americans, who saw in Said someone who could articulate their cause passionately and who could put the Palestinian case to Americans in basic, human terms. Not surprisingly, he gained the enmity of AIPAC and other Zionist organizations, which vilified him as an anti-Semite or, most typically, as "anti-Israel," as if hatred of Israel rather than justice for the Palestinians was what motivated him and other advocates of Palestinian rights. Said, however, pressed liberal Americans, especially Jewish Americans, to confront the contradiction in their commitment to secular equality in the United States and their attachment to a state that was based fundamentally upon the discrimination between Jew and non-Jew.

Such a state of affairs was, he knew, radically different from the American idea of civil rights. As he pointed out repeatedly, Israel conceived of itself as the state of the Jews worldwide, not of its citizens. On this basis it barred (as it still does) its non-Jewish—that is to say, Palestinian—citizens from ownership of land held in trust on behalf of the Jewish people worldwide by organizations such as the Jewish National Fund, and from equal educational and employment opportunities. The state also forbids intermarriage between Jews and non-Jews and explicitly encourages Jews from anywhere in the world to become citizens of Israel, but it refuses the Palestinians their right of return.[26] The United States, by contrast, is the state of all its citizens regardless of their race, religion, or ethnicity.

From early on, Said advocated a way out of the impasse of the Arab denial of Israel and the Israeli negation of the Palestinians. Pointing out that neither Arabs nor Israelis could ultimately impose a military solution on the other, he called instead for them to understand their interdependency. For Arabs, such an understanding required grappling with the history of anti-Semitism, especially what the Nazi Holocaust meant to the Jews, hence understanding the importance to them of the idea of a Jewish homeland and security. The Israelis needed to understand the nature of the Palestinian struggle for self-determination and also the inherently discriminatory nature of Zionism in Palestine. For Said, "security" and "justice" had to be mutually reinforcing concepts. One without the other was simply a prescription for further enmity. "Unhappily," he wrote in the late 1970s, "the question of Palestine will renew itself in all too well-known forms. But so too will the people of Palestine—Arabs and Jews—whose past and future ties them inexorably together. Their encounter has yet to occur on any important scale. But it will occur, I know, and it will be to their mutual benefit."[27]

Such an encounter was hard to imagine in 1967. The paradox of American support for Israel—made sacrosanct by U.S. domestic politics and yet itself a lightning rod for anti-American sentiment among Arabs—deepened profoundly following the Six-Day War. As Israel confronted the implications of its success, the Arab states were traumatized by their failure. Unable to go to war against Israel successfully, they were unprepared as yet to make peace on American terms. For the second time in twenty years, they had to draw on reserves of defiance built up in response to Western colonialism and by the fact of the Israeli occupation of Arab lands.

Although Nasser euphemistically referred to the war as the "setback," or the *naksa*, as opposed to the *nakba* ("catastrophe") of 1948, the totality of Arab defeat could not be denied. Nasser blamed the Americans for misleading him in the run-up to the war and also for colluding with the Israelis militarily during the war. He blamed his chief of staff, Field Marshal Abdel-Hakim Amer, for his incompetence, although it was Nasser who had trusted and promoted Amer over the years. But Nasser also understood his overall responsibility for the defeat that had befallen Egypt and the Arabs. He resigned, therefore, on June 9. "The forces of imperialism believe that Gamal Abdel-Nasser is their enemy," said Nasser. "I want it to be clear to them that it is the whole Arab nation, not just Gamal Abdel-Nasser, that is their enemy."[28] The basic truth of Nasser's assertion that the United States and Israel had confused the person with the cause of Arab unity could have equally been applied to the Arabs of his day.

Most of his own people had sublimated their political aspirations into one man. They could imagine no alternative. They had lost sight of the fact that Nasser was meant to symbolize Arab unity, not monopolize it.

The news of Nasser's resignation was met at first with disbelief, especially since the conflict was still raging on the Syrian front and because Arab propaganda in the first days of the war had indicated the imminence of an Arab victory, not the comprehensiveness of their defeat. Thousands of Egyptians surged into the streets of Cairo demanding that Nasser stay in his post. In Qatar the police force in Doha wept openly when they heard Nasser's broadcast, and a British official there remarked spitefully that they lamented the "downfall of their god."[29] Hundreds of thousands of Egyptians and other Arabs were stunned by the prospect of being left leaderless. Their demonstrations of support reflected a desperate faith in the first modern Arab leader who had successfully attracted a genuinely pan-Arab following. Nasser all too quickly withdrew his resignation.

At the Arab summit at Khartoum, Sudan, in late August 1967, Egypt accepted its financial dependency on the Saudis; the two formerly bitter rivals closed ranks and declared that they would fight politically "to eliminate the effects of the aggression and to ensure the withdrawal of the aggressive Israeli forces from the Arab lands which have been occupied since the aggression of June 5." Egypt and Saudi Arabia implicitly recognized that Israel within its pre-1967 borders now constituted a fait accompli that they would no longer challenge; henceforth, the occupied Palestinian territories of the West Bank, East Jerusalem, and Gaza, the Egyptian Sinai, and the Syrian Golan Heights were to be the primary arenas of Arab resistance. As a sop to the more radical elements among the conferees and to assuage the bitter hatred of Israeli colonialism among Arabs, they also vowed to abide by general Arab principles, including "no peace with Israel, no recognition of Israel, no negotiations with it, and the insistence on the right of the Palestinian people in its [original] homeland."[30]

The contradictions of the Arab position that emerged from Khartoum were matched by the ambiguity of UN Security Council Resolution 242, which was passed in November 1967. On the one hand, the resolution, which became the foundation of all future Arab-Israeli peacemaking, declared the "inadmissibility of the acquisition of territory by war and the need to work for a just and lasting peace in which every State in the area can live in security." On the other hand, it did not demand that Israel withdraw unconditionally from all its recently conquered territories. Rather, it merely admitted that any just solution would have to be based upon the "withdrawal of Israel armed forces from territories occupied in the recent conflict" and called vaguely for a "just settlement of the refugee problem."[31] The Arab states understood immediately that this formulation suited Israel far more than it suited them, for it evaded the root of the problem of Zionist colonization of Palestine and left the Palestinian refugees in limbo for the foreseeable future. Indeed, the resolution reflected a further alignment of the United States behind an Israeli conception of future peace that would be based upon bilateral relations with Arab states but not on the establishment of an independent Palestinian state.

Syria regarded the UN resolution as wholly inadequate. Jordan and Egypt accepted it. At the same time, however, they were themselves not yet able or willing to formally accept the fait accompli of Israel's creation. Though Israel also accepted the resolution, it believed that time was on its side. Israeli leaders were in no hurry to make peace with Arab states, let alone acknowledge the rights and aspirations of the Palestinian people. "There was no such thing as Palestinians," Israeli prime minister Golda Meir informed the British *Sunday Times* in 1969, justifying the Zionist colonization of Palestine. "It was not as though there was a Palestinian people in Palestine considering itself a Palestinian people and we came and threw them out and took their country away from them. They did not exist."[32] The cycle of mutual denial continued.

With Israel emboldened by its victory, an exhausted and disillusioned Nasser stayed in power for three more years, during which time he oversaw the rebuilding of the Egyptian army with yet more Soviet weapons and advisers. He engaged in a war of attrition between 1969 and 1970 against the Israelis, who dug in on the East Bank of the Suez Canal. As with every Arab-Israeli war, the cost to the Egyptians was far greater than the cost to the Israelis, especially after the Israelis began devastating Egyptian cities along the Nile delta with American-made Phantom bombers, attacks to which the Egyptians initially had no answer. Ultimately, Nasser accepted an initiative by U.S. Secretary of State William Rogers to achieve a durable cease-fire between the Israelis and the Egyptians, as a prelude to more substantial peace talks based upon Resolution 242. The peace talks did not occur, but the cease-fire held in August 1970.

At the twilight of his rule, the Egyptian leader was bitterly criticized by other so-called progressive Arab states and by new groups of Palestinian revolutionaries who feared that Egypt might sign a separate peace with Israel and thus abandon the Palestinians to their fate as a stateless people. Nasser responded by dismissing the self-styled Palestinian, Algerian, Syrian, and Iraqi revolutionaries who attacked him. They insisted on vigilance against "the capitulationists"—that is, those who would allegedly capitulate to U.S. and Israeli hegemony—but they offered no coherent plan to effect the liberation of occupied Arab lands.[33]

The trauma of their dispersal in 1948 had left Palestinians in disarray. A shattered society could not easily reconstitute itself in exile. Palestinians found work where they could—the Arab Gulf states were an especially attractive magnet for those fortunate enough to find their way there—but in the squalid refugee camps in Lebanon, Syria, and Jordan to which they had been consigned, younger Palestinians ineluctably grew restless and dissatisfied with their state of subsistence as stateless Arabs in Arab states and Palestinians without Palestine. In an era when Vietnam and Algeria were being decolonized, it was to be expected that Palestinians would organize themselves into a nationalist movement.

Nasser, of course, had encouraged the formation of the Palestine Liberation Organization (PLO) and for over a decade had articulated the grievances of the Palestinians to the world; they, in turn, had put their faith in him, until the crushing defeat of Egypt in 1967 galvanized Palestinian guerrilla factions to take their destiny into their own hands. Their most important leader was Yasser Arafat, whose family was from Gaza and who had studied civil engineering at Cairo before moving to Kuwait. There, in the mid-1960s, he had established an organization called Fatah, whose goal—directly inspired by the success of the Algerian war of independence—was to liberate Palestine through an "armed struggle" that relied on Palestinian strength and initiative.

Fatah had begun launching attacks on Israeli targets even before the 1967 war, and after the conflict ended, Palestinian fighters, reinforced by Jordanian army units, fought a much larger Israeli military force backed by the Israeli air force in what became a legendary battle in the village of Karameh in Jordan in March 1968. Although his fighters were militarily inferior to the Israelis and suffered heavy casualties as a result, Arafat ordered his men to stand their ground. That day, 156 Palestinians, 84 Jordanians, and 33 Israelis were killed, and the Israelis, surprised by the tenacity of the resistance they encountered, withdrew.[34]

Coming so soon after the disaster of 1967, the battle had an enormous psychological impact among Palestinians and Arabs. It proved that with enough motivation and a willingness to sacrifice, Arabs could fight and not retreat precipitously, as the Egyptian army had been ordered to do during the Six-Day War. That Karameh means "dignity" in Arabic and that the Palestinian fighters were known as the *fedayeen* (those who sacrificed themselves for the cause of Palestine) only added to the mystique of the battle. Overnight Arafat became a new Arab hero, and Fatah's ranks swelled with volunteers. The same enthusiasm that had greeted Nasser's act of defiance at Suez was transferred to Arafat at Karameh.

Karameh, however, had not changed the military balance of power; the guerrilla raids into Israel that occasionally killed Israeli civilians and soldiers more often than not ended with the deaths of the guerrillas themselves. Palestinian civilians in the West Bank and Gaza suffered in the collective punishment that invariably followed the raids, which included blanket curfews, deportations, torture, and home demolitions. The Israeli military was not afraid of the Palestinian commandos, no matter how greatly Fatah exaggerated its own prowess; sporadic Palestinian attacks solidified, rather than sapped, Israeli morale and did nothing to liberate occupied territory. The initial concept of armed struggle, moreover, left no room for any possible accommodation with Israeli Jews because it was premised on their return to their countries of origin as the sole means to rectify the injustice of 1948. It consolidated American Jewish support for Israel and antagonized host Arab states, such as Jordan, where Fatah now based itself, and Lebanon, where large refugee camps bore the brunt of Israeli retaliations. Unlike Nasser, who led the most populous Arab country with the most significant Arab army of his day, Arafat had neither a proper army nor a state to call his own. The exchange of Nasser's mystique for Arafat's was hardly auspicious for the actual freedom of the millions of Palestinians in exile or under occupation, but it appeared to be a step on the path toward Palestinian self-determination.

Military victory, in any case, was not the immediate goal of the armed struggle of the Palestinians. Rather, as was the case with the National Liberation Front in Algeria, their violence was meant to visibly and rapidly establish Palestinians as the central actors of their own drama, bring them to the attention of their fellow Arabs, and thrust their saga before a world that had studiously ignored their national aspirations up until this point. Arafat's portrait, with what would become his trademark kaffiyeh and sunglasses, appeared on the cover of *Time* magazine on December 13, 1968, under the title "The Arab Commandoes: Defiant New Force in the Middle East." For many Americans, this was their first glimpse of a Palestinian, and it provided the first inkling that besides the heroic story of Israel and Zionism that they knew so well, there might also be an Arab story to be heard.

Arafat took over the PLO's leadership in early 1969. From the outset, however, he had to contend with competing Palestinian factions, each with a different strategy and, often, a different patron. The Palestinian revolutionary George Habash was Arafat's most serious rival. During 1947, Habash had been enrolled as a medical student at AUB. By his own admission, he was not initially politicized. But after the UN partition of Palestine, he found himself demonstrating against Zionism and attending lectures by the Arab nationalist professor Constantine Zurayk. He assumed at first, like many Arabs outside of Palestine, that the Zionist forces would be easily routed. It was only when he returned in 1948 to his hometown of al-Lydd (today Lod in Israel) and witnessed how Israeli soldiers turned the Arab population out of their homes that the full reality of the *nakba* struck him. Helpless at the time, he returned to AUB to specialize in pediatric medicine and graduated from AUB in 1951. Habash exemplified the nationalist mood that had overtaken the venerable American missionary institution in the post-1948 era. He had been instrumental in the formation of the Movement of Arab Nationalists, which was an outgrowth of the radicalization of Christian and Muslim Arab students following the *nakba*. A charismatic orator, he believed that Palestine was a pan-Arab question that required a pan-Arab political and military strategy.

After the 1967 war, however, Habash understood that he could no longer pin his hopes for liberation on existing Arab leadership, and especially not on Nasser. He founded, therefore, the Popular Front for the Liberation of Palestine (PFLP), which was explicitly Marxist in its ideology. Although the PFLP's ethos tied the liberation of Palestine to the liberation of all Arabs from what he called "reactionary" regimes, the apparent success of Fatah at Karameh demanded equivalent action. Even more so than Arafat, Habash wished to shatter Western complacency and to remind Americans and Europeans of their culpability in his people's dispossession. Instead of Fatah's emphasis on armed struggle against Israel, Habash advocated uncompromising militancy against the "Arab bourgeoisie" and "world imperialism."[35] By any means necessary, the PFLP was determined to bring Palestine to the attention of the world.

On July 23, 1968, PFLP members hijacked an Israeli civilian airliner from Rome and diverted it to Algiers. Within a year, Israeli aircraft and interests were attacked in Athens, Zurich, London, the Hague, Brussels, and Bonn. In late August 1969, two Palestinians hijacked a TWA airliner over the Adriatic, reportedly because the Israeli ambassador to the United States, Yitzhak Rabin, who had overseen the ethnic cleansing of Habash's al-Lydd in 1948, was onboard. The hijackers said that they belonged to the "Che Guevara" commando unit of the PFLP and did not intend to harm any of the other passengers, but that they wanted to bring one of the men responsible for the misery of their people before a "revolutionary Palestininan court."[36]

One of the hijackers was a twenty-four-year-old Palestinian woman by the name of Leila Khaled; born in Haifa, she and her family had been expelled from there in 1948. Khaled became a refugee in Tyre in south Lebanon, dependent on UNRWA rations. She was educated at a local Protestant school and eventually enrolled at AUB. One form of American involvement in the Arab world had enabled and legitimated her dispossession; the legacy of another, much older, engagement educated her. Khaled was both embittered and radicalized by her people's tragedy. She was also determined to do something about it. She dogmatically dismissed AUB as a "provincial school that only excelled in producing CIA spies and ministers,"[37] and yet there she became involved with the Arab Nationalist Movement, which eventually drew her to the PFLP. She divided her world, which revolved around the idea of Palestine, into revolutionaries and counterrevolutionaries, nationalists and CIA spies, democrats and imperialists.

Leila Khaled encountered only a couple of Americans in Lebanon—a schoolteacher and a YWCA staff member. She debated the question of Palestine with them, but rejected their censure of Palestinian violence and their calls for peace and coexistence between Arab and Jew. For her, such a sentiment reflected a facile Western liberalism that was out of touch with her own experience of statelessness, that was ignorant of the nature of Zionism in Palestine, and that little comprehended the degree to which the United States remained complicit in her people's misery. So intense was her political hostility to America, and so beguiled was she by the revolutionary slogans of her era, that Khaled described the TWA plane she hijacked as an "imperialist" plane. She told air traffic controllers that "we have kidnapped this American plane because Israel is a colony of America and the Americans are giving the Israelis Phantom planes."[38] The plane was diverted to Damascus, where the hijackers released the passengers but destroyed the plane.

Thus was the age of Palestinian violence born—out of two decades of oppression at the hands of Israel, frustration at the lot of Palestinians in the Arab world, and almost total disinterest of the West in the Palestinian experience. The defeat of the Arab states in 1967 was the catalyst for action, but colonial Zionism was the root cause. The Palestinians who engaged in these early operations usually released the crew and passengers, but in several operations they either wounded or killed civilians. That these attacks were illegal, terrifying to those who endured them, and universally condemned in the West as reprehensible was not lost on the Palestinians. For twenty years, however, the Arab appeals to justice had fallen on deaf ears in the United States and Europe. America, Leila Khaled had said, was not innocent and therefore had to accept its responsibility as a party to the Arab-Israeli conflict. A PFLP journal in Beirut at the time declared that "America is Israel, and Israel is America."[39]

The targeting of civilian airliners, especially American ones, was another turning point in U.S.-Arab relations. The phenomenon of hijacking would estrange Americans from the Arabs as much as the Arabs had become estranged from America because of the 1967 war. In both instances, the Palestinian-Israeli conflict was at the heart of the issue. Although Arafat condemned the hijackings because they harmed the image of the Palestinians, there was little he could do to prevent the identification of many Arabs with Leila Khaled and her fellow hijackers. Quite simply, violence was seen as the response to injustice. The *nakba* came first—then the Arab reaction. Leila Khaled did not hate American society or culture, but quite clearly she and most Palestinians, who were in the midst of a struggle to survive as a people, saw the U.S. government, because of its financial, political, and military support for Israel, as unremittingly—and unjustly—hostile to them.

Americans, predictably, saw things differently. For them, hijackings and attacks on civilians inside Israel and abroad erupted out of the blue and became for them the essence of the Palestinian question rather than a sign of it. The reality of the suffering and violence endured by the Palestinians could hardly come across in the coercive crash course in the *nakba* represented by the hijackings. The language of "revolutionary violence" and "resistance" was also jarring to Americans; most of them had no knowledge of the history of Palestine and related to the passengers of the hijacked planes rather than to the hijackers.

Like Fatah's armed struggle, hijacking was a method with diminishing returns. Both were tactics designed at once to give voice to the Palestinians and to give authority and power to the leaders of the "revolution." Leila Khaled and others like her may have indeed brought the Palestinian question to the attention of the world, but the chorus of international condemnation of air piracy and the "dedicated, vicious political fanatics" who practiced it played directly into Israeli hands.[40] The hijackings (and subsequent bloody operations such as those of Munich in 1972) carried out by secular revolutionaries firmly identified to Americans the Palestinians with terrorism, and Israelis as their victims. The slogans used by the PFLP to justify its actions—"world imperialism," "colonialism," and "revolutionary violence"—were as hollow to Americans as had become the American evocations of "freedom," "democracy," and the "free world" to Arabs. The hijackings, moreover, were bound, sooner rather than later, to lead to an overwhelming response from more powerful enemies. Israel crushed the *fedayeen* in Gaza and pacified the West Bank; security was tightened at European airports; Israelis became more vigilant; and the Arab states that hosted Palestinians feared for their own sovereignty and worried about Israeli reprisals.

When the PFLP hijacked several New York–bound American and Swiss airliners and a Beirut-bound British aircraft in September 1970, they forced the planes to an abandoned former Royal Air Force landing strip in Jordan called Dawson's Field. Leila Khaled failed in her attempt to hijack a New York–bound El Al plane and was arrested in London. The PFLP, meanwhile, demanded the release of Palestinians jailed in Israel and the West. The hijackers eventually released all of the passengers, but to demonstrate their intent they blew up the empty planes. At Cairo Airport, the PFLP also blew up a hijacked Pan Am 747 in an act of defiance against Nasser, who had accepted a cease-fire with Israel.

The PFLP may have insisted that its guerrillas were not criminals but freedom fighters, and that they bore no malice toward their captives. In reality, the Palestinians faced a contradiction from which they could not escape. If they did nothing, the world would continue to ignore the plight of the Palestinians. If they fought the Israelis directly, they would be crushed; if they hijacked airplanes, they were outlaws; and if they killed, they were fanatics. They wanted the West to understand the history and the rights of their people, but the methods they chose isolated them from the very people they tried to reach. Inspired by the anticolonial struggles in Algeria and Vietnam, they conflated resistance with violence. In their struggle against a self-declared Jewish state, the Palestinians claimed that they made a distinction between Zionism and Judaism. Yet the PFLP fighters in Jordan separated the Jewish passengers from the rest on the grounds that they needed to determine whether any of them held dual Israeli citizenship. The PFLP evidently wanted to improve its bargaining position with Israel. Instead, Israel denounced Palestinian "blackmail" and then seized 450 Palestinians in the West Bank and Gaza.[41] The guerrillas were amateurs in the spectacle of propaganda they had precipitated at Dawson's Field.

They had also greatly overplayed their hand. King Hussein of Jordan, whose relationship with the PLO had been extremely tense for well over a year, decided that the time had finally come to rout the overconfident Palestinian groups. In their exuberance at their self-determination, or what passed for it in their refugee camps, the Palestinians had steadily alienated their Jordanian hosts. Their armed struggle and the unstinting rhetorical support it had received across the Arab world had encouraged a Palestinian chauvinism, for many Palestinian guerrillas believed that their cause was more important than either Jordan or Lebanon. They also relied on the fact that Jordan's population was mostly Palestinian and that the messages of solidarity from Iraqi and Syrian political and military circles would forestall any draconian action on the part of the Hashemite king.

Encouraged by the United States, however, King Hussein declared martial law. His army then broke the back of the disorganized Palestinian guerrilla movement inside the refugee camps of Jordan following several days of fierce fighting that became known as "Black September." The king secretly appealed for Israeli help in case the Syrians made any attempt to save the PLO. The Iraqis, who had troops in Jordan, did not come to the aid of the Palestinians. The Syrians sent tanks without air cover, but these were quickly repulsed. The Palestinians were on their own: Their leaders went into hiding or exile, or were arrested, their camps were ravaged, and the guerrillas were hunted down. Several thousand Palestinians, most of them civilians, were killed; at least fifteen thousand more were incarcerated. Arafat was forced to uproot the "revolution" and take it to Lebanon.[42]

So it was that the age of Nasser drew to a close, with the Arabs more bitterly divided than at the outset of his rule. At an Arab summit in Cairo in late September 1970 Nasser attempted to heal this latest round of internecine Arab warfare by appealing to both King Hussein and Arafat to set aside their differences in the interests of the greater Arab good. The two men signed a cease-fire accord on September 27, not so much because Nasser had called for it, as because the Palestinians had been routed. The next day, at the age of fifty-two, Nasser died of a heart attack. His vice president, Anwar al-Sadat, broke the news to his nation.

Sadat's eulogy glossed over the dark side of Nasser's regime, his repression of opposition, his stifling of press and political freedoms in the name of liberation, the enormous economic and social problems within Egypt, and the state of disarray of Arab politics that awaited his successor. Sadat himself was of humble origins and had been attracted to the Muslim Brotherhood before joining the army, where Nasser recruited him into the Free Officers. Few expected Sadat to be able to hold on to the reins of power, for he had none of Nasser's natural ability to connect to his people.

Nasser had always lived modestly, and his people could relate to him in spite of the layers of security and intelligence men and hangers-on who stood between the masses and their idol. Millions of Egyptians thronged the streets of Cairo to bid farewell to the first Egyptian leader who had given them a voice, while tens of millions of other Arabs followed the procession on their televisions and radios. In the rush of emotion that late September day, with men and women pressed together as far as the eye could see, police struggled to keep back the crowds that sought to touch Nasser's flag-draped coffin. Men sobbed openly. Nasser, for all his flaws, had tapped a powerful impulse among Egyptians and Arabs for dignity and independence. His bitterest Arab rivals acknowledged this and dutifully came to Egypt to pay their respects.

The genuine outpouring of grief, however, could not conceal some other stark realities. Nasser had failed to deter the Israelis, whose occupation of the Sinai tarnished his great achievement at Suez. The Americans were more firmly allied with Israel at his death than they had been in 1952, and the Israelis were more powerful because of this. Nasser had been unable, furthermore, to detach the Saudis from the Americans. Eager for Jordan's King Hussein to complete the task of ridding Jordan of "radical" elements, the United States had resupplied him within a month of Black September, thus bolstering a pro-American axis across the Middle East that had weathered the pan-Arab storm. U.S. hegemony in the region had been severely challenged, but the Americans had survived the test, even though they had all but declared war on the greatest of modern Arab heroes.

The condolences offered by the United States to Egypt following Nasser's death, therefore, could hardly conceal the obvious, Israel-centered breach that undermined America's relationship to the Arabs. "The world has lost an outstanding leader who tirelessly and devotedly served his countrymen and the Arab world," said Johnson's successor, Richard Nixon, aboard the USS *Saratoga* in the Mediterranean.[43] The United States hoped that, with Nasser's demise, it would now be able to pick the fruits of its antinationalist policy. It had boxed Nasser in and worn him out. American Cold Warriors and their Israeli counterparts exploited the enormous expectations that Nasser had awakened among Arabs, for they understood that when great expectations are raised and not met, they are inevitably followed by terrible disappointment. But the Americans who had worked for and celebrated Nasser's political demise misjudged quite profoundly the building sense of resentment against the United States that was developing in both the Arab world and, for different reasons, Iran.

The United States, preoccupied with China and Vietnam, allowed Israel to settle into its new role as the conqueror of occupied Palestinian territories. Under Golda Meir's Labor Party, Israel began to build Jewish settlements inside the West Bank and in East Jerusalem. It had no intention of returning East Jerusalem to Arab hands or of withdrawing to its pre-1967 boundaries. The Israeli-American relationship continued to build, and the United States openly became Israel's main military, political, and economic patron. In return for U.S. largesse, Israel was expected to act as America's principal weapon against Arab radicalism, yet paradoxically, and more than any other factor, it was the cause of Arab anger at America.

The result of the 1967 war all but assured the demise of the original, benevolent Arab interpretation of America. It also consolidated the emergence in the region of a far more widespread understanding of the United States as an aggressive anti-Arab empire. The Syrian poet Adonis, who had been jailed in his country before moving to Beirut in 1956 to establish a famous journal of poetic modernism, described the United States in terms that captured the sense of Arab disillusionment with America. "A woman—the statue of a woman / lifting in one hand a rag called liberty by / a document called history, and with the other / hand suffocating a child called Earth," he wrote in "A Grave for New York" in 1971.[44]

Never before were so many Arabs of different faiths and walks of life willing to believe in the idea of American imperialism, not because they were particularly given to conspiracy theories, but because the evidence around them overwhelmingly pointed in one direction. The United States pursued an openly hostile attitude toward the Arabs on the question of Israel and Palestine, and it supported regimes that had little popular support. When Britain removed its remaining military bases in the Persian Gulf in 1971, the United States alone came to dominate the oil-rich Arabian Peninsula. America now supplied Israel and the shah of Iran with copious quantities of advanced weaponry. The shah soon established himself as the largest purchaser of American weapons in the world, buying nearly $4 billion worth in 1974.[45] It was left to Wahabist Saudi Arabia to temper Arab frustration with U.S. policies.

Surveying U.S.-Arab relations in the aftermath of the 1967 war, the Saudi oil expert and former minister of petroleum and mineral affairs,

Abdullah Tariqi, offered a scathing, but by now quite typical, indictment of American policy and Arab conservatism. The Muslim Tariqi was yet another in a long line of Arab reformers who noticed the enormous gap that separated American professions of democracy and freedom from the reality of U.S. actions in the region. He was the first Saudi to graduate from the University of Texas at Austin, where he acquired a master's degree in petroleum engineering in 1947, and where he was occasionally mistaken for a Mexican in what was then a segregated U.S. South.

Tariqi nevertheless admired many aspects of the United States, especially its industry and its commitment to education, and his first wife was an American. He returned to Saudi Arabia in 1948. Because of his qualifications and background, the Saudi government insisted that he participate in ARAMCO's management. He moved to Dhahran, but he was not allowed to live in the senior ARAMCO compound because he was an Arab. Tariqi came face to face with the ugly side of ARAMCO, but he was more anxious about his own country's backwardness—his native town did not open its first elementary school until 1948. He understood how ARAMCO exploited this backwardness. It routinely concealed its true profits; moreover, it monopolized the refining, sale, and transportation of petroleum, and therefore, together with Western oil companies, it kept the price of oil low, a practice that aided Western economies at the expense of an oil-producing country such as Saudi Arabia. Tariqi devoted himself to breaking ARAMCO's stranglehold on Saudi oil wealth. He wanted the oil company to be subject to Saudi direction, to begin refining in Saudi Arabia, to pay greater royalties, and to hire qualified Saudis in senior production and management positions.

Tariqi was one of the visionaries behind the creation of the Organization of the Petroleum Exporting Countries (OPEC) in 1960 in an effort to shift the control in oil pricing away from Western oil companies and toward the oil-exporting countries. Inspired by Nasser, Tariqi understood that he struggled against the tribalism and nepotism of the Saudi monarchy as much as against a powerful American oil company. Despite his pioneering work in giving Saudi Arabia vastly more control over ARAMCO, and encouraging and recruiting educated Saudis to run

Saudi ministries, Tariqi was dismissed from government service in 1962 by King Faysal, who feared Nasserist pan-Arabism and rejected Tariqi's liberal thinking. Tariqi went into exile from Saudi Arabia, much to the relief of ARAMCO officials.

One question haunted Tariqi in the aftermath of the 1967 war: Why was it that the Arabs, who had done nothing historically to harm the United States and who had oil that Americans desired, had gained the enmity of so powerful a country? Tariqi was especially taken aback by how American politicians explicitly demanded Israel's military superiority over the Arabs, even though it was the Arabs who had been forced out of their homes, who had been denied their rights, and whose lands were occupied. Tariqi dismissed the idea that the United States supported Israel out of a sense of atonement for Western anti-Semitism, or for religious reasons; the average American, he pointed out, did not particularly like Jews and was not particularly interested in the long history of their persecution. He acknowledged that there had been "modest" and genuinely benevolent Americans, such as the missionaries and doctors who had traveled through Arabia in the first part of the twentieth century, and he praised Dr. Louis Dame as an exemplary figure. But times had changed. The new, "coarse" oil-company Americans whom he had witnessed at the ARAMCO camps, who lived in isolated compounds and discriminated against Arabs and Iranians, represented a new American approach to the Arabs.

For Tariqi, the answer, then, to the question of why the Americans had such contempt for the Arabs was both economic and political. He understood more than most Arabs that the United States led the world in the consumption of oil; he also understood that it had a dwindling domestic output that would be far outstripped by demand by 1980. America therefore had an unavoidable, escalating dependency on foreign energy. Not only did the Arabs possess vast quantities of proven oil reserves, but their oil was the cheapest to extract and refine in the world. As a result, the United States actively worked for a quiescent, divided Arab world, just as it had promoted dictatorships in Latin America. The emergence of a unified, powerful, industrial Arab state would not only have its own energy needs, but would be in a far stronger position than the existing weak Arab states to determine where to refine and market its oil, which could include China. The United States, in a word, was opposed to what Tariqi regarded as progressive political movements such as Nasser's because they carried within them the potential for a new balance of power. In this view, then, Israel was not a state of the Jews as much as it was "a 100% American base," utterly dependent on the United States and at the same time an extension of U.S. influence in the area.[46]

The implications of this analysis were evident to Tariqi. The problem was not Israel as much as it was the United States. Once again, Palestine revealed itself as a bedrock of modern Arab attitudes toward America. Upon this bedrock, Tariqi elaborated a case of U.S. oil imperialism, with Israel as its spearhead. Tariqi offered a bleak prognosis. He insisted that the American view of the Arabs was similar to how American colonists once viewed the Indians of the New World. The United States had divided the Arabs into "moderates" and "radicals," just as it had once distinguished between the "troublesome" Indians it subjected to unremitting warfare and the "moderate" Indians who were allowed to subsist temporarily until those who offered resistance had been destroyed. Schematic as Tariqi's interpretation of U.S. relations with the Indians was, it provided him with a highly instructive history. The "moderate" Arabs, such as the Hashemites and the Saudis, who put their faith in U.S. pledges of friendship despite the obvious partiality of America toward Israel would ultimately be consumed by the same avarice for power and oil that vanquished the "radical" Nasser. To survive, therefore, the Arabs had no choice but to unite and resist the United States. "The war between us and America and Israel is a war of life and death for us, and those who don't place all their resources into this battle now will lose these resources and will regret it when it will be too late to regret."[47]

Tariqi's existential cry exposed once again the gap that separated the idea of an "Arab nation" and the reality of a fragmented Arab world. He feared for the survival of the Arab nationalism espoused by Nasser after 1967, and yet he continued to believe in the vision of unity, dignity, and a better life for ordinary Arabs that underlay Nasser's phenomenal appeal. The questions begged by Tariqi, however, concerned the nature and costs of an Arab resistance to American imperialism, and which Arab states or organizations were going to lead this resistance.

As a committed Arab nationalist, he could not bring himself to confront the contradiction inherent in tying resistance to "progressive" Arab states that ruthlessly suppressed all forms of dissent, including Nasser's but especially Iraq and Syria, where Baathists had seized power. Arab nationalist hostility toward Israel was based on the naked (to Arab eyes at least) oppression of millions of their fellow Arabs, but it routinely overlooked the humiliations endured by entire communities and dissenters in Saudi Arabia, Syria, Iraq, Algeria, Libya, Sudan, and Egypt.

Although Tariqi pleaded for Arab unity and action, he implicitly admitted that the Arabs could for the foreseeable future play a defensive role at best: They could remain steadfast and foil the alleged plans and plots of the imperialists, but they could not actually advance the cause of the liberation of Palestine. Moreover, because the various Palestinian factions did not constitute a state and had no central authority, these factions competed with each other and were often bankrolled by one or another Arab intelligence service. Their actions therefore had as much to do with their struggle for position and authority within Palestinian ranks as it had to do with opposing imperialism. The Syrian scholar Sadiq al-'Azm admitted what Tariqi could not: The idea of the liberation of Palestine not only seduced Palestinian refugees in a fantasy of restoration—the idea that somehow the clock could be turned back to the period before 1948—but also lent itself to "demagogy pure and simple."[48]

More troubling still was that twenty years of rejecting Israel, of confrontations and wars, had cost the Arabs far more than it had cost Israel. While the American and Israeli governments wagered that the Arabs would eventually tire of fighting what appeared to be a losing battle for Palestine, Tariqi hoped that his generation of Arabs could keep alive the idea of resistance until a future date when the Arabs were better organized, more united, and more capable of asserting themselves on the world stage, and until a new leader could emerge to lead them again down the path of self-determination. Given the disarray and weakness in the Arab ranks, however, further resistance in the face of brute Israeli power suggested that the Arabs would continue to pay the cost of their idealism but reap few, if any, of its rewards. In the long run, such a political strategy was hardly sustainable. A half-century of ardent Arab belief in the question of Palestine had also become a millstone around Arabs' necks.

Tariqi, despite his continuing faith in the necessity of Arab unity, understood that Nasser's death had left a void and that Egypt after Nasser was the key to future developments in the Arab world. Tariqi was convinced that the Western powers—"colonialism," as he called them collectively—would do their utmost to separate Egypt from the Arab fold. He also understood that in the wake of 1967 the path was now open for an alternative form of Arab thinking to rise to the fore, one based not on the secular unity of the Arabs advocated by Nasser, but on the unity of Muslims in the face of Western imperialism. Tariqi cautioned against traveling down such a path, for the unity of the Arabs, as difficult as that was to achieve, was still far more feasible than the unity of Muslims. Either way, the "reservoir of goodwill for Americans" that William Eddy had spoken about in his Naval War College speech in 1953 finally appeared empty.

Meanwhile, as if to underscore the problems of resistance that Tariqi had spoken of in general, romantic terms, a Palestinian group called Black September announced itself to the world. The group, which was connected to Arafat's Fatah, was named after the events in Jordan that had seen the Palestinian guerrilla movement crushed. It sought to strike at the Israelis and what it regarded as their Arab "collaborators." It wanted revenge for the Jordanian repression of the PLO. Above all, it wanted to demonstrate the viability of resistance to imperialism. Leila Khaled's hijackings were quickly eclipsed by the ruthlessness of the Black September group. In Cairo in November 1971, agents of the group assassinated Jordanian prime minister Wasfi al-Tal, who had led the brutal campaign against the Palestinians in 1970.

Black September's most infamous action occurred a year later. During the Olympic Games held at Munich in September 1972, Palestinian guerrillas, recruited from the refugee camps in Lebanon, Syria, and

Jordan, attacked the Israeli pavilion in the Olympic village. They killed an Israeli trainer and an athlete and took nine other Israeli athletes hostage. Their goal was to secure the release of two hundred Palestinian prisoners held in Israel. For twenty-four hours, the world media was fixated on Munich, where German police surrounded the Palestinians and their hostages. When Israeli officials refused to release any Palestinians, German negotiators brokered an apparent compromise. The Black September guerrillas were to be allowed to fly to Cairo, where they would turn over their hostages to Egyptian authorities. At a German military airport, however, German police snipers shot dead several of the Palestinian guerrillas, and in the ensuing battle the other Palestinian gunmen killed all nine Israeli hostages.[49]

The operation was a shambles. Israel took revenge in its customary manner. It launched massive air raids against defenseless refugee camps in Lebanon, killing and wounding over two hundred Palestinians, most of whom were civilians. The Palestinian leadership obdurately justified the Munich operation. "World opinion was forced to take note of the Palestinian drama," insisted Fatah leader Abu Iyad, "and the Palestinian people imposed their presence on an international gathering that had sought to exclude them."[50] Yet far from convincing "world opinion" of the justice of the Palestinian cause, the Munich massacre served to further obscure the history of dispossession and exile that was the initial impetus for Palestinian violence. The attack brought in its wake a renewed wave of American and European sympathy for Israel. To American observers who followed the spectacle on their televisions, the Munich tragedy emphasized the humanity of the Israeli amateur athletes participating in a global sporting event. At the same time, it accentuated the apparent perversity of the Palestinians, who seemed to have no motivation or aspiration other than being "dedicated to the destruction of Israel," as John Chancellor explained to his viewers on the NBC evening news broadcast of September 5, 1972.[51]

Nixon immediately condemned the attack and expressed the solidarity of the American people with Israel. On March 1, 1973, Black September struck again. Its operatives took over the Saudi embassy in the Sudan during a reception in honor of the departing American chargé d'affaires, Curtis Moore. They took several hostages, including the American ambassador, Cleo Noel, and Moore. Once more, they demanded the release of Palestinian prisoners, this time from Jordanian as well as Israeli prisons. They also demanded the release of Sirhan Sirhan, who had assassinated Bobby Kennedy in 1968. When their ultimatum was rejected, the guerrillas executed both American hostages, who thus became the first U.S. diplomats killed directly as a result of the Arab-Israeli conflict. The United States expressed outrage but was otherwise unmoved. Palestinian guerrilla action had reached a dead end. The allure of Algeria and Vietnam had misled the *fedayeen*. Their militancy was proving to be futile. Through their much-vaunted armed struggle, Palestinians were unable to alter the fact that the pro-U.S. Hashemite Jordan had rejected resistance in the name of sovereignty. They could do nothing, moreover, to alter America's open, strategic embrace of their principal oppressor. And they could not liberate their country.

7

REAPING THE WHIRLWIND

The downward spiral in U.S.-Arab relations quickened pace in the last decades of the twentieth century. The themes that had first emerged in 1947 and 1948 intensified dramatically: The U.S. alignment with Israel strengthened, and aid to it increased exponentially, making Israel, remarkably, the single largest recipient of U.S. foreign aid in the world by the mid-1970s. Arab disillusionment with America also deepened, as did the negative stereotyping of Arabs in America. The difference between Eisenhower's time and those of subsequent administrations, however, lay in the final fracturing of even the appearance of a united Arab front against Israel. Yet the decline of secular Arab nationalism widened rather than diminished the rupture between Arabs and Americans. The historic decision of the United States to support oppressive, unpopular regimes in the Middle East, while also doing little to oppose Israel's anachronistic colonialism in the Arab territories it occupied during the 1967 war, ensured that the U.S. victory over secular Arab nationalism would create its own terrible dynamic. Nasser may have fallen, and with him the dreams of a generation, but pax Americana helped usher in an age of defiant religiosity, resistance, and cynicism. Having sown the wind, the United States now reaped the whirlwind.

But before the full extent of the coming storm was to reveal itself, there was one final war to be fought between the Arab states and Israel. The role played by the United States during the 1973 Ramadan or October War—or the Yom Kippur War, as it is known in the West—gave more credence to Abdullah Tariqi's belief that the United States was an outright enemy of the Arabs. From an Arab perspective, this was the first Arab-Israeli war that the Arabs had initiated. Egypt's president, Anwar Sadat, made several overtures to the United States about peace, even expelling thousands of Soviet military advisers from Egypt in 1972. Nixon, preoccupied with elections and the Watergate crisis, was confident that U.S. military aid to Israel, which increased tenfold between the fiscal years of 1970 and 1973 (from $30 million to $307.5 million), would maintain the docility of the Arab states.[1] He felt that he could ignore Sadat. His secretary of state, Henry Kissinger, allegedly dismissed the Egyptian president as a "buffoon."[2] In July 1973, the United States vetoed a UN Security Council resolution that deplored Israel's continued occupation of Arab territory. Israel therefore was supremely confident that its hold on the Arab lands occupied in 1967 was both secure and indefinite. But the Arab states were growing increasingly restless with the status quo. Kissinger admitted to the Israeli ambassador to the United States, Simcha Dinitz, on September 10, 1973, that the U.S. government was under "overwhelming" pressure, especially from the Egyptians and the Saudis, to do something. Strategizing with Dinitz, Kissinger said, "We have to find a way of splitting the Arabs."[3]

But it was Egypt and Syria that acted first. Simultaneously, they initiated hostilities in the afternoon of October 6. They had one overriding goal in mind: to regain their lands occupied by Israel. The Egyptians crossed the Suez Canal, smashed through the Israeli defenses at the Bar Lev Line, which consisted of concrete and sand fortifications built on the eastern bank of the canal, and neutralized the Israeli air force with their new Soviet-supplied air defense system. At the same time, the Syrian army threatened to break through the Israeli-occupied Golan Heights. Sadat hoped that his resort to war would force the Americans to take him more seriously. He was not disappointed.

Kissinger initially thought that the Egyptians and Syrians would be quickly defeated. He was shocked when he was informed by Dinitz on October 9 of the magnitude of Israeli losses, which amounted to an estimated five hundred tanks on both fronts and numerous aircraft.[4] The United States intervened openly on Israel's side during the war. It urgently resupplied Israel with military hardware (while the Soviets resupplied the Arabs) and, through the frenetic work of Kissinger, not only coordinated with Israel throughout the war but rejected any notion of linking a cease-fire to an Israeli withdrawal to the 1967 lines. Nixon believed that U.S. Cold War prestige was tied to Israeli success on the battlefield against the Soviet-sponsored Arabs. He also hoped for increased leverage with Israel in the aftermath of the war so that it could be "dragged kicking and screaming to the table." Both he and Kissinger understood, and accepted as a fait accompli, Israel's remarkable reach into the U.S. Congress. "We can't get so much to them that they will be arrogant," the president said of the Israelis even as he authorized a massive resupply of weapons to Israel, "but we can't be in the position where Israel puts pressure on Congress for us to do more."[5]

Egypt and Syria were exhausted by their one final effort at open warfare against Israel. They regarded the Canal crossing, or *al-'ubur*, as a historic victory. But ultimately the United States and Israel prevailed militarily. When the war ended on October 23, Israel not only had regained its control over all the Arab territories it held at the outset of the war but had even advanced across the Suez Canal. Its victory, however, was not nearly as resounding as it had been six years earlier, and the price it paid in matériel and lives was far greater. The mobilization of its reservists cost the Israeli economy dearly; Egypt and Syria had shattered Israel's military confidence, and the country's total dependence on the United States became obvious.[6]

The corollary to this Israeli dependence on the United States, however, was that the outright identification of the United States with Israel also became more extreme than it had ever been before. Before the outbreak of hostilities, King Faysal of Saudi Arabia had warned the United States that the Arabs would use oil as a weapon if America continued to favor Israel. Under severe pressure from the Saudi government, which had already acquired a 25 percent stake in the company, ARAMCO and other U.S. oil executives with interests in the Middle East pleaded with the U.S. government to take a more evenhanded approach during the war. They feared the nationalization of their companies. Libya had nationalized a small U.S. oil company in June, citing U.S. support for Israel as a primary reason. Immediately after the outbreak of the war, the Iraqi government nationalized American holdings in the Basrah Petroleum Company. Despite repeated Arab warnings, Kissinger dismissed the possibility of the Arabs resorting to their oil weapon. On October 17, the day Arab oil ministers were assembled in Kuwait to discuss what steps to take to pressure the United States, Kissinger remained confident that the Saudis would do nothing. At a National Security Council meeting he exclaimed, "Did you see the Saudi Foreign Minister come out like a good little boy and say that they had had very fruitful talks with us?"[7]

Kissinger's arrogance was soon tempered. With the war still raging, the Saudis bowed to enormous Arab pressure to retaliate against Western countries that supported Israel, especially the United States. The Arab oil ministers underscored their despair that the "United States is the principal and foremost source of the Israeli power which has resulted in the present Israeli arrogance and enabled the Israelis to continue to occupy our territories." They said they were determined to pressure the United States to adopt a more impartial Middle East policy.[8]

The initial Arab goal was to reduce oil production by 5 percent of the September level, and then a further 5 percent per month "until such time as total evacuation of Israeli forces from all Arab territory occupied during the June 1967 war is completed, and the legitimate rights of the Palestinian people are restored."[9] Yet on October 19, Nixon, on Kissinger's strong recommendation, requested that Congress provide Israel with a staggering $2.2 billion in aid.

Faysal was incredulous. As much as he wanted to avoid a confrontation with the Americans, he felt that he had no choice but to proceed with an embargo on oil shipments to the United States. However, he delayed the enforcement of the boycott and privately reassured the U.S. government that he was doing his utmost to diffuse Arab anger at the

United States for its support of Israel. He understood that the Saudi monarchy depended on the United States and that the oil-producing countries were entangled in a symbiotic relationship with the industrialized West.

Yet Faysal had also long decried Israeli oppression of the Palestinians. The preeminent Saudi position in the Islamic world, moreover, increased the pressure on him, especially after Israel's occupation of East Jerusalem, but it was America's blatant support of Israel that forced his hand. The Arab oil weapon, which Abdullah Tariqi had long seen as the most "potent" Arab weapon in the struggle against colonialism, was unleashed reluctantly, but the consequences of its deployment were immediately felt. Oil prices shot upward nearly 70 percent.

The Japanese and the Europeans, who were the most dependent on Arab oil, were also the most affected by the embargo, but oil continued to flow into Europe and Japan. Although the United States imported relatively little Arab oil, it was already facing an energy crisis before the 1973 war and was counting on an increase in Saudi production to keep down the price of oil. The pro-American shah of Iran refused to participate in the embargo. Iran, Indonesia, and Nigeria helped make up the shortfall in supply but nevertheless benefited from the resultant price increase. By January 1, 1974, the price of oil had increased nearly 470 percent over what it had been a year earlier, but this increase had less to do with the Arab embargo than with a consensus among oil-producing nations to end the era of cheap oil.[10] The costs of America's embrace of Israel had increased, but not nearly enough to force the United States to alter fundamentally its policy on the Arab-Israeli conflict.

On the contrary, it was the outwardly impressive Arab demonstration of unified action that was short-lived. Iraq refused to go along with cutbacks and demanded instead nationalization of foreign oil companies. The major political consequence of the embargo was to confirm the leading role of Saudi Arabia in Arab politics in the era after Nasser. Saudi revenues, and therefore influence, increased dramatically as oil prices moved from $3 to $17 a barrel.[11] Yet, rather than carry on with an embargo, Faysal went out of his way to limit its duration. He not only secretly authorized ARAMCO to resupply the U.S. navy with oil during the embargo but pressured the Arabs to end their boycott within six months of its initiation.

He had an ally in Sadat, who, through Kissinger's mediation, had brokered a disengagement plan with Israel in January 1974 that pulled the Israelis back from the western bank of Suez but left them in occupation of the Sinai. The Egyptians would be allowed to leave a token force on the eastern bank, but only in return for abandoning the Syrians to the prospect of an indefinite Israeli retention of the Golan Heights. Sadat now toured Arab capitals lobbying for an end to the oil embargo. The Arab oil ministers formally lifted their embargo on the United States on March 18, 1974. They insisted that there was evidence of a shift in U.S. public opinion and U.S. policy toward an understanding of the Arab position that, "if reinforced, would lead to the adoption by the U.S. of a position more consistent with the principles of right and justice as regards the occupied Arab territories and the legitimate rights of the Palestinian people."[12]

Their claim was misleading. As with his father in 1948, Faysal's relationship to the United States was ultimately more important to him than were the Palestinians, no matter how genuinely outraged and appalled Saudis continued to be with American support for Israel. The Arab oil-producing states had used their oil weapon, but they had not followed through. They had initially demanded impartiality and a full withdrawal of Israeli forces from occupied Egyptian and Syrian lands, and they had insisted on a "just" resolution to the Palestinian question—both demands that effectively conceded an Arab acceptance of Israel within its pre-1967 borders. They received, however, nothing more than standard U.S. assurances that it was committed to a peaceful resolution of the Arab-Israeli conflict. The Israelis still occupied Arab lands. They exhibited no appetite for compromise with the Palestinians and were not encouraged to do so by Kissinger. The major Arab states, Egypt and Saudi Arabia, thus resigned themselves to the power of the United States. They were effectively suing for peace. All they needed to completely come out in the open was the fig leaf of U.S. moderation, some acknowledgment of the rights of the Palestinians, and some small movement toward achieving them.

The irony is that even this enormous Arab concession was not enough to spark any U.S. interest in resolving the Palestinian question. From

Kissinger's perspective, there was no need to. To the extent that the Arab embargo had any success, it was not in moving America to compromise. Rather, it was limited to the wresting of formal statements by both Japan and the European community that paid lip service to UN Resolution 242 (which many Arabs had previously found unpalatable because it was so vague), that acknowledged the "inadmissible" nature of Israel's conquest of Arab lands, and that mentioned the "legitimate rights of the Palestinians" without specifying what these rights were or what steps either Japan or the European community would take to help ensure that they were minimally respected. No sooner were these statements issued than the Arab embargo was softened and subsequently lifted against the European states—except the Netherlands, which had taken an unabashedly pro-Israeli stand during the war and had facilitated the U.S. airlift to Israel. By July 1974, even the embargo against the Netherlands was ended. No sooner had the Arab embargo collapsed than the Saudis entered into negotiations with the United States to expand, equip, and train the Saudi National Guard, which was responsible both for the royal family's security and for protecting the kingdom's oil installations. Envious and fearful of the favored position of the shah of Iran in America and his ability to buy U.S. equipment for his army and air force, the Saudis lobbied to purchase major weapons system from the United States. Together with the shah, therefore, they recycled their petrodollar windfall in America.[13]

Even as Egypt and Saudi Arabia backed away from confrontation, anti-Arab xenophobia in America ratcheted up in the wake of the Arab oil embargo. Henry Kissinger publicly deplored the Arab "blackmail" of America in December 1973, and so too did major U.S. newspapers. Senator Henry Jackson, an ardent Zionist and patron to what was then a budding movement of neoconservatives, evoked a sense of humiliation that a great power was held hostage to Arabs in collusion with Big Oil. "I think," Jackson said in September 1974, "the entire industrialized world faces a clear and present danger of economic destruction by the Arab oil cartel."[14] The idea of an Arab boycott of America was not just economically frightening. It was politically and culturally intolerable.

Sketches and caricatures depicting menacing, hook-nosed Arab sheiks appeared in the American press. These images reinforced an already negative image of the masked, gun-toting Palestinian evoked by the Black September attacks. In this period, as American consumers lined up at gas stations and paid far more for gasoline, OPEC became synonymous with Arabs, Arabs with Muslims, Iranians with Arabs, and Arabs with terrorism. Hollywood caricatured Arabs, further enhancing the image of Israel and the United States as common victims of irrational—and fundamentally ahistorical—Arab Muslim hatred, and therefore engaged in a common struggle against ruthless Arab and Islamic economic and political terrorism. Whether a millionaire, greedy, licentious sheik engaged in slavery in the 1979 film *Ashanti* or the kaffiyeh-clad Palestinian terrorists represented in the 1977 film *Black Sunday*, the stereotype of the fanatical "Arab" recalled that of the "terrible Turk," albeit in a more potent and widely circulating form.[15]

Lost in the wave of anti-Arab invective was a crucial point. Although the groundwork for the demonization of the Arab had been laid before the 1973 war and drew on a panoply of racial stereotypes that had previously encompassed Jews, blacks, and Turks, the intense American antipathy to the Arabs was a direct consequence of the Arab-Israeli conflict. Yet, on the Arab side, there was no equivalent caricature of the figure of the "American," though the United States was often represented in Arab newspapers by the image of Uncle Sam with a dollar sign in his top hat. This was in large part because Arab nationalist hostility was directed not at Americans per se, but at abstractions such as "colonialism" or "imperialism." These epithets were understood to refer to the United States as a political, but not cultural, actor, just as they had previously referred to Great Britain. Anti-Arabism in the United States, therefore, was a phenomenon based upon the mystification of the origins of the Arab-Israeli conflict; anti-Americanism in the Arab world remained a phenomenon based upon a reasonably accurate understanding of the consistent U.S. role in the creation and promotion of Israel at the expense of the Arabs.

When the dust of the 1973 war and the consequent embargo had settled, Kissinger, who personally identified with Israel, went out of his way to ensure that the Palestinian question was avoided as much as possible. Rather than seizing the opportunity to resolve the Arab-Israeli conflict at its roots, Kissinger focused instead on drawing Sadat into a separate peace with Israel. Egypt restored its severed relations with the United States in November 1973. At the time, Kissinger flattered Sadat, who in turn confided in Kissinger. To Kissinger's surprise and delight, Sadat told Kissinger that not only did he look forward to the prospect of full peace with Israel, but that he desired to subordinate Egypt to America. Sadat impulsively and unilaterally offered concessions, in contrast to the Israeli side, which bargained hard and relentlessly during the disengagement talks following the war. Without consulting his military commanders or negotiators, he informed Kissinger that he had no objection to leaving only a token force of thirty Egyptian tanks in the Sinai—a prospect that appalled his own army commander, who reminded Sadat of the terrible cost that Egypt had paid in the lives of its soldiers to cross the canal. Israel was allowed to deploy fully behind its defensive lines in Sinai.[16]

Almost overnight Sadat had become America's man. He soon befriended the shah of Iran, and he traveled in a lavishly equipped Boeing airplane paid for by the Saudis. If Kissinger was a latter-day Lawrence, albeit an agent of American hegemony rather than British empire, Sadat was a latter-day Emir Faysal. The difference was that Sadat was far more cynical than Faysal, and Kissinger far less romantic than Lawrence. Both men understood at an early point that the Palestinians were to be left out of the negotiations, not necessarily because Sadat wanted it so, but because Israel, with Kissinger's blessing, insisted upon it.

The PFLP's George Habash remained unrepentant. He rejected Sadat's embrace of Kissinger. "Our primary enemy is American imperialism," Habash declared in an interview with a leading Lebanese newspaper in December 1973, "and we shall not permit Arab reactionaries to appear nationalistic through their enmity to Israel while simultaneously rushing to the arms of the United States."[17] Yasser Arafat was less sanguine about the ability of the Palestinians to stifle Egyptian, let alone U.S., ambitions. His Fatah faction was, in any case, more popular than Habash's PFLP and was receiving copious Arab diplomatic and financial support.

Arafat depended on the goodwill of the Arab states, especially the Gulf states. Less rigid than Habash, he focused instead on consolidating the Palestinian guerrilla presence in its new home in Lebanon, whose weak government and army had no choice but to accede to Palestinian autonomy in the sprawling refugee camps. The PLO used southern Lebanon as a staging ground for its armed struggle against Israel. It exploited and exacerbated the absence of Lebanese authority in the neglected, predominantly Shi'a south of the country.

The Arab League formally recognized the PLO as the "sole legitimate representative of the Palestinian people" in Rabat, Morocco, in October 1974.[18] The UN, whose General Assembly Dwight Eisenhower had once conceded represented the true voice of the international community, acknowledged in October, in General Assembly Resolution 3210, that the "Palestinian people is the principal party to the question of Palestine."[19] The United States and Israel had opposed this resolution (along with Bolivia and the Dominican Republic), but it nevertheless passed with an overwhelming majority. Because of its support for Israel, the United States found itself isolated from world opinion. The General Assembly had changed enormously from the days of the UN partition plan of 1947. From being completely overlooked as a player in the Arab-Israeli conflict, the Palestinians, with solid Arab support, began to make impressive diplomatic gains. Israel, along with apartheid South Africa, with which it maintained a close relationship, remained glaring exceptions to the wave of decolonization that had swept the world.

Yasser Arafat was thus invited to speak at the United Nations on November 13, 1974. Buoyed by the support of King Faysal, whose bid for Arab leadership had been enhanced by the imposition of the oil embargo, Arafat desperately sought international, and especially American, recognition. He understood that Palestinian militancy had damaged his cause in the West and hoped therefore to demonstrate before the world that he was both a statesman and a revolutionary. He wanted to show how far the Palestinians had come as a people, and how great were their expectations for a just and comprehensive solution to their tragedy.

On the eve of Arafat's historic appearance at the UN, Edward Said and several colleagues worked into the night in his Columbia apartment overlooking Morningside Park. They prepared the English translation of the speech originally written by the Palestinian poet Mahmoud Darwish. For all of them, the moment seemed to be a major event, cultural as well as political. The world at last was willing to hear the Palestinian side of the story of the Arab-Israeli conflict. Yet when the kaffiyeh-clad Arafat was ferried to the UN building on an American military helicopter, a paradox confronted him. Inside the building, over one hundred delegations representing the nations of the world eagerly awaited him. To them, he was a Third World hero in an age of heroes, from Che Guevara to Ho Chi Minh. Outside the building, a massive demonstration of American Zionists and their congressional supporters gathered. The protesters considered him the devil incarnate, yet they knew nothing of, or vigorously denied, that part of Israel's past and present that made Arafat into the leader of what they denounced as "Murder International."[20]

A roar of applause and a standing ovation met Arafat as he walked up to the UN rostrum. The U.S. delegation remained seated. The indignant Israeli representatives boycotted the session, for Israel considered Arafat a "murderer" who was directly responsible for the killing of Israeli civilians. It pointed to the attack at Maalot that had occurred in May, in which Palestinian guerrillas had taken one hundred Israeli high school students hostage. The Israeli commandos stormed the building and killed the Palestinians, but not before the latter had killed twenty-three Israelis, most of whom were schoolchildren. The next day Israel killed sixty civilians in an air raid on the refugee camps of Ain al-Hilweh and Nabatiyya in southern Lebanon.[21]

Arafat spoke for over an hour and a half. "I am a rebel and freedom is my cause," he said, stirring up a mixture of heady optimism and anticolonial rhetoric, but also providing a Palestinian account of their own tragedy. He pointed to the historical context of Zionist colonization of his homeland that was so often missing in American understandings of the Arab-Israeli conflict. But Arafat also reached out to Americans and Israelis—the former on terms they could easily understand if they were prepared to listen, the latter on terms they could not accept, no matter how intently they might have listened, without first abandoning Zionism.

Arafat noted that the U.S. government supplied Israel with weapons that were used against his people. He said, however, that he admired the American people and that the U.S. government's enmity toward the Palestinians served neither the cause of peace nor the interests of Americans. In language that recalled how an earlier generation of Arab nationalists had appealed to Wilson, Arafat pleaded with the American people to live up to their own professed ideals.

> I ask [them] whole-heartedly to endorse right and justice, to recall George Washington to mind, heroic Washington whose purpose was his nation's freedom and independence, Abraham Lincoln, champion of the destitute and the wretched, also Woodrow Wilson, whose doctrine of Fourteen Points remains subscribed to and venerated by our people. I ask the American people whether the demonstrations of hostility and enmity taking place outside this great hall reflect the true intent of America's will? What, I ask you plainly, is the crime of the people of Palestine against the American people? Why do you fight us so? Does such unwarranted belligerence really serve your interests?

He urged the Israeli people to forgo the "Masada complex" that he said their leaders were trying to instill in them, and he appealed to Jews worldwide to distinguish between their faith and Zionism, which promised Jews only "endless war." Rather than a Jewish state that existed in perpetual defiance of its Arab Muslim and Christian environment, Arafat called for a secular, democratic state to be established in Palestine, one that would include "all Jews now living in Palestine who choose to live there in peace and without discrimination." Once again, amid the revolutionary and diplomatic rhetoric, there was an Arab signal for compromise.

Arafat was tacitly repudiating a tenet of the PLO's own charter, which at that time called for the return to their countries of origin of all Jews who had emigrated to Palestine after the Balfour Declaration. He was risking the further enmity of men like Habash who held to the position that violent resistance alone could liberate Palestine. Arafat's final words were his most evocative. "Today I have come bearing an olive branch and a freedom fighter's gun," he declared. "Do not let the olive branch fall from my hand. I repeat: Do not let the olive branch fall from my hand."[22]

The PLO was granted observer status at the UN on November 22. A year later the General Assembly determined that "Zionism is a form of racism and racial discrimination."[23] But these diplomatic triumphs were quickly soured by another reality. The U.S. government would not countenance the idea of Palestinian liberation.

Henry Kissinger acceded to an Israeli demand in 1975 that the U.S. government not negotiate with or recognize the PLO until the latter first recognized Israel's "right to exist" and formally accepted UN Resolution 242. The conditions imposed on the PLO were predictably one-sided. America required no reciprocal Israeli recognition of Palestinian sovereignty. Rather, the U.S. acceptance of these conditions indicated how little Kissinger thought of the Palestinians and how marginal they were to his vision of an American-brokered peace between Israel and Egypt.

Arafat, in any event, embroiled the PLO in a Lebanese civil war that had begun in April 1975. As the fighting in Lebanon dragged on, pitting Lebanese Maronite militias intent on upholding Maronite privilege in the country and driving out the PLO against an alliance of Lebanese Muslim and Palestinian factions, the Palestinian "revolution" looked increasingly like a mirage. As his speech at the UN hinted, Arafat vacillated between posing as a Che Guevara and a Gamal Abdel Nasser; he wanted to be both, but proved to be neither. Lebanon, in effect, consumed the PLO: The bitterness and duration of the war distracted it from what was ostensibly its main task—liberating its homeland. Israel continued to consolidate its grip on the Arab territories it occupied, showing no desire to relinquish them in the near future.

In fact, the opposite was true. Menachem Begin's Likud coalition won the Israeli parliamentary elections in May 1977. Begin had been a leader of the extremist Zionist organization, the Irgun, that had carried out both the bombing of the King David Hotel in 1946 and the massacre of

Palestinian civilians in Deir Yassin in 1948. He remained proud and unrepentant for his involvement with the Irgun and still counted himself a loyal disciple of the militant Vladimir Jabotinsky. Like so many of Israel's prime ministers of the era, he too was born outside of Palestine, having immigrated there from Poland.

Begin was a man obsessed and tormented by the legacy of the Holocaust, which colored completely how he viewed the Palestinians. He perpetuated the Israeli consensus regarding the Palestinians, namely, that they would be allowed to remain on a portion of their lands, but only if they submitted themselves to Jewish Israeli domination. The messianic Begin vastly expanded the Israeli expropriation of Arab land in the occupied West Bank, which he called "Judea and Samaria" and judged not to be occupied territories but "liberated" Jewish lands and therefore beyond the scope of UN Resolution 242. He continued Israel's drive to consolidate Jewish control over East Jerusalem. He consolidated the Israeli grip on the Golan and Gaza.

Anwar Sadat pursued his ambition of bringing Egypt firmly into a U.S. orbit. He liberalized the Egyptian economy, a change that especially benefited wealthier Egyptians but that also saw consumer and luxury goods flood into Egypt—"for richer, for poorer," as the embittered, sarcastic Mohamed Heikal quipped.[24] Under pressure from the International Monetary Fund (IMF), Sadat cut food subsidies to the poor in an attempt to dismantle Nasser's pan-Arabist and socialist legacy. When food riots followed in January 1977, they were bloodily suppressed by the armed forces. Sadat disbanded Nasser's ruling party and also initially eased Nasser's persecution of the Muslim Brotherhood, hoping to find in them allies to mobilize against the anticipated Nasserist opposition to his economic policies. Yet Sadat was as committed to dictatorship as Nasser had been. From his position as the "victor" in the October war, Sadat again broached the subject of a comprehensive Arab-Israeli peace with the new Democratic U.S. administration of Jimmy Carter.

The American president would decades later acknowledge that during his first trip to Israel as governor of Georgia in 1973 he had equated Palestinians with the Creek Indians evicted from Georgia.[25] As a committed Christian who supported the desegregation of the U.S. South in the face of tremendous white southern opposition, Carter might well have understood the tribulations of the Palestinians in a manner that Ford, Nixon, Johnson, Eisenhower, and Truman could not have. His term in office began auspiciously enough with Carter suggesting that the Palestinians deserved a "homeland."[26]

But even this gesture, and Carter's accompanying call for Israel to stop building settlements in the West Bank, was met with a barrage of Israeli and American Zionist criticism. For Begin and Israel's many fervent American supporters, Carter was entering uncharted waters. A ranking Jewish member on the Senate Foreign Relations Committee, Jacob Javits of New York, publicly rebuked Carter for suggesting that Israel should withdraw to its pre-1967 borders. He asserted that Carter was only going to "feed Arab illusions" that an American president would be able to impose an Arab solution on Israel that the Arabs had been unable to impose themselves. Carter reassured the leader of the Conference of Major American Jewish Organizations that he did not support the creation of an independent Palestinian state and saw anything but a Jordanian-Palestinian federation as a "threat to peace."[27] Yet after meeting with Carter in Washington in July 1977, Begin returned to Israel and his government immediately authorized the construction of more illegal settlements. Israel openly defied its U.S. patron, knowing full well that it could count on the assertive AIPAC, among other American Zionist lobbying groups, to tame the enthusiasm of the Carter administration.

Sadat hoped that Carter could push Israel to relinquish its hold on Sinai, even if he was unable to loosen the Israeli control over the West Bank and Jerusalem. So it was that Sadat decided to make his historic trip to Jerusalem on November 19, 1977, to address the Israeli Knesset. His initiative surprised the Israelis, perplexed Egypt's own diplomatic corps, and made Sadat a household name in America. The Saudis, now under the leadership of King Khalid following the assassination of King Faysal in 1975, were taken aback. Not knowing what to expect next, they were fearful that Sadat's trip signaled his willingness to abandon an Arab claim to Jerusalem. Syria declared Sadat's visit to Jerusalem a "Day of National Mourning."[28] Most Arabs were stunned by Sadat's move, but also transfixed by the sight of Sadat shaking hands with Israeli leaders, including Begin, Rabin, and Meir. The tenor of Sadat's speech and the Israeli reply, however, augured poorly for a broader Arab peace with Israel. Sadat was conciliatory; his rhetoric was both suitably ecumenical and forward-looking. "Any life that is lost in war is a human life, be it that of an Arab or an Israeli," declared Sadat. And then he denied what had become obvious by his very visit to Israel. He claimed that he did not seek a "separate peace" between Egypt and Israel. Instead, he reminded Israelis that no "durable or just peace" could be had without addressing the rights of the Palestinians, including their right to self-determination.

Begin replied to Sadat with a belligerent affirmation of Zionism. He spoke of the Jewish people's "courage" and their "eternal and indisputable right" to independence that the Arabs had rejected. Once again, the Holocaust was Begin's singular point of reference. He presented the Israeli Jews as victims of an unprovoked Arab enmity and insisted that the Arabs had spurned what Begin described as Israel's outstretched hand of peace. "One day after the declaration of our independence," he said, "an attempt was made to strangle it with enmity, and to extinguish the last hope of the Jewish People in the generation of Holocaust and Resurrection." Begin too wanted peace, but it was a peace that pretended the Palestinians simply did not exist as a people. The prime minister spared not a conciliatory word for the history or political aspirations of his one million Palestinian subjects in the West Bank and Gaza, or for the Palestinians as a whole whose land he and other European Jewish immigrants had taken as their own. Begin's refusal to acknowledge the historical, legal, political, and moral Palestinian claim to what he referred to as "Eretz Israel" was predictable. He had remained faithful to his unreconstructed militant Zionism.[29]

It was Sadat who was now cultivating a new Western constituency, at the head of which was the United States. The favor of America was far more important to him than Arab dismay, although Sadat hoped, despite all the evidence before him, that somehow he might be able to link the liberation of Sinai with freedom for the Palestinians in the West Bank. Sadat was condemned in the non-Egyptian Arab press as an "agent of imperialism." Syria, Algeria, South Yemen, Libya, and the PLO were appalled and terrified at Sadat breaking ranks. They met in Tripoli and denounced Sadat's "grand treason."[30] They called for Egypt's isolation and assumed that if the Arabs held out longer, they could achieve better terms. Sadat believed that such an assumption was illusory. Egyptians, he knew, were tired of war, and the Arab states that bitterly condemned him offered no viable way to restore Egyptian sovereignty to the Sinai. In his own mind, a negotiated solution at least held out the faint possibility of future peace. Yet stung by the severity of the criticism directed at him by the Arab states represented at Tripoli, he severed diplomatic relations with them. Only Morocco, Jordan, and Sudan stood by Egypt.

Carter, witnessing the Arab disarray after Sadat's visit, sensed the impending breakthrough. From an American standpoint, Sadat had emerged as the quintessential "moderate" Arab leader willing to engage openly in a "peace process" that satisfied Israeli terms—gradual, direct negotiations between individual Arab states and Israel that shunted the Palestinian question to the side. Saudi Arabia was the only other significant Arab power, and it was now involved in negotiating a multibillion-dollar deal to purchase sixty-two U.S. F-15 fighter jets. Not much trouble, therefore, was expected from it.

The PLO, however, was determined to assert itself. It realized how little the American-sponsored process offered the Palestinians. Begin, like Israeli leaders before and after him, did not hide his intentions. The most he would concede to Palestinians would be some sort of native "home rule" in a manner that Afrikaner South Africa contemplated for its black majority. Arafat continued to seek U.S. recognition, but he refused to accept Israel's "right to exist" without corresponding Israeli recognition of Palestinian rights in return. The way forward remained blocked by the onerous conditions that Kissinger had placed to prevent any substantial U.S. dialogue with the PLO and by intense domestic Zionist pressure on Carter.

Arafat found himself in an intolerable position, checkmated whether he rejected an American peace or whether he embraced it. As a result,

Carter lost patience with the "negative" PLO and longed to find "moderate" Palestinians who would emulate Sadat's example and fall more quickly in line with the pax Americana. His national security adviser, Zbigniew Brzezinski, dismissed Arafat's relevance—"Bye-bye, PLO," he said.[31] Ruling out a Palestinian state, Carter timidly suggested in January 1978 that a solution to the Arab-Israeli conflict must "enable the Palestinians to participate in the determination of their own future."[32] Such circumlocution could hardly forestall Israel's plans to build dozens more settlements in the West Bank, much to Carter's dismay. As the minister of agriculture and head of the Israel Lands Administration, Ariel Sharon announced that Israel planned to settle one million Jews in the West Bank within twenty years. Begin's government openly supported the fanatical Jewish Israeli organization Gush Emunim, whose adherents believed, like Begin, that God had promised the land to the Jews, and who despised Palestinians in the West Bank. Begin's government also revealed that it planned to expand its settlements in the Sinai. Sadat was humiliated. Later, Sadat pleaded with Begin to provide a token of good faith to relieve some of the Arab pressure on him. The Israeli prime minister would respond by saying, "Not even one grain of desert sand as a present."[33]

Having been rebuffed by the United States and summarily cast aside by Egypt, and facing as tenacious a foe as it had ever faced in Begin, the PLO fell back on armed struggle. Arafat approved a Fatah guerrilla raid on Israel in March 1978, which resulted in the deaths of nine guerrillas and thirty-six Israelis, most whom were civilians. Tragedy was once again compounded by futility; the PLO's desperation to prove its continued relevance was matched by its callousness toward civilian suffering and by the savagery of the Israeli response. Begin ordered an invasion of southern Lebanon, unleashing artillery and air attacks on Lebanese villages and Palestinian refugee camps in a bid to punish both Palestinians and Lebanese. Israel uprooted nearly three hundred thousand Lebanese and killed and wounded several thousand civilians.[34] It occupied a large swath of southern Lebanon, calling it a "security belt." The PLO, however, survived the onslaught. Carter was furious with Begin, whose invasion jeopardized an Egyptian-Israeli deal. He had the United States vote for UN Security Council Resolution 425, which passed on March 19 and demanded that Israel "forthwith" end its occupation of Lebanon.

Israel ignored the UN resolution and would remain in occupation of southern Lebanon for another twenty-two years. America did not compel its ally to abide by this resolution, as it had not compelled it to abide by any other of the many UN resolutions that censured Israeli annexation or occupation of Arab lands. Rather, it pressed Begin to concede the Sinai, which he finally did at Camp David in September 1978. But he did so on his own terms, not Sadat's, prompting Egypt's foreign minister to resign at Camp David rather than implicate himself in an accord that gave Israel so much of what it wanted for so low a price. A full peace treaty between Israel and Egypt was signed just over six months later, on March 26, 1979. Israel pledged to withdraw gradually from the Sinai; in return, Israel gained a U.S. guarantee of its security, U.S. subsidies to cover Israel's oil needs for fifteen years, and $3 billion in aid to cover the costs of withdrawing the Israeli army and settlers from Sinai and for the construction of new military airfields in the Negev. Egypt was promised $1.5 billion over three years.[35]

Equally important, Israel gained diplomatic relations with Egypt despite its continued hold of Syrian, Palestinian, and now Lebanese territory. There was, in the end, to be no comprehensive peace despite all the American verbiage to that effect in the treaty. At Begin's insistence, Jerusalem was not mentioned, nor was the right of return of the Palestinian refugees brought up. Israel only accepted a timetable for "autonomy" talks for what it referred to as "the Arabs of the Land of Israel." Everyone, including Sadat, comprehended that these talks were a fig leaf for Egypt's abandonment of the Palestinians to their fate.[36]

Sadat understood how unpopular such a treaty with Israel was in the wider Arab world in which Nasser had loomed so large for so long. The Israeli Knesset voted to accept it; Sadat resorted to a referendum that indicated that 99.95 percent of Egyptians approved the treaty.[37] The difference was that Begin trusted his standing with Israeli Jews; Sadat did not trust his own people. He had Egypt's parliament dissolved and ordered new elections held with the proviso that the peace treaty with Israel could not be debated. Egypt was expelled from the Arab League, and Saudi Arabia cut off diplomatic ties. Sadat's rationale for accepting the treaty with Israel, however, was clear. The Arabs could not break Israel for the foreseeable future, and their policy of resistance and denial had led them into a situation that embittered them and consumed their resources but offered no prospect of peace or development, especially given the degree to which the United States stood behind Israel. He believed that the Arabs would bluster against any treaty with Israel, but that they were incapable, now or in the future, of acting together to liberate occupied Arab territory. Therefore, he decided, the time had come to act, not as an Arab leader, but as an Egyptian leader and to accept peace even if the terms were less than ideal.

The Arab dam of denial was finally burst. The Israeli denial of the Palestinians, however, was strengthened. With Egypt bowing out of the Arab-Israeli conflict, Israeli military superiority became that much greater in the face of Syria, and Israel's consequent ability to consolidate its colonization program in East Jerusalem, the West Bank, and the Golan Heights became that much more obvious. The number of Jewish settlers in the West Bank and Jerusalem increased dramatically under Begin, jumping from 57,000 to 122,000 in six years between 1977 and 1983.[38] Carter inadvertently, but knowingly, freed the Israelis to focus on what had become their main strategic concern: to take the West Bank.

"Camp David" became beguiling words in America, for they promised an end to an ostensibly age-old conflict. In the Arab world, the agreement left a bitter feeling that in peace, as in war, the Arabs were destined to be humiliated. Sadat had presented the United States with a golden opportunity to resolve the Arab-Israeli conflict comprehensively. Rather than restore U.S. credibility, Carter had bent to the will of a determined Begin and rewarded him lavishly in the process. When, in March 1979, the UN again passed a resolution—UN Security Council Resolution 446—deploring Israeli violations of the Fourth Geneva Convention for its illegal settlement construction, the United States abstained from the vote. Presidential elections were nearing, and Carter, unlike Eisenhower, felt that he could not afford to alienate American Jewish voters, many of whom thought that his administration was already too "pro-Arab." Then, in a so-called Basic Law of 1980, Israel declared occupied East Jerusalem part of the "complete and united" capital of Israel, in defiance of the international community. On August 20, the UN Security Council censured Israel in emphatic language in its Resolution 478, declaring all Israel's legislative and administrative actions that altered the character of Jerusalem "null and void."[39] The United States again abstained from voting for the resolution and took no steps to enforce its application. A year later, Begin annexed the Golan Heights. No matter how sincerely he wished Israel would stop colonizing Arab land, Carter found his options limited. The United States had provided Israel with such vast military advantage over its Arab foes that it had become very difficult to control. The influence, organization, success, and therefore confidence of the pro-Israel lobby had also grown enormously since Eisenhower's day. Whatever strategic asset Israel provided the United States in its battle against Arab "radicalism," Israel was no mere client of America, and Begin no puppet. To Arabs, it often seemed that the tail wagged the dog. The image of America among Arabs continued to free-fall.

Literary Arab portrayals of America in this period had an audience that took American imperialism for granted. The Egyptian writer Radwa Ashur specifically drew a contrast between her own experience of America and that of earlier generations of Arab travelers who had returned from the West "besotted with the bright lights of imperialism."[40] Hers was the era that finally lost faith in America. The Saudi author Abdelrahman Munif began writing what would become his masterful series of novels *Cities of Salt* (the first volume was published in Arabic in 1984), which depicted the transformation of an Arabian town in the age of oil, based on the history of ARAMCO in Saudi Arabia. Munif describes American oil men allying themselves with an Arab emir to drill for and export his country's oil. They promise prosperity for all the emir's subjects, and despite the initial fears of the foreign Americans expressed by some, the emir consents to an American-led transformation of a desert oasis into a company town where oil has been found. Although a tremendous material revolution becomes evident, so too does the emir's absolutism and corruption. The more dependent the emir becomes on the Americans, the more distant he grows from his people. He authorizes the bloody repression of poorly treated, striking workers. Dissenters are brutalized and tortured. The emir's regime ends up as a parable for the modern Arab national security state supported by the United States. The government's despotism, moreover, produces an anti-American fundamentalist backlash, but by then the traditional way of life and landscape of the area has irrevocably changed. "I told you," says a character at the end of the novel whose prophecies had been ignored at the outset, "I told every one of you, the Americans are the disease, they're the root of the problem, and what's happened now is nothing compared to what they have in store for us."[41]

With the signing of the Camp David Accords, the American wager that they could promote Israel and secure their need for Middle Eastern oil appeared to have paid off. The promise of Arab nationalism had clearly failed. Sadat, heir to Nasser, leader of the most populous Arab nation, which also possessed the strongest Arab army, had abdicated his pan-Arab role. The Arabs' collective will to resist Israel was sapped by Egypt's defection. There seemed to be little reason to alter the basic American approach that consistently privileged Israel over the Arabs and supported key pro-American rulers in Egypt and Saudi Arabia. Arab opinion, after all, hardly figured in how the current Arab leaders conducted their policies, whether in Baathist Iraq or Sadat's Egypt; there was no reason, therefore, why it should have mattered more to America.

But Nasser's ghost hovered over a region that craved a new hero. Sadat had become a pariah—idolized in the West, but isolated from his own people. His lavish lifestyle and the corruption that flourished among the Egyptian elite who took advantage of his economic liberalization put in bold relief the great distance that separated Sadat from millions of his poor subjects. His cultivation of the Muslim Brotherhood, which Nasser had suppressed, backfired on him. It gave Islamists more confidence, but the Muslim Brotherhood and several other Islamist organizations demanded more control of public life, harassed Coptic Christians, and, above all, bitterly opposed Sadat's treaty with Israel. As a result, they found themselves once again harshly persecuted at the same time that Sadat sought to exploit the religious card to mollify a growing opposition. Perhaps most indicative of Sadat's decline was the so-called Law of Shame that he had promulgated in 1980 and that criminalized advocating any doctrine "which impl[ies] a negation of divine teachings or which do not conform to the tenets thereof."[42]

In September 1981, Sadat ordered the mass arrest of secular and Islamist dissidents. Politicians, former judges, and journalists, including the loquacious Heikal, were all caught in the dragnet. Sadat even tried to depose the Coptic Pope Shenouda III after he protested a string of anti-Coptic attacks by Islamists in Egypt in the late 1970s. In Egypt and other Arab states, there was a growing turn to a more militant form of Islam inspired, in part, by the late prison writings and example of Sayyid Qutb, the Islamist leader who had been tortured and hanged by Nasser's regime in 1966. His sectarian vision of a great global clash between Muslim believers and infidels gained traction with the eclipse of credible secular nationalist leaders and with the continued domination of Jewish Israelis over Muslim Arabs. The widening gap between rich and poor across the Middle East further eroded the legitimacy of dictatorial regimes.

The Soviet Union invaded Afghanistan in 1979. In response, the CIA, along with the Pakistani and Saudi secret services, financed and encouraged a jihad against the Communists. The United States supported resistance to the Soviet invasion of Afghanistan without realizing that Arabs and Muslims would wonder why it did not support a similar resistance against the Israeli invasion of Arab lands. Hubris, a Cold War fixation on the Soviet foe, and a bureaucratic geographic compartmentalization (Afghanistan was related to South and Central Asian affairs, Palestine and Lebanon to the Middle East) blinded American policymakers to the obvious linkage between the struggle of one group of fighters to liberate Afghanistan (the "moral equivalents of America's founding fathers," as Ronald Reagan would hail the *mujahideen* in 1985) and another group struggling to liberate Palestine.[43]

Afghanis were at the forefront of this anti-Soviet campaign, but so too were an increasing number of Arabs who saw in Afghanistan a field of battle to redeem Muslim honor. A transnational band of like-minded men committed themselves to what they believed was the cause of freedom for Muslims everywhere. They believed that they were participants in a global struggle against the forces of atheism, apostasy, and heresy. Some of these volunteers were highly educated engineers and doctors, but most possessed only a rudimentary religious education. Although Afghanistan could never compensate for the loss of Palestine, the fact that there was success to be had there elevated its symbolic significance. In the mountains and valleys of Afghanistan, thousands of these so-called Afghan Arabs found a new calling. Among them was a Palestinian by the name of Abdullah Azzam, who had broken with Yasser Arafat years before because of the latter's secularism and who had been a member of the Muslim Brotherhood. In Afghanistan, Azzam sought to direct the energy of these radicalized young Muslims. He was a zealot inspired by the writings of the medieval Muslim jurist Ibn Taymiyya and by those of Sayyid Qutb and saw the world in Manichean terms, but he also carried with him the sorrow of the Palestinian *nakba*. He believed that Muslims were involved in an existential war against non-Muslims, but that pious Muslims also had to rid themselves of their internal enemies.

Among Azzam's disciples was Usama Bin Laden, the son of an extremely wealthy Saudi contractor, and Ayman al-Zawahari, an Egyptian doctor who had taken advantage of Sadat's Islamic policy to proselytize on Egyptian campuses before being jailed and tortured for his opposition to Sadat's regime. Zawahari was related on his father's side to the Shaykh al-Azhar who had led a campaign against American missionaries in the 1930s; on his mother's side, he was also related to the Arab League secretary general Azzam Pasha, who had warned the United States in 1946 of the negative consequences that Zionism was bound to have on the Arab world and on U.S.-Arab relations. For the time being, these two were prepared to exploit American and Saudi aid and work with the Pakistani military in order to defeat the Soviets. But this would change, for each carried within his heart a simmering hatred of the United States for its role in the Middle East.

As Afghanistan descended into a protracted war, one of the main pillars of American regional domination suddenly fell from power in neighboring Iran. The hated shah, whom Carter had hailed as the leader of an "island of stability" as recently as December 1977, was swept away in early 1979 by a genuinely popular revolution that shook Iran to its foundations.[44] Now kept at arm's length by the Carter administration, the shah took refuge in Sadat's Egypt. The new leader of Iran was Ayatollah Ruhollah Khomeini, who ushered in a revolutionary reign of terror as a prelude to the establishment of an Islamic republic. Puritanical, uncompromising, and anti-Western, Khomeini also swept aside secular and liberal alternatives to the shah. Secular Iranians and Arabs, the heirs to the liberal nationalists who had opened the century with such faith in America and themselves, ended the century contemplating their own irrelevance on an anti-American political stage.

Khomeini drew effortlessly on the insidious history of Russian, British, and American manipulation of Iran that had steadily embittered ordinary Iranians and driven them into the ranks of any leader who could tap into and mobilize their thirst for dignity, their desire for a better life, and their revulsion at the naked corruption and conspicuous consumption of the Iranian elites who had benefited from the post-1973 oil price boom. Khomeini was a master in this regard. He was as though a religious incarnation of Nasser, but unlike the Egyptian Free Officers when they instigated their coup of 1952, Khomeini began his revolution with an enormous following. American support for the shah, beginning with the overthrow of Mossadegh in 1953, was the principal reason why he called America the "Great Satan." But he also railed consistently against Israel, which had also supported the shah and helped set up his dreaded security apparatus, the SAVAK.

Like the Afghan Arabs, Khomeini did not speak, or bother to speak, a language that American audiences could easily understand. Unlike Sadat, he was not interested in cultivating a Western following at the expense of his own people. His rhetoric was heavily pietistic and fervent. It reflected his own Shi'a religiosity, social conservatism, and political opportunism, as well as an experience of degradation, exile, and political hardship to which Americans could not relate. Because of their similar experience of colonialism, Arabs could understand Khomeini, especially when he condemned American imperialism and "world Zionism." Far more successfully than the Saudi Wahabism, Khomeini's defiance initially captivated the Arab world. Khomeini represented the antithesis of Western liberalism, which had proved over half a century to be so vigilant against anti-Semitism but that had at the same time been mute about the ongoing colonial fate meted out by Jewish Israelis to the Christians and Muslims of Palestine.

In November 1979, Iranian students seized the U.S. embassy in retaliation for the shah's arrival in the United States for medical treatment. The long drama of the hostage crisis commenced. The students burned U.S. flags and chanted anti-American slogans. Americans were appalled at so abrupt a turn of events, but as with virtually every other moment of anti-American expression in the region, they were mostly unaware—and were kept ignorant—of the historical context that made such events intelligible, perhaps even inevitable. For Khomeini, the humiliation of Carter was sweet revenge against a U.S. president who had championed the idea of human rights but turned a blind eye to them in Iran.

Khomeini also mocked Arab leaders, exposing their hypocrisy and impotence in the face of Israel and America. Unlike the Saudis, who protested to the United States about Israeli actions but nevertheless protected their relationship with the U.S. government, Khomeini was confident enough in his own leadership to defy U.S. hegemony. "America is the number-one enemy of the deprived and oppressed people of the world," he said in September 1980 just after Saddam Hussein launched an ill-fated invasion of Iran with U.S. encouragement.[45] Although Saddam sought to portray Khomeini as a grave "Persian" threat to the Arabs, few Arabs regarded Iran as a greater menace than Israel, and fewer still were uncritical of the manner in which the United States had consistently turned its back on the Palestinians.

Given the total breakdown of relations between the United States and Iran, there was little left for Khomeini to lose, and only a global Muslim audience to gain, by playing up the intense injustice occurring in Palestine. This was not simply cynicism or shrewd politics. It was a swipe at the weakest point in American hegemony in the Middle East—America's Achilles' heel—and a reminder of what Albert Hourani, Philip Hitti, and William Eddy had each warned about a half-century earlier. Western imperialism would create its Islamist antithesis. If the United States exploited Arab military weakness to impose a colonial Israel on the Arabs, Khomeini exploited America's moral weakness over Palestine. He called Sadat a "traitor and servant of America, the friend and brother of Begin and the dead, deposed Shah."[46] Few Arabs outside of Egypt, and not a few inside, would have disagreed with such an assessment. Khomeini understood that every Israeli settlement built, every air raid and home demolition carried out, and every piece of Arab land expropriated constituted an indictment of America and its local allies.

On October 6, 1981, Islamist assassins murdered Sadat during a military parade to commemorate Egypt's crossing of the Suez Canal. The leader of the conspirators was a young lieutenant, Khalid al-Islambouli, who had been educated at what had once been an American missionary school nationalized after the Egyptian revolution. Unlike the intense outpouring of popular grief that accompanied Nasser's funeral, Sadat was taken to his grave followed by a large host of foreign leaders, including Menachem Begin and three former U.S. presidents, and an even larger security entourage. "He was admired and loved by the people of America," proclaimed President Ronald Reagan.[47] Egyptians, however, were kept away from the proceedings, and of all the Arab countries, only Sudan sent its head of state to offer condolences.

The following year, Israel evacuated its last Jewish settlement from Sinai and handed the area back to Egypt. Israel adhered to its part of the Camp David bargain. Now it fully expected that Egypt and America would adhere to theirs. Under Ariel Sharon's direction, and with Begin's blessing, Israel launched a massive invasion of Lebanon in June 1982 to finally be rid of the PLO and kill, once and for all, any prospect of Palestinian self-determination. The pretext that Israel used to justify its invasion was an assassination attempt on its ambassador in London by a Palestinian group that had broken away from the PLO long before and that was based in Baghdad, not Beirut.

The pretext mattered little. Egypt was no longer a threat, and the United States was now led by Reagan, who personally was far more sympathetic to Israel than Carter had been. His political base was made up of conservatives, many of whom were staunch Christian Zionists, such as the televangelist Jerry Falwell, who believed that "to stand against Israel is to stand against God."[48] Reagan's administration was also made up of enthusiastic Cold Warriors. They gave Israel the green light to attack.

As Israeli tanks and troops raced up the coast toward Beirut, the U.S.-equipped Israeli air force pounded the country. The world's cameras captured the sights and sounds of the terrifying air raids. There was no Arab army to speak of to stand in Israel's way, nor was there any significant air defense in Lebanon to withstand the aerial assault. Despite its best efforts, Israel could not pretend this time that it was a David fighting an Arab Goliath. Days turned into weeks and weeks into a two-month-long siege when the Israeli army and its Lebanese Maronite allies surrounded West Beirut, where the PLO and Arafat had sought refuge. To force the PLO's submission, the Israeli army cut electricity and water to the besieged inhabitants. Charles Malik, the man who had written one of the most astute commentaries on the state of U.S.-Arab relations in 1949 (see Chapter 5), but who had then turned into an ardent pro-Western Cold Warrior, sat and watched the indiscriminate Israeli bombardment of his capital city. He was old now, but like many other conservative Christians during Lebanon's civil war, he believed that the PLO was the greater threat to Lebanon than Israel. In putting his faith in Israeli violence to liberate his land, Malik had come full circle from his early days advocating Palestine's case at the United Nations in 1947.

Malik's transformation anticipated that of another Arab who was to become famous in America, Fouad Ajami. A Shi'a Lebanese from a small village in southern Lebanon, Ajami came to America in 1963. In his pursuit of higher education in the United States and his initial advocacy of Palestinian rights, Ajami traveled down a path well worn by many other Arab immigrants. But by 1982, Ajami had veered onto a new path. As a professor at Johns Hopkins University, he diagnosed what he described as an "Arab predicament" that he insisted could not be blamed on the West or on Israel.

Ajami described what he regarded as the dead end of modern Arab politics and decried the terrible hold that the "despotism and tribalism of Near Eastern traditions" had in stunting the contemporary Arab world. He pronounced secular Arab nationalism to have always been an illusion. The 1967 defeat revealed this, he wrote, and the Arab disarray in 1982 seemed to confirm his point. But rather than see the "Arab predicament" as part of a dialectic of action and reaction that implicated the West *and* the Arab world in the manner vividly described by the historian Albert Hourani in 1946, Ajami insisted that the "wounds that mattered were self-inflicted wounds."[49] His indictment of Arab political culture was adamant; it updated a lament voiced intensely for at least a generation in the Arab world, beginning with Constantine Zurayk, the Syrian Arab nationalist who had coined the term "the *nakba*" in 1948 and who had engaged in a deep criticism of the internal ills of Arab society.

What was new about Ajami, however, was the degree to which his furious, often harsh, criticisms of Arab failures went hand in hand with a stubborn refusal to acknowledge what was plainly evident in Lebanon itself: The United States and Israel had not only played but were *still* playing an enormous, consequential, damaging role in shaping an illiberal Middle East. "The outside world intruded," he said, "but the destruction one saw reflected the logic of Arab history," as though Arab and Western contexts could so easily be disentangled. If for anti-imperialist nationalist demagogues the fault lay entirely with imperialism or with alleged traitors, for Ajami the fault lay essentially with the Arabs. To suggest anything else was to indulge in what he would later, spitefully, characterize as Arab "victimology."[50] Meanwhile, Israeli aerial, naval, and artillery bombardments killed up to twenty thousand Lebanese and Palestinians, the vast majority of whom were civilians. Many more were wounded as a result of the use of U.S.-supplied cluster and phosphorous bombs.[51]

However, Egypt, now under the rule of Hosni Mubarak, did not cut its diplomatic ties with Israel. The Arab states protested loudly, but did nothing else. The Arab press reproached American complicity in the invasion; even those regimes that were pro-American, such as the Saudis, could not dampen anti-American criticism. "The U.S. must be seen in a new light," said the *Saudi Arab News*. "It is almost the sole supplier and benefactor of Israel. It has given it enough arms not only to protect itself but to invade and occupy any part of the Arab world." A reader from Medina, Saaed Al Hammad, wrote in to warn his fellow Arabs: "Do not be surprised at anything America does. For don't you know your enemy by now? For years it has exploited you and for years it has hit you hard at every available chance and it will continue to do so." He continued, "This Satan is now finished. For generation after generation of Arabs will now look at America as the arch-perpetrator of the inhuman atrocities against the Arab people. Bye Bye America." In Egypt the journalist Mustafa Amin echoed this refrain by writing: "We do not blame Israel alone for putting us to the dagger; we blame the United States first because it gave Israel the dagger with which to kill us."[52] Reagan watched impassively, giving Israel enough time to destroy the PLO and vetoing UN Security Council resolutions that urged Israel to stop the carnage in Lebanon.

Finally, Arafat understood, and was made to understand by war-weary Lebanese, that the PLO had been defeated. The United States mediated Arafat's surrender in early August. He would have to lead the PLO out of Lebanon and into a new exile in distant Tunis. His fighters were to be scattered throughout the Arab world. Despite defiant slogans and protests in the Arab world, including a demonstration of approximately one hundred thousand people in Kuwait on August 9 against the invasion, the PLO's armed struggle had reached its bitter end.[53] In return, the U.S. government solemnly pledged that the Palestinian civilians left behind in the refugee camps in Beirut would be protected. The Israelis undertook not to enter West Beirut. Yet even after the United States had brokered a draft agreement, Israeli defense minister Sharon ordered one final, murderous round of bombardment on August 12 that killed or wounded several hundred people in order to dispel any illusion as to who was victor and who was vanquished.[54] Then at last the Israeli guns fell silent. American marines, together with French and Italian soldiers, landed in Beirut to ensure the orderly departure of the PLO beginning on August 21. No sooner had they accomplished their task than the marines were ordered back to their waiting ships.

Hoping to capitalize on their military victory, the Israelis ensured that their local ally, Bashir Gemayel, was made president of Lebanon on August 23. Lebanese parliamentarians, several of whom were forcibly escorted to Parliament to ensure a legal quorum, were compelled to cast their votes under the shadow of Israeli tanks. But Israel's triumph was short-lived. Gemayel was killed in a massive bomb blast on September 14. Immediately after the assassination, for which Syria was blamed, Sharon ordered his army to occupy the rest of Beirut, ostensibly to maintain security. Israeli soldiers surrounded the Palestinian refugee camps of Sabra and Shatila. Israel army commanders authorized Lebanese Maronite militiamen to enter Sabra and Shatila to "clear out terrorist nests" that Sharon had insisted remained hidden in the camps.[55] Senior Israeli commanders knew full well that these militiamen desired vengeance for the murder of their leader and were, in any case, filled with hatred for Palestinians and Muslims. They also knew that the camps were filled with civilians. Nevertheless, the Israeli army provided the Maronite fighters with ammunition, wireless equipment, and food rations and transported them to the vicinity of the besieged Sabra camp during the day of September 16.

The militiamen entered the camp in the late afternoon. For forty hours, Israeli soldiers did not stop them as they raped, tortured, and murdered over 1,300 women, children, and men in a paroxysm of genocidal violence.[56] Rather, under orders, the Israeli soldiers prevented Palestinians from fleeing and fired flares to illuminate the camps at night.

As the news of the massacre leaked out and the images of the bloated corpses of victims were televised, the world was shocked. Bitter condemnations of Israel and America echoed across the Arab press. Mubarak urgently cabled Reagan, pleading with him to intervene decisively; he instructed his ambassador in Israel to express Egypt's "great disapproval and displeasure" at Israeli actions in Lebanon before recalling him to

Cairo on September 20. Still, Egypt had become too dependent on the United States to allow Mubarak to cut off ties with Israel. The new Saudi King Fahd also condemned the massacre and said that, although Muslims desired peace, they would react when they were humiliated. However, as if to underscore his impotence, he added, "I cannot say when this will take place but it will come."[57]

Hundreds of thousands of Israelis took to the street to protest their government's responsibility for what some of them likened to a pogrom. Reagan himself was moved enough to express "horror"—though his government voted, on September 24, 1982, against an emergency General Assembly resolution condemning the massacre. Israel's image was in tatters; inevitably, therefore, so too was America's. Arafat, now in exile, angrily said that the massacre was "an American-Israeli war of annihilation against us, and the Americans are responsible for it." He also said that "the Palestinian people are not red Indians to be chased and killed in collective massacres." The Israeli cabinet rejected all accusations against the Israeli army as "groundless." Begin even complained that "Goyim [a pejorative reference to non-Jews] are killing goyim, and the whole world is trying to hang Jews for the crime."[58]

In the aftermath of America's broken promise to protect the civilians in the refugee camps, an embarrassed Reagan ordered the U.S. marines back to Lebanon, but the situation there was chaotic. The Israelis occupied much of the country, provoking the inevitable resistance to their presence, initially led by mostly secular groups; meanwhile, Lebanese militias had resumed their struggle for power, which had been interrupted by Israel's invasion. Bashir Gemayel's older brother Amin was duly elected president, but his government was both unpopular and weak. It sought to take advantage of the U.S. presence to impose itself on its mostly Muslim and Druze opposition. U.S.-Iranian clashes in the Persian Gulf added to the tension.

On April 18, 1983, a bomb in a van ripped through the U.S. embassy in Beirut. Sixty-three people, mostly Lebanese, were killed, but seventeen of the victims were American, including several CIA operatives and analysts. A previously unknown group called Al-Jihad al-Islami took responsibility within minutes of the explosion. Nevertheless, U.S. Secretary of State George Shultz pressured the Gemayel government to sign a security treaty with Israel in May 1983. The treaty conceded control over southern Lebanon to Israel, forced the Lebanese army to integrate into its ranks militiamen who had openly collaborated with Israel, and thus further undermined Gemayel's legitimacy. As opposition to the Gemayel government escalated, the United States openly intervened to stave off its collapse, and the U.S. navy began to shell opposition forces in the mountains overlooking Beirut despite the reservations of the marine commanders on the ground.

In the early morning of October 23, 1983, a Mercedes truck loaded with explosives was driven by a suicide bomber into the main U.S. marine barracks at Beirut Airport. The deafening explosion killed 241 American marines, many of them still asleep, and wounded 100 more. This attack—the largest American military loss of life in a single day since the height of the Tet Offensive in Vietnam—was a staggering, terrifying blow. The French forces were also hit simultaneously by a suicide bomber, who killed fifty-eight of them.[59] American officials blamed Shi'a extremists backed by Iran. They were right, but in their shock and indignation they overlooked an equally salient point: The Israeli invasion had not only implicated America but led directly to the presence of U.S. marines in Lebanon. With U.S. approval, Israel had crushed the secular PLO, only to discover that it had cleared the ground for a more determined, more capable, more religious, and certainly more ruthless form of resistance to take its place.

The Arab press reaction to the bombing largely deplored the loss of American life, but also admonished the United States. It was reaping a fanaticism sown by its adamantly pro-Israel policy. Indeed, amid the recrimination and chaos in the aftermath of the bombing, a new Islamic movement was quietly taking shape in the villages of south Lebanon and in the slums of Beirut's southern suburbs. It grew out of a long-standing neglect of the south of the country and from a general radicalization of the Shi'a in the aftermath of the Iranian Revolution. But most of all, it drew strength from, and reflected, a desire for liberation felt by ordinary people who wanted to end Israel's occupation of their villages, lands, and lives. One of its youngest adherents was a Lebanese clergyman recently returned from Iraq, where he had studied at Najaf. Like so many other Shi'a Lebanese, he was also inspired by the example of Khomeini. His name was Hassan Nasrallah, and the movement he joined would eventually take the name of Hizbullah, or the Party of God. From despair was born a new generation of resistance, more hardened than the previous one and, like Khomeini himself, far less interested in dialogue with America or the West. But this resistance emerged at a moment when Arab leaders were less willing to fight America's relationship with Israel and the United States was less willing to examine critically the costs of its unique relationship to the self-proclaimed Jewish state. Between these two poles of resistance and acquiescence were millions of Arabs who were more desperate than ever to simply lead normal lives, but who were more than ever denied that opportunity.

The strike against the American marines signaled yet another turn in the long history of U.S.-Arab relations. In January 1984 the president of the American University of Beirut, Malcolm H. Kerr, was assassinated in his office in College Hall. Kerr was a well-regarded scholar of modern Middle Eastern politics and had taken up his post in September 1982 in the immediate aftermath of the Israeli invasion of Lebanon. The son of an AUB professor, he was born in Beirut in 1931 in a more tranquil era. He was eulogized as a "modern missionary," but his killing was an expression of just how much the Middle East, and the U.S. role in it, had changed in the intervening decades since the missionary age. The outpouring of grief among the AUB community was immediate and virtually universal, just as it had been when Daniel and Howard Bliss had passed away nearly a century earlier. But there was now a deep sense of apprehension and tragedy, not only because of the death of the well-liked Kerr, but because his murder constituted another refutation of the historical memory of peaceful interactions between Arabs and Americans that his own life had represented. President Reagan declared that "his work strengthened the historical, cultural, and academic ties between the United States and Lebanon and other countries in the Middle

East." Unacknowledged, however, was the degree to which U.S. policies and decisions had undermined these ties.[60]

The irony of anti-American acts such as the attack on the U.S. Marines and Kerr's assassination was that they drove the United States even closer to Israel in the name of a common fight against Arab and Muslim terrorism. To the extent that Reagan had outlined a peace plan to resolve the Arab-Israeli conflict, he had merely recycled Carter's failed Camp David formula for a vague Palestinian self-rule in the West Bank and Gaza subject to Israel's "security" requirements. Once again, the United States explicitly ruled out a Palestinian state. American protests against Jewish Israeli settlements—or what the U.S. administration now referred to meekly as "obstacles to peace"—became rhetorical exercises, issued without any conviction and without any intention of actually stopping them. Israel, as a result, continued to expand into the occupied West Bank and in East Jerusalem at the same time as AIPAC set out to mend Israel's image in America. In 1985 the U.S. Congress authorized over $3 billion in aid to Israel, nearly half of which was in the form of a military grant.[61]

In August 1990, Saddam Hussein ordered his army to invade Kuwait. His decision to occupy and annex a neighboring Arab country was extraordinary, reckless, and manifestly illegal. More than any other single act over the past half-century, the Iraqi invasion of Kuwait exposed the deep fractures of Arab countries and confirmed the demise of Arab nationalist politics. In addition, it revealed the vulnerability of the oil-rich Gulf states, including Saudi Arabia, despite the several billion dollars they had spent purchasing U.S. weapons over a decade and a half. More immediately, the conquest of Kuwait openly defied U.S. hegemony in the Arabian Peninsula. Oil had always been America's paramount interest in the Middle East, and though President George H. W. Bush would not explicitly say that the United States was fighting a war for oil (instead, he claimed that it was about the "hard work of freedom," the integrity of the UN, and the will of the international community),

American presidents had made it abundantly clear for decades that they would brook no challenge to the pro-Western petroleum order.[62] The United States had supported Saddam during his war against Iran, and it had largely ignored the atrocities he committed during the conflict, including both his use of poison gas against Iranian soldiers and his terrible massacre of Iraqi Kurdish civilians at Halabja in 1988 that left several thousand men, women, and children dead. Kurdish suffering meant little to Cold War Washington, which, along with Iran and Israel, had encouraged Kurdish resistance against the Iraqi regime in the 1970s until Iraq conceded a territorial dispute with the shah's Iran. Then support had been cut off abruptly, and the Kurdish guerrillas were crushed by the Iraqi military. Henry Kissinger had said in 1975 that "covert action should not be confused with missionary work."[63] In 1983 and 1984, Donald Rumsfeld, who was then head of a multinational pharmaceutical company, had been sent as a presidential envoy to Iraq to pave the way for a restoration of U.S. diplomatic relations with Saddam's regime. There he had lobbied for Iraq's permission to have a new oil pipeline constructed to Aqaba in Jordan. Human rights violations, democracy, and chemical weapons were simply not his priority; rather, they were seen as obstacles in the way of a mutually beneficial relationship that tied Washington to Baghdad. (Meanwhile, another U.S. covert operation, later known as the Iran-Contra scandal, supplied Iran with U.S.-made Tow anti-tank missiles and Hawk anti-aircraft missiles, which Iran immediately deployed against Iraq in return for Iranian help in freeing U.S. hostages held in Lebanon.) When an Iraqi plane fired two Exocet missiles that killed thirty-seven Americans and severely damaged the USS *Stark* in 1987, an incident reminiscent of Israel's attack on the USS *Liberty* in 1967, the United States quickly accepted Iraq's apology.

But Iraq's invasion of Kuwait in 1990 could not be tolerated by the United States. Bush rushed troops to the area and built up a massive force in Saudi Arabia in order to expel Iraq from Kuwait. Syria and Egypt subordinated themselves to the U.S. military effort against Iraq—the former in partial exchange for U.S. acceptance of its domination of Lebanon following the end of the civil war there, and the latter in return for the wiping out of Egypt's considerable U.S. debt. Yasser

Arafat, however, would not condone the U.S.-led military operation against Iraq, despite its occupation of Kuwait, and thus lost the sympathy and financial support of the Arab Gulf states.

In January 1991, the United States unleashed its fearful power on Iraq, starting the Gulf War, known as Desert Storm. Iraq's infrastructure, already debilitated because of the Iran-Iraq War, which had just ended in 1988, was systematically destroyed. Water treatment plants, oil refineries, railroads, bridges, the electricity grid, telecommunications, and government buildings were all targeted. In so uneven a war, Iraqi soldiers were inevitably slaughtered, and an unknown number of Iraqi civilians were killed. The United States lost 382 soldiers in the entire campaign.[64] By March 1991, the war was over. By stopping short of an occupation of Iraq, and by not deposing Saddam Hussein, Bush and his secretary of state, James Baker, believed that the United States could not be accused of being a colonial power.

The Saudis and Kuwaitis defrayed much of the approximately $60 billion cost of the war and allowed for the establishment of U.S. military bases or facilities in their respective countries.[65] Bahrain was the headquarters of the U.S. navy's Fifth Fleet. U.S. marines were also deployed on amphibious vessels in the Persian Gulf. The restored Kuwaiti ruling family, secure in its knowledge that the United States was supreme, expelled nearly three hundred thousand Palestinians who had been living in the country for decades in the vindictive anti-Palestinian and anti-Iraqi mood that permeated Kuwait after its liberation. The Arab League was paralyzed. Israel, which like Saudi Arabia had been subjected to random Iraqi Scud missile attacks, was amply compensated. Whereas Saudis paid a premium for their protection, Israel received $650 million for the damage caused by the missiles over and above the now-routine several-billion-dollar annual U.S. aid package.[66]

Saddam Hussein's inexplicable military challenge to the United States and the consequent crushing defeat to which his nation was subjected demoralized most Arabs outside the Gulf. Syrians, Lebanese, Palestinians, Algerians, Yemenis, and Egyptians had initially rallied around Saddam as a symbol of defiance of the West. Saddam, in turn, had sought to exploit this sympathy by launching Scud missiles at Israel. Like his nemesis Khomeini, Saddam played the Palestine card. However, as easy as anti-Israeli anger was to manipulate, it did little to satisfy the yearning for a more dignified life across the Arab world.

Arab nationalist rhetoric, to be sure, remained evident in Saddam's Baathist Iraq, but its utterances constituted a travesty given the violence that permeated his regime. The Iraqi dictator's clinging to power and his unleashing of the remnants of his defeated army (with U.S. acquiescence) to crush a Shi'a rebellion in the war's aftermath reflected the terror that had long been at the heart of his regime. His abrupt, cynical turn to Islam during the war exemplified the ostensibly secular regime's ideological and political bankruptcy. Saddam destroyed the lives and future of millions of his own people simply in order to survive. But despite U.S. vilification of him, he was not alone. Autocracy was the rule across the Arab world—much of it now supported by the United States, including once-radical Algeria, whose military annulled the results of democratic elections won comprehensively by Islamists in 1991.

From an Arab perspective, what was most striking about Desert Storm was that the United States devastated an Arab country in a manner scarcely imaginable a decade before. Equally striking was America's resorting to the UN to legitimate its use of crushing violence. In the name of enforcing UN resolutions, Iraq was placed under the most stringent sanctions regime in modern history. Between 1990 and 2003, Iraq was a nation besieged. Indeed, between 1990 and 1995, despite the destruction of its health and sanitation infrastructure, Iraq was blocked from importing generators or virtually any substance or product that the United States deemed might be used for industrial or military purposes. According to UN estimates, tens of thousands of Iraqi children under five died as a result, with some studies putting the figure as high as five hundred thousand. Iraqis also coped with chronic malnutrition, stunted development, and enormous unquantifiable social costs associated with the sanctions policy.[67] The United States, of course, blamed Saddam for bringing this misery on his own people, and to a large extent it was correct. But it was America that insisted upon the stringent application of the sanctions, and it was U.S. officials who were callously indifferent to the mass suffering that they knew was occurring in Iraq. When asked in

May 1996 by Lesley Stahl on CBS's *60 Minutes* whether the deaths of so many children—"I mean, that's more children than died in Hiroshima," Stahl exclaimed incredulously—could possibly be worth the effort to contain Saddam Hussein, Secretary of State Madeline Albright replied, "I think this is a very hard choice, but the price—we think the price is worth it."[68]

Iraq had been in plain violation of UN Security Council Resolution 660 passed in August 1990, which had demanded its immediate withdrawal from Kuwait. But so too, as every Arab knew, was Israel in violation of UN Security Council resolutions on multiple counts, the most pertinent of which was Resolution 425, related to its initial invasion of Lebanon in 1978, and Resolution 476 from 1980, which demanded that Israel cease all attempts to alter the character of occupied East Jerusalem. In Lebanon the United States simply turned a blind eye to Israel's defiance of the UN, even after the Shi'a Muslim Lebanese Hizbullah emerged as a potent force seeking to liberate the south of Lebanon. Not surprisingly, Hassan Nasrallah lashed out at America, saying that it was "responsible for all Israel's massacres and all the destruction, murder, and displacement it wreaks. Everybody knows that Israel would not have been able to stand on its own in the region had it not been for Western and American support."[69]

In the Palestinian territories, a popular and relatively nonviolent uprising, or *intifada*, against the Israeli military occupation between December 1987 and 1990 garnered considerable sympathy for the Palestinians on the world stage, including in America itself. Yet the United States government contented itself with issuing halfhearted calls for restraint even as Israel crushed the *intifada*. No sanctions were placed on Israel. And yet when Arabs pointed to the blatant double standard in the enforcement of UN Security Council resolutions in the Middle East, the United States went out of its way to deny publicly any linkage between the two situations and to insist that it was an "honest broker" in the Arab-Israeli conflict.[70]

But there was, and remains, an obvious linkage. As President Dwight Eisenhower said at the height of the Suez crisis in 1956, "There can be no peace—without law. And there can be no law—if we were to invoke one code of international conduct for those who oppose us—and another for our friends" (see Chapter 5). The initial, festering wound of Palestine was now compounded by the war on Iraq and the sanctions regime imposed upon it. Arab anger at American hypocrisy reached a boiling point. Still, the Arab states were in no position to alter the fundamental dynamic of the relationship that bound them at their nadir to the United States at the height of its post–Cold War power. "I think that anger in the Arab street is real," admitted Martin Indyk before the U.S. Congress in 1991; Indyk was then executive director of the AIPAC-affiliated Washington Institute for Near East Policy and later one of the architects of the Middle East policy of the Clinton administration. "It is produced by a number of different factors. But in the end, what matters is not whether they hate us or love us—for the most part, they hate us. They did before. But whether they are going to respect our power."

In a prepared statement he submitted separately, Indyk further dismissed the nature of anti-Americanism in the Arab world. "The antipathy towards the West that is likely to follow this war," wrote Indyk, "has long been present in the Arab world. It cannot be resolved through accommodation."[71] The implication of Indyk's words was clear: Anti-Americanism had no obvious origins, and therefore no obvious cure. For him, there was no need to delve into the reasons why so many Arabs felt so alienated from the United States.

The Bush administration, nevertheless, made an effort at resolving the Arab-Israeli conflict following the end of Desert Storm. It pressured Israel and the Arab states, including Saudi Arabia, to meet face to face for the first time at Madrid in October 1991. Once again, the United States accepted Israeli preconditions about which Palestinians could participate in the negotiations and under what conditions. President Bush and Secretary of State Baker famously demanded that Israel stop its settlement construction in the occupied territories. Given how much aid the United States supplied Israel, including $10 billion in loan guarantees to allow it to absorb hundreds of thousands of new Soviet Jewish immigrants, Bush believed that he had leverage over Israel. A solution to the Palestinian-Israeli conflict was clearly in America's national interest, for it would diffuse anti-American sentiment considerably. For a moment, it appeared as if Baker and Bush might give some credence to the notion of the United States as an "honest broker." Yet Israel refused to stop settlement construction. Unlike Eisenhower in 1956, this U.S. administration simply could not sustain effective pressure on Israel, which ultimately pressed ahead with its colonization program of East Jerusalem and the West Bank under the pretense of the "natural growth" of existing Jewish settlements. Another opportunity for a comprehensive settlement passed. Arab nationalism had been crushed, but Israeli Jewish nationalism was rampant. Meanwhile, the sanctions on Iraq continued.

The downward spiral in U.S-Arab relations accelerated even more under President Bill Clinton. He appointed Indyk and Dennis Ross—who, like Indyk, was Jewish and affiliated with AIPAC—to oversee his administration's Middle East policy; not surprisingly, they encouraged a further U.S. alignment behind Israel. What little pressure Bush and Baker had brought to bear was lifted. Clinton, however, applied the Iraq sanctions tightly and enforced "no-fly" zones over northern and southern Iraq. U.S. warplanes routinely bombed the country while UN inspectors scoured Iraq to find and destroy its stocks of chemical and biological weapons. Saddam Hussein nevertheless remained in power, heedless of the consequences of his catastrophic rule.

Having taken refuge under the U.S. security umbrella, Saudi Arabia was unwilling to challenge Indyk or Ross. Nor would Egypt defy the United States, for the rulers in both countries were now invested heavily in U.S. power, an erosion of which would undermine their own authority. Both countries, meanwhile, were dealing with the problem of the so-called jihadists who had been mobilized, trained, and equipped by the United States and the Saudis for the Afghan war, but who now found themselves turning their attention back to the "apostate" regimes that dominated the Arab world and to the military presence of the United States in the region.[72] Arab autocracies allied with the United States understood that among ordinary people across the Arab world dismay at the U.S. double standard over Iraq and Israel was almost universal. In addition, the U.S. troop presence in Arabia fueled anger within Saudi Arabia. The Saudi royal family could pressure the United States to keep a low military profile in its country, but they could not hide their dependency on America. A group called al-Qa'ida, whose origins lay in the U.S.-backed jihad in Afghanistan, emerged on the scene.[73]

In August 1996, the leader of this group, Usama Bin Laden, delivered a *fatwa*, or a religious opinion, to a London-based Arabic newspaper in which he declared war on the "Americans Occupying the Land of the Two Holy Places [Saudi Arabia]." The fatwa was laced with Koranic verses and references to medieval Islamic jurists and figures, but the salience of the declaration rested in its interpretation of the recent tribulations of the Arabs and the U.S. role in them. "It should not be hidden from you that the people of Islam had suffered from aggression, iniquity and injustice imposed on them by the Zionist-Crusaders alliance and their collaborators; to the extent that the Muslims' blood became the cheapest and their wealth as loot in the hands of the enemies," said Bin Laden. "Their blood was spilled in Palestine and Iraq. The horrifying pictures of the massacre of Qana, in Lebanon [in 1996, when an Israeli bombardment killed and wounded over two hundred Lebanese civilians who had sought shelter in a UN base] are still fresh in our memory."[74] Bin Laden rejected the secular, liberal language of universal human rights and international law. They had done nothing to protect Muslims around the world. The answer to the continuing injustice, he said, had to come from within, a return to the Sharia (Islamic law), a turning inward of Muslims, a renunciation of the world, and with it the promise of fiery blows to be struck at America and its allies.

Bin Laden, by now, had become in the eyes of young Arab Sunni militants a veritable holy warrior because of his conduct in Afghanistan, where he renounced the opulent lifestyle of his fellow Saudis, took to the caves of Afghanistan like other Arab Afghans, and spent millions of dollars from his own fortune in the anti-Soviet struggle. In February 1998, he and his right-hand man, the Egyptian Ayman al-Zawahari, announced the formation of the World Islamic Front, consisting of Bin Laden's al-Qa'ida and several other Egyptian, Pakistani, and Bangladeshi extremist groups. Like Bin Laden's prior fatwa, the declaration was a rambling document, also filled with Koranic references, but it was far more violent in tone. It declared openly that to "kill the Americans and their allies—civilian and military—is an individual duty for every Muslim" until the "Crusader-Zionist alliance" left Muslim lands and stopped oppressing Muslims.[75] The exhortation dehumanized Americans, rendering them an abstraction, the "collateral damage" in what its authors regarded as a defensive and religious war. It was also rabidly anti-Jewish and anti-Christian. Bin Laden counted on the fact that few, if any, Arabs would deny that rank injustice was occurring in Palestine and Iraq, that human rights abuses were rampant across the Arab world, that the Saudi royal family was corrupt, and that Arab regimes were undemocratic and out of touch with their people.

Yet the vast majority of Arabs had no desire to use these indisputable facts to return to a mythical golden age of Islam, and still less desire to carry out the kind of horrific acts in the name of ending injustice that Bin Laden and his associates carried out and condoned. Most Islamists, moreover, were not followers of Bin Laden but belonged to more established, or at least legitimate, organizations that operated in distinct national settings. Crucially, most Arabs still were able to discriminate between American society and American policy. The leading Shi'a cleric in Lebanon was (and remains) Muhammad Husayn Fadlallah. He had been affiliated with Hizbullah and therefore targeted for assassination in 1985, allegedly at the behest of the CIA, following the marine barracks bombing and the kidnapping of CIA operative William Buckley. A car bomb in the crowded Beirut neighborhood where he worked injured or killed nearly three hundred civilians, though he was not wounded. Yet, although Fadlallah repeatedly noted U.S. hostility to the Arabs and Muslims and justified violent resistance as a defensive reaction to Western aggression, he very clearly demarcated what he called the "arena of struggle" as a local one. "We consider our struggle is with American policy and not the American people," he insisted.[76]

There is no indication that most Arabs had even heard of Bin Laden at this point in the late 1990s, but there was every indication that his discussion of Arab suffering in Palestine and Iraq was bound to strike a chord. The establishment of an Arabic satellite news station known as Al-Jazeera in Qatar in 1996 added heart-rending visual documentation of the violence inflicted upon Arabs by both Americans and Israelis in Iraq and the occupied Palestinian territories. That Arabs were not collectively moved about the systematic injustice occurring *within* Iraq at the behest of the Iraqi regime—or for that matter within Egypt, Saudi Arabia, and most other Arab countries—did not in any way lessen the real concern and anger stoked by hostile and harsh American actions in the Middle East. Indeed, the high noon of official Arab surrender to America was not accompanied by any equivalent Israeli surrender to the United States. No matter how much the question of Palestine now embarrassed pro-American Arab regimes, and how greatly it inflamed and consolidated anti-American opinion among Arabs, Israeli actions ensured that it persisted.

Yasser Arafat's secular PLO had been in a state of terminal decline since its exile from Lebanon. In 1993, desperate to be brought back in from the cold following the Persian Gulf War, Arafat and his deputy, Mahmoud Abbas, cut a secret deal with Israel in Norway known as the Oslo Accords. (A second "interim" agreement was made in 1995.) In signing the Oslo Accords, Arafat bypassed his own formal negotiating team, which had been working assiduously, but unsuccessfully, since the Madrid conference for a comprehensive, just solution to the Palestinian-Israeli conflict based on international law and genuine reciprocity. The Oslo Accords, however, were anything but reciprocal and comprehensive. In return for Israeli recognition of the PLO (but not a Palestinian state), the PLO formally recognized Israel. It entered into essentially the same autonomy framework presented at Camp David in 1978, which it had vehemently rejected at the time. The Oslo Accords spelled out a "declaration of principles" that created islands of Palestinian self-rule in the West Bank, to be administered by an entity called the Palestinian Authority, surrounded by either Israeli settlements or Israeli military installations; the agreement tacitly allowed Israel to maintain all its Jewish settlements, for it avoided any reference to Israel's occupation of Palestinian land, the status of Jerusalem, a future Palestinian state, or the right of return of refugees.[77]

Instead, Arafat accepted, and Clinton quickly blessed, the fiction of an autonomous Palestinian entity that was bound to ensure Israel's security, not ensure the Palestinians' liberation. The ubiquitous references in the years that immediately followed the Oslo Accords to a Palestinian "government," with "ministers" in a place called "Palestine" despite the glaring absence of any such sovereign country constituted a charade of the most grotesque sort. Edward Said, who perhaps had put too much of his early faith in Arafat as he grappled with his Palestinian identity in the aftermath of 1967, was by now thoroughly disenchanted with Arafat and the PLO. He described the Oslo Accords as a "Palestinian Versailles" and an "instrument of Palestinian surrender."[78] The Americans called the agreement a victory for the "peace process," and Arafat immediately fell in line; he even banned Said's books from the few parts of the West Bank under his authority, claiming that Said was an intellectual in New York out of touch with reality. The truth was that the Arabs were deeply divided by the Oslo Accords. Many, like Said, were scandalized by them because they consolidated Israeli hegemony in most of the West Bank and fell so obviously short of meaningful self-determination. But many Palestinians and other Arabs also hoped that they represented a first step toward a comprehensive solution and felt that it behooved Arafat to finally seize an opportunity to end the misery of his people. The Oslo Accords were meant to pave the way for discussions that would deal with all the "outstanding" issues that separated Israel and the Palestinians.

With his recognition of Israel, Arafat had finally become a "moderate" in American eyes. He was rewarded with numerous invitations to the White House to confer with Clinton and Albright. Initially, Palestinians in the West Bank were eager to give Arafat, who had for so long embodied the cause of Palestine, the benefit of the doubt. They elected him "president" in 1996. Israel allowed the Palestinian leader to establish his headquarters in the West Bank town of Ramallah, and it withdrew its soldiers from several other densely inhabited towns.

But at the same time, and under a variety of pretexts, Israel continued to expropriate Palestinian land, to build Jewish-only bypass roads and colonies, and to fragment the West Bank into isolated pockets of Palestinian life hemmed in by Jewish Israeli settlers and soldiers. Between 1993 and 2000, the number of Jewish Israeli settlers in the West Bank nearly doubled, from 111,600 to 192,976 (and in East Jerusalem the number went from 152,800 to 172,250).[79] The former U.S. president Jimmy Carter belatedly realized that rather than setting the stage for peace, Israel accomplished, and Arafat inadvertently acquiesced to, a form of "apartheid" in the West Bank under Israeli domination. There was one rule, despite the existence of the Palestinian Authority, for Palestinians—who had to contend with military occupation in most of the West Bank, a system of passes that hindered their movement, and a separate, inferior road system—there was another, civilian rule for Israeli Jews, and there was paramount Israeli control over both groups. In the case of the peace treaty that Sadat had signed in 1979, at least Egyptian land had been regained, if at the expense of the Palestinians and Syrians. The desperation at Oslo was far more palpable, because the PLO's position was that much weaker. Egypt and the Gulf states had washed their hands of the Palestinian question. Arafat and Abbas misleadingly promised their people imminent liberation, but could do nothing but hope in vain that the United States would pressure Israel to live up to its side of a nebulous bargain.

Hamas, a fundamentalist movement that grew out of the Egyptian Sunni Muslim Brotherhood in the 1980s, objected vehemently to the Oslo Accords. Like Hizbullah, Hamas maintained a grassroots network and ran extensive social services, but it exclusively focused on Palestine. Hamas advocated an Islamic state, which most Palestinians did not want. It also vowed to continue the "armed struggle" that the PLO had formally abandoned. Although initially far less popular than Arafat's Fatah, Hamas was strengthened by the fact that life for the ordinary Palestinians under occupation deteriorated significantly during the "peace process." This was due in part to the corruption within the Palestinian Authority. But it was mainly due to the Israeli policy of fragmenting the West Bank into various areas, most of which were no longer accessible to Palestinians, and to its routine ban on the freedom of movement of Palestinians. Jewish settlers, including many from the United States, also terrorized Palestinians openly. In al-Khalil, or Hebron, 450 Jewish settlers had implanted themselves in a town in which over 130,000 Palestinians lived. Protected by Israeli soldiers, the settlers would eventually force a partition of Hebron in 1997 into two sections known as H1 and H2, although the settlers constituted less than 1 percent of the overall population. Along with other Jewish extremists in the West Bank, they routinely harassed Palestinians in streets, burned their outlying fields, cut down their orchards, and beat up and often killed Palestinians, whom they described as "Arab" interlopers on the land of Israel. One of them, Baruch Goldstein, who was originally from Brooklyn, massacred twenty-nine Palestinian worshipers in the Mosque of Ibrahim in Hebron in February 1994.[80]

Hamas also resorted to terrorism in the context of Israel's unyielding occupation. It succeeded in killing dozens of Israeli civilians in four suicide bombings between February and March 1996, without effecting their stated goals of liberating Palestinians and creating an Islamic state. Unlike Hizbullah's resistance against the Israeli soldiers, which was part of a clear strategy to force Israel out of Lebanon and which was predicated on a steady supply of weapons from Iran via Syria, Hamas's violence was not part of any obvious liberation strategy as much as it was a reactionary assertion of its presence. Rather than creating the "balance of terror" that its advocates claimed, Hamas bombings energized Israeli opposition to the Oslo Accords, increased Israeli repression, and thus made Palestinian life even more intolerable. The Palestinian Authority, in line with its obligations under the Oslo Accords, arrested and often tortured Hamas members. Israel refused to dismantle a single settlement and, citing terrorism, delayed its withdrawal from other Palestinian towns and cities. The "peace process" was unraveling.

At this very moment, in July 2000, Bill Clinton demanded that Arafat come to Camp David to iron out a final agreement with the then Israeli prime minister, Ehud Barak. Despite his strong reservations given the impasse in the West Bank, Arafat felt compelled to attend. He was coaxed by Clinton's promise not to blame him if the summit failed. With Clinton's connivance, Barak presented Arafat with a take-it-or-leave-it deal that on the face of it offered, at last, the promise of an independent, demilitarized

Palestinian state. But the devil lay in the details, and these were ominous. Israel demanded or expected control of Palestinian airspace, the water aquifers under the West Bank, and the borders of the proposed rump state, including all the land running alongside the border with Jordan, which it would "lease" for a prolonged period. Israel would also annex large chunks of the West Bank that included the major Jewish settlements (Palestinians would be compensated with less valuable land), and it would exercise sovereignty over most of Jerusalem and the bypass roads that crisscrossed the West Bank. The Palestinian refugees from 1948 and their descendants, in essence, would have to abandon their right of return and formally declare an end to the conflict. This was what Israel and its supporters in America hailed as Israel's most "generous" offer and "extraordinary concessions" to the Palestinians.[81]

In reality, Barak was demanding nothing more than a formal surrender. He was utterly contemptuous of the Palestinians. "They are products of a culture in which to tell a lie . . . creates no dissonance," he informed the Israeli historian Benny Morris in the wake of the Camp David summit, adding that they suffered from a "salmon syndrome," that is, they had a compulsive need to return to their birthplaces to die. He believed that as soon as the generation that had lived through the *nakba* passed from the scene, Palestinians would abandon their desire to return to their lands and their struggle for their rights.[82] For Barak, Jews had history and Arabs had only impulses. In any case, he had reason to believe that Arafat might accept the *diktat*, for over the decades the Palestinian leader had repeatedly conceded ground. He had moved the PLO from its original goal of a single democratic state, to accepting a two-state solution, to something that merely suggested sovereignty in the Oslo Accords. The significant Arab countries, moreover, had long since withdrawn from the military confrontation with Israel. AIPAC maintained a stranglehold over a supine U.S. Congress. Yet, for all of Israel's power, Barak himself was politically weak at home and under pressure from a resurgent opposition led by none other than Ariel Sharon, who believed that Barak's offer at Camp David was far too generous to the Palestinians. Clinton pressured Arafat to capitulate.

Arafat, however, balked. He felt that the Palestinians had conceded enough and would not consent to this final deal that so egregiously "ended" the conflict on terms so manifestly unjust. Camp David represented a humiliation too far. A furious Clinton turned on Arafat and, despite his prior assurance, blamed him publicly for the failure of the summit. In truth, Arafat and his aides did have themselves to blame. They had allowed themselves to be led to Camp David. And having sacrificed international law and UN-affirmed rights in favor of what he thought was pragmatism as the basis for his feeble authority, Arafat had little to offer when both rights and law were inevitably brushed aside by Israel and the United States. Arafat had been coddled and feted by the West, and especially by Clinton, with the full expectation that at the end of the day he would sign away his people's rights. When he did not, he was simply discarded. The "moderate" Arafat had run his course—a quintessentially tragic Arab figure in a modern American age that has been ruthlessly unkind to the Arabs.

Inevitably, Arabs contrasted Arafat's dismal showing at Camp David with the successful war of liberation fought in southern Lebanon by Hizbullah. The Islamic organization had grown from a shadowy, militant Shi'a group linked to the attacks on the U.S. embassy and marine barracks into a major movement in the course of a decade. Although the United States consistently regarded Hizbullah as a terrorist organization, the Arab view of it and its dynamic leader, Hassan Nasrallah, was radically different. Between 1985 (when it formally emerged as an organization advocating an Islamic state) and 2000, Hizbullah waged a long, relentless campaign against Israel's army in Lebanon. Its success ensured that it would eclipse all previous Palestinian and Lebanese resistance groups.

The small band of Hizbullah guerrillas fought on, and for, their land. They were well trained, relatively well equipped by Iran and Syria, and highly motivated and disciplined, and by the mid-1990s they were engaged in a classic guerrilla war. They set the stage for a new round of the

Arab-Israeli conflict just as the United States and Israel had hoped to gain Arafat's capitulation to "end" it. Nasrallah studied Israeli society and identified its obvious weakness: It was not willing to endure indefinite casualties in a land that most Israelis did not consider strategically important for them. He traded war crime for war crime, Katyusha rocket for Israeli aerial bombardment. Rather than strive for military parity with Israel, Nasrallah achieved—temporarily at least—the so-called balance of terror that Hamas had sought in vain. Attacks on Lebanese civilians were answered by rocket attacks on northern Israel.

In the event, such a balance was an illusion given the awesome firepower at Israel's disposal. However, Hizbullah and its masses of supporters in southern Lebanon were willing to endure enormous hardship to liberate their country. Nasrallah's predecessor and mentor, Abbas al-Musawi, with his wife and children, had been assassinated by the Israelis in 1992; Nasrallah's own son Hady was also killed in a guerrilla operation in 1997. Unlike Sadat or Saddam or any other Arab leader, Nasrallah commanded the respect and devotion of his people. Though Shi'a, he was also admired in the predominantly Sunni Arab world. He came closest to wearing the mantle of Gamal Abdel Nasser. His message was far more pietistic than Nasser's, and his religious fervor was intense, but his underlying appeal to Arab dignity and pride was identical to Nasser's in its affirmation of the ideal of self-determination.

In both 1993 and 1996, Israel launched massive bombing campaigns against southern Lebanon in the hopes of bludgeoning Hizbullah into ending its resistance. In the midst of an ostensible peace process with the Palestinians, Israel deliberately uprooted hundreds of thousands of Lebanese civilians from their villages, bombed indiscriminately, and committed atrocities in the name of fighting Hizbullah's "terror." In the 1996 assault, the Israeli army shelled a UN station in the village of Qana that was filled with refugees who had sought shelter in it. Over two hundred Lebanese civilians, many of them children, were wounded or killed. The Qana massacre, however, simply strengthened Hizbullah's resolve and cemented its standing as a popular resistance movement. In May 2000, harassed and harried, Israel finally pulled out of Lebanon. For the first time in the history of the Arab-Israeli conflict, Israel was compelled to withdraw from occupied Arab land without preconditions. The Shi'a Hassan Nasrallah became a new Arab hero, and he marked the occasion with a famous speech before one hundred thousand people in Bint Jbeil, a town in the far south of Lebanon close to the border with Israel.

The message Nasrallah delivered then was cutting in its sharpness. He and his people put no stock in the international community; they had no faith in the UN, which had done nothing to enforce its own resolutions in the case of Israel; they had no faith in America, which they recognized had enabled and justified their torment for decades; they had no faith in the West. Rather, Nasrallah noted—correctly—that Israel had been compelled to withdraw "through resistance and the force of arms." He therefore juxtaposed, unfairly but nonetheless poignantly, the success achieved in Lebanon by an armed, disciplined, uncompromising Islamist resistance, with Arafat's fruitless moderation, which had gained his people no respite from occupation and no prospect of imminent liberation. "To our Arab and Muslim people, I say," Nasrallah cried, "O, Arab nation, dear Arab and Islamic nation, shame, defeat, and humiliation are a thing of the past. This victory paves the way for a new historical era, and closes the door on what is past."[83]

Hizbullah's triumph at the dawn of a new century was thus accompanied by a new wager that Islamist politics would succeed in bringing freedom to the Arabs where secular Arab nationalist politics had clearly failed. Nasrallah turned on its head the U.S. and Israeli assumption that the historic failure of Arab states to defeat Israel would inevitably lead to a victor's peace. For over fifty years, anti-Americanism had been tied inexorably to the question of Palestine and to the visible role played by the United States in legitimating, financing, and protecting Israel at the expense of the indigenous Arab population. Yet rather than resolving anti-Americanism by resolving its obvious root cause in a manner that could win Arabs over to America—that is, by supporting the struggle for a just, secular solution that encompasses the rights and security of Palestinians and not simply those of the Israelis—the United States during and after the Cold War has banked on Arab exhaustion and Israeli strength.

Indeed, since 1967 at least, U.S. presidents have believed that the Arabs must eventually accept Israel regardless of how it treats the Palestinians, and that the resistance of Arab states to Israel will wither in the face of Israel's apparently insurmountable military strength and the U.S. commitment to that strength. To a large extent, this belief has been vindicated at the level of Arab regimes. Sadat was the first Arab ruler to embrace openly the American vision of the Middle East. But this major American and Israeli victory was only partial, and the price paid to achieve it was extraordinarily high, for it involved sacrificing the possibility of a pro-Western Arab world in favor of pro-American Arab dictatorships. The age of secularism was made to give way to Islamism in various forms.

As Nasrallah stood in Bint Jbeil to mark a historic Israeli defeat in May 2000, it was clear to him that Arab faith in America had been shattered. He knew that both Sunni and Shi'a Arabs resented U.S. policy because it had enabled, justified, and protected Israeli colonialism. Hizbullah drew strength from this fact. So too did Hamas. Their Islamist politics, however, was fraught with enormous problems. Both movements appropriated the mantle of freedom from their Arab nationalist antecedents, but they rejected their secularism. They drew instead on an unvarnished religiosity, a deep belief in sacrifice, and a commitment to continue by modern means a long-standing rejection of Israel. But to what end? Hizbullah may have chased Israel out of Lebanon, but Israel remained powerful, and the Palestinians were no closer to liberation than they were before. American aid continued to pour into Israel. The gulf between people and rulers expanded in the Arab world; democracy and freedom of expression remained stifled; and militant Islamists continued to gather strength, exploiting and acting upon the loss of faith in the West that has permeated Arab societies.

Without fully realizing it, Nasrallah spoke on the cusp of an even more violent era, the latest and most cataclysmic installment of a struggle between Americans and Arabs whose ultimate end remains uncertain but whose origin can be dated with fair accuracy. Fateful British and then American decisions, first to colonize the Arab world and then to partition Palestine, and the Arab reactions to these decisions fundamentally altered the Arab relationship to the United States. Each new episode of destruction and death compounds the tragedy of U.S.-Arab relations, obscuring its origins and creating new points of conflict that, in turn, have led, and will continue to lead, to further tragedy.

EPILOGUE

A New Beginning?

A decade into our new century, despite occasional talk of peace and progress, the unhappy relationship between Americans and Arabs has continued to deteriorate. President Barack Obama, it is true, was quick to address the Arab and Muslim world. He gave his first television interview as president to the Saudi satellite station Al-Arabiyya in January 2009 and delivered a highly anticipated speech in Cairo in June 2009. In both instances, he spoke of hope; in both he insisted that the conflict that now separates Americans and Arabs is not historically preordained. To his Arab audience, Obama evoked the history of American cooperation with Arabs. "America," the president said on Al-Arabiyya, "was not born as a colonial power, and that same respect and partnership that America had with the Muslim world as recently as 20 or 30 years ago, there's no reason why we can't restore that."[1]

Every situation indeed can change. But to lay the foundations for a new beginning, we need to address where and why the original relationship between Arabs and Americans went astray. Comprehension comes through context, but this context has been obscured or overlooked in many presentations of current U.S.-Arab relations. For most Americans, understandably, the horror of the attacks of September 11, 2001, and, just as important, the way in which these attacks have been interpreted as a war on American "values" and on the American "way of life" continue to frame their view of the Middle East.[2] But reasonable fear has given way to a U.S. "war on terror" (the name of which President Obama has disavowed) that constantly fights symptoms of a malaise without acknowledging or addressing its underlying causes. The end result is that Arabs and Muslims are collectively seen and treated as potential enemies, rather than as necessary allies in what ought to be a joint struggle against the extremism that has blighted the Arab world just as much as, if not more than, it has America. American security ultimately is bound up with Arab security; American militarism merely fans Arab militancy.

I have no particular reason to be sanguine about the prospect for such an alliance between America and the Arab world. According to a CNN poll taken just before Obama's Cairo speech, 46 percent of Americans surveyed had an unfavorable view of Muslim countries. An earlier Pew poll indicated that a plurality of Americans viewed Islam as a religion that was "more likely to encourage violence."[3] But this book has argued that these American views are themselves not set in stone, nor have they been uncontested within the United States. They are, in large part, a consequence of America's role in the Arab-Israeli conflict, subsequent, often related, policies in the Middle East, and Arab reactions to this role and these policies. I sincerely believe, moreover, that many Americans who use the language of religious and cultural stereotype and prejudice to define Arabs do so largely out of ignorance rather than malice. At the same time, I know that far too many people still believe in the spurious thesis of a "clash of civilizations" first posited by Bernard Lewis and popularized by the late Harvard political scientist Samuel Huntington.[4] No matter what evidence to the contrary is amassed in this book to illustrate a far more complex story with interdependent elements, these people will continue to cling to their predetermined convictions that the world is divided into rival monoliths of right and wrong, black and white, believer and nonbeliever, "Islam" and the "West."

In the meantime, the decontextualized present continues to haunt us, to distract us, to overwhelm us. The attacks of September 11, 2001, marked not so much the sudden, surprising birth of a dangerous new world, but the continuation of an older order of things, albeit on an appalling scale and with a fury that few could have imagined. That the perpetrators of the attacks of September 11 were mostly Saudi citizens, led and inspired by Usama Bin Laden, is obviously significant. Of all the Arab countries, Saudi Arabia stands out for its official espousal of an antisecular and intensely discriminatory and intolerant Wahabi ideology, which has for decades coexisted uneasily with the country's pro-American foreign policy. That the perpetrators were inspired by a Manichean view of the world is equally significant. Scholars and journalists, in addition to U.S. federal investigators, have painstakingly recreated how al-Qa'ida operated; how jihadists imagined the world; how their "political Islam" functioned; how Bin Laden used Afghanistan as a base of operations; how before that Saudi, U.S., and Pakistani secret services had helped finance and organize an anti-Soviet jihad in the 1980s; and how, finally, U.S. intelligence failures led to the deadliest terror attack on U.S. soil. Yet the overarching question that has always needed an honest answer is not simply what could possibly explain such a manifestation of rage against America, but why is there among Arabs the widespread, pervasive disillusionment with the United States upon which this rage feeds?

This book has provided a historical answer and suggested, I hope, that this disenchantment was not inevitable. It was unnecessary. There is no U.S. innocence to speak of when it comes to the Arab world. Now there is no longer any Arab innocence either. There have been decisions, however rationally made by the United States, that have incurred predictable, if deferred, costs. Anti-Americanism, in other words, did not emerge organically in the region, and it does not flow naturally from medieval Islam. It was produced recently, and it has been relentlessly stoked by political and historical realities.

The broken promise of U.S.-Arab relations is the result of a chain of actions and reactions that stretches back to at least the First World War and to the betrayal of the principles of Wilsonian self-determination with which many Arabs had become familiar and to which they were deeply devoted. Anti-Americanism as a distinctly Arab phenomenon began with the U.S. support for the creation of Israel. The evidence is overwhelming. Blunt warnings were issued at the time—and since then—by countless Arab politicians, military leaders, intellectuals, novelists, filmmakers, and artists. In addition, U.S. consuls, ambassadors, educators, and missionaries in the area clearly recorded the depth of Arab resentment and disillusionment with America; as individuals and as a group, they had carefully listened to, and urgently registered, what Arabs had been telling them in unequivocal terms.

Middle Eastern oil, it is true, has since the 1940s been a paramount U.S. interest. Many scholars who are fiercely critical of U.S. foreign policy, such as Noam Chomsky, insist that the fundamental problem of U.S.-Arab relations is rooted in U.S. imperialism and its need for oil, not in the U.S. commitment to Israel. This line of argument suggests that even without Israel's creation, the United States would have still supported dictatorships in the Middle East, as it did in Latin America and Indonesia and elsewhere during the Cold War. The United States did not, for example, overthrow Iran's Mossadegh on account of Israel. The decision to ally itself with unpopular and unrepresentative regimes in the Arab world in the name of stability has produced its own corrosive dynamic. However, U.S. support for repressive regimes in Mexico, Indonesia, and other oil-producing states has not entailed the same degree of intense, enduring anger within these countries as has been provoked in the Arab world.

Oil, in this sense, is a red herring. It explains why the United States is in the Middle East. It explains, in large part, why the United States currently occupies Iraq. It explains why the United States has major military bases across the Persian Gulf in Kuwait, Bahrain, Qatar, Saudi Arabia, and Iraq. Oil is at the heart of the persistence and power of Saudi autocracy. It is also a major factor in what the authors of the widely circulated United Nations *Arab Human Development Reports* refer to as the "freedom deficit" in the Arab countries.[5] But on its own, the American quest for oil hegemony explains neither the depth and nature of Arab disillusionment with America nor the peculiarities of the American relationship to Israel.

It is the American decision to privilege Israel over the Arabs in 1948 and the subsequent, strident reiterations of this privilege that have precluded the possibility of a less fraught American relationship with the Arab world. This is, and has always been, an inevitable trade-off. A very clear trajectory of U.S.-Arab relations was profoundly altered in 1948; so too, of course, was the Arab world. There is a reason why every Arab and, since the revolution in Iran, every Iranian and perhaps every Muslim opponent of the United States inevitably turns to the question of Palestine, for it continues to exemplify Western injustice against the Arabs more completely than any other issue.

The U.S. occupation of Iraq since 2003 under false pretenses and the torture scandal at Abu Ghraib have greatly exacerbated Arab and Muslim alienation. Certainly, the U.S. role in Iraq demands serious analysis that this book, given its historical nature, does not offer. Suffice it to say that the gross violations of human rights in Iraq do not make those in Palestine any less real or visible; they actually underscore them more emphatically, just as they underscore the key role of the United States in both. Many of President George W. Bush's neoconservative advisers who championed the Iraq War also openly expressed their sympathy for Israel and conflated America's alleged interests with Israel's. Millions of Arab viewers of Al-Jazeera have watched the same American-made weapons wreak havoc on Arab civilians in three different places in a single decade: in the occupied Palestinian territories, Lebanon, and Iraq. What has taken place over the past decade is a revivification of the initial Arab disillusionment in 1948, albeit with ever more complex and contradictory manifestations in the wake of America's catastrophic war against Iraq and its ongoing war on terror that seems to have no end.

Palestine is not, then, the only question that defines American-Arab relations. Most Arabs would like nothing better than to be done with the question and have despaired at their collective inability to force Israel into compromise. If anything, beginning with the 1979 peace treaty between Egypt and Israel, Arab regimes have conceded their military inferiority to Israel and all but abandoned any meaningful struggle to restore Palestinian rights. Moreover, Sunni and Shi'a divisions have also come to the fore in the past decade, most dramatically in U.S.-occupied Iraq. The Middle East remains obviously polarized, but no longer between the secular revolutionary Arab nationalist regimes and the pro-Western monarchies of Nasser's day. Rather, two antagonistic camps vie for control of Arab public opinion. The first, led by oppressive and undemocratic Arab states, includes the moribund Palestinian Authority, almost all of whose members accept U.S. hegemony and either formally or de facto recognize Israel. The second, backed by both Iran and Syria, is led by nonstate Islamist groups such as Hizbullah and Hamas, which have contested and won democratic elections in Lebanon and the Palestinian territories because of the corruption of extant regimes, because they have been able to provide crucial social services, and because they fill the leadership vacuum left by the withdrawal of most of the Arab states from the ongoing confrontation with Israel. The Muslim Brotherhood of Egypt, though not engaged in armed struggle, also falls within this camp. There are, to be sure, countless Arabs—writers, teachers, doctors, lawyers, trade unionists, workers, artists, and citizens from all walks of life—who refuse to belong to either camp. They do not indulge in the abject sycophancy of the pro-American camp, nor do they necessarily share the militant faith of the anti-American camp. Instead, these groups and individuals struggle in myriad ways for more decent, tolerant, and just Arab societies.

These voices have been drowned out by the prevailing, unequal contest that now dominates the Arab world. Israel's rejection of the Arab Peace Plan of 2002, which called for a two-state solution based on the 1967 boundaries, and its continued oppression and colonization of the Palestinians (building more Jewish settlements even as I write these lines in early 2010) only strengthen Arab and Muslim disillusionment with America and embarrass and further delegitimize pro-U.S. Arab regimes.

The irony of the U.S. position, then, is not simply that it lacks any kind of popular support in the Arab world and directly contradicts repeated U.S. assertions about its concern for human rights and democracy. Rather, the true irony of the strategic U.S. decision not to compel Israel to address the rights of the Palestinians is that this decision has consolidated the position of nonstate—what the United States considers "radical"—groups. These groups constitute the main organized expression of protest in a region tormented by a unique combination of harsh colonial and postcolonial rule represented by Israel and the Arab regimes. Thus, on the eve of Obama's Cairo speech, a leading member of Egypt's opposition Muslim Brotherhood stressed that Arabs and Muslims do not need "more promises and eloquent words" but American actions that are consistent with, not contradictory to, the values of the U.S. Constitution.[6]

Virtually every poll taken of Arab opinion since 2001 affirms a central point of this book: that anti-Americanism has been, and generally remains, an expression of profound Arab opposition to U.S. bias and support in favor of Israel, rather than hostility to American culture or values. For example, according to the Pew Research Center's December 2001 global opinion poll on attitudes toward America, an overwhelming 95 percent of respondents in the Middle East and 90 percent in the larger Islamic world insisted that the United States "has been too supportive of Israel"; some 82 percent in Asia, 78 percent in Latin America, and 68 percent in Western Europe agreed. In 2003 reports by both the Brookings Institution and the James A. Baker III Institute for Public Policy of Rice University echoed these findings. In September 2004, the Pentagon's own 102-page Defense Science Board Task Force on Strategic Communication report stated that "U.S. policies on Israeli-Palestinian issues and Iraq . . . have damaged America's credibility and power to persuade." It added that

> Muslims do not "hate our freedom," but rather, they hate our policies. The overwhelming majority voice their objections to what they see as

> one-sided support in favor of Israel and against Palestinian rights, and the longstanding, even increasing support for what Muslims collectively see as tyrannies, most notably Egypt, Saudi Arabia, Jordan, Pakistan, and the Gulf states. Thus when American public diplomacy talks about bringing democracy to Islamic societies, this is seen as no more than self-serving hypocrisy.[7]

Another Pew Research Center poll released in July 2009 indicated that President Barack Obama has been able to lift America's image around the world, including in several Arab Muslim countries. Israel was the only country in which confidence in Obama was less than confidence had been in Bush. However, in not a single Arab country did a majority believe that Obama would be "fair" in his approach to the Middle East.[8]

As if to confirm this very point, in November 2009 the U.S. Congress voted overwhelmingly (344–36) to censure the respected Jewish South African judge Richard Goldstone for producing an allegedly "irredeemably biased" report for the UN Human Rights Council because it condemned both Israel's and Hamas's war crimes in Gaza.[9] The Obama administration condemned the report out of hand as both "deeply flawed" and "unbalanced" (and voted against it in the General Assembly on November 5, 2009, along with Israel and 16 other countries; 114 voted for it and 44 abstained) without, predictably enough, actually rebutting the substance of the report itself.[10] Evenhandedness remains a derogatory term in the American political lexicon when it comes to the Arab-Israeli conflict.

How, then, is one to understand the emphatic quality of U.S. support for Israel that has so clearly antagonized Arabs for so long? A large part of the answer lies in the agency of many Americans, particularly within American Jewish communities, who strongly believe in the necessity and legitimacy of Israel. Another part of the answer, however, lies in the nature of power. Israel's military successes on the ground have gone a long way in shaping what can and cannot be said about Israel in America. Moreover, President Obama delivered the message to his Arab audience in Cairo that the United States shares an "unbreakable" bond with Israel not simply to reassure American supporters of Israel who were nervous about his outreach to Muslims. That message was also very clearly a reiteration of the U.S. victory over the secular Arab nationalism that the defiant Gamal Abdel Nasser had so famously represented. Rather than bend Israel to the will of international law and justice, U.S. policy presumes that it is the Arabs who must and will be made to bend to Israel.

Another explanation for the nature of American support for Israel lies in a general, though historically recent, American and Western European sympathy with the plight of Jews, especially in the wake of the Nazi Holocaust. Obama made it a point to remind the Arabs of the persecution that Jews had endured, and he decried what he strongly implied was Arab denial of the Holocaust. He explicitly justified the creation of Israel as making amends for a long history of anti-Semitism. "Around the world," said Obama pointedly, "the Jewish people were persecuted for centuries, and anti-Semitism in Europe culminated in an unprecedented Holocaust. Tomorrow, I will visit Buchenwald, which was part of a network of camps where Jews were enslaved, tortured, shot and gassed to death by the Third Reich." Yet Obama made no indication that an American president, at long last, was also prepared to acknowledge the great Western, and American, moral failure in having made another people, the Palestinian Arabs, pay the principal price for a Western atonement for its own anti-Semitism in which the Arabs had played no part.

A third reason that explains U.S. support for Israel lies in the ability of the pro-Israel lobby to shut down debate about U.S. policy toward Israel in political circles. There can be an open discussion between, and among, Republicans and Democrats about U.S. policy regarding Iraq and Afghanistan, but there is virtually no discussion when it comes to Israel. Even secular liberal Americans and religiously conservative American Christian Zionists, who disagree vehemently and openly on questions such as abortion and evolution, routinely find themselves standing together behind Israel. This is not because of a conspiracy; rather, it is because the confluence of factors sketched here has made it a virtual taboo to question American support for Israel. In colleges and universities throughout the United States, it is true, this taboo has finally been broken, or at least is being openly and consistently challenged. There are signs of dissent in the wider public as well, including in significant parts of the American Jewish community as well as among elder statesmen like former president Jimmy Carter. Freethinking Americans of all faiths, like freethinking Arabs and Israelis, do have far more in common than current politics suggests. In time, educated Americans may well think of Palestinians in much the same manner they today think of black South Africans or African Americans who fought for equal rights—that is, as protagonists in a struggle for long-overdue liberation that does not require special pleading.

There is, however, a crucial fourth reason for the nature of U.S. support for Israel, and this reason lies with the Arabs themselves and with the formidable gap that has long separated Arab rhetoric about freedom for Palestine from the obvious absence of political, press, and juridical freedoms within Arab countries. The struggle for human liberation and security, after all, is a common one.[11] The great historic failure of Arab nationalist regimes such as Nasser's was their inability to recognize this basic fact; today, indeed, virtually all Arab states remain undemocratic. Instead of reconciling a commitment to Palestinian freedom with liberty for their own citizens, these states have chosen instead to wash their hands of the Palestine question and to remain unaccountable before their own people.

What has occurred over the past sixty years, in other words, has been the development of an association of the United States with Israel at several distinctive political, economic, and military levels but also at institutional, educational, and cultural ones. This itself has been the product of enormous effort, representation, and politics on the part of myriad individuals and organizations. Alongside this association—and indeed, as a direct result of it—has been an active dissociation of Americans and Arabs and a decontextualization of modern Arab politics. It is my hope that this book goes some way toward contextualizing Arab history, but the problem remains that the American identification with

Israel is potent and has a wide, overlapping array of ideological, political, historical, institutional, and emotional buttresses that cannot be simply wished away. These exist and will do so for some time to come, especially given Arab disunity and Israeli military hegemony.

Every indication, therefore, is that for the immediate future, the United States will continue with a misguided policy of an almost blind support for Israel at the expense of the Palestinians and that it will persist with an overtly militaristic approach to the Middle East and to Afghanistan, Pakistan, and wherever else its "war on terror" takes it. Were the United States to remain a superpower forever, and were the costs of its policies negligible to Americans, there would be little need to amend such an approach, no matter how unjust and arrogant it appears to Arabs and Muslims.

For decades, it is true, the United States has been able to reconcile its pro-Israel posture with its manifest interest in Middle Eastern oil. For decades, it is also true, one consequence of this approach has been to consolidate an illiberal Arab world, for which ordinary Arab citizens have paid the principal price. But the direct and indirect costs to Americans have been rising steadily and obviously. Several thousand Americans have already died, and tens of thousands more have been wounded, in what are essentially unwinnable wars in Iraq and Afghanistan. There is also a massive financial cost to these wars, borne by U.S. taxpayers. The Nobel laureate and economist Joseph Stiglitz estimates the long-term cost of the Iraq War alone to be $3 trillion.[12] These costs come over and above the routine annual infusion of several billion dollars into Israel and Egypt that has essentially subsidized the Israeli oppression of the Palestinians and authoritarianism in Egypt. The collective predicament of Americans and Arabs should be evident by now to every rational observer.

How, then, to achieve the "new beginning" that President Obama called for in his Cairo speech? There is, it is clear, no going back in time, and there is no undoing the damage that has been done or the history that has been made. The era of misplaced faith in America is over. So too is the ascendancy of secular Arab nationalism. Islamic politics today dominates the Arab world, but such a politics is neither monolithic nor uncontested and impervious to profound, positive change. The current turn to Islamic parties throughout the Arab world is not because Arabs are more pious than they were a century ago. It follows, instead, the shattering, demoralizing defeats of 1948 and 1967 that have greatly determined the course of the Arab world and the nature of its leadership. That the Shi'a Hassan Nasrallah was able to sustain his popularity in the predominantly Sunni Arab world at a moment of extraordinary sectarian violence in Iraq is remarkable.[13] In his pan-Arab appeal during Israel's 2006 war on Lebanon, Nasrallah appeared to be a latter-day Gamal Abdel Nasser and stood for much the same secular desire for self-determination. The attraction to Bin Laden, who has become the face of the Arab world to Americans, has proved ephemeral to the vast majority of Arabs. They are deeply opposed to both his intolerant message and his brutal methods.[14]

There is no reason to believe that anti-Americanism, since it was produced by politics, cannot also be resolved through politics. The French, after all, colonized Algeria for over a century, and anti-French sentiment was once rife across the Middle East. Today, following decolonization, this is no longer the case. It is common sense, therefore, that one essential step down the path of healing requires the closing of the oldest of the open wounds that has deterred Americans and Arabs from collectively following the path of coexistence.

I do believe, in any case, that the struggle for Palestinian liberation must continue unequivocally, and not simply because a resolution to this conflict is essential to normalizing U.S.-Arab relations, but because it is the moral thing to do. Every struggle for justice has been sustained in its darkest and most apparently hopeless hours by faith in that justice, a faith that some have dismissed as foolish, others as naive, but a faith that nevertheless endures and leads ultimately to resolution. That this will be the case for the Palestinians I have no doubt, but how much longer the road is, and how many more unexpected bends in it remain, I, of course, do not know. But the argument for liberation, I also believe, has to be made ultimately in positive terms rather than in simply negative ones—rather than only decrying injustice, there has to be a vision of secular justice and a platform of equal rights and equal humanity that can bring together Muslims, Christians, and Jews. Only this platform can be the basis for a successful international struggle against a state of affairs so injurious to human dignity, to professed American values, and to historic Arab aspirations.

The idea, in a word, is not to dismiss the fears of Israeli Jews or to subject Palestinians to perpetual inferiority, but to work for a real solution that looks forward, not to the past. To my mind, this will come only with the establishment of a genuinely democratic, secular state in which the rights of all citizens are enshrined as equal before the law. The point, however, is not to be dogmatic about the form of a solution, but to insist that it be based on basic notions of justice and equality, not on a denial of these notions, as has been the case with every single recent American and Israeli scheme for renewal of "the peace process" in which no one believes. That a solution will not happen for some time to come is obvious, and even if it were to come sooner rather than later, it would not be a panacea for all that is wrong in U.S.-Arab relations. But a just resolution of the Arab-Israeli conflict remains urgent for the sake of the millions of Muslims, Christians, and Jews who do not want an even more violent, racist, or theocratic future. The occupation of Iraq and Afghanistan will end sooner or later, just as the Vietnam War and most other modern imperial ventures have ended. Arabs have always said that a resolution to the plight of the Palestinians is the key to unlocking the door to more productive and positive relations between America and the Arab world. They have been ignored. But they have not, as yet, been proven wrong. Precisely because Arabs do not hate America but rather have genuinely opposed deeply unjust U.S. policies, beginning but not ending with the question of Palestine, there remains some basis for faint optimism.

NOTE ON TRANSLITERATION

Arabic names have been transliterated according to a simplified system based on that used in the *International Journal of Middle East Studies*. All diacritical marks have been omitted. I have not changed the transliterations of names adopted by authors who have been published in English (Ameen, not Amin). Arabic words widely used in English such as Koran or Beirut or Saud are left in the familiar form. Similarly, I have elected to use the term Shi'a as both noun and adjective rather than Shi'a and Shi'i.

ACKNOWLEDGMENTS

I am grateful to the Carnegie Corporation for appointing me a Carnegie Scholar for the academic year 2009–2010; a leave from my normal teaching and service duties allowed me to complete this book. I am appreciative of the following individuals who supported this project, helped me with the research, or read chapters of the manuscript: Mustafa Aksakal, Betty Anderson, T. J. Fitzgerald, Rashid Khalidi, Walid Khalidi, Michael Maas, Bruce Masters, Mark Pegg, George Sabra, Mariam Said, Yasser Shaib, Malik Sharif, and Gary Wihl. I am especially grateful to colleagues who read and commented on versions of the entire manuscript: As'ad AbuKhalil, Nate Citino, Daniel Cohen, Fady Joudah, Akram Khater, Dina Rizk Khoury, Ilham Khuri Makdisi, Allen Matusow, Alan Mikhail, Caroline Quenemoen, Wadie Said, Heather Sharkey, Martin Weiner, and Salim Yaqub. I also acknowledge the able research assistance provided by Joelle Boutros, Alex Casarez, and Zafir Khan. I alone, of course, am responsible for the views expressed in this book. My editor at PublicAffairs, Clive Priddle, and my agent, Jeff Gerecke, have both guided me in navigating the thickets of the trade press world. I am grateful, as well, to the project editor at PublicAffairs, Michelle Welsh-Horst. I am greatly indebted to my parents, Jean and Samir, as well as to my brothers, Saree and Karim, for reading this book at various stages of its production. My wife, Elora Shehabuddin, has had to put up with my writing this book for the better part of two years. She has been a constant source of intellectual and emotional support in more ways than one, reading and listening to various iterations of this book as it has taken shape during a crucial moment in her career and in the growth of our family. It is to our two young children, Sinan and Nur, that I dedicate this book. May they live to see an age of genuine understanding between Americans and Arabs.

NOTES

INTRODUCTION

1. "The Case Against a Jewish State in Palestine: Albert Hourani's Statement to the Anglo-American Committee of Enquiry of 1946," *Journal of Palestine Studies* 35 (2005): 90.

CHAPTER 1

1. Kamal Salibi and Yusuf K. Khoury, eds., *The Missionary Herald: Reports from Ottoman Syria 1819–1870* [hereafter MHROS], 5 vols. (Amman: Royal Institute for Interfaith Studies, 1995), 1:7.

2. Levi Parsons, *The Dereliction and Restoration of the Jews: A Sermon, preached in Park-Street Church Boston, Sabbath, Oct. 31, 1819, just before the Departure of the Palestine Mission* (Boston: Samuel T. Armstrong, 1819), 12.

3. Ibid., 13, 5.

4. MHROS, 1:6.

5. For more on the concept of "disinterested benevolence," see Stephen Post, "Disinterested Benevolence: An American Debate over the Nature of Christian Love," *Journal of Religious Ethics* 14 (1986): 356–368.

6. Cotton Mather, *Magnalia Christi Americana, or, The Ecclesiastical History of New-England*, 2 vols. (Hartford: Silas Andrus, 1820), 1:23.

7. On the money contributed for the mission of Fisk and Parsons, see MHROS, 1:7.

8. Cited in Ussama Makdisi, *Artillery of Heaven: American Missionaries and the Failed Conversion of the Middle East* (Ithaca, NY: Cornell University Press, 2008), 67.

9. Daniel Oliver Morton, *Memoir of Rev. Levi Parsons, Late Missionary to Palestine* (Poultney, VT: Smith and Shute, 1824), 223.

10. MHROS, 1:14.

11. MHROS, 1:124.

12. On the English connection, see Makdisi, *Artillery of Heaven*, 85–87.

13. Boston Athenaeum, "Collection of Arabic and Oriental Manuscripts, ca. 1799–ca. 1830."

14. For figures on the distributions of Bibles and religious tracts between 1820 and 1825, see MHROS, 1:405–406. The description of the American missionaries draws on A. L. Tibawi, *American Interests in Syria, 1800–1901: A Study of Educational, Literary, and Religious Work* (Oxford: Clarendon Press, 1966), and Makdisi, *Artillery of Heaven*. For the opium trade, see James A. Field Jr., *America and the Mediterranean World, 1776–1882* (Princeton, NJ: Princeton University Press, 1969), 114.

15. Papers of the American Board of Commissioners for Foreign Missions, deposited at Houghton Library, Harvard University, Cambridge, MA [hereafter ABC], 16.6, "Palestine Mission, 1820–1824, Letters, Journals," vol. 1, Fisk to Van Lennep, August 19, 1823.

16. Alvan Bond, *Memoir of the Rev. Pliny Fisk, A.M., Late Missionary to Palestine* (Boston: Crocker and Brewster, 1828), 112, 376.

17. ABC 1.01, "Preliminary Series, Letters 1812–1839," vol. 6, Evarts to King, June 24, 1825.

18. MHROS, 1:220.

19. MHROS, 1:234.

20. MHROS, 1:242.

21. MHROS, 1:191. The comment by Bashir was made to Fisk and King in Egypt in 1823.

22. Michel Feghali, *Proverbs et Dictons Syro-Libanais* (Paris: Institut d'Ethnologie, 1938), 602–603.

23. MHROS, 1:243.

24. Tibawi, *American Interests*, 32–33.

25. Cited in Makdisi, *Artillery of Heaven*, 95.

26. Cited in ibid., 99.

27. David Urquhart, *The Lebanon: (Mount Souria) A History and a Diary*, 2 vols. (London: Thomas Cautley Newby, 1860), 1:208.

28. For an English-language version of Jonas King's "Farewell Letter," see Jonas King, *The Oriental Church and the Latin* (New York: John A. Grey & Green, 1865). Citations are from 1–9, 23, 29.

29. The information on the story of As'ad Shidyaq is reproduced from Makdisi, *Artillery of Heaven*, 103–137.

30. MHROS, 2:119.

31. W. F. Lynch, *Narrative of the United States' Expedition to the River Jordan and the Dead Sea* (Philadelphia: Blanchard and Lea, 1858), 26.

32. Edward W. Hooker, *Memoir of Mrs. Sarah L. Huntington Smith, Late of the American Mission in Syria*, 3rd ed. (New York: American Tract Society, 1845), 168.

33. Ibid., 272–273.

34. Cited in Paul William Harris, *Nothing but Christ: Rufus Anderson and the Ideology of Protestant Foreign Missions* (New York: Oxford University Press, 1999), 75.

35. Daniel Bliss, *The Reminiscences of Daniel Bliss, Edited and Supplemented by His Eldest Son* (New York: Fleming H. Revell Co.), 134.

36. Cited in Marwa El-Shakry, "The Gospel of Science and American Evangelism in Late Ottoman Beirut," *Past and Present* (August 2007): 188.

37. Cited in Harris, *Nothing but Christ*, 128.

38. "Hatt-i Hümayun of 1856," reprinted in *The Middle East and North Africa in World Politics: A Documentary Record*, vol. 1, *European Expansion, 1535–1914*, edited by J. C. Hurewitz (New Haven, CT: Yale University Press, 1975), 315–318.

39. MHROS, 4:261.

40. William M. Thomson, *The Land and the Book, or Biblical Illustrations Drawn from the Manners and Customs, the Scenes and Scenery, of the Holy Land: Southern Palestine and Jerusalem* (New York: Harper and Brothers, 1886), v.

41. William M. Thomson, *The Land and the Book*, vol. 3, *Lebanon, Damascus, and Beyond Jordan* (Hartford, CT: S. S. Scranton Co., 1910), 67.

42. ABC 30.10(2), "Meeting at Mission House, 20 March 1844." The words are Anderson's notes of Thomson's statement at the meeting.

43. *The Missionary Herald* 40 (1844): 352.

44. *Morning Herald* (New York), May 19, 1840, 1, 3, 4, in Eli Smith Family Papers, record group 124, box 3/2, Divinity Library Special Collection, Yale University, New Haven, CT.

45. MHROS, 4:358.

46. MHROS, 4:310.

47. MHROS, 4:342.

48. MHROS, 4:384.

49. See Leila Tarazi Fawaz, *An Occasion for War: Civil Conflict in Lebanon and Damascus in 1860* (London: I.B. Tauris, 1994), 132.

50. Cited in Tibawi, *American Interests*, 162. Anderson's chief concern was that the missionaries would no longer focus on the development of "simple" native churches.

51. Daniel Bliss to his brother, August 30, 1869, box 10, file 3, Daniel Bliss Papers, Special Collections and Archives, Jafet Library, American University of Beirut.

52. Bliss, *Reminiscences*, 198.

CHAPTER 2

1. Butrus al-Bustani, *Da'irat al Ma'arif*, 11 vols. (Beirut: Dar al-ma'rifa, n.d.), 4:380. See also Ami Ayalon, "The Arab Discovery of America in the Nineteenth Century," *Middle Eastern Studies* 20 (1984): 5–17.

2. Rifa'a Rafi' al-Tahtawi, *An Imam in Paris: Al-Tahtawi's Visit to France (1826–1831)*, translated and introduced by Daniel L. Newman (London: Saqi Books, 2004), 117–118.

3. For more on missionary arrogance and the Smith quotation, see Makdisi, *Artillery of Heaven*, 145–147.

4. Faris Shidyaq to Tannus Shidyaq, March 12, 1841, reprinted in *Awraq Lubnaniyya*, 3 vols., edited by Yusuf Ibrahim Yazbak (Hazmiyya, Lebanon: Dar al-ra'id al-lubnani, 1983), 1:41.

5. Mikhayil Mishaqa, *Murder, Mayhem, Pillage, and Plunder: The History of the Lebanon in the Eighteenth and Nineteenth Centuries*, translated by Wheeler M. Thackson Jr. (Albany: State University of New York Press, 1988), 236–237.

6. Tibawi, *American Interests in Syria*, 181–182.

7. This section is derived from Jean Said Makdisi, *Teta, Mother, and Me: Three Generations of Arab Women* (New York: Norton, 2006).

8. For "undying race," see Henry Harris Jessup, *Syrian Home Life*, compiled by Isaac Riley (New York: Dodd and Mead, 1874), 365.

9. *Al-nashra al-shahriyya* (June 1870): 1.

10. See *Al-Muqtataf* 7 (November 1882): 233–236, and (December 1882): 287–292.

11. Cited in Shafiq Jeha, *Darwin and the Crisis of 1882 in the Medical Department*, translated by Sally Kaya and edited by Helen Khal (Beirut: American University of Beirut Press, 2004), 66–67.

12. Cited in ibid., 64.

13. D. S. Dodge to Daniel Bliss, September 29, 1882, box 5, file 2, Daniel Bliss Papers, Special Collections and Archives, Jafet Library, American University of Beirut.

14. *Al-Muqtataf* 9 (1884–1885): 633.

15. *Al-Hilal* 1 (1892–1893): 168–172.

16. Ibid., 172.

17. Qasim Amin, *The New Woman: A Document in the Early Debate About Egyptian Feminism*, translated by Samiha Sidhom Peterson (Cairo: American University in Cairo Press, 1995), 7–8.

18. *Al-nashra al-usbu'iyya* 1758 (October 6, 1899): 389.

19. *Al-Muqtataf* 18 (1893): 188.

20. *Al-Muqtabas* 2 (1907): 152–155.

21. *Al-Muqtataf* 19 (1895): 882.

22. Jurji Zaydan, *Tarajim mashahir al-sharq fi al-qarn al-tasi' 'ashar*, 2 vols. (Cairo: Matba'at al-hilal, 1902–1903), 2:43.

23. Ibid., 2:46–47; *Al-Muqtataf* 14 (1889–1890): 323.

24. Earl of Cromer (Evelyn Baring), *Modern Egypt*, 2 vols. (New York: Macmillan Co., 1908), 2:229; 1:328, 335.

25. Henry Harris Jessup, "Introductory Paper," in *The Mohammedan World of To-day: Being Papers Read at the First Missionary Conference on Behalf of the Mo-*

hammedan World Held at Cairo April 4th–9th, 1906, edited by S. M. Zwemer, E. M. Wherry, and James L. Barton (New York: Fleming H. Revell Co., 1906), 14.

26. Statistics taken from Julius Richter, *A History of Protestant Missions in the Near East* (New York: Fleming H. Revell Co., 1910), 412–421.

27. William R. Hutchison, *Errand to the World: American Protestant Thought and Foreign Missions* (Chicago: University of Chicago Press, 1987), 119.

28. Samuel M. Zwemer and James Cantine, *The Golden Milestone* (New York: Fleming H. Revell Co., 1938), 138.

29. Samuel M. Zwemer and Arthur Judson Brown, *The Nearer and Farther East: Outline Studies of Moslem Lands and of Siam, Burma, and Korea* (New York: Macmillan, 1908), 8.

30. Theodore Roosevelt, *African and European Addresses* (G. P. Putnam's Sons, 1910). For more information, see Donald Reid, *Cairo University and the Making of Modern Egypt* (Cambridge: Cambridge University Press, 1990), 42–43.

31. *Al-Muqtataf* 36 (1910): 424.

32. Cited in Karl K. Barbir, "Alfred Thayer Mahan, Theodore Roosevelt, the Middle East, and the Twentieth Century," *Journal of Middle Eastern and North African Intellectual and Cultural Studies* 2 (2004), available at: http://mena.binghamton.edu/karlkbarbir.htm.

33. Cited in Sheikh Ali Youssuf (Ali Yusuf), "Egypt's Reply to Colonel Roosevelt," *North American Review* 191 (June 1910): 735. The *New York Times* dispatch from Cairo adds that protesters did not mention Roosevelt by name and also decried "despotism" and "hypocrisy" in French; see "Egyptians Resent Roosevelt Speech," *New York Times*, March 29, 1910.

34. Youssuf, "Egypt's Reply to Colonel Roosevelt," 729.

35. Ibid.

36. See Cemil Aydin, *The Politics of Anti-Westernism in Asia: Visions of World Order in Pan-Islamic and Pan-Asian Thought* (New York: Columbia University Press, 2007), 47–54.

37. Cited in Benjamin Fortna, *Imperial Classroom: Islam, the State, and Education in the Late Ottoman Empire* (New York: Oxford University Press, 2002), 217.

38. Yusuf al-Nabhani, *Tahdhir al-muslimin min madaris al-nasara*, 2nd ed. (Aleppo: Al-matba'a al-'ilmiyya, 1932), 8.

39. *Al-Manar* 6 (1903): 567.

40. *Al-Manar* 12 (1909):18.

41. Cited in Stephen B. L. Penrose Jr., *That They May Have Life: The Story of the American University of Beirut 1866–1941* (Beirut: American University of Beirut Press, 1970), 135.

42. David S. Dodge to Howard Bliss, February 9, 1909, box 6, Howard Bliss Papers, Special Collections and Archives, Jafet Library, American University of Beirut.

43. From "Remarks of President Bliss before the Faculty, April 26, 1909, regarding the subject of Required Chapel and Bible Class Attendance," AA/1/70,

"Events and Issues: 1909 Crisis," Special Collections and Archives, Jafet Library, American University of Beirut.

44. Howard Bliss to David S. Dodge, March 3, 1909 (emphasis added), box 6, Howard Bliss Papers, Special Collections and Archives, Jafet Library, American University of Beirut.

45. From "Remarks of President Bliss before the Faculty, April 26, 1909, regarding the subject of Required Chapel and Bible Class Attendance," AA/1/70, "Events and Issues: 1909 Crisis," Special Collections and Archives, Jafet Library, American University of Beirut.

46. *Al-Manar* 12 (1909): 16–18.

47. *Al-Manar* 12 (1909): 637–640.

48. Ameen Rihani, *The Book of Khalid* (New York: Dodd, Mead and Co., 1911), 25.

49. The following section relies on Akram Khater's *Inventing Home: Emigration, Gender, and the Middle Class in Lebanon, 1870–1920* (Berkeley: University of California Press, 2001); and Gregory Orfalea's *The Arab Americans: A History* (Northampton, MA: Olive Branch Press, 2006).

50. Cited in Orfalea, *The Arab Americans*, 58.

51. For immigrant statistics, see Gregory Orfalea, *The Arab Americans: A History* (Northhampton, MA: Olive Branch Press, 2006), 436–437.

52. Mikha'il As'ad Rustum, *Kitab al-gharib fi al-gharb, rihlat Mikha'il As'ad Rustum ila Amirka, 1885–1894*, 2nd ed. (Beirut: Dar al-hamra', 1992), 115.

53. Ibid., 121–122, 97.

54. Ibid., 123.

55. "Masters of Mendicants; Syrian Arabs Infesting the Cities. How They Squeeze Through Castle Garden—Pen Pictures of the Most Filthy Immigrants," *New York Times*, February 21, 1888, 3.

56. S. A. Mokarzel, "Turkish Subjects," *New York Times*, October 3, 1909, 12.

57. Layyah A. Barakat, *A Message from Mount Lebanon* (Philadelphia: Sunday School Times Co., 1912), 130.

58. Rihani, *The Book of Khalid*, 39. For Rihani bibliographical details see www.alhewar.com/Bushrui_Rihani.html.

59. Ibid., 128. See also Rasheed El-Enany's discussion of Rihani in *Arab Representations of the Occident: East-West Encounters in Arabic Fiction* (London: Routledge, 2006), 154–158.

60. Cited in Donald M. Reid, *The Odyssey of Farah Antun* (Minneapolis: Bibliotheca Islamica, 1975), 124.

61. This section borrows from the work of Khater, *Inventing Home*; Sarah M. A. Gualtieri, *Between Arab and White: Race and Ethnicity in the Early Syrian American Diaspora* (Berkeley: University of California Press, 2009); and El-Enany, particularly his discussion of "The Cuckoo Clock," in *Arab Representations*, 161–163.

62. Kahlil Gibran, *The Kahlil Gibran Reader: Inspirational Writings* (New York: Kensington Publishing, 1979), 50.
63. Rihani, *Book of Khalid*, 246.

CHAPTER 3

1. Frederick Davis Greene, *Armenian Massacres, or The Sword of Mohammed. Containing a Complete and Thrilling Account of the Terrible Atrocities and Wholesale Murders Committed in Armenia by Mohammedan Fanatics* (American Oxford Publishers, 1896), 431.
2. Figures from Jeremy Salt, *Imperialism, Evangelism, and the Ottoman Armenians, 1878–1896* (London: F. Cass, 1993), 31. The following discussion is indebted to Jeremy Salt and to Joseph L. Grabill's classic *Protestant Diplomacy and the Near East: Missionary Influence on American Policy, 1810–1927* (Minneapolis: University of Minnesota Press, 1971).
3. Greene, *Armenian Massacres*, 444. Like all such figures, they are to be treated with caution.
4. Edwin Munsell Bliss, *Turkey and the Armenian Atrocities: A Reign of Terror from Tartar Huts to Constantinople Palaces* (Philadelphia: Keystone Publishing Co., 1896), 483, 514.
5. Cited in Tibawi, *American Interests in Syria*, 297.
6. Frances E. Willard, introduction to Bliss, *Turkey and the Armenian Atrocities*, 2.
7. Bliss, *Turkey and the Armenian Atrocities*, title page.
8. Ibid., vii.
9. Willard, introduction to Bliss, *Turkey and the Armenian Atrocities*, 2.
10. Henry Harris Jessup, *Fifty-Three Years in Syria*, 2 vols. (Reading, U.K.: Garnet Publishing, 2002 [1910]), 2:606–607.
11. Textbook information drawn from Norbert J. Scholz, "Foreign Education and Indigenous Reaction in Late Ottoman Lebanon: Students and Teachers at the Syrian Protestant College in Beirut," 2 vols. (PhD diss., Georgetown University, 1997).
12. Jessup, *Fifty-Three Years in Syria*, 2:689–690.
13. Zwemer and Cantine, *The Golden Milestone*, 142.
14. Cited in Victoria Clark, *Allies for Armageddon: The Rise of Christian Zionism* (New Haven, CT: Yale University Press, 2007), 77.
15. William E. Blackstone, *Jesus Is Coming*, 2nd ed. (London: Partridge, 1889), 95.
16. Cited in Clark, *Allies for Armageddon*, 83. This section is based on readings from Clark, *Allies for Armageddon* and from articles in Yaacov Ariel and Ruth Kark, "Messianism, Holiness, Charisma, and Community: The American-Swedish Colony in Jerusalem, 1881–1933," *Church History* 65 (1996): 641–657; and Peter Amann, "Prophet in Zion: The Saga of George J. Adams," *New England Quarterly* 37 (1964): 477–500.

17. Cited in Hilton Obenzinger, "In the Shadow of 'God's Sun-Dial': The Construction of American Christian Zionism and the Blackstone Memorial," *Stanford Electronic Humanities Review* 5–1 (1996). Available at: http://www.stanford.edu/group/SHR/5–1/text/obenzinger.html. My discussion of Blackstone's Memorial draws on Obenzinger's essay.

18. Jessup, *Fifty-Three Years in Syria*, 2:688.

19. "'Palestine for the Jews': A Copy of the Memorial Presented to President Harrison, March 5, 1891, Oak Park, Illinois," reprinted in *Christian Protagonists for Jewish Restoration* (New York: Arno Press, 1977), 1.

20. William E. Blackstone, "May the United States Intercede for the Jews," *Our Day* (1891), reprinted in *Christian Protagonists for Jewish Restoration*, 15.

21. Trade figures from John De Novo, *American Interests and Policies in the Middle East 1900–1939* (Minneapolis: University of Minnesota Press, 1963), 38.

22. Cited in Grabill, *Protestant Diplomacy*, 63.

23. Henry Morgenthau, *Ambassador Morgenthau's Story* (New York: Doubleday, Page and Co., 1918), 306–307.

24. James L. Barton, *The Story of Near East Relief (1915–1930): An Interpretation* (New York: Macmillan Co., 1930), xi.

25. Grabill, *Protestant Diplomacy*, 77.

26. Cited in ibid., 96.

27. James L. Barton, "Shall the Land Be Healed?" in William H. Hall, *The Near East: Crossroads of the World* (New York: Interchurch Press, 1920), 212.

28. Howard S. Bliss, *The Modern Missionary* (Beirut: Trustees of the Syrian Protestant College, 1920), 4–5. This was reprinted from the article originally published in the *Atlantic Monthly* in May 1920.

29. Howard Bliss to Azmi Bey, "Memoranda/Documents Re: World War One; 1914, 1916, 1917," box 1, file 4, Howard Bliss Papers, Special Collections and Archives, Jafet Library, American University of Beirut.

30. Edward F. Nickoley, "Historic Diary Written During the Year 1917," box 2, file 3, Edward F. Nickoley Papers, Special Collections and Archives, Jafet Library, American University of Beirut.

31. Bayard Dodge, "Relief Work in Syria During the Period of the War" (description of relief work taken from Dodge report), mss. AUB 21, 2/3, Special Collections and Archives, Jafet Library, American University of Beirut.

32. Text of Wilson's speech available at http://wwi.lib.byu.edu/index.php/President_Wilson%27s_Fourteen_Points.

33. Cited in *Al-Manar* 21 (1918): 28.

34. Cited in Erez Manela, *The Wilsonian Moment: Self-Determination and the International Origins of Anticolonial Nationalism* (New York: Oxford University Press, 2007), 151. My discussion of Wilsonianism draws on Manela's work.

35. Cited in George Antonius, *The Arab Awakening: The Story of the Arab National Movement* (London: Hamish Hamilton, 1938), 442.

36. See Secretariat of H.E. the High Commissioner for Iraq, "Intelligence Report No. 17" (Baghdad, 1922), L/PS/10, vol. 2, no. 39. I thank David Getman for this reference.

37. Cited in George Antonius, *The Arab Awakening*, 419; see also A. L. Tibawi, *Anglo-Arab Relations and the Question of Palestine 1914–1921* (London: Luzac & Co., 1978), 87–88.

38. Rashid Rida, *Maqalat Al-Shaykh Rashid Rida al-siyasiyya*, 5 vols., edited by Yusuf Ibish and Yusuf Quzma Khuri (Beirut: Dar ibn 'Arabi, 1994), 3:1195.

39. Oskar K. Rabinowicz, *Winston Churchill on Jewish Problems*, reprinted in *From Haven to Conquest: Readings in Zionism and the Palestine Problem Until 1948*, edited by Walid Khalidi (Washington, DC: Institute for Palestine Studies, 1987), 112.

40. "Balfour Declaration 1917," reproduced at Yale Law School, Avalon Project: http://avalon.law.yale.edu/20th_century/balfour.asp.

41. Rida, *Maqalat Al-Shaykh Rashid Rida*, 3:1205.

42. Cited in Tibawi, *Anglo-Arab Relations*, 301.

43. Cited in Lawrence Davidson, "Debating Palestine," in *Arabs in America: Building a New Future*, edited by Michael W. Suleiman (Philadelphia: Temple University Press, 1999), 231.

44. Cited in Zeine N. Zeine, *The Struggle for Arab Independence: Western Diplomacy and the Rise and Fall of Faisal's Kingdom in Syria* (Beirut: Khayat, 1960), 250. But Tibawi disputes this strongly (*Anglo-Arab Relations*, 342–343), claiming that Lawrence deliberately distorted what Faysal said and that nobody on his delegation spoke English. 'Awni Abdel Hadi, who was one of Faysal's key advisers in Paris, denies the authenticity of the memorandum of January 1, 1919, alleging that Lawrence may have had a role in it; see 'Awni Abdel Hadi, *Mudhakkirat 'Awni Abdel Hadi*, edited by Khayriyya Qasmiyya (Beirut: Markaz dirasat al-wahda al-'arabiyya, 2002), 66–67; see also Khayriyya Qasmiyya, *Al-Hukuma al-'arabiyya fi Dimashq 1918–1920* (Beirut: Al-mu'assasa al-'arabiyya lil-dirasast wa al-nashr, 1982), 97.

45. See Tibawi, *Anglo-Arab Relations*, 355–357.

46. Cited in Zeine, *The Struggle for Arab Independence*, 252.

47. Robert Lansing, *The Big Four and Others of the Peace Conference* (Boston: Houghton Mifflin, 1921), 170.

48. Edward M. House and Charles Seymour, eds., *What Really Happened at Paris: The Story of the Peace Conference, 1918–1919, by American Delegates* (New York: Charles Scribner's Sons, 1921), 432.

49. Rustum Haydar, *Mudhakkirat Rustum Haydar*, edited by Najda Fatha Safwa (Beirut: Al-dar al-'arabiyya lil-mawsu'at, 1988), 237.

50. A summary of the translation of Faysal's speech is available in U.S. Department of State, *Papers Relating to the Foreign Relations of the United States [hereafter FRUS]: The Paris Peace Conference 1919*, vol. 3 (Washington, DC: U.S. Government Printing Office, 1919), 889–891. Available at: http://digital.library.wisc.edu/1711.dl/FRUS.FRUS1919Parisv03.

51. Chaim Weizmann to Balfour, May 30, 1918, in *The Letters and Papers of Chaim Weizmann*, series A, 23 vols. (New Brunswick, NJ: Transaction Books, 1977), 8:197–206.

52. Zionist Organization Statement on Palestine, 3 February 1919. Available online at http://www.ipcri.org/files/wzo1919.html.

53. See Grabill, *Protestant Diplomacy*, 156, for a similar point.

54. *FRUS: The Paris Peace Conference 1919*, 3:1016–1021.

55. Harry N. Howard, *The King-Crane Commission: An American Inquiry in the Middle East* (Beirut: Khayat, 1963), 35.

56. Ibid., 25.

57. Ibid., 45.

58. Cited in F. W. Brecher, "Charles R. Crane's Crusade for the Arabs, 1919–1939," *Middle Eastern Studies* 24 (1998): 50.

59. For "virtually" closed, see Arthur S. Link, ed., *The Papers of Woodrow Wilson*, vol. 58. May 10–31, 1919 (Princeton, NJ: Princeton University Press, 1988), 373–374.

60. Howard, *The King-Crane Commission*, 89.

61. See the full text of the King-Crane Commission report of August 28, 1919, reproduced at: http://www.hri.org/docs/king-crane/. For "passion for democracy," see: http://www.hri.org/docs/king-crane/asiaminor-recomm.html. For "utter unfitness," "hideous mis-government," "quietism," and "pragmatism," see: http://www.hri.org/docs/king-crane/asiaminor-div.html.

62. For recommendations on Syria and Palestine, see King-Crane Commission report of August 28, 1919: http://www.hri.org/docs/king-crane/syria.html. See also Antonius, *The Arab Awakening*, 443–458; Howard, *The King-Crane Commission*, 345–361.

63. Ibid., 196. This discussion is based upon Howard's analysis.

64. Haydar, *Mudhakkirat Rustum Haydar*, 245.

65. For a discussion of Montgomery and Yale, see Howard, *The King-Crane Commission*, 196–209.

66. Ameen Rihani, "The American Commission in Syria," *The Review* 12 (1919): 252–253.

67. "Memorandum by Mr. Balfour (Paris) Respecting Syria, Palestine and Mesopotamia, 1919," reprinted in Khalidi, *From Haven to Conquest*, 208.

68. From the papers of Muhibb al-Din al-Khatib, reprinted in Qasmiyya, *Al-Hukuma al-'arabiyya fi Dimashq*, 279.

Chapter 4

1. Cited in Antonius, *The Arab Awakening*, 442.

2. Haydar, *Mudhakkirat Rustum Haydar*, 187–188.

3. Muhammad Kurd Ali, *Memoirs of Muhammad Kurd 'Ali: A Selection*, translated by Khalil Totah (Washington, DC: American Council of Learned Societies, 1954), 43.

4. Anis Khuri Makdisi, *Ma' al-zaman* (Beirut, n.d.), 40.

5. Cited in Tibawi, *Anglo-Arab Interests*, 396.

6. House and Seymour, *What Really Happened at Paris*, 200–201.

7. Lord Balfour memorandum (1919), reprinted in Khalidi, *From Haven to Conquest*, 208.

8. Abd al-Rahman Shahbandar, *Al-Maqalat*, edited by Muhammad Kamil al-Khatib (Damascus: Matabi' wizarat al-thaqafa, 1993), 251, 255.

9. Cited in Sven Lindqvist, *A History of Bombing* (New York: New Press, 2001), 43.

10. Michael Provence, *The Great Syrian Revolt and the Rise of Arab Nationalism* (Austin: University of Texas Press, 2005), 104.

11. *Krayn wa Suriyya* (Cairo: Al-matba'a al-salafiyya, 1927), 55, 57.

12. Rida, *Maqalat Al-Shaykh Rashid Rida*, 3:1125.

13. Shahbandar, *Al-Maqalat*, 238.

14. *Krayn wa Suriyya*, 67.

15. Lansing, *The Big Four and Others of the Peace Conference*, 170.

16. Lowell Thomas, *With Lawrence in Arabia* (New York: P.F. Collier & Son, 1924), 3, 374.

17. See "Resolution Taken by the Arab Club in Damascus, Addressed to the Faculty of the American Protestant College, May 16, 1920," box 12, Howard Bliss Papers, Special Collections and Archives, Jafet Library, American University of Beirut.

18. Edward Nickoley to D. S. Dodge, August 12, 1920, Edward F. Nickoley Papers, Special Collections and Archives, Jafet Library, American University of Beirut.

19. Edward Nickoley to D. S. Dodge, June 30, 1920, Special Collections and Archives, Jafet Library, American University of Beirut.

20. Information derived from Lawrence R. Murphy, *The American University in Cairo: 1919–1987* (Cairo: AUC Press, 1987).

21. Quotes from Charles R. Watson, *What Is This Moslem World?* (New York: Friendship Press, 1937), 97, x.

22. Cited in Heather J. Sharkey, *American Evangelicals in Egypt* (Princeton: Princeton University Press, 2008), 133. This section on the American missionaries in Egypt and the backlash against them is taken from her book and from Khalid Na'im, *Tarikh jam'iyat muqawamat al-tansir al-misriyya 1933–1937* (Cairo: Kitab al-mukhtar, 1987).

23. Amir Buqtur (Boktor), *Al-dunya fi Amrika* (Cairo: Al-matba'a al-'asriyya, 1926), dedication, facing page 3.

24. Ibid., 203.

25. Howard Bliss to Edward Nickoley, September 8, 1919, in Edward F. Nickoley Papers, Special Collections and Archives, Jafet Library, American University of Beirut.

26. Philip K. Hitti, "America in the Eyes of an Easterner," in *America in an Arab Mirror: Images of America in Arab Travel Literature: An Anthology*, edited by

Kamal Abdel-Malek (New York: Palgrave Macmillan, 2000), 49. The translation is Abdel-Malek's.

27. Philip K. Hitti, *Syrians in America* (New York: George H. Doran, 1924), 120.

28. U.S. Congress, House Committee on Foreign Affairs, hearings on H. Con. Res. 52, "Expressing Satisfaction at the Re-creation of Palestine as the National Home of the Jewish Race," 67th Cong., 2nd sess., April 18, 19, and 21, 1922, 168.

29. This section is based on Rashid Khalidi, *Palestinian Identity: The Construction of Modern National Consciousness* (New York: Columbia University Press, 1997).

30. Information on Shatara is drawn from Lawrence Davidson, "Debating Palestine: Arab-American Challenges to Zionism 1917–1932," in Suleiman, *Arabs in America*, 227–240.

31. Figures cited in Fred J. Khouri, *The Arab-Israeli Dilemma*, 3rd ed. (Syracuse, NY: Syracuse University Press, 1985), 18.

32. Information taken from Joseph B. Glass, *From New Zion to Old Zion: American Jewish Immigration and Settlement in Palestine, 1917–1939* (Detroit: Wayne State University Press, 2002), 182.

33. Judah L. Magnes, *Dissenter in Zion: From the Writings of Judah L. Magnes*, edited by Arthur A. Goren (Cambridge, MA: Harvard University Press, 1982), 34.

34. Vladimir Jabotinsky, "Iron Wall (We and the Arabs)," *Rassvyet*, November 4, 1923, reproduced at: http://www.marxists.de/middleast/ironwall/ironwall.htm.

35. *Palestine Royal Commission Report* (London: H.M. Stationery Office, 1937), 396 ("rights and aspirations") and 395 ("generosity").

36. U.S. Department of State, *FRUS: The Paris Peace Conference, 1919*, vol. 4 (Washington, DC: U.S. Government Printing Office, 1919), 169. Available at: http://digital.library.wisc.edu/1711.dl/FRUS.FRUS1919Parisv04.

37. See Ameen Rihani, *The Fate of Palestine: A Series of Lectures, Articles, and Documents About the Palestinian Problem and Zionism* (Beirut: Rihani Printing and Publishing House, 1967).

38. Information on Antonius taken from Susan Silsby Boyle, *Betrayal of Palestine: The Story of George Antonius* (Boulder, CO: Westview Press, 2001), 214–218.

39. Antonius, *The Arab Awakening*, 13.

40. Ibid., 411.

41. Cited in Shabtai Teveth, *Ben-Gurion and the Palestinian Arabs: From Peace to War* (Oxford: Oxford University Press, 1985), 189.

42. Declaration adopted by the Extraordinary Zionist Conference, Biltmore Hotel, New York, May 11, 1942; available at: http://unispal.un.org/UNISPAL.NSF/0/F86E0B8FC540DEDD85256CED0070C2A5.

43. Magnes quoted in Magnes, *Dissenter in Zion*, 46; "new democratic world" quote from the program for the Extraordinary Zionist Conference, Biltmore Hotel, New York, May 11, 1942.

44. U.S. Congress, House Committee on Foreign Affairs, hearings on H. Res. 418 and H. Res. 419, "The Jewish National Home in Palestine," 78th Cong., 2nd

sess. (Washington, DC: U.S. Government Printing Office, 1944), 1. The testimony that follows is derived from the same report.

45. Ibid., 241–250.

46. Cited in U.S. Congress, House of Representatives, Report submitted by Mr. Bloom to accompany H. Res. 418, "The Jewish National Home in Palestine," 78th Cong., 2nd sess. (Washington, DC: U.S. Government Printing Office, 1944).

47. Information on Crane's visit to Arabia taken from David Hapgood, *Charles R. Crane: The Man Who Bet on People* (Hanover, NH: Institute of Current World Affairs, 2000), 74–84.

48. Cited in David Schoenbaum, *The United States and the State of Israel* (New York: Oxford University Press, 1993), 32. For Ibn Saud quote, see William A. Eddy, *FDR Meets Ibn Saud* (New York: American Friends of the Middle East, 1954), 34.

49. Musa Alami speech reproduced in Bayan Nuwayhid al-Hut, *Al-qiyadat wa al-mu'assasat al-siyasiyya fir Filastin 1917–1948* (Beirut: Mu'assasa al-dirasat al-filastiniyya, 1981), 810.

50. Anglo-American Committee of Inquiry, hearing, Mena House Hotel, Cairo, March 2, 1946, reprinted in *Policies and Position of the Arab League Toward Palestine and Zionism: Collected Documents, 1915 to 1946, Including Those of Its Predecessor, the Arab Palestine Congress* (s.i., s.n.), 111.

51. Cited in Amikam Nachmani, *Great Power Discord in Palestine: The Anglo-American Committee of Inquiry into the Problems of European Jewry and Palestine, 1945–1946* (London: Frank Cass, 1987), 165.

52. Ibid., 161.

53. Hourani testimony from "The Case Against a Jewish State in Palestine: Albert Hourani's Statement to the Anglo-American Committee of Inquiry of 1946," reprinted in *Journal of Palestine Studies* 35 (2005): 80–90.

54. See "The Arab Attitude," in Anglo-American Committee of Inquiry, "Report to the United States Government and His Majesty's Government in the United Kingdom," Lausanne, Switzerland, April 20, 1946, available at Yale Law School, Avalon Project: http://avalon.law.yale.edu/subject_menus/angtoc.asp.

55. "President Roosevelt's Answer to King Ibn Saud's Letter," April 5, 1945, *Congressional Record*, 79th Cong., appendix vol. 91, part 13, October 15, 1945, to December 21, 1945, A4815.

56. Citations taken from United Nations Special Committee on Palestine, "Recommendations to the General Assembly," A/364, September 3, 1947.

57. For figures, see Walid Khalidi, "Revisiting the UNGA Partition Resolution," *Journal of Palestine Studies* 27 (1997): 5–21.

58. Magnes, *Dissenter in Zion*, 510.

59. King Abdullah, "As the Arabs See the Jews," *American Magazine* (November 1947).

60. "Against Palestine Partition," *New York Times*, November 21, 1947.

61. Peter Kurth, *American Cassandra: The Life of Dorothy Thompson* (Boston: Little, Brown, 1990), 423–425.

62. Ibid., 422.

63. Cited in Lawrence Davidson, *America's Palestine: Popular and Official Perceptions from Balfour to Israeli Statehood* (Gainesville: University Press of Florida, 2001), 184. For Kermit Roosevelt, see his "The Partition of Palestine: A Lesson in Pressure Politics," *Middle East Journal* 2 (1948): 1–16.

64. Central Intelligence Agency, "The Consequences of the Partition of Palestine," November 28, 1947, 1, 9, 16; available at: http://www.foia.cia.gov/.

65. Cited in Davidson, *America's Palestine*, 190.

66. For Khalidi quotation, see "Palestine's Arabs Kill Seven Jews, Call Three-Day Strike," *New York Times*, December 1, 1947; see also "Damascus Rioters Affront U.S. Flag," and "Arab States Call Meeting; Riots over Palestine Go On," *New York Times*, December 2, 1947; for Iraqi protests, see "Iraqis Protest 'Tyranny'" and for jihad, see "Moslem Sages Ask Holy War as Duty to Bar Palestine Split," *New York Times*, December 3, 1947; Ghada Hashem Talhami, *Palestine in the Egyptian Press* (Lanham, MD: Lexington Books, 2007), 86.

67. See Talhami, *Palestine in the Egyptian Press*, 86; see also "20,000 Demonstrate in Cairo," *New York Times*, December 6, 1947.

68. "Huge Cairo Crowd Meets in Protest," *New York Times*, December 15, 1947.

69. *Foreign Relations of the United States 1948,* vol. 1: General; The United Nations (in two parts); Part 2, 521–529. Available at: http://digital.library.wisc.edu/1711.dl/FRUS.FRUS1948v01p2.

70. The ethnic cleansing of the Palestinians is now a well-documented fact thanks to the work of Israeli historians such as Benny Morris and Ilan Pappe. See their respective accounts of the creation of Israel: Benny Morris, *1948: A History of the First Arab-Israeli War* (New Haven, CT: Yale University Press, 2008); and Ilan Pappe, *The Ethnic Cleansing of Palestine* (Oxford: Oneworld, 2006).

71. Pappe, *Ethnic Cleansing*, xxiii; Morris, *1948*, 407, estimates seven hundred thousand.

72. On the destruction of villages, see Walid Khalidi, ed., *All That Remains: The Palestinian Villages Occupied and Depopulated by Israel in 1948* (Washington, DC: Institute of Palestine Studies, 2006); see also Meron Benvenisti, *Sacred Landscape: The Buried History of the Holy Land Since 1948* (Berkeley: University of California Press, 2000).

73. Rony E. Gabbay, *A Political Study of the Arab-Jewish Refugee Conflict* (Geneva: Librairie E. Droz, 1959), 110.

CHAPTER 5

1. *An Arab-Syrian Gentleman and Warrior in the Period of the Crusades: Memoirs of Usamah Ibn Munqidh*, translated by Philip K. Hitti (Princeton, NJ: Princeton University Press, 1987 [1929]).

2. *Swift Seasons Roll: A Tribute to Philip K. Hitti by Charles Malik and a Response by Professor Hitti* (New York: American Friends of the Middle East, 1954), 10.

3. *Sharl Malik wa al-qadiyya al-filastiniyya* (Beirut: A. Badran, 1973), 59–123.

4. Dorothea Seelye Franck, ed., *Islam in the Modern World* (Washington, DC: Middle East Institute, 1951), 7–8.

5. Mohamed Hassanein Heikal, *Cairo Documents: The Inside Story of Nasser and His Relationship with World Leaders, Rebels, and Statesmen* (New York: Doubleday, 1973), 33.

6. "Airlift for Allah," *Time*, September 8, 1952. I am grateful to Sean Foley for pointing out this episode.

7. CIA, *National Intelligence Survey: Iraq* (Washington, DC: CIA, 1951), 42–21, available at: www.foia.cia.gov.

8. CIA, *National Intelligence Estimate: Probable Developments in Egypt* (March 25, 1953), 6, available at: www.foia.cia.gov.

9. Constantine Zurayk, *Al-a'mal al fikriyya al-'amma lil-duktur Qustantin Zurayq*, vol. 1 (Beirut: Markaz dirasat al-wahda al-'arabiyya, 1994), 253.

10. Zurayk, "Ma'na al-nakba," in *Al-a'mal al fikriyya*, 195–239.

11. Ibid., 1:227.

12. Ibid., 1:230.

13. Charles Malik, "The Relations of East and West," *Proceedings of the American Philosophical Society* 97 (1953): 3–5.

14. Charles Malik, "The Basic Issues of the Near East," *Annals of the American Academy of Political and Social Science*, 258 (1948), 3.

15. Zurayk, *Al-a'mal al fikriyya*, 1:220.

16. Cited in Adnan M. Musallam, *From Secularism to Jihad: Sayyid Qutb and the Foundations of Radical Islamism* (Westport, CT: Praeger, 2005), 95.

17. Cited in ibid., 86.

18. Cited in John Calvert, "'The World Is an Undutiful Boy!': Sayyid Qutb's American Experience," *Islam and Christian-Muslim Relations* (2000), 94.

19. Sayyid Qutb, "The America I Have Seen," in Abdel-Malek, *America in an Arab Mirror*, 14–15.

20. *Sharl Malik wa al-qadiyya al-filastiniyya*, 74.

21. Khaled Mohi El Din, *Memories of a Revolution* (Cairo: American University in Cairo Press, 1995), 61.

22. Cited in Jon B. Alterman, *Egypt and American Foreign Assistance, 1952–1956: Hopes Dashed* (New York: Palgrave Macmillan, 2002), 54.

23. Gamal Abdel Nasser, "The Egyptian Revolution," *Foreign Affairs* 33 (1955): 199–211. For this section, I have also relied on Alterman, *Egypt and American Foreign Assistance*.

24. Figures from Avi Shlaim, *The Iron Wall: Israel and the Arab World* (New York: Norton, 2001), 124.

25. National Security Council (NSC) 5428, "United States Objectives and Policies with Respect to the Near East," 4. Available at the National Security

Archive at: http://www.gwu.edu/~nsarchiv/NSAEBB/NSAEBB78/propaganda%20127.pdf.

26. For U.S. aid figures and contacts with Syria, see Joshua Landis, "Early U.S. Policy Toward Palestinian Refugees: The Syria Option," in *The Palestinian Refugees: Old Problems, New Solutions*, edited by Joseph Ginat and Edward J. Perkins (Norman: University of Oklahoma Press, 2001), 77–87.

27. Heikal, *Cairo Documents*, 56.

28. This section draws from Michelle Mart, "Eleanor Roosevelt, Liberalism, and Israel," *Shofar: An Interdisciplinary Journal of Jewish Studies* 24, no. 3 (2006): 58–89; and also from *The Eleanor Roosevelt Papers*, vol. 1, *The Human Rights Years, 1945–1948* (Detroit: Thomson Gale, 2007).

29. *Eleanor Roosevelt Papers*, 1:819–820.

30. Cited in Mart, "Eleanor Roosevelt, Liberalism, and Israel," 79.

31. Leon Uris, *Exodus* (New York: Doubleday, 1958), 285, 291, 483.

32. Ibid., 575.

33. Slogans from Robert Faherty, *In Human Terms: The 1959 Story of the UNRWA-UNESCO Arab Refugee Schools* (Paris: UNESCO, 1959), 12.

34. Roy Lebkicher, George Rentz, and Max Steineke, *ARAMCO Handbook* (Arabian American Oil Co., 1960), 1.

35. Ibid., 54.

36. Ibid., 81.

37. Cited in *Eleanor Roosevelt Papers*, 1:748; for Roosevelt's reply, see her column "My Day," March 1, 1948.

38. For conspiracy quote, see William Eddy to Philip Hitti, April 22, 1953, AA: 6.2.8, Philip Khoury Hitti Collection, 1886–1976, Special Collections and Archives, Jafet Library, American University of Beirut.

39. William A. Eddy, *The Political Temperature in the Near East Today and U.S. Strategy in the Cold War* (Beirut: private printing, July 1953).

40. Lebkicher, *Aramco Handbook*, 149–150.

41. Eddy, *FDR Meets Ibn Saud*, 11.

42. Quoted in George Ibrahim Kheirallah, *Arabia Reborn* (Albuquerque: University of New Mexico Press, 1952), 193; the quote is attributed to the Saudi crown prince.

43. "Remarks by all classes" and "pigs" cited in Robert Vitalis, *America's Kingdom: Mythmaking on the Saudi Oil Frontier* (Stanford, CA: Stanford University Press, 2007), 105, 157. The description of ARAMCO's policies and practices is based upon Vitalis, *America's Kingdom*. The description of U.S.-Saudi relations is drawn from Nathan J. Citino, *From Arab Nationalism to OPEC: Eisenhower, King Saud, and the Making of U.S.-Saudi Relations* (Bloomington: Indiana University Press, 2002).

44. ARAMCO figures from Madawi al-Rasheed, *A History of Saudi Arabia* (Cambridge: Cambridge University Press, 2002), 97.

45. For U.S. coup and bribery information, see Miles Copeland, *Game of Nations: The Amorality of Power Politics* (New York: College Notes and Texts, 1969), 50, 177.

46. Dorothy Thompson, introduction to Gamal Abdel Nasser, *Egypt's Liberation: The Philosophy of the Revolution* (Washington, DC: Public Affairs Press, 1955), 8.

47. *Proceedings of the First Annual Conference of the American Friends of the Middle East, Inc., New York, January 29–30, 1953* (New York: American Friends of the Middle East), 14.

48. Foreign Service dispatch, Baghdad to State Department, April 28, 1952, reproduced in the National Security Archive at: http://www.gwu.edu/~nsarchiv/NSAEBB/NSAEBB78/propaganda%20074.pdf (emphasis in original). This section draws also on Joyce Battle, ed., "U.S. Propaganda in the Middle East: The Early Cold War Version," available at: http://www.gwu.edu/~nsarchiv/NSAEBB/NSAEBB78/essay.htm.

49. Stephen B. L. Penrose, comment on "The Soviet Challenge in the Near East," June 2, 1951, reproduced in the National Security Archive at: http://www.gwu.edu/~nsarchiv/NSAEBB/NSAEBB78/propaganda%20024.pdf.

50. Cited in Said K. Aburish, *Nasser: The Last Arab* (New York: Thomas Dunne Books, 2004), 107.

51. Gamal Abdel Nasser, *The Philosophy of the Revolution* (Buffalo, NY: Economica Books, 1959), 61.

52. *FRUS*, "Memorandum of a Conference with the President, White House, Washington, July 31, 1956," Suez Crisis, July 26–December 31, 1956 (Washington, DC: U.S. Government Printing Office, 1990), 62–68.

53. Citino, *From Arab Nationalism to OPEC*, 100.

54. Anthony Eden to Dwight Eisenhower, November 5, 1956, *FRUS*, "Suez Crisis, July 26 to December 31, 1956," vol. 16 (1955–1957) (Washington, DC: U.S. Government Printing Office), 984, available at: *http://digital.library.wisc.edu/1711.dl/FRUS.FRUS195557v16.*

55. "Jewish Units Ask U.S. Appraisal," *New York Times*, November 1, 1956; Wagner quoted in *New York Times*, November 3, 1956.

56. Dwight Eisenhower to Swede Hazlett, November 2, 1956, *FRUS*, "Suez Crisis, July 26 to December 31, 1956," vol. 16 (1955–1957), 944, available at: http://digital.library.wisc.edu/1711.dl/FRUS.FRUS195557v16.

57. "Radio and Television Report to the American People on the Developments in Eastern Europe and the Middle East," October 31, 1956, *Public Papers of the Presidents of the United States, Dwight D. Eisenhower: 1956: Containing Public Messages, Speeches, and Statements of the President* (Washington, DC: U.S. Government Printing Office, 1958), 1064–1066, available at: http://name.umdl.umich.edu/4728413.1956.001.

58. "Eisenhower: Ma wara' siyasatihi?" *Al-Hayat*, December 2, 1956.

59. "Mawqif maqdur li-Amrika," *Al-Ahram*, November 9, 1956.

60. Stephen E. Ambrose, *Eisenhower*, vol. 2, *The President* (New York: Simon & Schuster, 1983), 386.

61. "Aide-Mémoire from the Department of State to the Israeli Embassy," February 11, 1957, *FRUS*, "Arab-Israeli Dispute, 1957," vol. 17 (1955–1957), 133; see

also "Telegram from the Embassy in Egypt to the Department of State," February 15, 1957, *FRUS*, "Arab-Israeli Dispute, 1957," 173; on American "weakness," see "Du'f Amrika," *Al-Ahram*, February 14, 1957.

62. "Radio and Television Address to the American People on the Situation in the Middle East" February 20, 1957, *Public Papers of the Presidents of the United States, Dwight D. Eisenhower: 1957: Containing Public Messages, Speeches, and Statements of the President* (Washington, DC: U.S. Government Printing Office, 1958), 147–156, available at: http://name.umdl.umich.edu/4728417.1957.001.

63. "Al ra'is Gamal Abdel Nasser yaqul: lan nasir wara' al-duwal al-kubra," *Al-Ahram*, February 12, 1957.

64. The phrase "Moslem Billy Graham" was used by former CIA agent Miles Copeland in his account of CIA activities in the Middle East, *The Game of Nations*, 58.

65. Cited in Matthew F. Jacobs, "The Perils and Promise of Islam: The United States and the Muslim Middle East in the Early Cold War," *Diplomatic History* 30 (2006): 734.

66. See ibid., 711, for more information on this point. See also Bernard Lewis, "Communism and Islam," *International Affairs* (1954): 12.

67. For the "holy war" quotation, see Salim Yaqub, *Containing Arab Nationalism: The Eisenhower Doctrine and the Middle East* (Chapel Hill: University of North Carolina Press, 2004), 167.

68. This section is based on ibid. and on Douglass Little, *American Orientalism: The United States and the Middle East Since 1945* (Chapel Hill: University of North Carolina Press, 2002).

69. Cited in Hanna Batatu, *The Old Social Classes and the Revolutionary Movements of Iraq* (Princeton: Princeton University Press, 1978), 802.

70. Eisenhower used the term "peace-loving" in reference to Lebanon. See "Statement by the President on the Lebanese Government's Appeal for United States Forces," July 15, 1958, *Public Papers of the Presidents of the United States, Dwight D. Eisenhower: 1958: Containing Public Messages, Speeches, and Statements of the President*, 171.

71. "Saud Talks Peace as Arrival Stirs Dissension in City," *New York Times*, January 30, 1957.

72. Cited in Yaqub, *Containing Arab Nationalism*, 25.

73. Cited in Matthew Connelly, *A Diplomatic Revolution: Algeria's Fight for Independence and the Origins of the Post–Cold War Era* (Oxford: Oxford University Press, 2002), 211.

74. United Arab Republic (UAR), "Speech Delivered by President Gamal Abdel Nasser to Members of the United Nations General Assembly," September 27, 1960, in *President Gamal Abdel Nasser's Speeches and Press Interviews, October–December 1960* (Cairo: Information Department, 1960), 81, 96.

75. UAR, "Address by President Gamal Abdel Nasser on Victory Day Celebrations," December 23, 1960, in *President Gamal Abdel Nasser's Speeches and Press*

Interviews, October–December 1960 (Cairo: Information Department, 1960), 165, 167.

76. Ibid., 175.

CHAPTER 6

1. Muhammad Hasanayn Haykal (Mohamed Hassanein Heikal), *Nahnu wa Amrika* (Cairo: Dar al-'asr al-hadith, 1967), x.

2. See Anthony Nutting, *Nasser* (New York: E. P. Dutton & Co., 1972), 338–357. This section on Nasser is indebted to Nutting's biography of the Egyptian leader.

3. Cited in Malik Mufti, "The United States and Nasserist Pan-Arabism," in *The Middle East and the United States: A Historical and Political Reassessment*, edited by David W. Lesch, ed., 4th ed. (Boulder, CO: Westview, 2007), 155.

4. Cited in Michael Brecher, with Benjamin Geist, *Decisions in Crisis: Israel, 1967 and 1973* (Berkeley: University of California Press, 1980), 100.

5. "Report by the Chief of Staff of the United Nations Truce Supervision Organization in Palestine to the Secretary-General Concerning the Incident Which Took Place on 13 November 1966 in Jordan," available at: http://www.state.gov/r/pa/ho/frus/johnsonlb/xix/28059.htm.

6. Cited in Walter Laqueur and Barry Rubin, eds., *The Israel-Arab Reader: A Documentary History of the Middle East Conflict*, 6th ed. (New York: Penguin, 2001), 105–106.

7. Cited in Moshe Shemesh, *Arab Politics, Palestinian Nationalism, and the Six-Day War* (Brighton, U.K.: Sussex Academic Press, 2008), 237.

8. For Israeli interpretations of 1967, see Shlaim, *The Iron Wall*, 241–256, and Benny Morris, *Righteous Victims: A History of the Zionist-Arab Conflict, 1881–2001* (New York: Vintage Books, 2001), 327–333; see also David Hirst, *The Gun and the Olive Branch: The Roots of Violence in the Middle East*, 3rd ed. (New York: Nation Books, 2003), 332–385.

9. Rostow quoted in Donald Neff, "Lyndon Johnson Was First to Align U.S. Policy with Israel's Policies," *Washington Report on Middle East Affairs* (November–December 1996): 96, available at: http://www.wrmea.com/backissues/1196/9611096.htm; see also Kathleen Christison, *Perceptions of Palestine: Their Influence on U.S. Middle East Policy*, updated ed. (Berkeley: University of California Press, 1999), 109–123.

10. For the USS *Liberty* incident, see James Scott, *The Attack on the* Liberty*: The Untold Story of Israel's Deadly 1967 Assault on a U.S. Spy Ship* (New York: Simon & Schuster, 2009).

11. Deputy Assistant Secretary of Defense for International Security Affairs Townsend Hoopes, memorandum to Secretary of Defense Robert McNamara, June 8, 1967. Available at http://history.state.gov/historicaldocuments/frus1964-68v19/d226.

12. Notes of a Meeting of the Special Committee of the National Security Council, notes of meeting of June 9, 1967, 6:30 PM, Washington, DC. Available at http://history.state.gov/historicaldocuments/frus1964-68v19/d236.

13. *Sharl Malik wa al-qadiyya al-filastiniyya* (Beirut: A. Badran, 1973), 59–123.

14. Melani McAlister, *Epic Encounters: Culture, Media, and U.S. Interests in the Middle East Since 1945* (Berkeley: University of California Press, 2005 [2001]), 111.

15. Elmer Berger, "Memoir of an Anti-Zionist Jew," *Journal of Palestine Studies* 5 (1975): 46.

16. *Near East Report* (October 1964): B-4.

17. See Michael Suleiman's analysis of U.S. mass media and the 1967 war in Ibrahim Abu-Lughod, ed., *The Arab-Israeli Confrontation of June 1967: An Arab Perspective* (Evanston: Northwestern University Press, 1970), 138–154.

18. See "3,742 American Professors Ask U.S. to Break Blockade" and "The Moral Responsibility in the Middle East" (advertisement), *New York Times*, June 4, 1967.

19. Timothy P. Weber, *On the Road to Armageddon: How Evangelicals Became Israel's Best Friend* (Grand Rapids, MI: Baker Academic, 2004), 191.

20. Ibid., 186.

21. This section is based on Heather Sharkey's research in *American Evangelicals in Egypt*, 179–214.

22. Information about the evangelical Coptic Church and the situation in Egypt is derived from Heather Sharkey, "Presbyterian Church Politics in the Middle East, 1948–2008" (unpublished manuscript).

23. Americans for Justice in the Middle East, *The Middle East Newsletter* (September 1, 1967): 6.

24. Cited in Gualtieri, *Between Arab and White: Race and Ethnicity in the Early Syrian American Diaspora*, 171.

25. Edward W. Said, *Orientalism*, 25th anniversary ed. (New York: Vintage, 2003 [1978]), 286.

26. Edward W. Said, *The Question of Palestine* (New York: Vintage Books, 1992 [1979]), 104–114; for Israeli discrimination laws, see Jonathan Cook, *Blood and Religion: The Unmasking of the Jewish and Democratic State* (London: Pluto Press, 2006), 12–18.

27. Said, *The Question of Palestine*, 238.

28. "Nasser's June 9 Speech," *Al-Ahram Weekly*, June 7–13, 2007, available at: http://weekly.ahram.org.eg/2007/848/sc5.htm.

29. Cited in Rosemarie Said Zahlan, *Palestine and the Gulf States: The Presence at the Table* (London: Routledge, 2009), 44.

30. See the text of the Khartoum resolutions, September 1, 1967, at the Arab League website: http://www.arableagueonline.org.

31. For the text of UN Resolution 242, see: http://daccess-ods.un.org/TMP/4198217.html.

32. *Sunday Times*, June 15, 1969.

33. Malcom H. Kerr, *The Arab Cold War: Gamal 'Abd al-Nasir and His Rivals 1958–1970*, 3rd ed. (Oxford: Oxford University Press, 1971), 146.

34. Morris, *Righteous Victims*, 369.

35. Popular Front for the Liberation of Palestine Platform (1969) in Laqueur and Rubin, eds., *The Israeli-Arab Reader*, 140.

36. Leila Khaled, *My People Shall Live: The Autobiography of a Revolutionary*, ed. George Hajjar (London: Hodder and Stoughton, 1973), 136–137.

37. Quoted in Khaled's autobiography, *My People Shall Live*, 59.

38. As reported in "U.S. Jet with 113 Hijacked to Syria by 2 Young Arabs," *New York Times*, August 29, 1969; see also Khaled, *My People Shall Live*, 138, where Khaled denies that Rabin was the intended target.

39. *Al-Hadaf*, August 20, 1969, 6–7. I thank Bayan al-Hout for this reference.

40. Cited in *Time*, September 21, 1970.

41. *Middle East Journal* 25 (1971): 59–60.

42. The description of Black September is taken from Yezid Sayigh, *Armed Struggle and the Search for State: The Palestinian National Movement, 1949–1993* (Oxford: Clarendon Press, 1997), 267.

43. "Statement on the Death of President Gamal Abdel Nasser of the United Arab Republic," September 28, 1970, *Public Papers of the Presidents of the United States, Richard Nixon: 1970: Containing Public Messages, Speeches, and Statements of the President* (Washington, DC: U.S. Government Printing Office, 1971), 782, available at: http://name.umdl.umich.edu/4731750.1970.001.

44. Adonis, "A Grave for New York," translated by Salma Khadra Jayyusi, in *Modern Arabic Poetry*, edited by Salma Khadra Jayyusi (New York: Columbia University Press, 1987), 141.

45. Leslie M. Pryor, "Arms and the Shah," *Foreign Policy* 31 (1978): 57.

46. On Israel as a "100% American base," see *Abdullah al-Tariqi: Al-a'mal al-kamila*, edited by Walid Khadduri (Beirut: Markaz al-dirasat al-wihda al-'arabiyya, 1999), 552; for the description of Louis Dame as "modest" and American oil men as "coarse," see pages 926–927.

47. Ibid., 555.

48. Cited in David Hirst, *The Gun and the Olive Branch* (New York: Nation Books, 2003), 418.

49. Sayigh, *Armed Struggle*, 309; Hirst, *The Gun and the Olive Branch*, 439–447.

50. Abou Iyad, with Eric Rouleau, *My Home, My Land: A Narrative of the Palestinian Struggle* (New York: Times Books, 1981), 112.

51. For John Chancellor's comment, see the Vanderbilt Television News Archive, available at: http://tvnews.vanderbilt.edu/program.pl?ID=466535.

CHAPTER 7

1. For aid figures to Israel, see Jeremy M. Sharp, "U.S. Foreign Aid to Israel," Congressional Research Service report for Congress, available at: http://www.fas.org/sgp/crs/mideast/RL33222.pdf.

2. This according to Israeli journalist Matti Golan's *The Secret Conversations of Henry Kissinger: Step-by-Step Diplomacy in the Middle East* (New York: Quadrangle/New York Times Book Co., 1976), 145.

3. National Security Archive, George Washington University, "Memcom Between Kissinger and Israeli Ambassador Simcha Dinitz, September 10, 1973," document 5, available at: http://www.gwu.edu/~nsarchiv/NSAEBB/NSAEBB98/index.htm.

4. For information on Israeli tank losses, see National Security Archive, "Memcom Between Dinitz and Kissinger, October 9, 1973," document 21A, available at: http://www.gwu.edu/~nsarchiv/NSAEBB/NSAEBB98/index2.htm#III.

5. National Security Archive, "Memcom: WSAG Principles: Middle East War, October 17, 1973," document 36B, available at: http://www.gwu.edu/~nsarchiv/NSAEBB/NSAEBB98/index.htm.

6. This section borrows from Eqbal Ahmad's analysis of the 1973 war, "What Washington Wants," in *Middle East Crucible: Studies on the Arab-Israeli War of October 1973*, edited by Naseer Aruri (Wilmette, IL: Medina University Press International, 1975), 227–264.

7. National Security Archive, "Washington Special Action Group Meeting, October 17, 1973," document 36A, available at: http://www.gwu.edu/~nsarchiv/NSAEBB/NSAEBB98/index.htm.

8. Cited in Ibrahim F. I. Shihata, *The Case for the Arab Oil Embargo: A Legal Analysis of the Arab Oil Measures* (Beirut: Institute for Palestine Studies, 1975), 4.

9. Cited in ibid., 77.

10. On the oil price increase, see Joe Stork, "The Oil Weapon," in Aruri, *Middle East Crucible*, 352.

11. Rosemarie Said Zahlan, *The Making of the Modern Gulf States*, rev. ed. (Reading, U.K.: Ithaca Press, 1998), 146.

12. Cited in Shihata, *The Case for the Arab Oil Embargo*, 96.

13. This section is based on Stork, "The Oil Weapon," 340–385, and Zahlan, *Palestine and the Gulf States*, 47–65.

14. Jackson quoted in "Sen. Jackson Urges Food Uses on Arabs," *Denver Post*, September 22, 1974.

15. See Melani McAlister, *Epic Encounters: Culture, Media, and U.S. Interests in the Middle East Since 1945*, updated ed. (Berkeley: University of California Press, 2005 [2001]), 134–140 and 187–197. For the point about OPEC and Hollywood, see Jack G. Shaheen's analysis in *The TV Arab* (Bowling Green, OH: Bowling Green State University Popular Press, 1984), and also Jack G. Shaheen, *Reel Bad Arabs: How Hollywood Vilifies a People* (New York: Olive Branch Press, 2001); see Said, *Orientalism*, 285–288.

16. For more on the negotiations, see Muhammad Hasanayn Haykal (Mohammed Heikal), *Uqtubir 73: Al-silah wa al-siyasa* (Cairo: Markaz al-ahram, 1993), 669–695.

17. George Habash, interview with *An-Nahar*, December 18, 1973, translated and published in *MERIP Reports* 24 (1974): 27.

18. See Arab League resolution from the Rabat summit of October 29, 1974, available at: http://www.arableagueonline.org/las/arabic/details_ar.jsp?art_id=403&level_id=202.

19. For the text of the General Assembly resolution, see: http://daccess-ods.un.org/TMP/1720419.52610016.html.

20. Cited in David Hirst, *The Gun and the Olive Branch: The Roots of Violence in the Middle East* (New York: Nation Books, 2003), 463.

21. Figures from Yezid Sayigh, *Armed Struggle and the Search for State: The Palestinian National Movement, 1949–1993* (Oxford: Clarendon Press, 1997), 341.

22. For the text of Arafat's speech at the UN, see "Palestine at the UN," *Journal of Palestine Studies* 4 (1975): 181–194.

23. UN General Assembly Resolution 3379 was adopted November 10, 1975.

24. Mohammed Heikal, *Autumn of Fury* (New York: Random House, 1983), title of chapter 4, 84.

25. Jimmy Carter, *Palestine: Peace Not Apartheid* (New York: Simon & Schuster, 2006), 33.

26. This section borrows from Kathleen Christison's *Perceptions of Palestine*, 158–194.

27. Javits and Carter quotations from *American Jewish Year Book, 1979* (Philadelphia: American Jewish Committee, 1979), 136–137.

28. Sabri Jiryis, "The Arab World at the Crossroads: An Analysis of Arab Opposition to the Sadat Initiative," *Journal of Palestine Studies* 7 (1978): 26.

29. The texts of Sadat's and Begin's Knesset speeches are available at the Israel Ministry of Foreign Affairs website: http://www.mfa.gov.il/.

30. "Grand treason" cited in Sayigh, *Armed Struggle*, 424; for "agent of imperialism," see Jiryis, "The Arab World at the Crossroads," 27.

31. Cited in Hirst, *The Gun and the Olive Branch*, 490.

32. Cited in Christison, *Perceptions of Palestine*, 180.

33. "Statement to the Knesset by Prime Minister Begin," 24 July 1978, available at http://www.mfa.gov.il/. The Sharon figures are from Ian S. Lustik, *For the Land and the Lord: Jewish Fundamentalism in Israel* (New York: Council on Foreign Relations, 1988), 46–47.

34. For the Fatah raid figures and Israel's 1978 invasion of Lebanon, see Sayigh, *Armed Struggle*, 426–427.

35. For the terms of the Camp David peace treaty, see William B. Quandt, *Camp David: Peacemaking and Politics* (Washington, DC: Brookings Institution, 1986), 270, 313; Morris, *Righteous Victims*, 485–486.

36. Cited in Avi Shlaim, *The Iron Wall: Israel and the Arab World* (New York: Norton, 2001), 375.

37. For the Egyptian referendum on the peace treaty with Israel, see David Hirst and Irene Beeson, *Sadat* (London: Faber and Faber, 1981), 325–326.

38. Cited in Donald Neff, "Sadat's Jerusalem Trip Begins Difficult Path of Egyptian-Israeli Peace," *Washington Report on Middle East Affairs* (October–November 1998): 83–85.

39. See Israel's Basic Law, Jerusalem, 30 July 1980. For UN Resolution 478 see www.un.org/documents/sc/res/1980/scres80.htm.

40. Cited in Michelle Hartman, "'Besotted with the Bright Lights of Imperialism'? Arab Subjectivity Constructed Against New York's Many Faces," in *U.S.–Middle East Historical Encounters: A Critical Survey*, edited by Abbas Amanat and Magnus T. Bernhardsson (Gainesville: University Press of Florida, 2007), 177.

41. Abdelrahman Munif, *Cities of Salt* (New York: Vintage, 1989), 578.

42. Cited in Kirk J. Beattie, *Egypt During the Sadat Years* (New York: Palgrave, 2000), 262.

43. Cited in Mahmood Mamdani, *Good Muslim, Bad Muslim: America, the Cold War, and the Roots of Terror* (New York: Pantheon Books, 2004), 119.

44. "Itinerary Is Shifted," *New York Times*, January 1, 1978.

45. *Islam and Revolution*, vol. 1, *Writings and Declarations of Imam Khomeini (1941–1980)*, translated by Hamid Algar (Berkeley: Mizan Press, 1981), 305.

46. Ibid., 301.

47. "Proclamation 4872. Death of Anwar Sadat, October 7, 1981," *Public Papers of the Presidents of the United States, Ronald Reagan: 1981: Containing the Public Messages, Speeches, and Statements of the President, January 20 to December 31, 1981*, 902.

48. Cited in McAlister, *Epic Encounters*, 194.

49. Fouad Ajami, *The Arab Predicament: Arab Political Thought and Practice Since 1967* (Cambridge: Cambridge University Press, 1981), 3; for "despotism," see p. 195. This section on Fouad Ajami also draws on Adam Shatz, "The Native Informant," *The Nation*, April 28, 2003.

50. Fouad Ajami, *The Foreigner's Gift* (New York: Free Press, 2006), 211.

51. For estimates of casualties in the 1982 Lebanon war, see "The 1982 Israeli Invasion of Lebanon: The Casualties," *Race and Class* 24 (1983): 340–342. See also Robert Fisk, *The Great War for Civilization* (London: Fourth Estate, 2005), 1037, estimates 17,500 deaths.

52. Arab press citations are from "Arab Media Reaction," *Journal of Palestine Studies* 11–12 (September–Autumn 1982): 193–207.

53. For the demonstration figure in Kuwait, see *Journal of Palestine Studies* 11 (1982): 207–208.

54. "Beirut Hit by 11-Hour Air Raid," *New York Times*, August 13, 1982.

55. Noam Chomsky, *The Fateful Triangle: The United States, Israel, and the Palestinians*, updated ed. (Cambridge, MA: South End Press, 1999), 364.

56. Bayan Nuwayhed al-Hout, *Sabra and Shatila: September 1982* (London: Pluto Press, 2004), 296.

57. For Fahd quotation, see U.S. Foreign Broadcast Information Service (hereafter FBIS), *Middle East and South Asia Review*, September 24, 1982.

58. For information on the Sabra and Shatila massacre, see Sayigh, *Armed Struggle*, 539; see also Bayan Nuwayhid al-Hout, *Sabra and Shatila: September 1982* (London: Pluto Press, 2004); for Reagan "horror," Arafat "American-Israeli massacre" and "Red Indians," and Israeli cabinet claim of "groundless" accusation, see FBIS, *Middle East and South Asia Review*, September 20, 1982. For Begin "goyim" quote, see Shlaim, *Iron Wall*, 416.

59. For figures of U.S. embassy bombing, Robert Fisk, *Pity the Nation: Lebanon at War*, 3rd ed. (Oxford: Oxford University Press, 1991), 479–480; for Marine barracks, 515.

60. For quotations regarding the Kerr assassination, see AUB Newsletter on Kerr's assassination, available at: http://www.aub.edu.lb/themes/1999/Kerr/newsletter.html.

61. Sharp, *U.S. Foreign Aid to Israel*, 22.

62. George H. W. Bush, "Address Before a Joint Session of the Congress on the Cessation of the Persian Gulf Conflict," March 16, 1991.

63. Cited in Rashid Khalidi, *Sowing Crisis* (Boston: Beacon Press, 2009), 152.

64. For U.S. casualties in the Persian Gulf War, see Anne Leland and Mari-Jana Oboroceanu, "American War and Military Operations Casualties: Lists and Statistics," Congressional Research Service report for Congress, September 15, 2009, available at: www.fas.org/sgp/crs/natsec/RL32492.pdf.

65. For Persian Gulf War contributions by Saudi Arabia and Kuwait, see "Cost of Operation Desert Shield and Desert Storm and Allied Contributions," U.S. General Accounting Office, May 15, 1991, available at: archive.gao.gov/d38t12/143921.pdf.

66. Sharp, *U.S. Foreign Aid to Israel,* 20; for the expulsions of Palestinians from Kuwait, see Philip Mattar, "The PLO and the Gulf Crisis," *Middle East Journal* 48 (1994): 42–43.

67. For Iraqi children and UN sanctions, see Anup Shah, "Effect of Iraq Sanctions," available at: http://www.globalissues.org/article/105/effects-of-sanctions#UnitedNationsreportsonmassivedeathtollfromsanctions; for social costs, see Dennis J. Halliday, "The Impact of the UN Sanctions on the People of Iraq," *Journal of Palestine Studies* 28 (1999): 29–37. See also Sarah Graham-Brown, *Sanctioning Saddam: The Politics of Intervention in Iraq* (London: I.B. Tauris, 1999), 70–80.

68. CBS, "60 Minutes," May 12, 1996.

69. Nicholas Noe, ed., *Voice of Hezbollah: The Statements of Sayyed Hassan Nasrallah* (London: Verso, 2007), 53.

70. Edward P. Djerejian, *Danger and Opportunity: An Ambassador's Journey Through the Middle East* (New York: Threshold Editions, 2008), 164.

71. U.S. Congress, House Committee on Foreign Affairs, Subcommittee on Europe and the Middle East, *Postwar Policy Issues in the Persian Gulf,* 102nd Cong., 1st sess., February 21, 1991, pp. 120, 85 (emphasis added).

72. Abdel Bari Atwan, *The Secret History of Al-Qaeda*, updated ed. (Berkeley: University of California Press, 2008), 78.

73. Ibid., 50.

74. Translation available at: http://www.pbs.org/newshour/terrorism/international/fatwa_1996.html.

75. Translation available at: http://fas.org/irp/world/para/docs/980223-fatwa.htm.

76. Al-Sayyid Muhammad Husayn Fadlallah, *Umara' wa qaba'il* (Beirut: Riad El-Rayyes Books, 2001), 64.

77. For the text of the Oslo Accords, see *Journal of Palestine Studies* 23 (1993): 115–121, and 25 (1996): 123–137.

78. Edward Said, "The Morning After," *London Review of Books* 15 (October 21, 1993): 3–5.

79. Foundation for Middle East Peace, "Comprehensive Settlement Population Growth 1972–2008," available at: http://fmep.org/settlement_info/settlement-info-and-tables/stats-data/comprehensive-settlement-population-1972–2006.

80. For Hebron settlement figures, see Saree Makdisi, *Palestine Inside Out: An Everyday Occupation* (New York: Norton, 2007), 211–212; for the Hebron massacre, see Charles D. Smith, *Palestine and the Arab-Israeli Conflict*, 6th ed. (Boston: Bedford/St. Martin's, 2007), 459.

81. See Seth Ackerman, "The Myth of the Generous Offer: Distorting Camp David Negotiations," Fairness and Accuracy in Reporting (July–August 2002), available at: http://www.fair.org/index.php?page=1113; see also Makdisi, *Palestine Inside Out*, 87–89. See also Akram Hanieh, "The Camp David Papers," *Journal of Palestine Studies* 30 (2001): 75–97.

82. Benny Morris, "Camp David and After: An Exchange: 1. An Interview with Ehud Barak," *New York Review of Books* 49 (June 13, 2002).

83. Noe, *Voice of Hezbollah*, 242.

EPILOGUE

1. The full text of President Obama's Al-Arabiyya interview is available at: http://www.alarabiya.net/articles/2009/01/27/65087.html#004. The text of Obama's Cairo speech is available at: http://www.whitehouse.gov/the_press_office/Remarks-by-the-President-at-Cairo-University-6–04–09.

2. See transcript of President George W. Bush's address to a joint session of Congress, September 20, 2001, available at: http://archives.cnn.com/2001/US/09/20/gen.bush.transcript.

3. CNN Opinion Research Poll, May 14–17, 2009. For Pew poll of 2004, see: http://people-press.org/commentary/?analysisid=96.

4. The phrase "clash of civilizations," popularized by Samuel Huntington in his essay "The Clash of Civilizations?" *Foreign Affairs* 72 (Summer 1993): 22–49, was first used in the context of Islam and the West by Bernard Lewis in his essay "The Roots of Muslim Rage," *Atlantic Monthly* 266 (September 1990): 47–60.

5. The term is coined in *Arab Human Development Report 2002: Creating Opportunities for Future Generations* (New York: United Nations Development Pro-

gram [UNDP], 2002). See also *Arab Human Development Report 2009: Challenges to Human Security in the Arab Countries* (New York: UNDP, 2009). For another recent analysis, see Ibrahim el-Badawi and Samir Makdisi, eds., *Democracy in the Arab World: Explaining the Deficit* (London: Routledge, 2010).

6. "Risala ila Barak Obama," *Al-Akhbar*, June 3, 2009.

7. Office of the Under Secretary of Defense for Acquisition, Technology, and Logistics, *Report of the Defense Science Board Task Force on Strategic Communication* (Washington, DC: Department of Defense, September 2004), 18, 40.

8. See Pew Global Attitudes Project, "Confidence in Obama Lifts U.S. Image Around the World," Pew Research Center (July 23, 2009), available at: http://pewglobal.org/reports/display.php?ReportID=264.

9. Cited in "U.S. House Rejects Goldstone Report," AlJazeera.net, November 4, 2009.

10. "U.S. Response to the Report of the United Nations Fact-Finding Mission on the Gaza Conflict," September 2009, available at: http://geneva.usmission.gov/2009/09/29/gaza-conflict/.

11. This is the principal, and correct, point of the latest *Arab Human Development Report 2009: Challenges to Human Security in the Arab Countries* (UNDP, 2009).

12. Joseph E. Stiglitz and Linda J. Bilmes, *The Three-Trillion-Dollar War: The True Cost of the Iraq Conflict* (New York: Norton, 2008).

13. See Amal Saad Ghorayeb, "What the Moderate Arab World Is," *Al-Ahram Weekly*, April 26–May 2, 2007.

14. See Shibley Telhami, "2008 Annual Arab Public Opinion Poll Survey of the Anwar Sadat Chair for Peace and Development at the University of Maryland (with Zogby International)."

BIBLIOGRAPHIC ESSAY

One of the problems that bedevils the allegedly "controversial" field of study that is the Middle East is that pundits, journalists, and even outright propagandists hold forth regularly on the problems of Islam, the Middle East, and the Arabs in a blatantly ahistorical and crudely chauvinistic manner. In the post-9/11 landscape of apparently universal expertise, widely read individuals such as the *New York Times* columnist Thomas Friedman and Michael B. Oren in his *Power, Faith, and Fantasy: America in the Middle East, 1776 to the Present* (New York: Norton, 2007) have offered a variety of prescriptions for what America should do next in this "troubled" region of the world, from bombing it to reforming Islam. The vast majority of these commentators do not seriously engage with contemporary Middle Eastern perspectives, and they are to be taken as authoritative sources by readers much as one would take seriously an Arab journalist who speaks no English, has no real familiarity with American society, and yet makes categorical statements about the nature of "the Americans" and U.S. history based on Arabic sources.

In the academic realm, thankfully, the situation is no longer nearly as bleak. There is, to be sure, no unanimity among scholars of the Middle East about America's relationship with the region they study. But discomfort with representations of the region has been widespread among scholars at least since the publication of Edward Said's enormously influential book *Orientalism* in 1978. As I indicated in Chapter 6, Said criticized what he described as the Orientalist dogma that perpetuated notions of the rational, advanced West and the backward, inferior East, generalizations about the timeless, monolithic nature of Islam or "the Muslim," and, above all, reliance on "classical" texts rather than modern realities to make arguments about contemporary Arab or Muslim societies. Said's criticism of the Orientalists, chief among them the now-emeritus Princeton historian Bernard Lewis, signaled a revolution in the manner in which many, if not most, academics viewed and studied the Middle East. The influence of Lewis and other scholars who have vociferously justified U.S. imperialism, such as Fouad Ajami, endures in the public realm to be sure, but Said's insistence on self-awareness and self-criticism in place of Orientalist omniscience has had a deep academic impact.

Following Said, scholars in American studies, literature, history, art history, and, most clearly, Middle East studies have so systematically deconstructed Western assumptions about the East that criticism of Orientalist bias has long since ceased to be original. Despite the many serious and substantive criticisms of *Orientalism*, Said's intervention has become academic common sense, and readers interested in this topic would do well to consult Zachary Lockman's *Contending Visions of the Middle East: The History and Politics of Orientalism*, 2nd ed. (Cambridge: Cambridge University Press, 2009). Representations of all cultures must be interrogated and not taken at face value. Although there is no *one* right book to read, the best historical work on the United States and the Middle East clearly acknowledges that both American and Middle Eastern understandings of self and other fluctuate, rather than adhering to basic, unchanging civilizational tropes. Rather than assuming American benevolence toward the East, or accepting nationalist assumptions about what America or the Arab world is or who Americans or Arabs are, these new studies underscore complexity and contingency.

My suggestions for further reading are very much influenced by these criteria, and for the most part they offer far more detailed explanations of various facets that I have taken up in *Faith Misplaced*. One of the most readable recent books is Rashid Khalidi, *Resurrecting Empire: West-*

ern Footprints and America's Perilous Path in the Middle East (Boston: Beacon Press, 2004), which covers much of the recent history of American policies in the Middle East in the twentieth century and compares them to those of the British. For a more detailed, administration-by-administration account, see *The Middle East and the United States: A Historical and Political Reassessment*, edited by David W. Lesch, 4th ed. (Boulder, CO: Westview Press, 2007). I have found Kathleen Christison, *Perceptions of Palestine: Their Influence on U.S. Middle East Policy* (Berkeley: University of California Press, 1999), extremely useful, and also Douglass Little, *American Orientalism: The United States and the Middle East Since 1945*, 3rd ed. (Chapel Hill: University of North Carolina Press, 2008 [2002]).

The most recent as well as classic accounts of American missionaries to the Arab world are certainly one place to begin reading about the origins of U.S.-Arab relations. There are plenty of interesting primary sources, missionary hagiographies, and general histories of the missions that I refer to in the text and in the notes. The most important classic work remains A. L. Tibawi, *American Interests in Syria, 1800–1901* (Oxford: Clarendon Press, 1966). For more recent accounts, see Ussama Makdisi, *Artillery of Heaven: American Missionaries and the Failed Conversion of the Middle East* (Ithaca, NY: Cornell University Press, 2008), Heather J. Sharkey, *American Evangelicals in Egypt: Missionary Encounters in an Age of Empire* (Princeton, NJ: Princeton University Press, 2008), and Thomas S. Kidd, *American Christians and Islam: Evangelical Culture and Muslims from the Colonial Period to the Age of Terrorism* (Princeton, NJ: Princeton University Press, 2009). For general accounts on the Barbary Wars, see Robert J. Allison, *The Crescent Obscured: The United States and the Muslim World, 1776–1815* (New York: Oxford University Press, 1995), and Richard B. Parker's *Uncle Sam in Barbary: A Diplomatic History* (Gainesville: University Press of Florida, 2004); for an older diplomatic and economic history that is useful for providing American views and statistics for trade in the Orient, see James A. Field Jr., *America and the Mediterranean World, 1776–1882* (Princeton, NJ: Princeton University Press, 1969); for an excellent cultural history of nineteenth-century American views of the Orient and Islam, see Timothy Marr, *The Cultural*

Roots of American Islamicism (Cambridge: Cambridge University Press, 2006). For a general history of the Arab provinces of the Ottoman Empire, see Bruce Masters, *Christians and Jews in the Ottoman Arab World: The Roots of Sectarianism* (Cambridge: Cambridge University Press, 2001); for a general history of the entire Ottoman empire, see Donald Quataert, *The Ottoman Empire, 1700–1922*, 2nd ed. (Cambridge: Cambridge University Press, 2005). See also Jeremy Salt, *The Unmaking of the Middle East: A History of Western Disorder in Arab Lands* (Berkeley: University of California Press, 2008), and James L. Gelvin, *The Modern Middle East: A History*, 2nd ed. (New York: Oxford University Press, 2008).

A classic and still highly readable work on Arabic thought in the nineteenth and early twentieth centuries is Albert Hourani, *Arabic Thought in the Liberal Age, 1798–1939* (London: Oxford University Press, 1962), or his more recent *A History of the Arab Peoples*, 2nd ed. (Cambridge, MA: Belknap Press of Harvard University Press, 2003). A new book by Eugene Rogan, *The Arabs: A History* (New York: Basic Books, 2009) will also be of general interest, although readers with more academic inclinations should consult Ilham Khuri Makdisi, *The Eastern Mediterranean and the Making of Global Radicalism, 1860–1914* (Berkeley: University of California Press, 2010), or Elizabeth Suzanne Kassab, *Contemporary Arabic Thought: Cultural Critique in Comparative Perspective* (New York: Columbia University Press, 2010). For the wider Muslim intellectual currents across the empire, see Cemil Aydin, *The Politics of Antiwesternism in Asia: Visions of World Order in Pan-Islamic and Pan-Asian Thought* (New York: Columbia University Press, 2007), and for Ottoman approaches to education and their competition with Western missionaries, see Benjamin C. Fortna, *Imperial Classroom: Islam, the State, and Education in the Late Ottoman Empire* (Oxford: Oxford University Press, 2002). On the Armenian question and its relationship to U.S. and Western missionaries, see Jeremy Salt, *Imperialism, Evangelism, and the Ottoman Armenians: 1878–1896* (London: Frank Cass, 1993), but for the actual Armenian genocide, see Donald Bloxham, *The Great Game of Genocide: Imperialism, Nationalism, and the Destruction of the Ottoman Armenians* (Oxford: Oxford University Press, 2005). For Ottoman entry into World War I, see Mustafa Aksakal, *The Ottoman Road to War: The Ottoman Empire and the First World War* (Cambridge:

Cambridge University Press, 2008). For Arab emigration to the United States, see the important work by Akram Fouad Khater, *Inventing Home: Emigration, Gender, and the Middle Class in Lebanon, 1870–1920* (Berkeley: University of California Press, 2001), and Sarah M. A. Gaultieri, *Between Arab and White: Race and Ethnicity in the Early Syrian American Diaspora* (Berkeley: University of California Press, 2009). For a less academic overview, see Gregory Orfalea, *The Arab Americans: A History* (Northampton, MA: Olive Branch Press, 2006). For Arab literary representations of the West, including America, see Rasheed El-Enany, *Arab Representations of the Occident: East-West Encounters in Arabic Fiction* (London: Routledge, 2006), and Kamal Abdel Malak, *America in an Arab Mirror: Images of America in Arabic Travel Literature: An Anthology, 1895–1995* (New York: St. Martin's Press, 2000). For cultural histories of American interest in the Holy Land, see Hilton Obenzinger, *American Palestine: Melville, Twain, and the Holy Land Mania* (Princeton, NJ: Princeton University Press, 1999), and Burke O. Long, *Imagining the Holy Land: Maps, Models, and Fantasy Travels* (Bloomington: Indiana University Press, 2003). For more personal and poignant accounts of individuals and families influenced by missionaries in this period, see Jean Said Makdisi, *Teta, Mother, and Me: Three Generations of Arab Women* (New York: Norton, 2006), and Wadad Makdisi Cortas, *A World I Loved* (New York: Nation Books, 2009). See also Susan Silsby Boyle, *The Betrayal of Palestine: The Story of George Antonius* (Boulder, CO: Westview Press, 2001). Readers may also want to peruse *Syrian Yankee* (Garden City, NY: Doubleday, Doran and Co., 1944), the humorous, anecdotal biography of Salom Rizk, who was an immensely popular speaker on the American lecture circuit before 1948. See also Suheil Bushrui and Joe Jenkins, *Kahlil Gibran: Man and Poet* (Oxford: Oneworld, 1998). Both books give a fair indication of the "pre-political" era of U.S.-Arab relations. It is far more difficult in the post-1948 era to find a fair portrait of the so-called "Arabists." The most popular account remains Robert D. Kaplan's vindictive and tendentious *The Arabists: The Romance of an American Elite* (New York: Free Press, 1993).

The seminal King-Crane Commission report has not received any recent treatment. The classic accounts therefore remain exceptionally important. I have relied mainly on Joseph L. Grabill, *Protestant Diplomacy and the Near East: Missionary Influence on American Policy, 1810–1927* (Minneapolis: University of Minnesota Press, 1971), John A. DeNovo, *American Interests and Policies in the Middle East 1900–1939* (Minneapolis: University of Minnesota Press, 1963), and Harry N. Howard, *The King-Crane Commission: An American Inquiry in the Middle East* (Beirut: Khayyat's, 1963). The most popular account of the post–World War I creation of the British-dominated Middle East remains David Fromkin, *A Peace to End All Peace: The Fall of the Ottoman Empire and the Creation of the Modern Middle East* (New York: Henry Holt and Co., 1989). Though interesting, it is replete with egregious clichés about the Ottomans and Arabs. Readers should consult instead Priya Satia's *Spies in Arabia: The Great War and the Cultural Foundations of Britain's Covert Empire in the Middle East* (Oxford: Oxford University Press, 2008). For the conflicting British First World War–era promises to Arabs and Zionists, scholars have not, honestly speaking, moved far beyond interpretations made decades ago. George Antonius's unrivaled *The Arab Awakening: The Story of the Arab Nationalist Movement* (London: Hamish Hamilton, 1938) is still a moving account and an important historiographical primary source, but it should be read alongside A. L. Tibawi, *Anglo-Arab Relations and the Question of Palestine 1914–1921* (London: Luzac & Co., 1978), Zeine N. Zeine, *The Struggle for Arab Independence: Western Diplomacy and the Rise and Fall of Faisal's Kingdom in Syria* (Beirut: Khayyat's, 1960), and Elie Kedourie, *In the Anglo-Arab Labyrinth: The McMahon-Husayn Correspondence and Its Interpretations, 1914–1939* (Cambridge: Cambridge University Press, 1976). For the Paris Peace Conference, Margaret MacMillan's *Paris 1919: Six Months That Changed the World* (New York: Random House, 2003) is comprehensive for a Western perspective, but by far the most interesting recent work on Wilsonianism and its application (or lack thereof) is Erez Manela, *The Wilsonian Moment: Self-Determination and the International Origins of Anticolonial Nationalism* (Oxford: Oxford University Press, 2007), though it does not deal with the King-Crane Commission.

The Arab-Israeli conflict, of course, remains immensely controversial, but there has been a remarkable convergence among serious historians over the past three decades as a number of important works have undermined the hegemonic Zionist narrative of 1948. Benny Morris is the most famous Israeli historian on the topic. See both his *Righteous Victims: A History of the Zionist-Arab Conflict, 1881–2001* (New York: Vintage, 2001) and *1948: A History of the First Arab-Israeli War* (New Haven, CT: Yale University Press, 2008). His interpretation must be read alongside Ilan Pappe, *The Ethnic Cleansing of Palestine* (Oxford: Oneworld, 2006), *The War for Palestine: Rewriting the History of 1948*, edited by Eugene L. Rogan and Avi Shlaim, 2nd ed. (Cambridge: Cambridge University Press, 2007), Shlaim's own *The Iron Wall: Israel and the Arab World* (New York: Norton, 2000), Nur Masalha, *The Politics of Denial: Israel and the Palestinian Refugee Problem* (London: Pluto Press, 2003), Meron Benvenisti, *Sacred Landscape: The Buried History of the Holy Land Since 1948* (Berkeley: University of California Press, 2000), *All That Remains: The Palestinian Villages Occupied and Depopulated by Israel in 1948*, edited by Walid Khalidi (Washington, DC: Institute for Palestine Studies, 2006), and Khalidi's still important source book *From Haven to Conquest: Readings in Zionism and the Palestine Problem Until 1948* (Washington, DC: Institute for Palestine Studies, 1987). The great problem, however, remains a lack of access to Arab government archives. See also Rashid Khalidi, *The Iron Cage: The Story of the Palestinian Struggle for Statehood* (Boston: Beacon Press, 2006), Edward Said's relatively neglected *The Question of Palestine* (New York: Vintage Books, 1992 [1979]), David Hirst's *The Gun and the Olive Branch: The Roots of Violence in the Middle East* (New York: Nation Books, 2003 [1977]), and Charles D. Smith, *Palestine and the Arab-Israeli Conflict*, 6th ed. (Boston: Bedford/St. Martin's, 2007). For relief work, see Nancy Gallagher, *Quakers in the Israeli-Palestinian Conflict: The Dilemmas of NGO Humanitarian Activism* (Cairo: American University in Cairo Press, 2007). For American liberalism and Israel, see Michelle Mart, *Eye on Israel: How America Came to View the Jewish State as an Ally* (Albany: State University of New York Press, 2006), and for an overview of American views about the necessity and creation of a Jewish state, see Lawrence Davidson's *American Palestine: Popular and Official Perceptions from Balfour to Israeli Statehood* (Gainesville: University Press of Florida, 2001). The *Journal of Palestine Studies* is an excellent resource for primary documents, and readers should also avail themselves of pertinent documents such as the UN resolutions at the "United Nations Information System on the Question of Palestine" website (unispal.un.org), as well as the copious oral histories of the Harry S. Truman Library and Museum online at http://www.trumanlibrary.org/library.htm and the declassified U.S. government documents available through the "Foreign Relations of the United States" series online at http://digicoll.library.wisc.edu/FRUS/.

For more recent academic works on Cold War U.S. relations with the Arab world, see, in addition to the general overview works already cited, Irene L. Gendzier, *Notes from the Minefield: United States Intervention in Lebanon and the Middle East, 1945–1958* (Boulder, CO: Westview Press, 1999), Nathan Citino, *From Arab Nationalism to OPEC* (Bloomington: Indiana University Press, 2002), and Salim Yaqub, *Containing Arab Nationalism: The Eisenhower Doctrine and the Middle East* (Chapel Hill: University of North Carolina Press, 2004). All these books, as well as the accounts by former CIA operatives Miles Copeland, *The Game of Nations: The Amorality of Power Politics* (New York: College Notes and Texts, 1969), and Wilbur Crane Eveland, *Ropes of Sand: America's Failure in the Middle East* (New York: Norton, 1980), corroborate information about U.S. coup and bribery attempts in the Middle East. For U.S. propaganda activities in this period, see James R. Vaughan, *The Failure of American and British Propaganda in the Arab Middle East, 1945–1957, Unconquerable Minds* (New York: Palgrave Macmillan, 2005). For cultural relations, see Melani McAlister, *Epic Encounters: Culture, Media, and U.S. Interests in the Middle East Since 1945*, updated ed. (Berkeley: University of California Press, 2005), and Brian T. Edwards, *Morocco Bound: Disorienting America's Maghreb from Casablanca to the Marrakech Express* (Durham, NC: Duke University Press, 2005). Of particular importance in relation to ARAMCO is Robert Vitalis, *America's Kingdom: Mythmaking on the Saudi Oil Frontier* (London: Verso, 2009), but this should be read alongside Abdelrahman Munif's novel *Cities of Salt* (New York: Vintage, 1989) as well as Anthony Cave Brown's *Oil, God, and Gold: The Story of ARAMCO and the Saudi Kings* (Boston: Houghton Mifflin, 1999) and Rachel Bronson's *Thicker Than Oil: America's Uneasy Partnership with*

Saudi Arabia (Oxford: Oxford University Press, 2006). For a pro-Nasser account of the 1956 Suez crisis, see Mohamed H. Heikal, *Cutting the Lion's Tail: Suez Through Egyptian Eyes* (London: Andre Deutsch, 1986), and for a 1967–1970 view of Nasser, see Abdel Magid Farid, *Nasser: The Final Years* (Reading, U.K.: Ithaca Press, 1994). For a recent critical appraisal of Arab nationalism, see Adeed Dawisha, *Arab Nationalism in the Twentieth Century: From Triumph to Despair* (Princeton, NJ: Princeton University Press, 2003), although readers should also consult *Rethinking Nationalism in the Arab Middle East*, edited by James Jankowski and Israel Gershoni (New York: Columbia University Press, 1997), *The Origins of Arab Nationalism*, edited by Rashid Khalidi (New York: Columbia University Press, 1991), and Basheer M. Nafi, *Arabism, Islamism, and the Palestine Question 1908–1941* (Reading, U.K.: Ithaca Press, 1998). For a new interpretation of the nuances of the Muslim Brotherhood and a reevaluation of Sayyid Qutb's ideological imprint upon it, see Barbara H. E. Zollner, *The Muslim Brotherhood: Husayn al-Hudaybi and Ideology* (London: Routledge, 2009).

For an American view of the Camp David negotiations, see the work of William B. Quandt, *Peace Process: American Diplomacy and the Arab-Israeli Conflict Since 1967*, rev. ed. (Berkeley: University of California Press, 2001); for an Arab perspective in English, readers may consult Mohamed Ibrahim Kamel's *The Camp David Accords: A Testimony* (London: KPI, 1986), although readers may also want to read Heikal's *Secret Channels: The Inside Story of Arab-Israeli Peace Negotiations* (London: HarperCollins, 1986). I have also relied on Yazid Sayigh's comprehensive *Armed Struggle and the Search for State: The Palestinian National Movement, 1949–1993* (Oxford: Clarendon Press, 1997), but this should be read alongside Rashid Khalidi's more recent *The Iron Cage*. The same caution one takes when reading about Palestine in 1948, of course, applies to all subsequent Arab-Israeli conflicts. The same problems—namely, those associated with a lack of access to declassified Arab government documents—are also evident. Nevertheless, several of the books referred to here, such as the works by Morris, Shlaim, and Hirst, more than adequately cover the wars of 1967 and 1973 and the Camp David negotiations, but readers can now consult declassified U.S. government documents that are available either at the State Department website (http://www.state.gov/r/pa/ho/frus/johnsonlb/xix/) or at the extremely important National Security Archive at George Washington University (http://www.gwu.edu/~nsarchiv/).

In addition to the sources noted here, a standard work on the Israeli invasion of Lebanon in 1982 remains Noam Chomsky's *Fateful Triangle: The United States, Israel, and the Palestinians*, updated ed. (Cambridge, MA: South End Press, 1999); see also Robert Fisk, *Pity the Nation: Lebanon at War*, 3rd ed. (Oxford: Oxford University Press, 2001). For Desert Storm, see Dilip Hiro, *Desert Shield to Desert Storm: The Second Gulf War* (London: HarperCollins, 1992). For U.S. policies toward Saddam Hussein's Iraq, see Joost R. Hilterman, *A Poisonous Affair: America, Iraq, and the Gassing of Halabja* (New York: Cambridge University Press, 2007); for sanctions, see H. C. von Sponeck, *A Different Kind of War: The UN Sanctions Regime in Iraq* (New York: Berghahn Books, 2006). For the emergence of Hizbullah, see Augustus R. Norton, *Hezbollah: A Short History* (Princeton, NJ: Princeton University Press, 2007), and *Voice of Hezbollah: The Statements of Sayyed Hassan Nasrallah*, edited by Nicholas Noe (London: Verso, 2007). There are, of course, dozens of other books on Hizbullah, but one advantage of Noe's work is that it provides readers with translations in context. For this very reason, readers should be highly cautious when dealing with the blatantly misleading Middle East Media Research Institute (MEMRI) and instead rely on Mideastwire.com, which provides decent translations of the Arab media without the obvious attempt to steer readers toward a pro-Israeli perspective.

On the U.S. cultivation of Islamic fundamentalism during the Cold War, see Fawaz A. Gerges's somewhat dated but still relevant book entitled *America and Political Islam: Clash of Cultures or Clash of Interests?* (Cambridge: Cambridge University Press, 1999). See also Mahmood Mamdani, *Good Muslim, Bad Muslim: America, the Cold War, and the Roots of Terror* (New York: Pantheon Books, 2004); for al-Qa'ida's formation, see the accounts of Abdel Bari Atwan, *The Secret History of al-Qaeda*, updated ed. (Berkeley: University of California Press, 2008), and Lawrence Wright, *The Looming Tower: Al-Qaeda and the Road to 9/11* (New York: Alfred A. Knopf, 2006). Juan Cole has recently written *Engaging the Muslim World*

(New York: Palgrave MacMillan, 2009), which also puts Islamic fundamentalism in perspective. For the politics of the pro-Israel lobby, the obvious place to begin reading is John J. Mersheimer and Stephen M. Walt's *The Israel Lobby and U.S. Foreign Policy* (New York: Farrar, Straus and Giroux, 2007) and the debates surrounding that book, particularly a roundtable on the topic held by the *London Review of Books* in 2006, available at: http://www.scribemedia.org/2006/10/10/transcript-israel-lobby/.

Needless to say, the closer one gets to contemporary politics the greater the number of books, essays, and blogs, but also the more classified government records become. This is precisely where a well-grounded historical perspective is crucial to navigation through a bewildering array of perspectives. I do not pretend that this list of books is at all exhaustive. There is ultimately no end to reading, but there is a beginning to understanding.

INDEX

Tommy Lavergne

Ussama Makdisi is a professor of history and the first holder of the Arab American Educational Foundation Chair of Arab Studies at Rice University. In April 2009, the Carnegie Corporation named Makdisi a 2009 Carnegie Scholar as part of its effort to promote original scholarship regarding the cultures and civilizations of Muslim societies and communities, both in the United States and abroad. Makdisi came to Rice in 1997 from Princeton University, where he earned a doctorate in history. He earned his bachelor's degree from Wesleyan University. His previous book, *Artillery of Heaven: American Missionaries and the Failed Conversion of the Middle East,* was the winner of the American Studies Association's John Hope Franklin Prize and the Middle East Studies Association's Albert Hourani Book Award.

PublicAffairs is a publishing house founded in 1997. It is a tribute to the standards, values, and flair of three persons who have served as mentors to countless reporters, writers, editors, and book people of all kinds, including me.

I. F. STONE, proprietor of *I. F. Stone's Weekly*, combined a commitment to the First Amendment with entrepreneurial zeal and reporting skill and became one of the great independent journalists in American history. At the age of eighty, Izzy published *The Trial of Socrates*, which was a national bestseller. He wrote the book after he taught himself ancient Greek.

BENJAMIN C. BRADLEE was for nearly thirty years the charismatic editorial leader of *The Washington Post.* It was Ben who gave the *Post* the range and courage to pursue such historic issues as Watergate. He supported his reporters with a tenacity that made them fearless and it is no accident that so many became authors of influential, best-selling books.

ROBERT L. BERNSTEIN, the chief executive of Random House for more than a quarter century, guided one of the nation's premier publishing houses. Bob was personally responsible for many books of political dissent and argument that challenged tyranny around the globe. He is also the founder and longtime chair of Human Rights Watch, one of the most respected human rights organizations in the world.

• • •

For fifty years, the banner of Public Affairs Press was carried by its owner Morris B. Schnapper, who published Gandhi, Nasser, Toynbee, Truman, and about 1,500 other authors. In 1983, Schnapper was described by *The Washington Post* as "a redoubtable gadfly." His legacy will endure in the books to come.

Peter Osnos, *Founder and Editor-at-Large*